AF531221

Art as Image

Art as Image

Prints and Promotion in Cincinnati, Ohio

Edited by

Alice M. Cornell

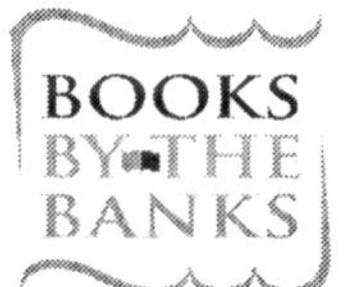

Ohio University Press / Athens
in association with the University of Cincinnati Digital Press

Ohio University Press, Athens, Ohio 45701

Ohio University Press books are printed on acid-free paper ∞™

09 08 07 06 05 04 03 02 01   5 4 3 2 1

Images and abstracts for this book can also be viewed on the
University of Cincinnati Digital Press Web site:
http://www.ucdp.uc.edu/ArtAsImage

Frontispiece: Danner's Original Revolving Book-Cases (lithograph; Cincinnati: Krebs Lithographing Co., n.d.). Courtesy of the Langstroth Collection, Art and Music Department.

Library of Congress Cataloging-in-Publication Data

Art as image : prints and promotion in Cincinnati, Ohio / edited by Alice M. Cornell.
p. cm.
Includes bibliographical references and index.
ISBN 0-8214-1335-X (cloth : alk. paper)
1. Prints, American—Ohio—Cincinnati. 2. Graphic arts—Ohio—Cincinnati—History. 3. Commercial art—Ohio—Cincinnati—History. I. Cornell, Alice, 1945–

NE538.C57 A78 2001
769.9771'78—dc21

00-054537

Contents

Preface

SINCE 1793, WHEN WILLIAM MAXWELL published the first newspaper in the Northwest Territory, Cincinnati has been a center of the midwestern printing industry and continues to loom large in the history and technology of American printing and prints. Highlights of this history—particularly in the nineteenth century—are presented in this series of essays. They are intended to provide both an introduction to Cincinnati printing history and a glimpse of some of the city's intriguing prints and printers. The common thread through prints, newspapers, posters, portfolios, playing cards, and expositions is the use of prints for promotion. They are advertisements, news media, advertising, propaganda, and educational tools. In some cases, they also provide some fascinating views of the city of Cincinnati and serve as documents of the physical, social, political, and commercial history of the Queen City of the West.

Our gratitude is extended to many. First to the authors, who assembled the essays and accommodated our editorial requirements. Several Cincinnati repositories with rich collections of images were most helpful in making these available for this publication. In particular, we acknowledge the Cincinnati Historical Society Library and The Public Library of Cincinnati and Hamilton County, whose old and distinguished collections are always a treasure to examine. Jay Yocis of UC Photographic Services did yeoman duty preparing photographs.

One of the goals of Ohio University Press and the University of Cincinnati Digital Press in publishing this work is to enhance the availability of information and images through the integration of old and new technology. This has been accomplished by combining a hard copy print publication with electronic publication of images on the World Wide Web at <http://www.ucdp.uc.edu/ArtAsImage>. It represents one approach and a beginning of continuing efforts to capitalize on the challenges and opportunities of new information delivery systems.

ALICE M. CORNELL
Head, Archives & Rare Books Department
University of Cincinnati

Chapter One

Early Printing and Publishing in Cincinnati

Noel Martin
Designer
Cincinnati, Ohio

The first downtown building of the Public Library of Cincinnati and Hamilton County complex was opened on January 31, 1955. The head of public relations for the library brought me in as a consultant designer for the opening and the subsequent exhibition and display program. At this time, I was working at the Cincinnati Art Museum as the designer and assistant to the director, teaching at the Art Academy of Cincinnati, and tending to an already demanding freelance practice. As I became familiar with some of the needs of the program, I met with Yeatman Anderson III, the library's curator of rare books and special collections. We considered the merits of doing an exhibition on nineteenth-century printing and publishing. Anderson had a remarkable knowledge of this subject and began to show me many examples from the collection.

My friend Edward H. Dwight, who was the curator of American paintings at the Cincinnati Art Museum, came down to give us a hand. Dwight possessed an abundance of curiosity and information about our visual world. He was to become the director of the Milwaukee Art Museum and later the Munson-Williams-Proctor Institute of Art in Utica, New York. While discussing the early history of the city, I learned that Anderson was a relative of Griffin Yeatman, one of the early Cincinnati settlers who in 1797 built a tavern at Front and Sycamore Streets on the public landing. For several years it served the community as city hall, hospital ward, courthouse, and registry.

The community now called Cincinnati got under way in November 1788, when the first group of twenty-six settlers arrived by flatboat and founded the village of Columbia, west of the mouth of the Little Miami River. Six weeks later, the second village, across from the mouth of the Licking River, was founded and named Losantiville. And by the next year the area west of Losantiville was settled and named North Bend. The combined settlement was located between the two Miamis for increased protection from flooding. On January 4, 1790, Arthur St. Clair, the governor of the Northwest Territory, renamed the city Cincinnati because he did not care for the name Losantiville.

In 1788 the printer William Maxwell crossed the Alleghenies westward with his printing equipment strapped to the backs of packhorses. The equipment consisted of a wooden press similar to the one used by Benjamin Franklin and cases of type, which could be carried downriver in a large canoe or flatboat. From Pittsburgh he began a river trip that took him as far as Maysville, Kentucky; then he traveled overland to Lexington, where he proceeded to set up shop despite the fact that this community had already subsidized John Bradford, a surveyor turned printer. By 1793 Maxwell had relocated to Cincinnati and printed the first issue of *The Centinel of the North-Western Territory*[1] (fig. 1.1), a weekly newspaper of four pages, thus becoming the first printer and publisher in Cincinnati—only four years after the settlement had been established.

The technology used by Maxwell hardly differed from that developed by Johann Gutenberg in the middle of the fifteenth century. Gutenberg invented type casting, and for the first time in history a true system of mass production was applied: from a punch cut in steel, a mold was produced by striking brass, a softer metal. This matrix formed the bottom of a two-part mold. The mold was filled with a lead alloy, and a letter was cast. Nearly three hundred characters were individually produced to cover the many versions of letters, punctuation marks, and ligatures of the handwritten manuscripts that he used as a model. The entire system included the proper alloy used for casting, a method for justifying lines, the wooden press, and the formulation of a suitable printing ink. With the production and distribution of books modern times began.

Gutenberg's heroic effort was his forty-two-line Bible, 1450–55, the earliest surviving book printed in the Western world, consisting of 1,286 pages and issued in two volumes. A single page was printed at a time. Then the type was put back in the case and used for another page. For more than four hundred years after the invention of printing all type was set by hand.

Maxwell produced his *Laws of the Territory of the United States North-West of the Ohio*[2] in 1796 for the territorial legislature. This 225-page book, printed in an edition of 1,000 copies, was the first book published in the Northwest Territory. The population of the entire territory was a mere fifteen thousand people. Cincinnati, centrally located between Pittsburgh and the Mississippi River, grew rapidly as an early frontier commercial center, providing for the physical needs of the thousands of settlers arriving from the East. The first military post in the territory was Fort Washington, built in 1789 and situated in

T H E

CENTINEL of the *North-Western TERRITORY.*

Open to all parties—but influenced by none.

(Vol. I.) SATURDAY, *November 9,* 1793. (Num. 1.)

The *Printer* of the CENTINEL of the *North-Western TERRITORY,* to the *Public.*

HAVING arrived at *Cincinnati,* he has applied himſelf to that which has been the principal object of his removal to this country, the Publication of a *News-Paper.*

This country is in its infancy, and the inhabitants are daily expoſed to an enemy who, not content with taking away the lives of men in the field, have ſwept away whole families, and burnt their habitations. We are well aware that the want of a regular and certain trade down the Miſſiſippi, deprives this country in a great meaſure, of money at the preſent time: Theſe are diſcouragements, nevertheleſs I am led to believe the people of this country are diſpoſed to promote ſcience, and have the fulleſt aſſurance that the *Preſs* from its known utility will receive proper encouragement: And on my part am content with ſmall gains, at the preſent, flattering myſelf that from attention to buſineſs, I ſhall preſerve the good wiſhes of thoſe who have already countenanced me in this undertaking, and ſecure the friendſhip of ſubſequent population.

It is to be hoped that the CENTINEL will prove of great utility to the people of this Country, not only to inform them of what is going on on the eaſt of the Atlantic in arms, and in arts of peace—but what more particularly concerns us, the different tranſactions of the ſtates in the union, and eſpecially of our own Territory, at ſo great a diſtance from the ſeat of general government—it is a particular grievance, that the people have not been acquainted with the proceedings of the legiſlature of the union, in which they are as much intereſted, as any part of the United States.—It is expected the CENTINEL, will in a great meaſure remedy this misfortune.

Theſe are ſubſtantial advantages, which will reſult from the publication of this *paper;* but it muſt be an agreeable amuſement to know a thouſand particulars which make up the intelligence, though not ſo immediately intereſting to the property & perſons of men, whether they be of a philoſophical, political, hiſtorical or moral nature.

The EDITOR therefore reſts his ſucceſs on the merits of the publication, but as an inducement to the people of this country, to make exertions to ſupport the *Preſs*, he muſt obſerve that they will have an opportunity, by means of this *paper* to make themſelves and their ſituations known abroad; if they have valuable lands to diſpoſe of, it can be made known; if they have grievences to lay before the public, it can now be done. I hope therefore, all men of public ſpirit will conſider the undertaking as a proper object of attention, and not conſult merely their own perſonal intereſt, but the intereſt of the public and the coming time.

The MONK.

CALAIS.

A POOR monk of the order of St. Francis came into the room to beg ſomething for his convent. No man cares to have his virtues the ſport of contingencies- or one man may be generous, as another man is puiſſant—*ſed non, quo ad hanc*—or be as it may—for there is no regular reaſoning upon the ebbs and flows of our humours; they may depend upon the ſame cauſes, for ought I know, which influence the tides themſelves—'twould oft be no diſcredit to us ſuppoſe it was ſo; I'm ſure at leaſt for myſelf, that in many a caſe I ſhould be more highly ſatisfied, to have it ſaid by the world, "I had an affair with the moon, in which there was neither ſin nor ſhame," than have it paſs altogether as my own act and deed, wherein there was ſo much of both.

—But be this as it may. The moment I caſt my eyes upon him, I was predetermined not to give him a ſingle ſous, and accordingly I put my purſe into my pocket—buttoned it up -ſet myſelf a little more upon my center, and advanced up gravely to him: there was ſomething I fear forbidding in my look: I have his figure this moment before my eyes, and think there was that in it which deſerved better.

The monk, as I judged from the break in his tonſure, a few ſcatter'd white hairs upon his temples being all that remained of it, might be about ſeventy—but from his eyes, and that ſort of fire which was in them, which ſeemed more temper'd by courteſy than years, could be no more than ſixty—Truth might lie between—He was certainly ſixty-five; and the general air of his countenance, notwithſtanding ſomething ſeemed to have been planting wrinkles in it before their time, agreed to the account.

It was one of thoſe heads, which Guido has often painted—mild, pale—penetrating, free from all common place ideas of fat-contented ignorance, looking downwards upon the earth—it look'd forwards; but look'd as if it look'd at ſomething beyond this world. How one of his order came by it, heaven above, who let it fall upon a monk's ſhoulders, beſt knows; but it would have ſuited a Bramin, and had I met it upon the plains of Indoſtan, I had revenced it.

The reſt of his outline may be given in a few ſtrokes; one might put it into the hands of any one to deſign, for 'twas neither elegant nor otherwiſe, but as character and expreſſion made it ſo: it was a thin, ſpare, form, ſomething above the common ſize, if it loſt not the diſtinction by a bend forwards in the figure—but it was the attitude of entreaty; and as it now ſtands preſented to my imagination, it gained more than it loſt by it.

When he had enter'd the room three paces, he ſtood ſtill; and laying his left hand upon his breaſt, (a ſlender white ſtaff with which he journey'd being in his right)—when I had got cloſe up to him, he introduced himſelf with the little ſtory of the wants of his convent, and the poverty of his order—and did it with ſo ſimple a grace—and ſuch an air of deprecation was there in the whole caſt of his look and figure—I was bewitched not to have been ſtruck with it——

—A better reaſon was, I had predetermined not to give him a ſingle ſous.

——'Tis very true, ſaid I, replying to a caſt upwards with his eyes, with which he had concluded his addreſs- —'tis very true —— and heaven be their reſource who have no other but the charity of the world, the ſtock of which, I fear, is no way ſufficient for the many *great claims* which are hourly made upon it.

As I pronounced the words *great claims,* he gave a ſlight glance with his eye downwards upon the ſleeve of his tunic—I felt the full force of the appeal—I acknowledge it, ſaid I—a coarſe habit, and that but once in three years, with meagre diet—are no great matters; and the true point of pity is, as they can be earn'd in the world with ſo little induſtry, that your order ſhould wiſh to procure them by preſſing upon a fund which is the property of the lame, the blind, the aged, and the infirm—the captive who lies down counting over and over again the days of his afflictions, languiſhes alſo for his ſhare of it; and had you been of the *order of Mercy,* inſtead of the order of St. Francis, poor as I am, continued I, pointing at my portmanteau, full cheerfully ſhould it have been open'd to you, for the ranſom of the unfortunate—The monk made me a bow—but of all others, reſumed I, the unfortunate of our own country, ſurely, have the firſt right; and I have left thouſands in diſtreſs upon our own ſhore——The monk gave a cordial wave with his head—as much as to ſay, No doubt there is miſery enough in every corner of the world, as well as within our convent—But we diſtinguiſh, ſaid I, laying my hand upon the ſleeve of his tunic, in return for his appeal—we diſtinguiſh, my good father! betwixt thoſe who

Fig. 1.1 ***The Centinel of the North-Western Territory.***
Vol. 1, no. 1 (November 9, 1793), title page. Facsimile. Author's collection.

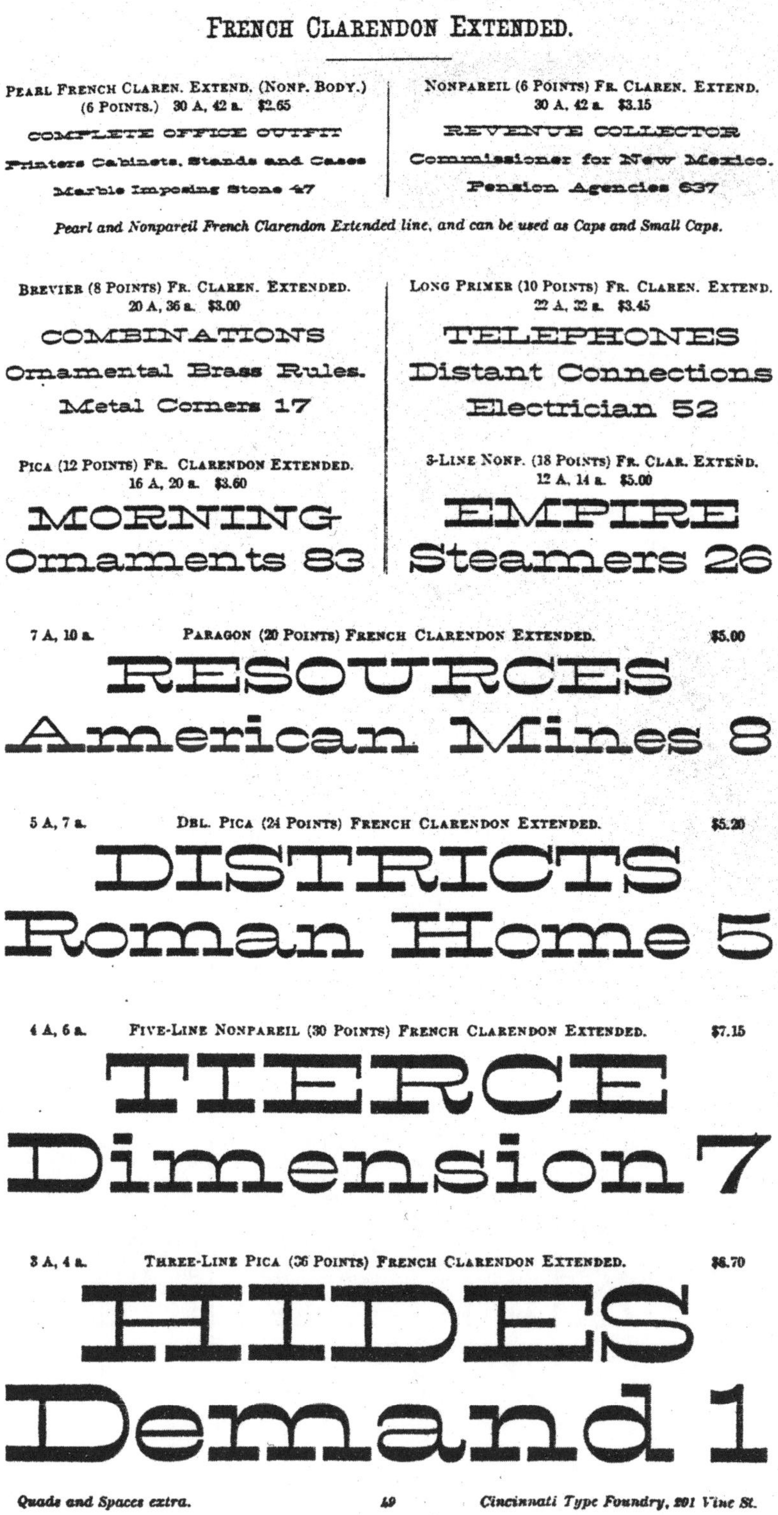

French Clarendon Extended.

Pearl French Claren. Extend. (Nonp. Body.) (6 Points.) 30 A, 42 a. $2.65

COMPLETE OFFICE OUTFIT

Printers Cabinets, Stands and Cases

Marble Imposing Stone 47

Nonpareil (6 Points) Fr. Claren. Extend. 30 A, 42 a. $3.15

REVENUE COLLECTOR

Commissioner for New Mexico.

Pension Agencies 637

Pearl and Nonpareil French Clarendon Extended line, and can be used as Caps and Small Caps.

Brevier (8 Points) Fr. Claren. Extended. 20 A, 36 a. $3.00

COMBINATIONS

Ornamental Brass Rules.

Metal Corners 17

Long Primer (10 Points) Fr. Claren. Extend. 22 A, 32 a. $3.45

TELEPHONES

Distant Connections

Electrician 52

Pica (12 Points) Fr. Clarendon Extended. 16 A, 20 a. $3.60

MORNING

Ornaments 83

3-Line Nonp. (18 Points) Fr. Clar. Extend. 12 A, 14 a. $5.00

EMPIRE

Steamers 26

7 A, 10 a. Paragon (20 Points) French Clarendon Extended. $5.00

RESOURCES

American Mines 8

5 A, 7 a. Dbl. Pica (24 Points) French Clarendon Extended. $5.20

DISTRICTS

Roman Home 5

4 A, 6 a. Five-Line Nonpareil (30 Points) French Clarendon Extended. $7.15

TIERCE

Dimension 7

3 A, 4 a. Three-Line Pica (36 Points) French Clarendon Extended. $6.70

HIDES

Demand 1

Quads and Spaces extra. 49 *Cincinnati Type Foundry, 201 Vine St.*

Fig. 1.2 Type specimens

The Sixteenth Specimen Book and Catalogue of Machinery from the Cincinnati Type Foundry (Cincinnati: Cincinnati Type Foundry, 1885), p. 42. Archives and Rare Books Department, University of Cincinnati.

what is now the Lytle Park area. Soldiers garrisoned there were trained for skirmishes with Indian tribes and offered a degree of security for the settlers.

Until the city's population increased, the demand for literature was limited to practical needs such as schoolbooks, almanacs, guides for immigrants and river men, songbooks, and religious works. Schoolbooks were responsible for half the output of local presses by 1825. The two newspapers, *Liberty Hall*[3] and the *Western Spy*,[4] each had an extra press for book printing.

A grave problem in the early years was the shortage of paper, which at that time was made from cotton rags. As one printer succinctly stated, "tis hard to print and get nothing, and find paper in the bargain."[5] The first paper mill west of the Alleghenies was established in Georgetown, Kentucky, in 1793. Transportation and the mill's limited output made it difficult to meet the needs of Cincinnati's presses. Ohio's first mill was founded upriver in East Liverpool in 1807. Finally, by 1811 two paper mills on the Little Miami River within thirty miles of the city eased the shortage.

Ten years later the Cincinnati Steam Paper mill, situated on the river in the western part of town, was the city's first steam-driven mill. It produced enough to supply the local market, as well as to ship surplus paper downriver to New Orleans. A continuous web of machine-made paper was a French invention by Louis Robart in 1798. The process was sold to the Fourdrinier family of England and revolutionized the production of paper. By 1840 manufacturing methods were developed using groundwood pulp, an abundant source of raw material. During the period before the Civil War, Ohio was the largest paper-producing state in the West, with mills operating not only the along the Miami River but also in Hamilton and Dayton.

Abel Buell of Connecticut made the first successful attempt to perform all functions of type founding in 1769. His letter was crude and had none of the design quality of the types imported from England and Holland. It was, however, a move to free the colonial printers from relying on England.

In 1772 Christopher Sauer II established the first regular type foundry in Germantown, Pennsylvania. There followed a number of other attempts to produce a decent product, but that was not accomplished until two Scots, Binny and Ronaldson, established a permanent type foundry in Philadelphia in 1796. The typeface, Binny, is still available today. Before this period the most widely used letter in America was that of Englishman William Caslon, popular because of its exceptional legibility and originally introduced by Benjamin Franklin. The Declaration of Independence was set in Caslon by a Philadelphia printer.

Local manufacture of type and related equipment began in 1820 with the establishment of the Cincinnati Type Foundry (figs. 1.2 and 1.3) by the bookdealer John P. Foote in partnership with Oliver Wells. Foote soon turned over the business to members of the Wells family, who continued to operate it for more than half a century. By 1826, with Cincinnati's population of sixteen thousand people and with efficient steamboat transportation available on the Ohio and Mississippi, the printers were turning out large quantities of books for the trade.

Letterpress printing had its start in the colonies with the installation of a wooden

EVANS & LINDSEY, General Insurance Agents, No. 65 West Third Street, Cincinnati.

APPLEGATE & CO.,

BOOKSELLERS, STATIONERS, PRINTERS,

AND

PUBLISHERS

OF

Clark's Commentary, Dick's Complete Works, Rollins' Ancient History, Plutarch's Lives, Spectator, Tatler and Guardian, Mosheim's Church History, Josephus, Gathered Treasures from the Mines of Literature, Dick's Theology, Chain of Sacred Wonders, Complete Works of Lorenzo Dow. Farmers' Hand Book, Shakspeare, Soden's German Grammar, Peterson's Familiar Science, Speeches of Hon. Thomas S. Marshall, Life of Dr. Daniel Drake, Guizot's History of the Decline and Fall of the Roman Empire, Nightingale, Universal Musician. Brownlow's Book,

TOGETHER WITH

WEBBS' FREE MASONS' MONITOR,

THE BEST MASONIC BOOK EXTANT. ALSO,

THE BROTHERHOOD, OR ODD FELLOWSHIP,

Published in English and German.

We invite the attention of Booksellers, Druggists, and General Dealers to our stock of Books, Paper and Stationery, Blank Books, etc., suitable to the wants of City Jobbers and Country Dealers. In addition to our own large list of Publications, we supply the trade with all Books at Publishers Prices. We Manufacture every variety of

BLANK BOOKS,

And offer them to the trade at the Lowest Wholesale Rates of Eastern Markets. Our extensive assortment of

Letter, Cap, Note Papers, Envelopes, Wrapping Paper, Bonnet Boards, etc.,

Enable us to compete successfully with Eastern Houses in supplying the Jobbing Trade with these articles and Stationery of every description. Our large and well furnished

PRINTING OFFICE AND BINDERY

Enable us to do JOB PRINTING of every description, and Publish Books for Authors in as good style and on as favorable terms as can be done anywhere,

JOBBERS AND DEALERS ARE INVITED TO CALL AND EXAMINE OUR STOCK.

All orders received by Mail filled promptly and with strict attention to the wishes of the customer.

APPLEGATE & CO.,

43 Main, Below Second Street, Cincinnati, O.

Fig. 1.3 Type specimens
Williams Cincinnati Directory. . . . (Cincinnati: Williams & Co., 1865), p. 46. Archives and Rare Books Department, University of Cincinnati.

press in Cambridge, Massachusetts, in 1638. This installation, by Stephen Daye, became closely associated with Harvard College. The press had been brought from England along with an assortment of English and Dutch type.

A problem common to wooden presses was the inability to produce enough pressure for a proper impression. This problem lead to the development of the all-metal press in 1799 by England's Lord Stanhope. The Columbian and Washington presses were of similar design. Some six thousand Washington presses were sold by 1900—one version being produced by the Cincinnati Type Foundry.

Next came the steam-powered flatbed cylinder press built in London by the German Frederick Koenig and used to print the *London Times* in 1814. The cylinder pressed paper against a type form. This improvement was followed by the invention of grippers for holding the sheet of paper while it was being run through the press.

An American contribution was the platen or job press, which served as an intermediary between the hand and the cylinder presses. The job press was very popular because of its low cost and versatility. At one time, more than seventy companies produced job presses. They were used primarily for short-run jobs such as business forms, letterheads, invitations, and announcements. In the job press the paper and type form were flat surfaces hinged together. After paper was inserted, the two surfaces came in contact for an impression. This press was first powered by a foot treadle and later by steam power and electricity.

Speed became an important factor in the effort to meet the ever-growing need for printed materials. Richard Hoe's sheet-fed rotary press, developed in 1847, had the desired speed and efficiency for long runs. By 1856 a roll-fed rotary press was patented by William Bullock—our first web press.

Setting type around a cylinder was a serious problem. Soon curved stereotypes were produced from conventional type forms. Attaching a folding mechanism as the work left the press came about in 1875.

The rapid development of all aspects of printing technology brought about increased production, and as early as 1830 Cincinnati became a center of the Western book market. Twenty years later it ranked fourth among the country's publishing leaders after New York, Philadelphia, and Boston. In 1830 stereotyping provided duplicate printing plates, and 1834 gave us the first steam-driven presses. But the much desired automatic typesetting did not happen until 1886, when Ottmar Merganthaler invented the Linotype machine, which cast justified slugs of type. Monotype came a year later, with its capability of casting lines of individual letters. The desire for display letters was solved by the Ludlow system, introduced in 1906, using manually assembled matrices.

Printing ink was produced locally by 1845—the inconvenience of waiting for delivery from the East was over. Bookbinding was transformed from a handcraft to a mechanical operation in the nineteenth century with machinery invented for folding, gathering, and sewing signatures, making cases, embossing presses, and casing-in procedures, which joined the sewn volume to make a finished book.

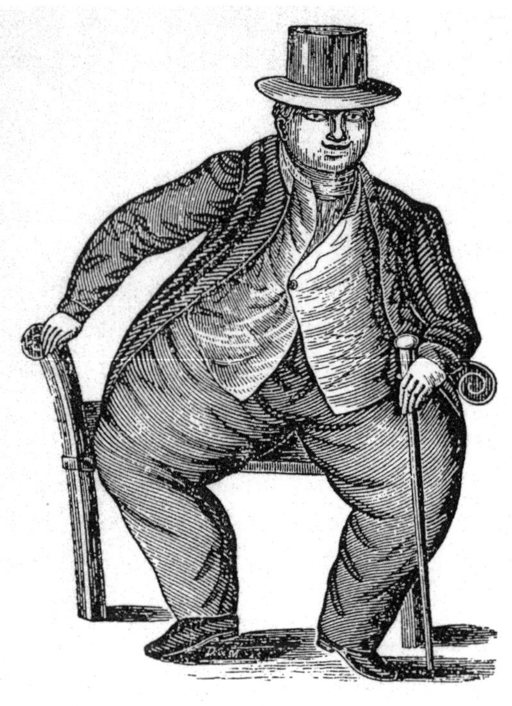

Fig. 1.4 Woodcut illustration by Doolittle & Munson
Woodcut. 3⅝ × 2⅝ in (9.2 × 6.7 cm). *The Cincinnati Directory Advertiser for the Years 1836–7* (Cincinnati: J. H. Woodruff, 1836), verso of title page. Archives and Rare Books Department, University of Cincinnati.

The demand for illustrations was first met by importing woodcuts. By the 1820s local craftsmen were turning out all that were needed (figs. 1.4 and 1.5). The blocks were locked in with the raised metal type and printed. Copper and steel engravings were also produced (figs. 1.6 and 1.7). These were printed separately by the intaglio method and bound in with letterpress signatures. Intaglio goes back to the fifteenth century, with an engraved line cut into a metal plate. Ink was rubbed into this groove, the top surface was wiped clean, and a dampened sheet of paper was run through a press similar to those used for making etchings, pulling ink from the groove to the paper.

Early Publications

Publishing schoolbooks became a profitable outlet for local printers, and they quickly grew in numbers. Noah Webster, who lived in Connecticut, turned out a much sought after

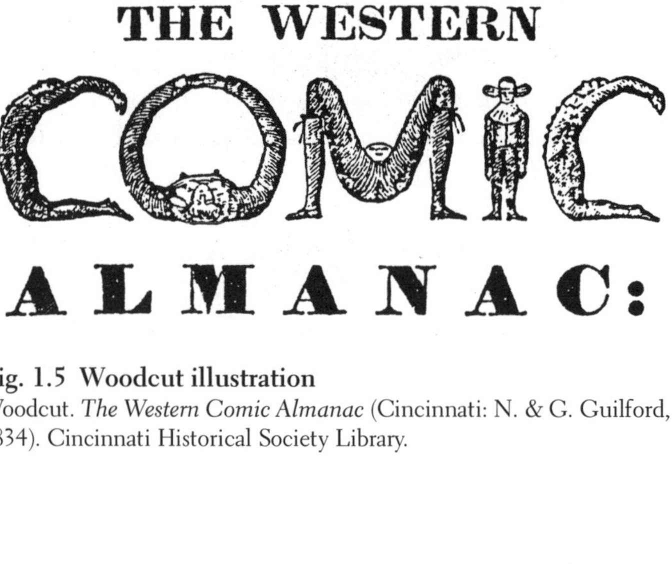

THE WESTERN
COMIC
ALMANAC:

Fig. 1.5 Woodcut illustration
Woodcut. *The Western Comic Almanac* (Cincinnati: N. & G. Guilford, 1834). Cincinnati Historical Society Library.

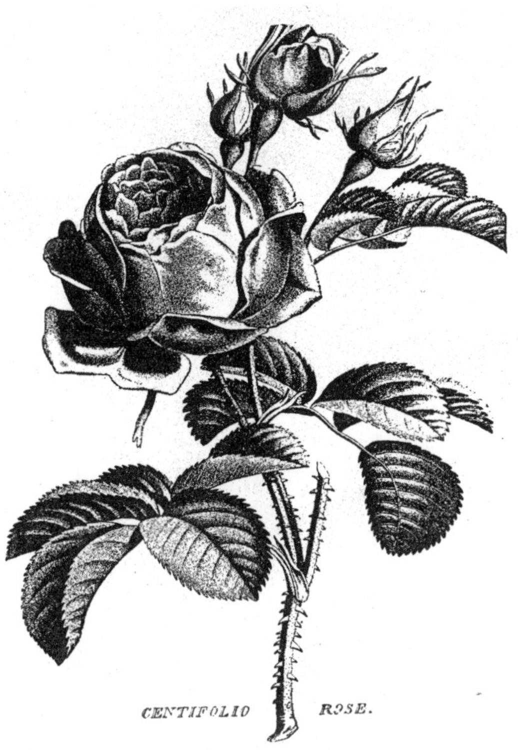

Fig. 1.6 (left) [Centifolio Rose]
Elijah C. Middleton. Copper engraving, ca. 1850. Probably from *The Ladies Repository.* Cincinnati Historical Society Library.

Fig. 1.7 (below) Text and illustrations
Engravings. Daniel J. Kenney, *Illustrated Cincinnati: A Pictorial Hand-Book of the Queen City* (Cincinnati: Robert Clarke & Co., 1875), pp. 182–83. Archives and Rare Books Department, University of Cincinnati.

182 *KENNY'S ILLUSTRATED CINCINNATI.*

which Carriages are constructed. The following is only a brief summary of some of the leading articles; namely: Springs, Axles, Bolts, Bands, Enameled Leather, Muslin, Drill, Duck, Cloths, Damask, Bent Timber Wheels, Bodies, Gold, Silver, and Ivory Mountings of all kinds, and American and English Varnishes. Their trade, which is almost exclusively confined to Carriage and Coach Builders, covers an immense territory, including all of the Southern and Western States. The members of the firm are Hugh F. Kemper, Henry L. Kemper, and Andrew C. Kemper.

LEATHER.
HIDES & OIL.
T.T.BROWN & CO.

T. T. BROWN & CO.

T. T. Brown & Co.'s wholesale Leather warehouse is at No. 166 Main Street. This building is 25 feet front and 156 feet in depth. It is fitted up in the most modern style, with every facility for the transaction of extensive business. The offices are on the second floor and are comfortably furnished. The firm were established in 1864. They deal in Leather, Hides, Oil, and Shoe Manufacturers' goods, and are Cincinnati agents for Wm. R. Stewart & Bros. Morocco, and sell at factory prices, and at all times keep a complete stock on

KENNY'S ILLUSTRATED CINCINNATI. 183

J. & A. J. NURRE.

hand. Their business extends over the States of the North-west and South and South-west, with a large city factory trade. They also do a large business, in Hides and Heavy Leather, with New England, New York State, and New Jersey. The members of the firm are Thomas T. Brown and George S. Brown.

The warerooms of **J. & A. J. Nurre**, manufacturers of Frame Mouldings, etc., are situated at No. 164 Main Street. The factory is situated at 276, 278, and 280 Broadway. The business was established in 1849. The firm manufacture all descriptions of Gilt, Imitation Rosewood, Walnut, and Imitation Walnut Frame Moldings, and Square Frames, besides Looking-glasses and Looking-glass Plates, and all necessaries for framing-Pictures. The warehouse has a frontage of 24 feet and a depth of 154 feet. It is four stories in height. The main floor is the salesroom and offices, the upper floors are devoted to the light manufacturing department of the business. The factory has a frontage of 60 feet and is 90 feet in depth. It is five stories in height. The business of the house covers a wide territory, embracing nearly every State in the Union. The members of the firm are Joseph Nurre and Aloys Joseph Nurre.

Pape Brothers & Kugemann's Molding, Picture-frame, and Looking-glass sales-room and office are situated at 137, 139, and

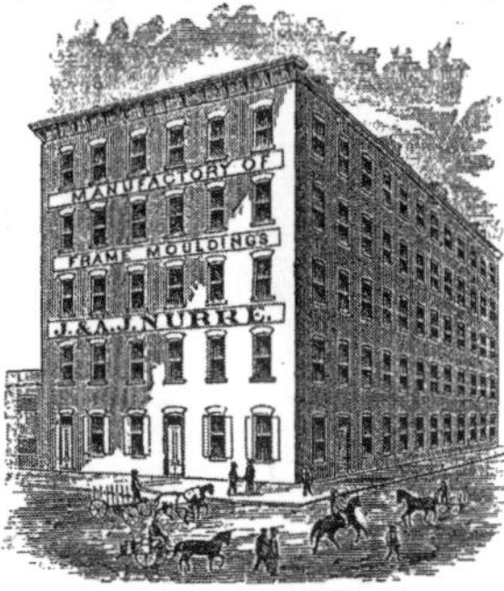

THE MANUFACTORY.

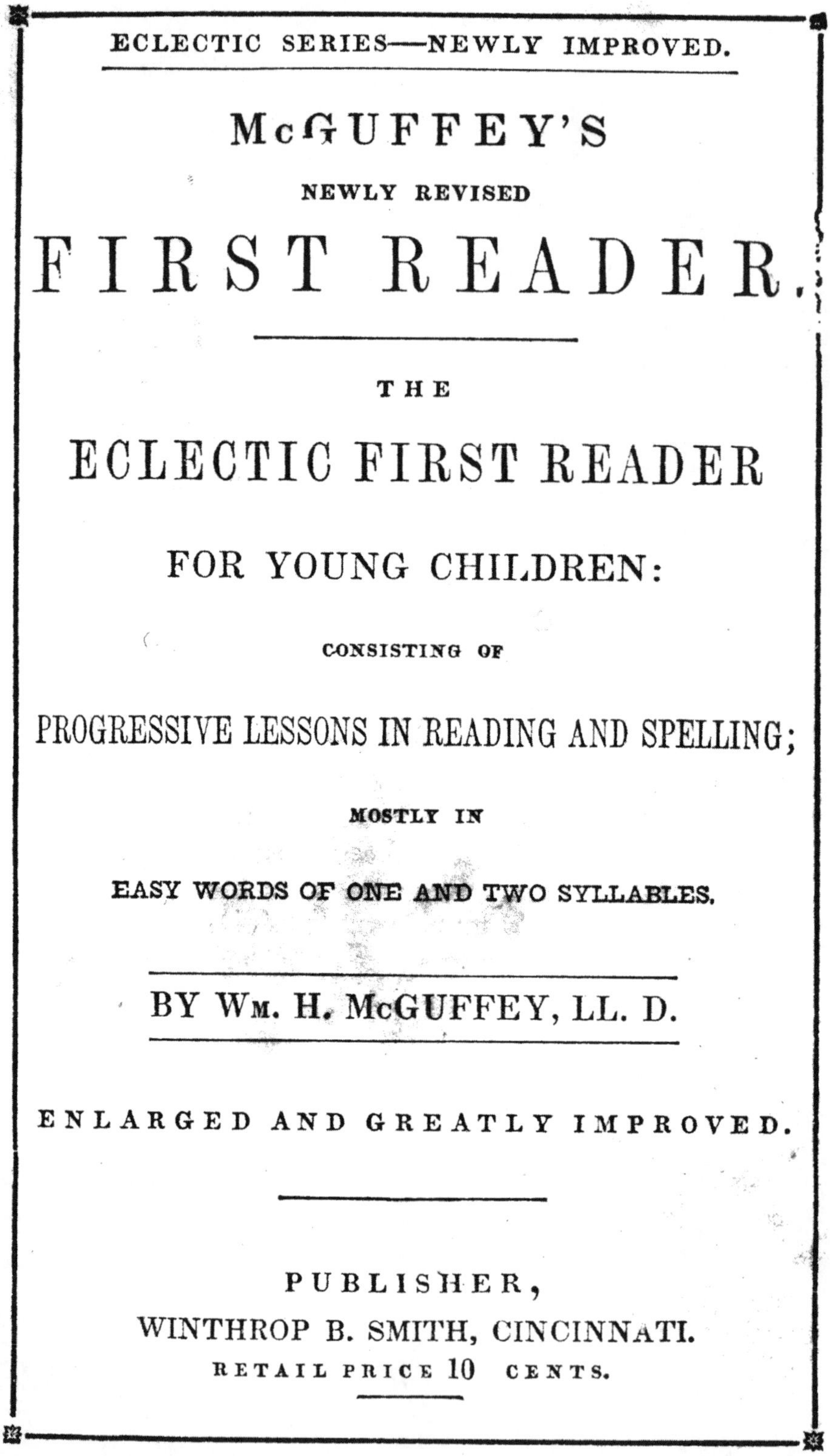

ECLECTIC SERIES—NEWLY IMPROVED.

McGUFFEY'S

NEWLY REVISED

FIRST READER.

THE

ECLECTIC FIRST READER

FOR YOUNG CHILDREN:

CONSISTING OF

PROGRESSIVE LESSONS IN READING AND SPELLING;

MOSTLY IN

EASY WORDS OF ONE AND TWO SYLLABLES.

BY WM. H. McGUFFEY, LL. D.

ENLARGED AND GREATLY IMPROVED.

PUBLISHER,

WINTHROP B. SMITH, CINCINNATI.

RETAIL PRICE 10 CENTS.

Fig. 1.8 McGuffey reader

William Holmes McGuffey, *McGuffey's Newly Revised First Reader* (Cincinnati: Winthrop B. Smith, 1843 [?]), title page. Rare Books and Special Collections Department, The Public Library of Cincinnati and Hamilton County.

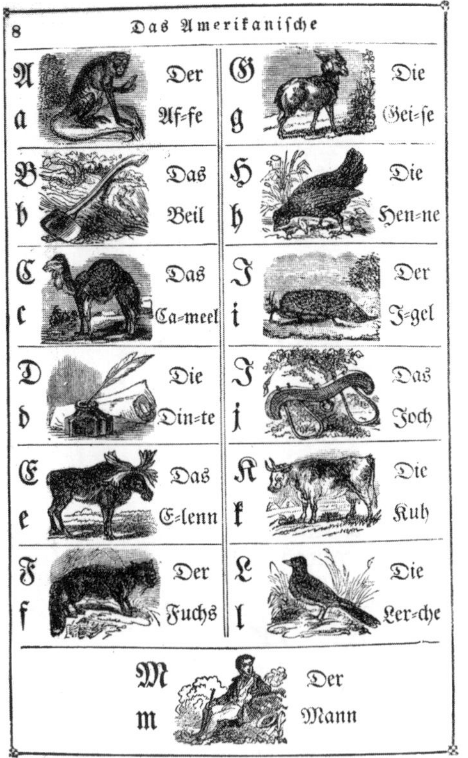

8 Das Amerikanische

A a Der Af-fe
B b Das Beil
C c Das Ca-meel
D d Die Din-te
E e Das E-lenn
F f Der Fuchs
G g Die Gei-se
H h Die Hen-ne
I i Der I-gel
J j Das Joch
K k Die Kuh
L l Die Ler-che
M m Der Mann

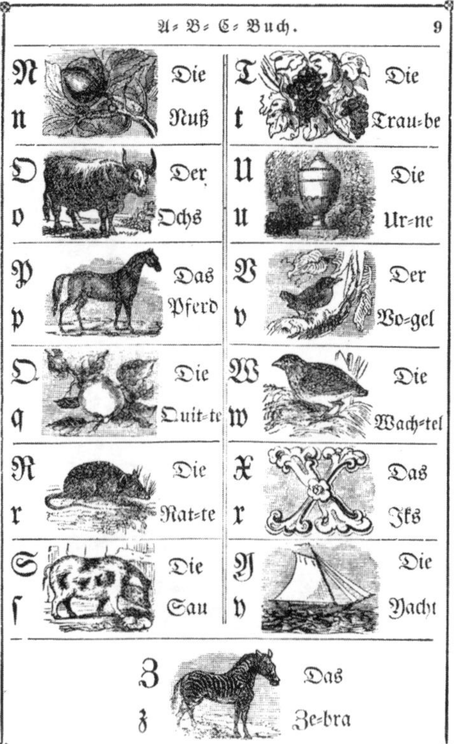

A- B- C- Buch. 9

N n Die Nuß
O o Der Ochs
P p Das Pferd
Q q Die Quit-te
R r Die Rat-te
S ſ Die Sau
T t Die Trau-be
U u Die Ur-ne
V v Der Vo-gel
W w Die Wach-tel
X x Das Ixs
Y y Die Yacht
Z z Das Ze-bra

Fig. 1.9 German spelling book
Letterpress with woodcuts. Germanus, *Das Amerikanische A-B-C Buch* (Cincinnati: Verlag von Wilde & Co., 1854), pp. 8–9. Rare Books and Special Collections Department, The Public Library of Cincinnati and Hamilton County.

classic with *The American Spelling Book*.[6] Webster gave permission to printers in strategic locations, such as Cincinnati's Truman and Smith, to produce and sell his book. William Holmes McGuffey was associated with Miami University when he began the famous *McGuffey Readers*[7] in the 1830s. These books were a special brand of literature that frontier readers found appropriate, differing from the more austere New England primers. McGuffey's series were filled with fables, mottoes, proverbs, and quotations that taught a stern code of honor, the Golden Rule, and the rewards of virtue and industry. McGuffey became president of the Cincinnati College and later, Ohio University. His *Eclectic Readers* (fig. 1.8) had between 200,000 and 300,000 copies in print by 1838; publication continued through the nineteenth century and into the twentieth.

A variety of schoolbooks began to appear. With the ever-increasing German population, a German spelling book (fig. 1.9) set in Fraktur type with woodcut illustrations, was published for elementary students in 1854.

Dr. Daniel Drake, who founded the Medical College of Ohio, wrote *Notices Concerning Cincinnati*[8] in 1810 and *Natural and Statistical View, or Picture of Cincinnati and the*

NO. VI.

Browne's

Cincinnati Almanac,

FOR THE YEAR OF OUR LORD,

BEING THE THIRD AFTER BISSEXTILE OR LEAP YEAR:

AND AFTER THE FOURTH OF JULY,

THE THIRTY SIXTH YEAR

OF AMERICAN INDEPENDENCE.

Calculated for the meridian of Cincinnati, in latitude 39 degrees 7 minutes N. longitude 84 degrees 15 minutes W

BY ROBERT STUBBS, PHILOM

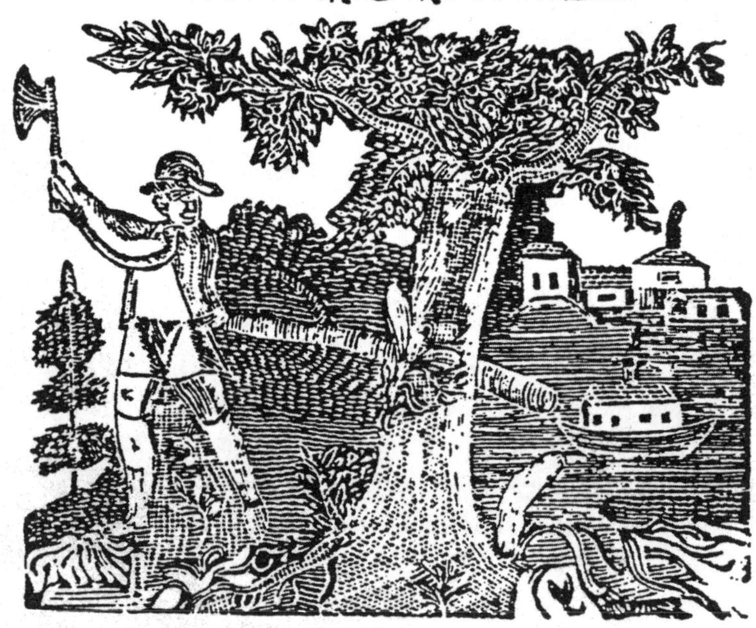

CINCINNATI:

PRINTED BY JOHN W. BROWNE AND COMPANY,

LIBERTY HALL OFFICE.

Fig. 1.10 ***Browne's Cincinnati Almanac***

Woodcut. $2\frac{3}{8} \times 2\frac{7}{8}$ in (6.0×7.3 cm). *Browne's Cincinnati Almanac, for the Year of Our Lord, 1811* (Cincinnati: printed by John W. Browne and Co., [1810]), title page. Rare Books and Special Collections Department, The Public Library of Cincinnati and Hamilton County.

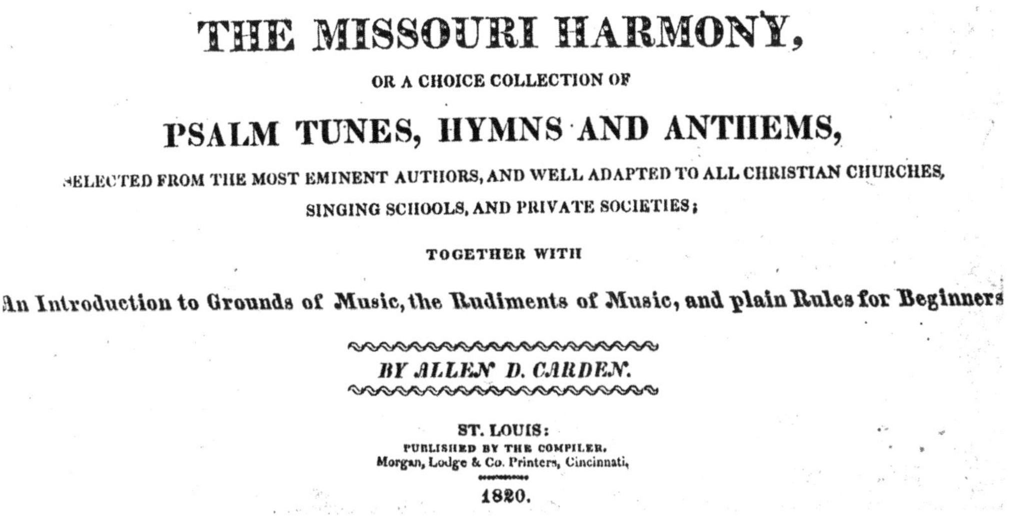

THE MISSOURI HARMONY,

OR A CHOICE COLLECTION OF

PSALM TUNES, HYMNS AND ANTHEMS,

SELECTED FROM THE MOST EMINENT AUTHORS, AND WELL ADAPTED TO ALL CHRISTIAN CHURCHES, SINGING SCHOOLS, AND PRIVATE SOCIETIES;

TOGETHER WITH

An Introduction to Grounds of Music, the Rudiments of Music, and plain Rules for Beginners

BY ALLEN D. CARDEN.

ST. LOUIS:
PUBLISHED BY THE COMPILER.
Morgan, Lodge & Co. Printers, Cincinnati,
1820.

Fig. 1.11 ***The Missouri Harmony***
Allen D. Carden, comp., *The Missouri Harmony, Or a Choice Collection of Psalm Tunes, Hymns and Anthems* (Cincinnati: Morgan, Lodge & Co., Printers, 1820), title page. Rare Books and Special Collections Department, The Public Library of Cincinnati and Hamilton County.

Miami Country in 1815.[9] His observations on the geography, flora, fauna, and agricultural and industrial possibilities, along with his writings on the relationship of disease and environment, were an invaluable contribution to those seeking information about the area.

An almanac published at Harvard College in 1639 was the first book printed in the colonies. Almanacs were being printed here in 1826 in quantities that rivaled the schoolbooks. *Browne's Cincinnati Almanac*[10] (fig. 1.10), first published in 1805, was a product of the Liberty Hall press. It began as a calendar with a collection of data on everything imaginable and was very popular with the reading public. *The Western Comic Almanac*[11] in the 1830s was an early version of the comic book. Another extremely useful publication was *The Cincinnati Directory*[12] of 1819, a guide to the growing community of ten thousand inhabitants. Over the years it continued to present evidence of the staggering number of people who were connected to the various aspects of the local printing community.

River guides and maps were much in demand. Useful navigational descriptions were a great help for those moving down the river. Other types of publications grew with the needs of the community—religious books containing sermons, catechisms, and hymnals and various songbooks, which took advantage of copper engraving and later lithography. However, one songbook, *The Missouri Harmony* (fig. 1.11),[13] published by Morgan, Lodge & Company in 1820, after close observation reveals music printed from metal type. This had been done in Europe as early as 1526, but having music type here in Cincinnati's early days comes as a surprise. There were pamphlets with instructions for playing the piano, guitar, and violin. Stephen Foster lived in Cincinnati between 1846 and 1850 and composed music that was published here.

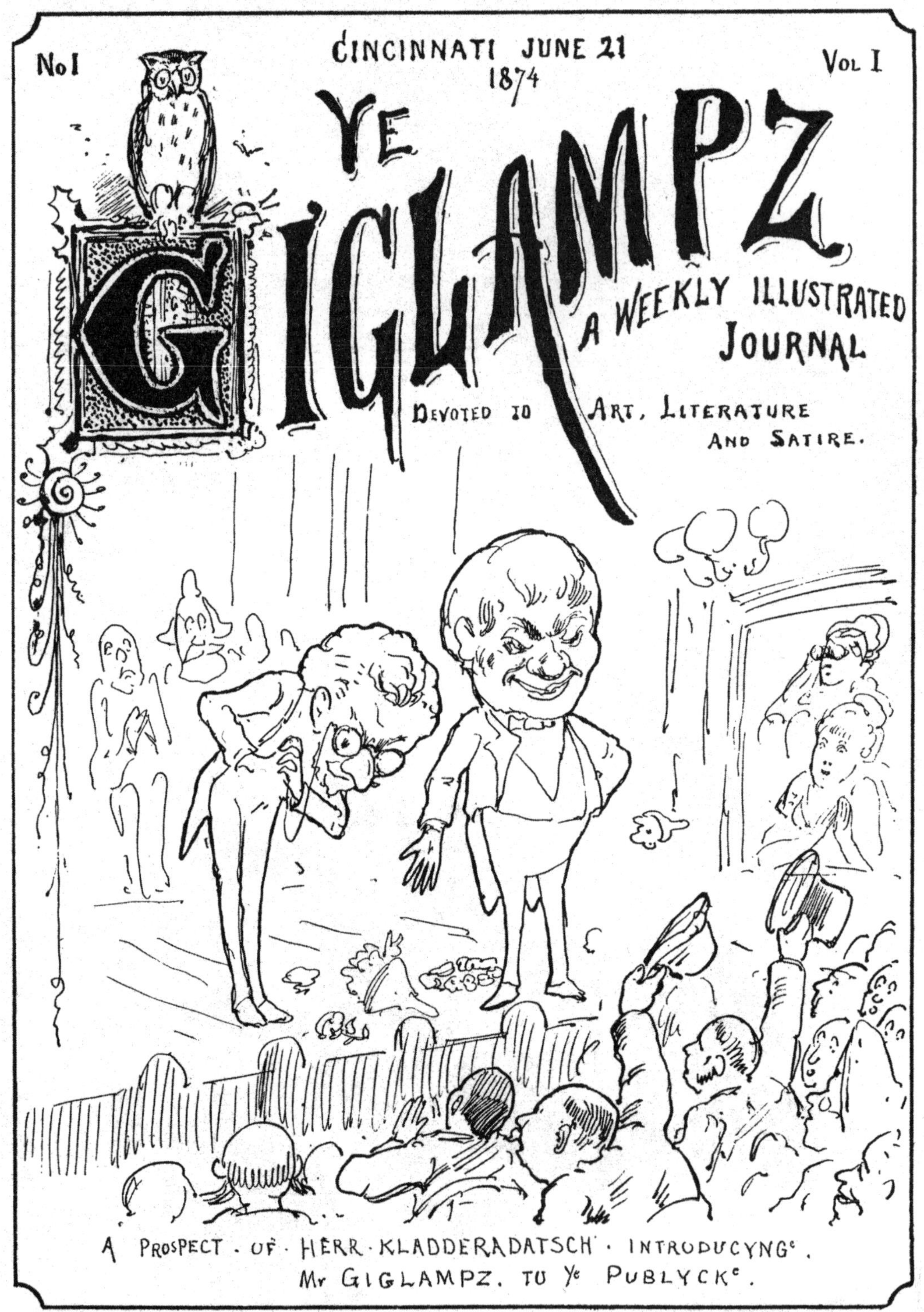

Fig. 1.12 ***Ye Giglampz***
Vol. 1, no. 1 (June 21, 1874), title page. Rare Books and Special Collections Department, The Public Library of Cincinnati and Hamilton County.

Finally the flourishing commerce had its own needs. These were legal books, ledgers, stationery, bills, notices, signs, contract forms, and blank books such as tablets—all of the many tools for conducting business—along with early forms of promotion and advertising.

Alsatian-born Henry François Farny did many illustrations for the *McGuffey Readers* and for *Harper's Weekly*, as well as an illustrated brochure for Procter and Gamble and circus posters. In 1874, at the age of twenty-six, he collaborated with Lafcadio Hearn, then a reporter on the *Cincinnati Enquirer*, on a unique but short-lived comic weekly, *Ye Giglampz* (fig. 1.12).[14] Farny later traveled to the American West and made studies of Indians for a series of paintings—works that were well received and exhibited in Cincinnati, Louisville, Chicago, New York, and Paris.

In the late 1840s, *The Sidereal Messenger* (fig. 1.13)[15] was a monthly journal devoted to astronomy and edited by O. M. Mitchell, director of the famous Cincinnati Observatory. The text was printed by letterpress but included lithographs of the planets and an outstanding engraving of the telescope (fig. 1.14), which had a twelve-inch lens that had been purchased in Munich. This carefully produced work was a fine combination of the three major printing methods.

Another work of interest was the *Manual of Phonography* by British-born Benn Pitman, which introduced his brother Isaac's system of shorthand to America. He also perfected the electroplating process of relief engraving and taught woodcarving at the Art Academy of Cincinnati from 1873 until 1892.

An extremely useful and well-executed catalog was D. J. Kenny's *Illustrated Cincinnati* (1875),[16] profusely illustrated with 320 engravings. More than two hundred photographs had been taken for the artists to use as reference, and a special type had been cast for this volume. The title page reads: "A Pictorial Hand-Book of the Queen City comprising its architectural, manufacturing, trade; its social, literary, scientific and charitable institutions; its churches, schools and colleges; and all other principal points of interest to the visitor and resident."

Photographic Reproduction

One of the outstanding discoveries of the nineteenth century was photography, offering mankind a new form of pictorial record. The invention of photography is credited to Joseph Niepce, a Frenchman who produced a photographic image when he was looking for a method to transfer drawings onto a printing plate. He shared his discoveries with Louis Jacques Daguerre, who pursued the process after Niepce's death. During the same period, an Englishman, William Henry Fox Talbot, pioneered a system that ultimately became the basis for photography and photomechanical plate making. In the graphic arts, photography was first used as a reference for wood engravings.

In 1871 John Calvin Moss of New York developed a procedure for turning line art into metal printing plates for letterpress. Many people were searching for a method to print

THE SIDEREAL MESSENGER.

DERBY, BRADLEY & CO.] [PUBLISHERS.

NO. 8. CINCINNATI, DECEMBER, 1846. VOL. 1.

SIDEREAL MESSENGER.

Published Monthly, at $3,00 per annum, payable in advance.

CINCINNATI ASTRONOMICAL SOCIETY.

(*Concluded.*)

Cincinnati Observatory,
14th Sept., 1846.

To the President and Board of Control of the Cincinnati Astronomical Society.

Gentlemen:—I have received the Preamble and Resolution adopted on the 12th inst. by your Board, and, in compliance, beg leave to submit the following statement:

The duplex character of Antares, the principal star in the constellation Scorpio, was discovered with the Cincinnati Refractor more than a year since. The particulars of this discovery were communicated to Prof. S. C. Walker, at his request, in a letter, dated July 9, 1846. On the receipt of this letter, Lieut. M. F. Maury, Director of the Washington Observatory, commenced an examination of Antares, and, on the 30th of July, in a communication addressed to the Hon. George Bancroft, Secretary of the Navy, announced the *triplicity* of this star. This remarkable discovery, according to Lieut. Maury, was confirmed by Prof. S. C. Walker, in charge of the Washington Equatorial, by Professors Coffin and Hubbard, and by Lieut. Page. In a communication from Prof. Walker, dated August 3, the particulars of the observations and measures on the evenings of the 29th and 30th July, and on the 1st, 2d and 3d of August, were fully given. In a like communication from Lieut. Maury, dated August 7, further particulars were stated; and the final results of all the measures for angle of position and distance, among the components of the triplet, were stated.

Prof. Walker's letter was received August 9th, and excited no little surprise among those familiar with the appearance of Antares in the Cincinnati Refractor. The evening of the 9th was cloudy, but the 10th and 11th of August were remarkably clear and steady, furnishing an excellent opportunity for the examination of difficult objects. On each of these evenings, full observations were made upon Antares. The small star discovered at this Observatory was seen readily three quarters of an hour before sunset, and on a subsequent occasion (Aug. 15) so early as 5h. 30m. P. M. But with all apertures from 4 inches to 12, and with all powers from 100 to 1400, the large star, pronounced by the Washington observers to be *double*, was seen entirely *round*, and without the *slightest elongation, or other indication of duplex character*. This result led to a more critical examination of the circumstances under which the star had been seen triple at Washington.

It appears from Lieut. Maury's communication, addressed to the Secretary of the Navy, and published in the Washington papers of the 30th July, that the discovery was made on the 15th of that month, but up to the 29th, the weather "had been exceedingly unfavorable." On the 23d, through *openings in the clouds*, he saw enough to confirm previous impressions, but on the evening of the 29th, from "9 *o'clock till the hour of setting, the star was in fine view, and was seen triple*," by all the observers already quoted.

The triplet is described as follows:

A	2d magnitude.	Fiery red.
B	3d "	Emerald green.
C	11th "	Sapphire blue.

The green star is the one discovered at Washington. At 9 o'clock, on the evening of the 29th of July, Antares had already passed the meridian of Washington city, and had sunk too near the horizon for very accurate observation. Indeed it was at that hour lower than the limit adopted by Struve in his examinations for double stars. The large star is represented as composed of two: the one *fiery red*, the other *emerald green*. These are precisely the *prismatic colors* which belong to the appearance of all bright stars, when near the horizon, and the direction in which the elongation is reported, excited a further suspicion that *possibly* a mistake had arisen from this source. Moreover, the reported distance from the center of the red star to that of the green one, (1.82) one second and eighty-two hundreths, was a quantity so large that the Cincinnati Refractor could not possibly fail to detect it. A fourth part of this distance is easily appreciated, and is a matter of every day examination.

In a letter recently received from Dr. Lamont, in charge of the great Refractor of the Observatory of Munich, Bavaria, he remarks that he had given special attention to Antares during two years, but had failed to see it *double*. The Munich Refractor is far more powerful than the Washing-

Fig. 1.13 ***The Sidereal Messenger.***
Vol. 1, no. 8 (December 1846), p. 1. Cincinnati Observatory Collection. Archives and Rare Books Department, University of Cincinnati.

photographs—a method to separate continuous tones into dots of different sizes. Stephen H. Hogan came up with a halftone screen used in 1890 for a New York newspaper. Then by 1893 Max and Louis Levy were producing consistent commercial halftones. The 1880s and 1890s accelerated the photomechanical revolution; full-color images were already being done, and with the twentieth century the reproduction of photographic graphic design was a reality. The principles of photoengraving are also applied in the production of intaglio and lithographic printing.

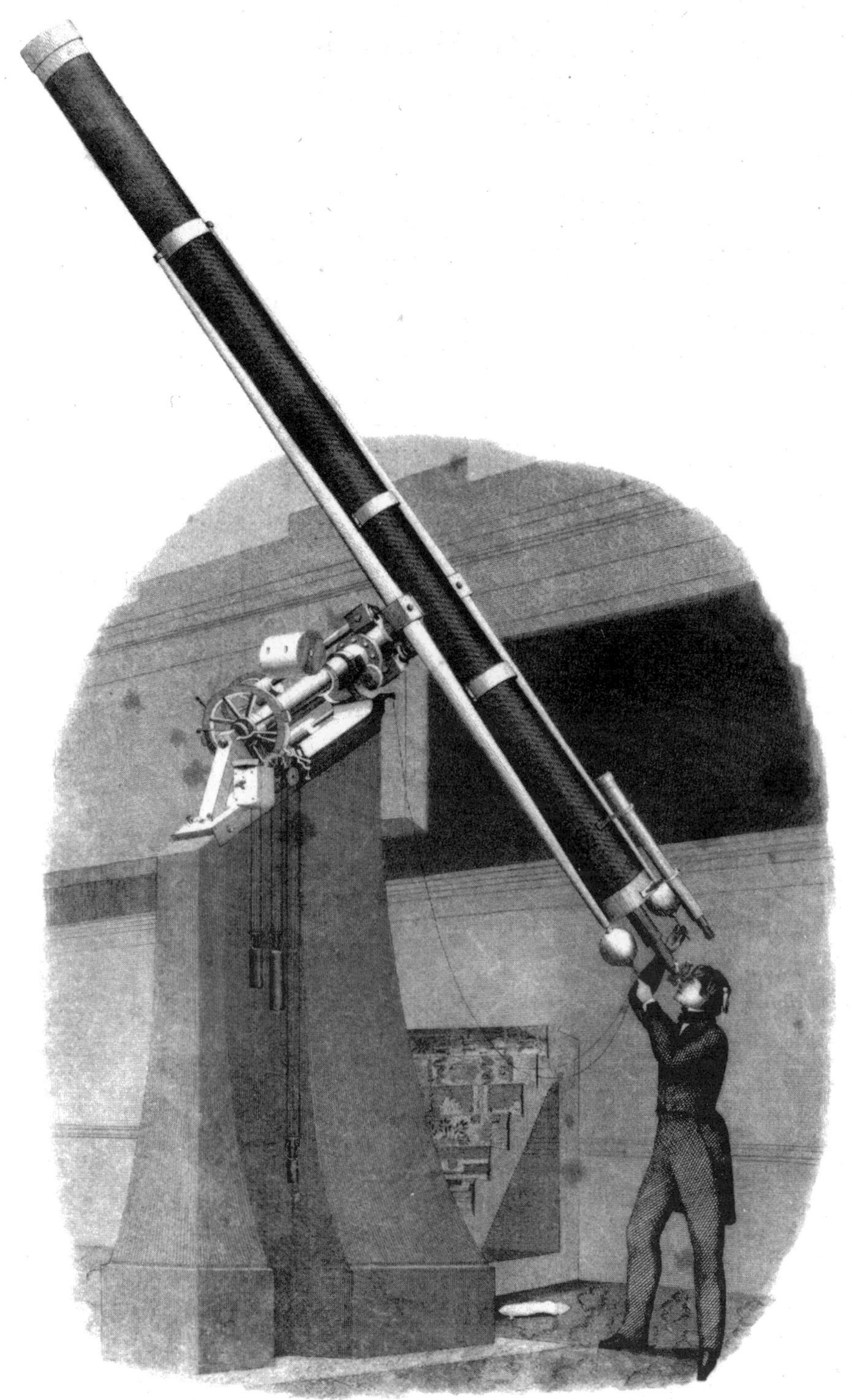

The Cincinnati Equatoreal Telescope.

Fig. 1.14 The Cincinnati Equatorial Telescope
Edward H. Knight. Engraving. Image: 7⅞ × 4⅞ in (20.0 × 12.4 cm). Sheet: 11³⁄₁₆ × 9 in (28.4 × 22.9 cm). *The Sidereal Messenger* 1, no. 1 (July 1846), frontispiece. Cincinnati Observatory Collection. Archives and Rare Books Department, University of Cincinnati.

Local Newspapers

The public's desire for newspapers had a great deal to do with the rapid advances that were made in all phases of printing technology. The need for speed and ease of operation contributed to the mechanization of the pressroom and improved typesetting machines, stereotyping, photoengraving, and the production of rolled pulp newsprint. This all happened before the nineteenth century ended. The transition from newspapers of opinion to those of service was gradual. After early starts of the *Centinel*, the *Western Spy*, *Liberty Hall*, and the *Gazette*, the first attempt at turning out a daily was the *Commercial Register* in 1825, but it found the going rough and suspended operation in six months. Local merchants, realizing the value of advertising, encouraged the *Gazette* eleven years later to start a modest daily that could actually manage to come out each day.

The *Times*, founded in 1840, and the *Star*, founded in 1872, merged in 1880 to become the *Times-Star*. The *Enquirer* began in 1841. It was the first to do a color Sunday supplement and was the first to print from photoengravings in the 1890s.

The Penny Post started up in 1881, and by 1887 it had a circulation of 55,000. The owner, Edward Wyllis Scripps, later joined by Roy Howard, established the Scripps-Howard organization, a major national newspaper chain. The paper had a very enlightened editorial policy: "We have no politics in the sense of the word as commonly used. We are not Republicans, not Democrats, not Greenback and not Prohibitionist. We simply intend to support good men and condemn bad ones, no matter what party they belong to. We shall tell no lies about persons or politics for love, malice or money. It is no part of a newspapers business to array itself on the side of this or that party, or fight, lie or wrangle for it."[17]

The newspaper business represented a wide range of specialized interests. The *Philanthropist*,[18] an Abolitionist weekly, was destroyed by a proslavery mob in 1839 because of stories about slavery written by its editors. Started during the Civil War, a black newspaper, the *Colored Citizen*,[19] existed for six years. Beginning in the 1830s, a number of German language papers were available: *Die Chronik*, *Die Weltburger*, the *Volksblatt*, and the *Freie Presse*. The *Irish Citizen* lasted from 1876 to 1880. Of the religious sheets, the earliest was the *Catholic-Telegraph*[20] in 1831. Isaac Mayer Wise, the father of Reform Judaism, was the founder and editor of the *American Israelite*[21] (1874–1900). Small specialized-audience newspapers for sports, markets, racing, stockyards, shopping, and neighborhood news were constantly being brought into existence. By 1900, increasing advertising enabled the dailies to expand the variety of features for their readers.

Senefelder's Gift

For those who have studied stone lithography, the understanding of the basic principles of the medium are apparent—oil and water do not mix. A concise description of the process was written by Peter Duval in Ringwalt's celebrated *American Encyclopedia of Printing* in 1871: "The process of lithography is founded—1st, upon the adhesion to the smooth face of a stone, of an encaustic fat, which forms the lines or traces; 2d, upon the power acquired by the parts penetrated by this encaustic of attracting to themselves and becoming covered with the printing ink; 3d, upon the interposition of a film of water, which prevents the adhesion of the ink in all parts of the surface of the stone not impregnated with the encaustic; and 4th, and lastly, upon a pressure applied by the stone sufficient to transfer to paper the greater part of the ink which covers the greasy tracing of the encaustic."[22]

Lithography was invented in 1798 by Alois Senefelder in Munich and it quickly spread to Vienna, Offenbach, then to England, Russia, and throughout Europe. It reached the New World in 1818 but was not practiced locally until around 1840. The speed of production and reduced cost favored lithography over copperplate engraving. Early lithography, as it developed, was a hit-or-miss activity—surfacing the stone, drawing an image, making an ink, dampening a suitable paper, etching the stone, then pulling an impression on a manual press.

Good craftsmanship made the difference; discoveries were guarded and unfortunately not freely shared. The various ways of generating suitable art for lithography were numerous, such as drawing with lithographic crayons and pencils or with a pen or brush using liquid tusche. Using water with the tusche to thin it and applying it with a brush produced the effect of a wash drawing. The stone could also be engraved with a steel point or graver, combining lithography and engraving by cutting through the crayon or tusche. Drawing or writing on a specially prepared paper could be transferred to the stone. Also impressions from the copper or steel plates, woodcuts, or type could be transferred to the stone.

Here in Cincinnati the lithographic industry expanded rapidly, possibly because of the influx of German immigrants, many with a knowledge of this new medium gained before their arrival in America. One of these was Emil Klauprecht, a native of Mainz, who in 1840, along with Adolphus Menzel, established what was considered the first genuine lithographic firm in the city. They published the *Fliegende Blätter*[23] in 1846–47, the earliest illustrated newspaper in the West.

By 1849 Elijah C. Middleton, an engraver in copper and steel, joined forces with W. R. Wallace, a lithographic engraver. Hines Strobridge entered the partnership in 1854 after working for the Methodist Book Concern, where he was in charge of the publishing department which produced the *Ladies Repository.*[24] Wallace and Middleton left within a few years, and the firm became Strobridge and Company in 1867. Strobridge enjoyed a long and successful career, becoming one of the leaders in the field, specializing in circus and theatrical work. Strobridge absorbed the Henderson Lithographic Company in Norwood and in 1925 moved from downtown. Various other lithographers of nineteenth-century fame had become part of the Henderson group, including names such as Ehrgott, Forbriger, Krebs, and Achert, among others.

In 1851 Otto Onken published some outstanding examples of stone lithography in his book *Western Scenery.*[25] He was responsible for employing and training many of the craftsmen who later started their own shops. Gibson Greetings, Inc., the renowned manufacturer of greeting cards, began around 1852 with George Gibson, who came from England, bringing along a French litho press, a wife, and seven children. Gibson and Company, as it was called, turned out a wide array of printed products, which were marketed through novelty and stationery stores—scenes and heroes of the Civil War were a specialty.

Charles Cist's *Cincinnati in 1859* stated that "the increase in business in this line from one lithographer with four hands turning out $40 worth of work, to four establishments in 1850 with 20 hands, and a product of $20,000, and now six lithographers with 65 hands exhibiting a product of $165,000 is not more remarkable than the continued advance in the art as respects taste in design and excellence in the finish of what is now executed here. It requires a good judge to distinguish some of our own Cincinnati lithographs from steel engravings."[26] During the latter part of the nineteenth century, Russell, Morgan & Company, with a huge downtown plant, was said to be the largest printing house on the continent and was doing more business than any other job printing house in the world, turning out playing cards, labels, and show business products. They moved to Norwood in 1902 and split into the U.S. Playing Card Company and the United States Printing and Lithography Company.

Donaldson and Elmes started up in the 1860s with two small presses. They began working with chromos (color lithographs), reproducing oil paintings using from four to eighteen colors. After a competing firm, Ehrgott & Forbriger, installed the first steam press west of the Alleghenies, they quickly ordered a similar press and changed their name to the Donaldson and Elmes Steam Lithographic Company.

So rather than 300 copies per day from a hand press, a pressman was now capable of producing 2,600 impressions. Zinc and aluminum printing plates were available by the 1890s. An almost simultaneous discovery in 1906 by A. Rubel of New Jersey and A. F. Harris of Ohio was the offset press. A metal press plate attached to a cylinder "offset" the image to another cylinder covered by a rubber blanket, and it was transferred to a sheet of paper run through the press on the impression cylinder, making a sharp printed image. The Cincinnati Lithographic Company installed the first Harris 22 × 30 single-color offset press the following year.

As a medium of self-expression, lithography attracted many outstanding fine artists, among them Goya, Daumier, Toulouse-Lautrec, and, in this century, Picasso. The work from the firm of Currier & Ives, which gained great popularity in America, was turned out by an unusual partnership, a businessman and an artist. Their success encouraged lithographers to find better and faster methods.

Persuasion Art

Much of our industrial progress has had to do with letting people know what we had to sell, or what services we had to offer. Advertising was salesmanship on a mass basis. The first advertisement in America appeared in the Boston, Massachusetts, *Spy* in 1780. P. T. Barnum nearly exhausted the possibilities by the 1850s with his heavy expenditures for ad space and his method of multiplying superlatives. Barnum's style was widely copied by others and might be explained in this early verse: "The man who has some goods to sell / And goes and shouts it down a well, / Is not so apt to reap the dollars / As he who climbs a tree and hollers."[27]

Advertising falls into two main categories: consumer advertising directed to the ultimate purchaser and trade advertising aimed at dealers and other middlemen. Either of these can be local, national, or international and reaches diverse audiences in amusement, food and farming, manufacturing, legal, political, financial, medical, educational, and charitable areas. The techniques of persuasion are many and can be found in newspapers, magazines, direct mail and mail order, billboards and signage, circulars, and, of course, today, in television and radio. What would our world be without comparative-price and promotional advertising? P. T. Barnum would be in for a surprise if he could look over today's excesses.

In 1870 Oscar Harpel, a local printer, produced a catalog containing examples of his firm's design of tickets, labels, letterheads, and other ephemeral printing, which he used for self-promotion—one of the first of its kind to be produced anywhere.[28]

The Victorian era, which spanned the last two-thirds of the nineteenth century, was influenced by Gothic architecture, ornament, and letterforms. It's love of business and complexity spread to work being done in this country. Lithography, which freed the artist from the constraints of letterpress, also provided a new freedom in solving problems. Advertising, illustration, and typography were given a free license for ornamental solutions that were seldom appropriate for clear visual communication. Many of these influences unfortunately lingered far into this century. Pictures dominated the type messages in advertisements appearing in newspapers and magazines. Book design in the nineteenth century was a disaster because of this wild preoccupation with overly decorative design and typography.

By the middle of the nineteenth century, William Pickering, one of the founders of the Arts and Crafts Movement in England, realized that graphic design should be separated from printing production, giving control over format design, type selection, illustration, binding, and other visual considerations to the planning stage of each job, following the wise old notion of think first, work later. This method quickly had an effect, producing a more classical simplicity. William Morris, probably the best-known designer of this movement, advocated a reunion of art with crafts. The problems created by the too rapid expansion of industrialization needed attention. This awareness helped fine book design and slowly spread to commercial design being done in England, as well as in America, which produced its own serious practitioners, such as Theodore Low DeVinne and later Frederic Goudy, T. M. Cleland, and Bruce Rogers.

For several decades at the turn of the century, Art Nouveau flourished in Europe, touching all aspects of design, including architecture, furniture, fashion, and graphic and industrial design, and provided a transition to the modern movement. Its free-flowing, linear, plantlike forms were handled with individuality by many outstanding practitioners, among them Victor Horta, Henri de Toulouse Lautrec, Peter Behrens, Charles Rennie Mackintosh, Aubrey Beardsley, Henri van de Velde, as well as the American Will Bradley.

In America, Art Nouveau influenced our developing advertising media, setting the style for bus and car cards, posters, billboards, direct mail, and catalogs. The General Electric trademark of this period still survives, but the individuality of the artists who were the original producers was imitated by many with less to offer. By World War I, the movement had dwindled out.

The Industrial Age

As the nineteenth century drew to a close, electricity and gasoline-fueled engines replaced handicrafts and the steam engine, greatly adding to productivity. Many who had counted on the land for subsistence found their way to the cities' factories. Mass production of goods reduced the cost and increased availability, thus stimulating the general economy. The development of new technologies went hand in hand with this movement. The rapid expansion of the reading public created a need for larger quantities of printed materials, in turn creating lower prices. The industrial age had started paving the way for a new century.

One is astounded at how quickly Cincinnati's industry and economy increased. An example is Procter and Gamble, which began in 1837 and by 1937 was generally acknowledged to be the world's largest individual advertiser. Another was the Fleischman Yeast Company, which made the first compressed yeast in 1868, a boon to the country's baking industry. Others starting up were the United Playing Card Company in 1880 and Kroger, the vast modern retail grocery chain, founded in 1883. The machine tool industry began with R. K. LeBlond in 1887 and the Cincinnati Milling Machine Company two years later. By the turn of the century Cincinnati was the national center for machine tools and eventually became the world center. R. K. LeBlond invented a gun-barrel boring lathe just in time for World War I.

In 1891, before the nineteenth century ended, there were 1,292 industrial establishments located here. Leaders by the year 1925 were soap, metal products, clothing, meat, printed matter, motorcars and trucks, bakery products, boots and shoes, and paints and varnishes. A 1937 census compiled by the U.S. Department of Commerce found the city represented in 250 of the 319 industrial classifications.

They Built a City, a book published in 1938 by the Cincinnati Federal Writers' Project of the Works Progress Administration in Ohio, tells of a decline in industry and commerce at the turn of the century. The expansion of rail transportation and road building spread production and population to other midwestern cities. However, this publication asserts that new trades, as well as many established ones, were soon enjoying a definite revival. In the printing industry the revival touched publishing, theatrical posters, and the ink manufacturers.

Notes

1. *The Centinel of the North-Western Territory* (Cincinnati: William Maxwell, 1793–96), weekly publication.

2. *Laws of the Territory of the United States North-West of the Ohio: Adopted and Made by the Governour and Judges, in Their Legislative Capacity, at a Session Begun on Friday, the XXIX Day of May, One Thousand, Seven Hundred and Ninety-five, and Ending on Tuesday the Twenty-fifth Day of August Following. With an Appendix of Resolutions and the Ordinance for the Government of the Territory* (Cincinnati: William Maxwell, 1796).

3. *Liberty Hall* (Cincinnati: J. W. Browne & Co., 1809–15), weekly.

4. *The Western Spy* (Cincinnati: Joseph Carpenter & Co., 1810–19), weekly.

5. Walter Sutton, *The Western Book Trade: Cincinnati as a Nineteenth-Century Publishing and Book-Trade Center* (Columbus: Ohio State University Press for the Ohio Historical Society, 1961), p. 11.

6. First published as Noah Webster, A *Grammatical Institute of the English Language: Comprising an Easy, Concise, and Systematic Method of Education: Designed for the Use of English Schools in America: In Three Parts: Part I Containing a New and Accurate Standard of Pronunciation* (Hartford: printed by Hudson & Goodwin for the author, [1783]). Subsequent revised editions of this part were published under the title *The American Spelling Book.*

7. First Edition: William Holmes McGuffey, *The Eclectic First Reader for Young Children: Consisting of Progressive Lessons in Reading and Spelling, Mostly in Easy Words of One and Two Syllables* (Cincinnati: Truman and Smith, 1836).

8. Daniel Drake, *Notices Concerning Cincinnati* (Cincinnati: printed for the author at the press of John W. Browne, 1810).

9. Daniel Drake, *Natural and Statistical View, or Picture of Cincinnati and the Miami Country, Illustrated with Maps. With an Appendix, Containing Observations on the Late Earthquakes, the Aurora Borealis, and South-West Wind* (Cincinnati: printed by Looker and Wallace, 1815).

10. *Browne's Western Calendar, or, The Cincinnati Almanac for the Year of Our Lord, Eighteen Hundred and Six. . .* (Cincinnati: printed at the press of John W. Browne, 1805).

11. *The Western Comic Almanac* (Cincinnati: N. & G. Guilford & Co., 1834).

12. *The Cincinnati Directory: Containing the Names, Profession and Occupation of the Inhabitants of the Town, Alphabetically Arranged; with the Number of the Building Occupied by Each. Also, an Account of its Officers, Population, Institutions and Societies, Public Buildings, Manufacturer, &c. . .* (Cincinnati: published by Oliver Farnsworth; Morgan, Lodge & Co., Printers, 1819). This was the first Cincinnati directory.

13. Allen D. Carden, comp., *The Missouri Harmony, or a Choice Collection of Psalm Tunes, Hymns and Anthems, Selected from the Most Eminent Authors, and Well Adapted to all Christian Churches, Singing Schools, and Private Societies; Together with an Introduction to Grounds of Music, the Rudiments of Music and Plain Rules for Beginners. . .* (Cincinnati: published by the compiler; Morgan, Lodge & Co., Printers, 1820).

14. *Ye Giglampz:* A *Weekly Illustrated Journal Devoted to Art, Literature and Satire. Edited by Lafcadio Hearn & Henry Farny* (Cincinnati: Giglampz, 1874), weekly.

15. *The Sidereal Messenger* (Cincinnati: Derby, Bradley & Co., 1846–48), monthly.

16. Daniel J. Kenny, *Illustrated Cincinnati: A Pictorial Hand-Book of the Queen City, Comprising Its Architecture, Manufacture, Trade; Its Social, Literary, Scientific, and Charitable Institutions; Its Churches, Schools and Colleges; and all Other Principal Points of Interest to the Visitor and Resident, Together with an Account of the Most Attractive Suburbs, by D. J. Kenny. Illustrated with over Three Hundred and Twenty Engravings and a New Complete Map* (Cincinnati: R. Clarke, 1875).

17. Federal Writers' Project, *They Built a City* (Cincinnati: Cincinnati Post, 1938), p. 249.

18. *The Philanthropist* (New Richmond and Cincinnati: James G. Birney, Ohio State Anti-Slavery Society, and William Birney, 1836–43), weekly (irregular).

19. *The Colored Citizen* (Cincinnati: Colored Citizen Co., 1863–69), weekly.

20. *The Catholic Telegraph* (Cincinnati: [Editors of the Catholic Telegraph], 1831–), weekly.

21. *The American Israelite* (Cincinnati: Bloch, 1874–), weekly.

22. J. Luther Ringwalt, *American Encyclopaedia of Printing* (Philadelphia: Menamin and Ringwalt [etc.], 1871), p. 276.

23. *Fliegende Blätter* (Cincinnati: Klauprecht & Menzel, 1846–47), weekly.

24. *The Ladies Repository* (Cincinnati: Methodist Episcopal Church, 1841–76), weekly.

25. William Franklin Wells, *Western Scenery; or, Land and River, Hill and Dale, in the Mississippi Valley, Superbly Lithographed from Original Sketches* (Cincinnati: O. Onken, 1851).

26. Charles Cist, *Sketches and Statistics of Cincinnati in 1859* (Cincinnati: printed and published for the author, 1859), p. 301.

27. Federal Writers' Project, *They Built a City*, p. 274.

28. Oscar Henry Harpel, *Harpel's Typograph, or Book of Specimens Containing Useful Information, Suggestions and a Collection of Examples of Letterpress Job Printing Arranged for the Assistance of Master Printers, Amateurs, Apprentices, and Others, by Oscar H. Harpel* (Cincinnati: author, 1870).

References

The American Israelite. Cincinnati: Bloch, 1874–. Weekly.

Berry, W. Turner, and Edmund H. Poole. *Annals of Printing.* London: Blandford Press, 1966.

Browne's Western Calendar, Or, The Cincinnati Almanac for the Year of Our Lord, Eighteen Hundred and Six. . . . Cincinnati: John W. Browne, 1805.

Carden, Allen D., comp. *The Missouri Harmony or a Choice Collection of Psalm Tunes, Hymns and Anthems, Selected from the Most Eminent Authors, and Well Adapted to All Christian Churches, Singing Schools, and Private Societies; Together with an Introduction to Grounds of Music, the Rudiments of Music and Plain Rules for Beginners. . .* Cincinnati: published by the compiler; Morgan, Lodge & Co., Printers, 1820.

The Catholic Telegraph. Cincinnati: [editors of the Catholic Telegraph], 1831–. Weekly.

The Cincinnati Directory: Containing the Names, Profession and Occupation of the Inhabitants of the Town, Alphabetically Arranged; with the Number of the Building Occupied by Each. Also, an Account of Its Officers, Population, Institutions and Societies, Public Buildings, Manufacturer, &c. . . Cincinnati: Oliver Farnsworth; Morgan, Lodge & Co., Printers, 1819.

Cist, Charles. *Sketches and Statistics of Cincinnati in 1859.* [Cincinnati: printed and published for the author, 1859].

The Centinel of the North-Western Territory. Cincinnati: William Maxwell, 1793–96. Weekly.

The Colored Citizen. Cincinnati: Colored Citizen Co., 1863–69. Weekly.

Drake, Daniel. *Natural and Statistical View, or Picture of Cincinnati and the Miami Country, Illustrated with Maps. With an Appendix, Containing Observations on the Late Earthquakes, the Aurora Borealis, and South-West Wind.* Cincinnati: printed by Looker and Wallace, 1815.

———. *Notices Concerning Cincinnati.* Cincinnati: printed for the author at the press of John W. Browne, 1810.

Dwight, Edward H., and Noel Martin, eds. *Modern Graphic Design. No. 1.* Cincinnati: J. W. Ford Co., 1955.

Federal Writers' Project. *A Guide to the Queen City and Its Neighbors.* Cincinnati: Wiesen-Hart Press, 1943.

———. *They Built a City.* Cincinnati: Cincinnati Post, 1938.

Fliegende Blätter. Cincinnati: Klauprecht & Menzel, 1846–47. Weekly.

Gutenberg Jahrbuch 1950. Mainz, Germany: Gutenberg Gesellschaft, 1950.

Harpel, Oscar Henry. *Harpel's Typograph, or Book of Specimens Containing Useful Information, Suggestions and a Collection of Examples of Letterpress Job Printing Arranged for the Assistance of Master Printers, Amateurs, Apprentices, and Others, by Oscar H. Harpel.* Cincinnati: author, 1870.

Hurley, Daniel. *Cincinnati: The Queen City.* Cincinnati: Cincinnati Historical Society, 1982.

Kenny, Daniel J. *Illustrated Cincinnati: A Pictorial Hand-Book of the Queen City, Comprising Its Architecture, Manufacture, Trade; Its Social, Literary, Scientific, and Charitable Institutions; Its Churches, Schools and Colleges; and All Other Principal Points of Interest to the Visitor and Resident, Together with an Account of the Most Attractive Suburbs, by D. J. Kenny. Illustrated with over Three Hundred and Twenty Engravings and a New Complete Map.* Cincinnati: R. Clarke, 1875.

Klein, Benjamin F. *Lithography in Cincinnati; Part I and II.* Cincinnati: Young & Klein, 1958–59.

The Ladies Repository. Cincinnati: Methodist Episcopal Church, 1841–76. Weekly.

Laws of the Territory of the United States North-West of the Ohio: Adopted and Made by the Governour and Judges, in Their Legislative Capacity, at a Session Begun on Friday, the XXIX Day of May, One Thousand, Seven Hundred and Ninety-five, and Ending on Tuesday the Twenty-fifth Day of August Following. With an Appendix of Resolutions and the Ordinance for the Government of the Territory. Cincinnati: William Maxwell, 1796.

Liberty Hall. Cincinnati: J. W. Browne & Co., 1809–15. Weekly.

McGuffey, William Holmes. *The Eclectic First Reader for Young Children: Consisting of Progressive Lessons in Reading and Spelling, Mostly in Easy Words of One and Two Syllables.* Cincinnati: Truman and Smith, 1836.

Meggs, Philip B. *A History of Graphic Design, Second Edition.* New York: Van Nostrand Reinhold, 1992.

The Philanthropist. New Richmond and Cincinnati: James G. Birney, Ohio State Anti-Slavery Society, and William Birney, 1836–43. Weekly (irregular).

Ringwalt, J. Luther. *American Encyclopaedia of Printing.* Philadelphia: Menamin & Ringwalt, 1871.

The Sidereal Messenger. Cincinnati: Derby, Bradley & Co., 1846–48. Monthly.

Sterne, Harold E. *Catalogue of Nineteenth Century Printing Presses.* Cincinnati: Ye Olde Printery, 1978.

Sutton Walter. *The Western Book Trade.* Columbus: Ohio State University Press, 1961.

Webster, Noah. *A Grammatical Institute of the English Language: Comprising an Easy, Concise, and Systematic Method of Education: Designed for the Use of English Schools in America: In Three Parts: Part I Containing a New and Accurate Standard of Pronunciation.* Hartford: Printed by Hudson & Goodwin for the author, [1783].

Wells, William Franklin. *Western Scenery; or, Land and River, Hill and Dale, in the Mississippi Valley, Superbly Lithographed from Original Sketches.* Cincinnati: O. Onken, 1851.

The Western Comic Almanac. Cincinnati: N. & G. Guilford & Co., 1834.

The Western Spy. Cincinnati: Joseph Carpenter & Co., 1810–19. Weekly.

Ye Giglampz: A Weekly Illustrated Journal Devoted to Art, Literature and Satire. Edited by Lafcadio Hearn & Henry Farny. Cincinnati: Giglampz Pub. Co., 1874. Weekly.

Chapter Two

Cincinnati as Seen by Some Early Engravers

Virginius C. Hall
Retired Associate Director
Virginia Historical Society

For the past few years, lithography has been in the spotlight, and rightly so. We have heard much and read much and seen much to celebrate the development of the lithographic art in this country. At an early date Cincinnati gained a place of prominence as a center of the lithographic trade, with such firms as Ehrgott & Forbriger and, later, Strobridge turning out work widely recognized for its technical and artistic excellence. Proud of their city, and eager to record its beauties, Cincinnatians commissioned artists to depict it. And increasingly, it was to lithographers that they turned. It was lithographers who produced and published those large colorful views suitable for framing and hanging over the fireplace that were both works of lithographic art and expressions of civic pride.

This essay is not about Cincinnati's lithographers or the views they produced. It is about a much more diverse group: Cincinnati's engravers—a gaggle of versatile artists who worked sometimes on wood, sometimes on metal, sometimes on both; artists of widely varying ability; jacks of many trades, prepared to engrave bill heads, banknotes, illustrations for books or periodicals, maps, invitations, or virtually any picture or decoration that might be called for. Much of their work was ephemeral, some signed, some unsigned. When I looked for a list of Cincinnati engravers, I found nothing at all, so I began gathering names from city directories and other sources. These are compiled in appendix A, which is necessarily a preliminary list. Inevitably, there will be additions and deletions—additions because new names will come to hand; deletions because some names will turn

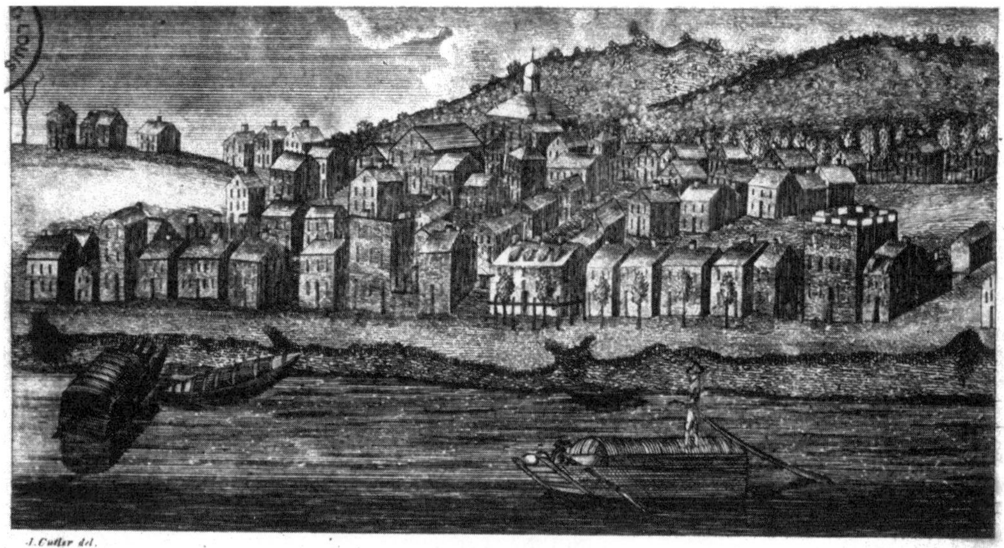

Fig. 2.1 A View of Cincinnati on the Ohio.
Jervis Cutler. Engraving. 3 × 5 1/16 in (7.62 × 12.86 cm). *A Topographical Description of the State of Ohio* . . . (Boston: published by Charles Williams; J. Belcher, Printer, 1812), facing p. 43. Cincinnati Historical Society Library.

out to belong to engravers who did only calling cards or lettering or scrollwork, and I have decided, arbitrarily perhaps, to include only pictorial engravers.

The first known published view of Cincinnati is a crude engraving drawn by Capt. Jervis Cutler, which was almost certainly engraved by him also. Cutler was born on Martha's Vineyard, and in 1788, as a youth of nineteen, he came to the Ohio country with a group of forty-eight adventurers under the command of Gen. Rufus Putnam. He is said to have been the first person to jump ashore at Marietta. Constantly on the move, he spent the next ten years up and down the east coast before returning to Marietta and Chillicothe in 1802. Like most frontiersmen, he was called on from time to time to perform military service. And so it happened that 1809 found him stationed at the Arsenal in Newport, Kentucky, just across the river from the little village of Cincinnati. In fact, for some time Captain Cutler served as post commander. It was doubtless at this time that he sketched his picture of Cincinnati, for we are told he "possessed great taste for the fine arts [and] sketched remarkably well."[1]

Later, having taken his command to New Orleans, he contracted yellow fever, which led to his discharge from the army and his return to New England. Here he devoted himself to writing *A Topographical Description of the State of Ohio*, published in Boston in 1812 and embellished with plates. One plate is a view of Cincinnati (fig. 2.1). It seems a curiously amateurish work for someone who sketched "remarkably well," but perhaps a promising effort on the part of someone just learning the art of engraving on copperplate. In time Cutler

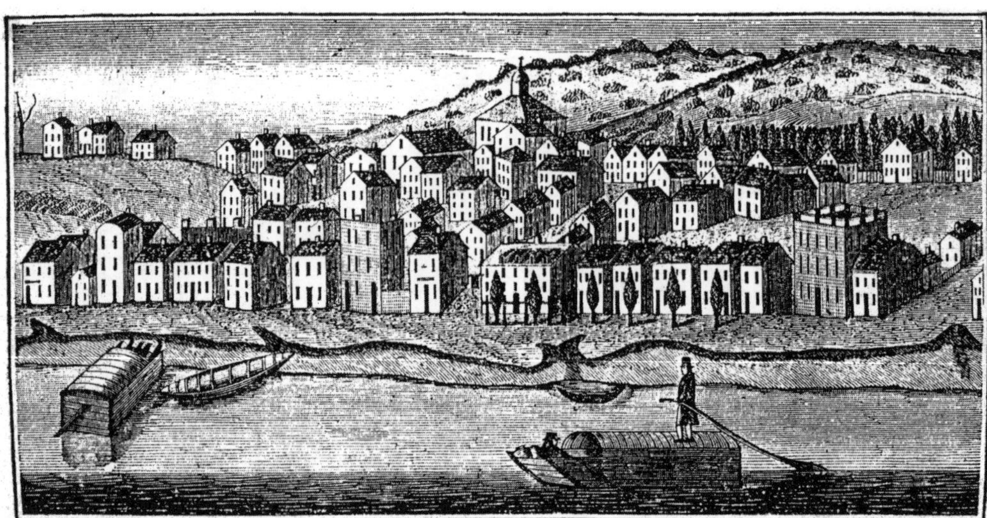

Fig. 2.2 Cincinnati in 1810.
Jervis Cutler. Wood Cut. $2\frac{15}{16} \times 5\frac{1}{16}$ in (7.46 × 12.86 cm). Henry Howe, *Historical Collections of Ohio* (Cincinnati: Derby, Bradley & Co., 1847 [1851?]), p. [217]. Archives and Rare Books Department, University of Cincinnati.

became a proficient engraver and in 1824 moved to Nashville, Tennessee, with his second wife to spend his remaining years working in a firm that engraved bank notes.

Cutler's view of the little town probably would not have gained much currency if it had not been reengraved on wood and used as an illustration in Henry Howe's highly successful book *Historical Collections of Ohio.* First published in 1847, Howe's book was popular enough to go through six editions. The reworking of Cutler's engraving brought the view into better focus, as it were, while at the same time retaining the naive vision and perspective of the original. Figure 2.2 is Howe's 1851 copy of Cutler's 1812 engraving of his own 1810 drawing, the 1812 engraving being the earliest published view of Cincinnati.

The versatile Dr. Daniel Drake deserves credit for compiling the first promotional pamphlets on Cincinnati. Credit for the first illustrated promotional pamphlet on Cincinnati goes to Dr. Drake's brother, Benjamin Drake, and his coauthor, Edward D. Mansfield. Bearing the straightforward title *Cincinnati in 1826*, the 100-page descriptive booklet was embellished with two engraved plates: one depicting the first home of the Medical College of Ohio (fig. 2.3), the other, the Cincinnati branch of the Bank of the United States (fig. 2.4). Both engravings are skillfully executed views of sophisticated buildings. William Woodruff engraved the view of the Medical College, which at the time was still under construction on Sixth Street between Vine and Race, and perhaps for that reason is shown sitting on a square tray in the middle of the sky. Ebenezer Martin's plate of the Branch Bank on the east side of Main between Third and Fourth Streets appears to be an accurate rendition of what the authors call "one of the chastest specimens of architecture within

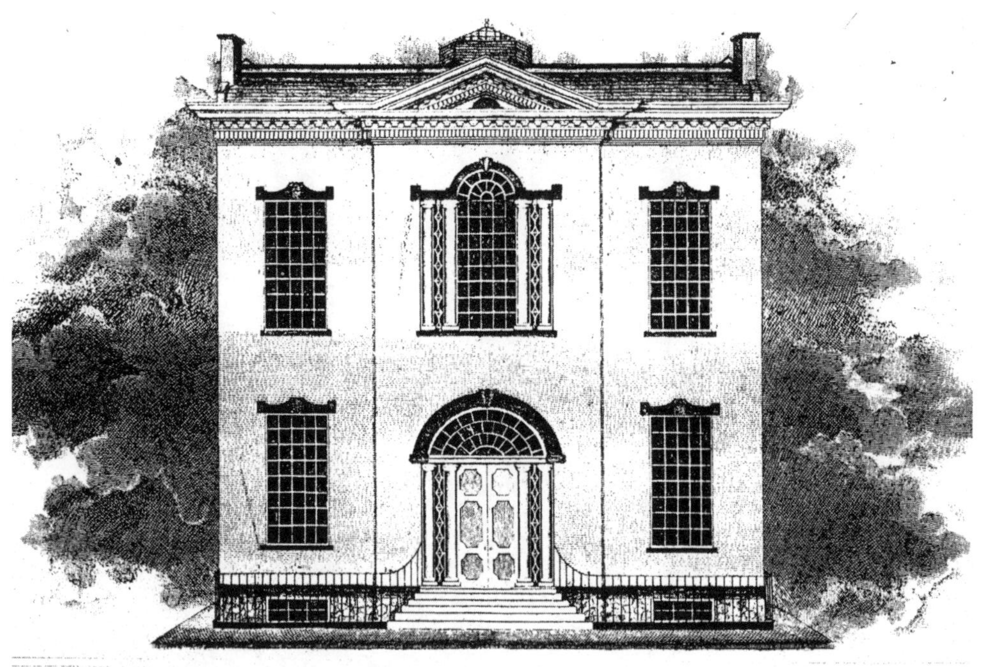

MEDICAL COLLEGE OF OHIO CINCINNATI

Fig. 2.3 Medical College of Ohio Cincinnati
William Woodruff. Engraving. 3 ⅞ × 5 $^{15}/_{16}$ in (9.84 × 15.08 cm). Benjamin Drake and E. D. Mansfield, *Cincinnati in 1826* (Cincinnati: printed by Morgan, Lodge and Fisher, February, 1847), frontispiece. Archives and Rare Books Department, University of Cincinnati.

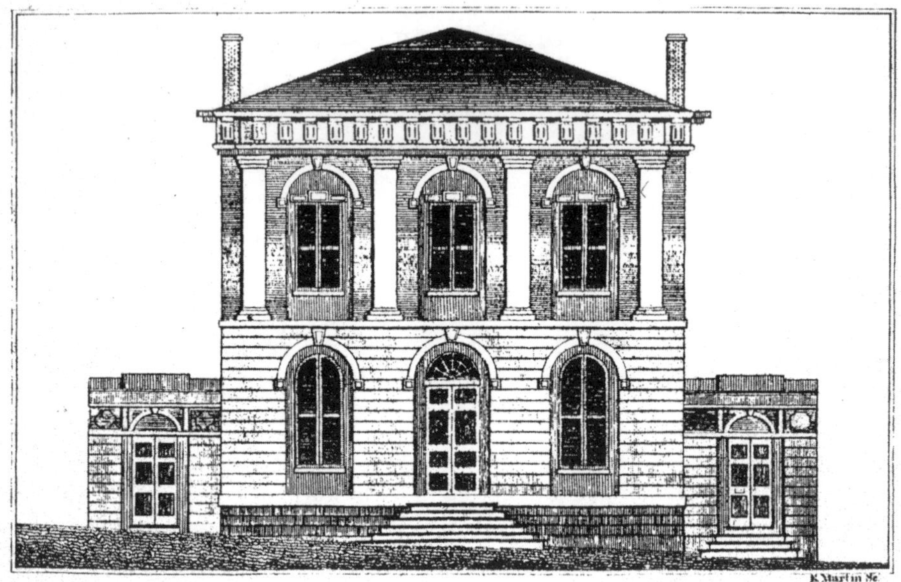

BRANCH BANK U.S. CINCINNATI.

Fig. 2.4 Branch Bank U.S. Cincinnati.
Ebenezer Martin. Engraving. 3 ¼ × 5 ¼ in (8.26 × 13.34 cm). Benjamin Drake and E. D. Mansfield, *Cincinnati in 1826* (Cincinnati: printed by Morgan, Lodge and Fisher, February, 1847), facing p. 29. Archives and Rare Books Department, University of Cincinnati.

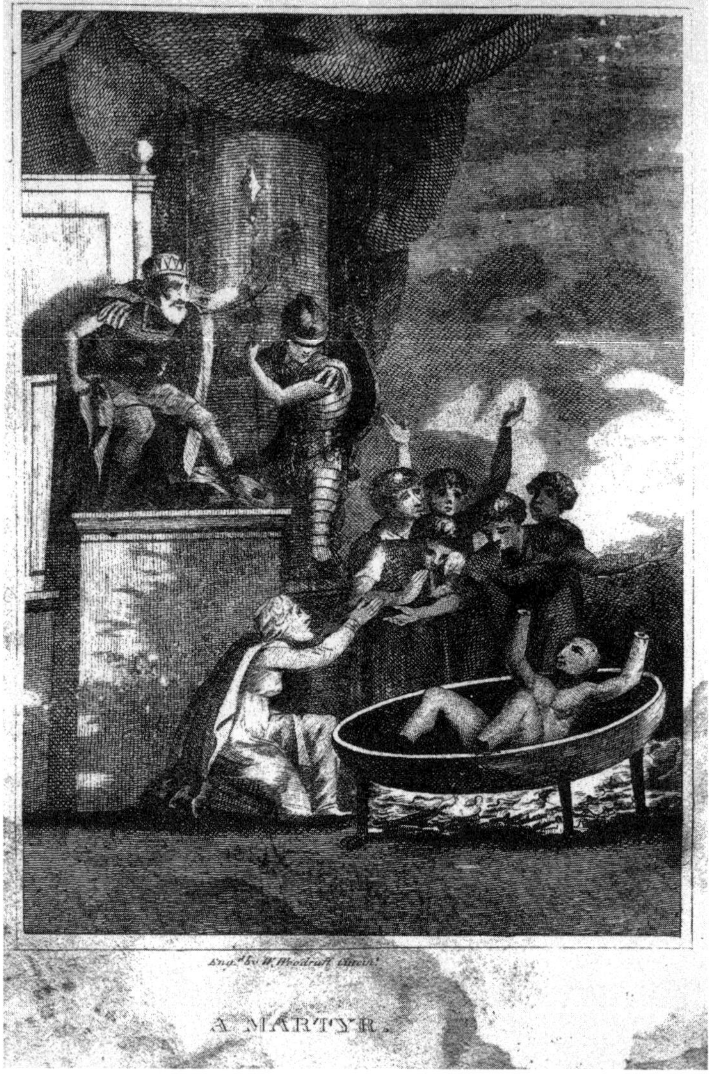

Fig. 2.5 A Martyr. William Woodruff. Engraving. 4⅞ × 3½ in (12.38 × 8.89 cm). Akins Wright, *A History of the Principal and Most Distinguished Martyrs. . .* (Cincinnati: Whetstone and Buston—Printers, 1829), frontispiece. The Public Library of Cincinnati and Hamilton County.

the city."[2] It even shows how the architect accommodated the building to its sloping site: with the downgrade door approached by steps and the upgrade door approached straight from the street.

These two 1826 engravings, one by William Woodruff, the other by Ebenezer Martin, are good, straightforward, competent architectural illustrations, suggesting that both men were trained in the East and knew what they were doing. Martin's is the only example of his work I have found. Woodruff, however, provided illustrations for a book published in Cincinnati in 1829 called *A History of the Principal and Most Distinguished Martyrs* (fig. 2.5). The martyrs may have been distinguished, but Woodruff's pictures of them are not. Undaunted, he later used his somewhat limited illustrative skills to produce five plates for *The Personal Narrative of James O. Pattie, of Kentucky,* edited by Timothy Flint and published

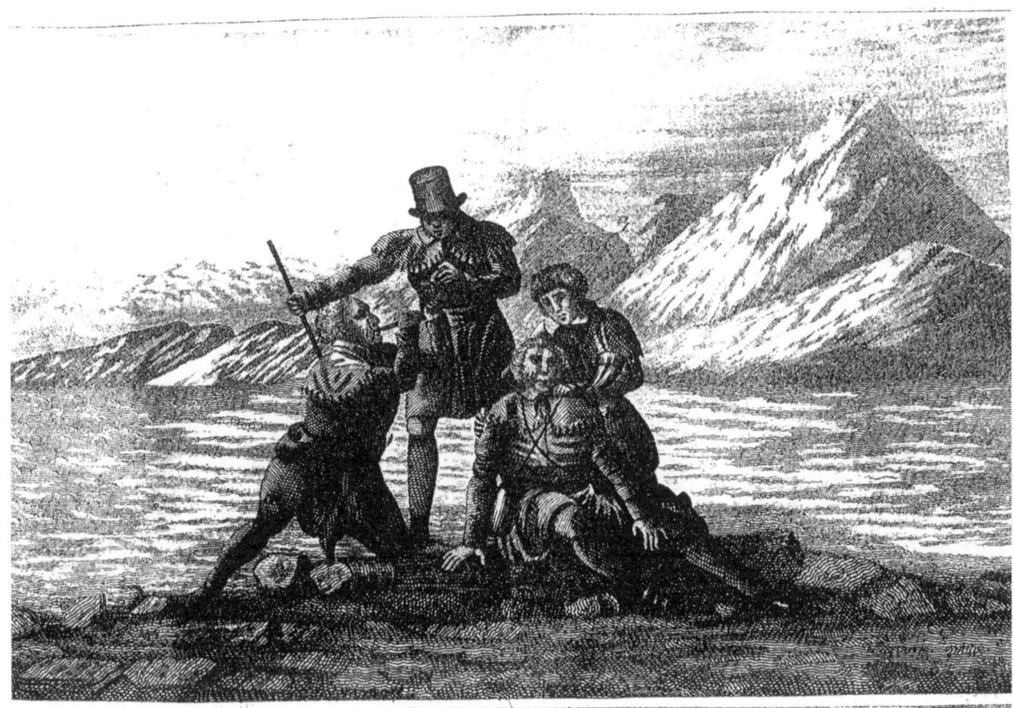

Fig. 2.6 Messrs. Pattie and Slover Rescued from Famish.
William Woodruff. Engraving. 3 × 4⁹⁄₁₆ in (7.62 × 11.59 cm). James O. Pattie, *The Personal Narrative of James O. Pattie, of Kentucky. . .* (Cincinnati: printed and published by John H. Wood, 1831), facing p. 165. The Public Library of Cincinnati and Hamilton County.

in Cincinnati in 1831 (fig. 2.6). Clearly, Woodruff was one of those engravers who is more comfortable with architecture than the human figure. He also did well with maps, as can be seen in the numerous plates he engraved for Samuel Cumings's *Western Pilot* (fig. 2.7).

As a visual footnote, figure 2.8 illustrates what happened to the elegant Medical College building when the college found itself needing more space. A second central bay and one side bay were added, resulting in a building that retained its symmetry but lost its focus. This wood engraving by George Whipple appeared in a Cincinnati newspaper in 1834, probably just a short time after the addition was completed. The building as shown here stood until about 1850, when it was torn down to make way for the new, gothic Medical College that remained a Cincinnati landmark for many years.

In 1831, five years after Benjamin Drake and Edward Mansfield commissioned the engravings for their booklet *Cincinnati in 1826*, two engravers from Connecticut, Curtis Doolittle and Samuel Munson, joined forces to establish Cincinnati's first engraving firm. In its first year of business (perhaps as an advertising piece to demonstrate the firm's capabilities), Doolittle & Munson issued a *Topographical Map of the City of Cincinnati*

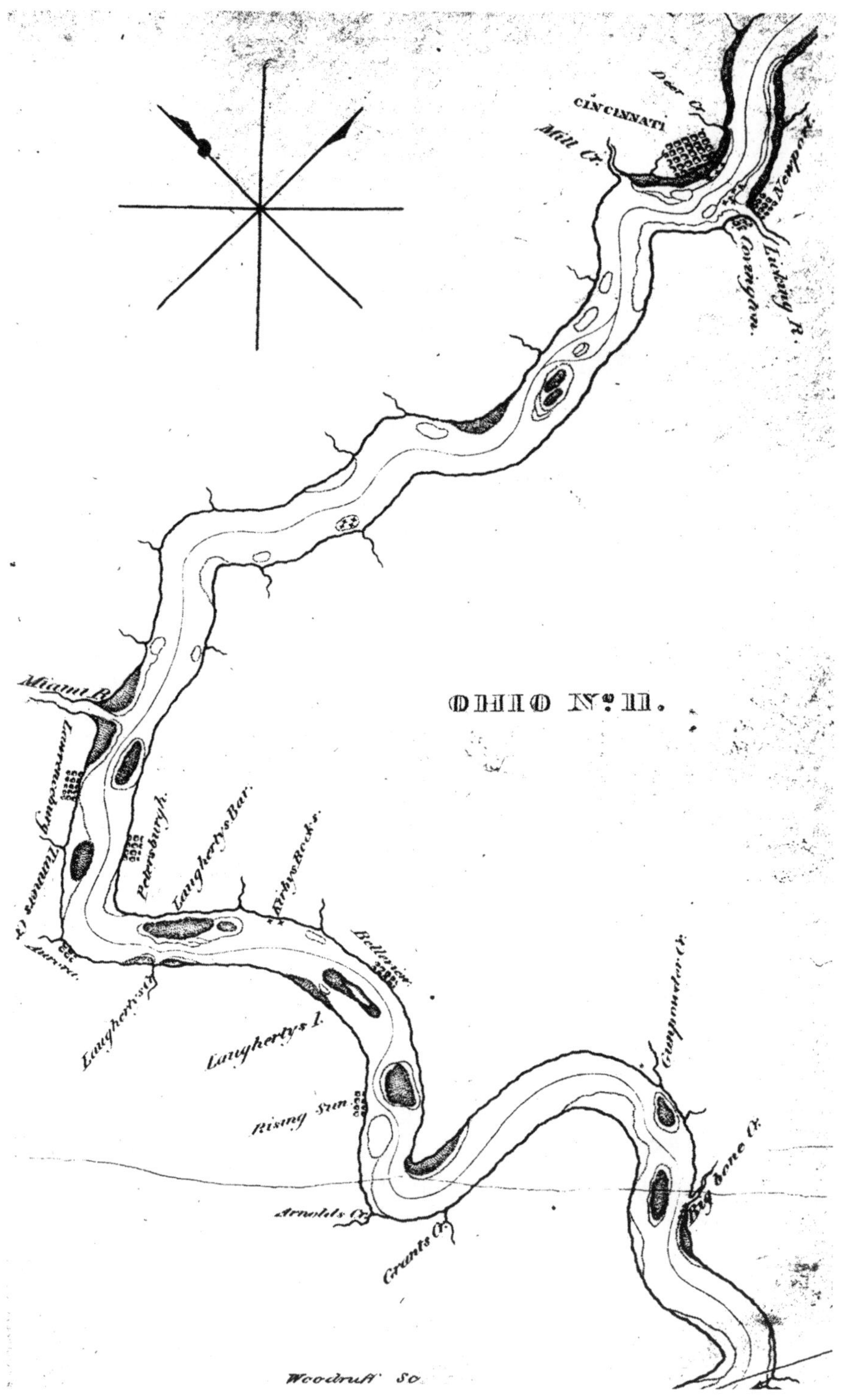

Fig. 2.7 Ohio No. 11.
William Woodruff. Engraving. 8 × 4¾ in (20.32 × 12.07 cm). Samuel Cumings, *The Western Pilot*. . . (Cincinnati: Morgan, Lodge and Fisher, 1825), facing p. 18. The Public Library of Cincinnati and Hamilton County.

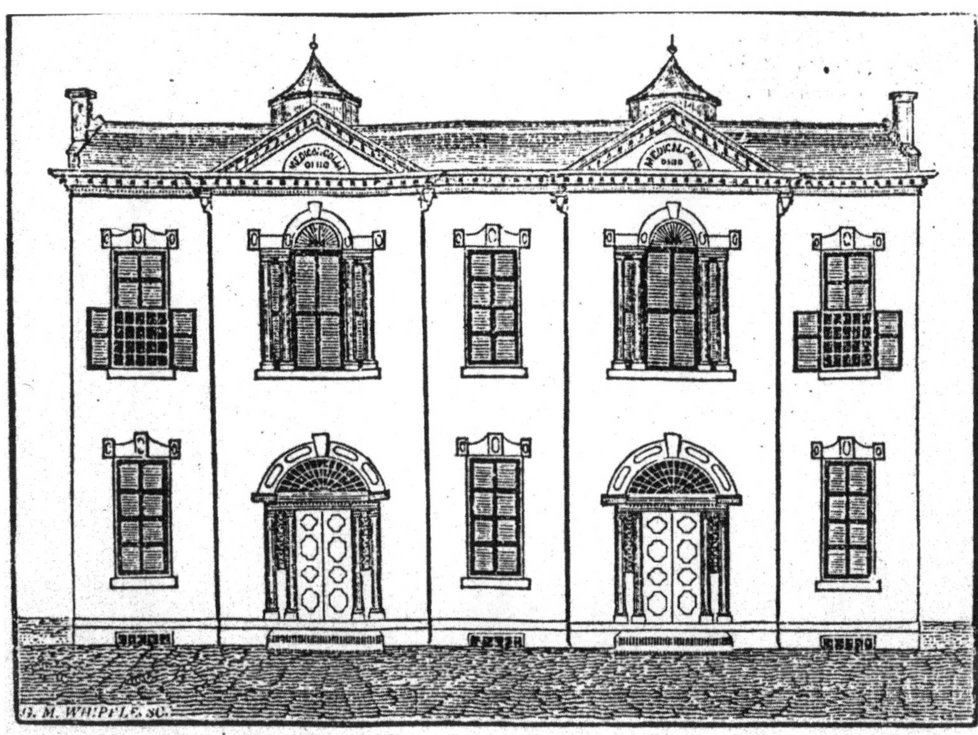

VIEW OF THE OHIO MEDICAL COLLEGE EDIFICE.

Fig. 2.8 View of the Ohio Medical College Edifice.
George M. Whipple. Engraving. $3\frac{3}{16} \times 4\frac{5}{16}$ in (8.10 × 10.95 cm). *Cincinnati Mirror and Western Gazette* 3, no. 15 (January 25, 1834), p. 120. Cincinnati Historical Society Library.

(fig. 2.9), a *tour de force* production with every line in the title engraved in a different style, a key for finding various important buildings, and along the top and sides a border of thirteen engraved views. Two of the views were of the Medical College and the Branch Bank, virtually identical to the ones used by Drake and Mansfield, and may have been the same plates slightly reworked. Five more of the views were done in the same two-dimensional style, more like elevations than views, though no less effective for that. Three more were treated more naturalistically, with perspective coming into play, and the three large ones across the top were views from the Ohio River. The map may be a show-off piece for Doolittle & Munson, but it is also a show-off piece for Cincinnati, a charming early expression of legitimate civic pride. The message is clear: You may have heard about tough frontiersmen and roughnecks off the riverboats, but these are the kinds of buildings we are putting up in Cincinnati. And in case anyone needs to know how far we've come in a short time, just glance at the box at the lower right where you will see that our population has grown from 2,300 in 1810 to 26,000 in 1830, a tenfold increase in just twenty years!

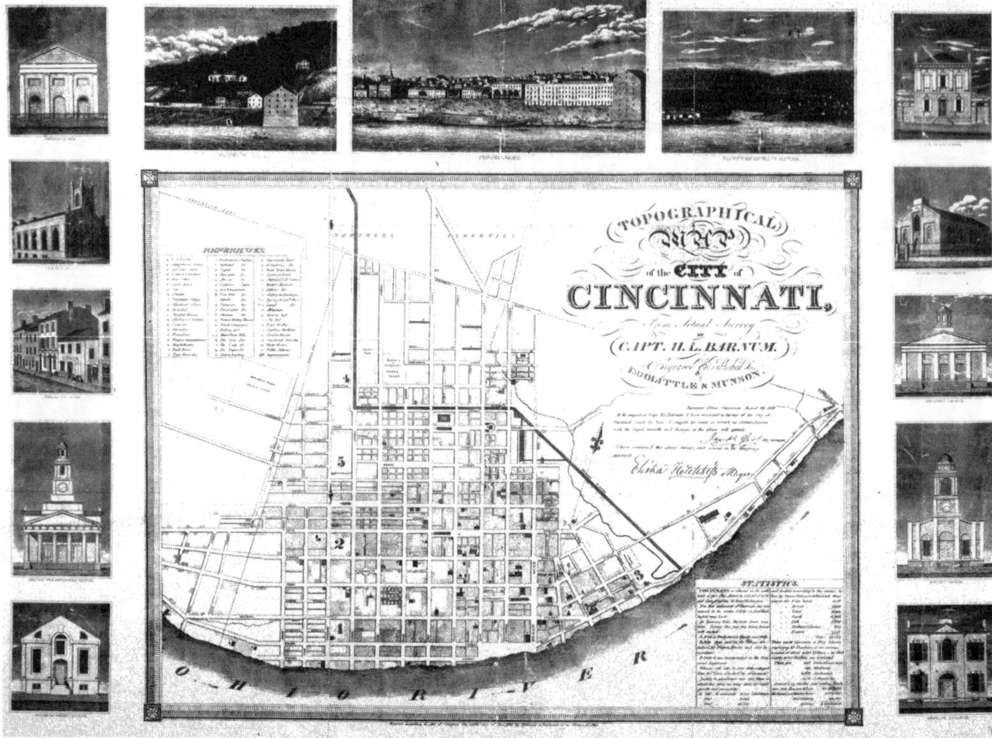

Fig. 2.9 Topographical / Map / of the City of / Cincinnati, / from Actual Survey / by / Capt. H. L. Barnum / Engraved and Published / Doolittle & Munson.
Doolittle & Munson. Engraving. 1831. 16 1/16 × 21 in (41 × 53.3 cm). Cincinnati Historical Society Library (Map 977.14CD691 1831A Copy 2)

For the decade 1831 to 1841 the firm of Doolittle & Munson did much of Cincinnati's illustrative engraving. The firm's office, shown in this early advertisement (fig. 2.10), was located on an upper floor of Thoms's Row at the northeast corner of Fifth and Main Streets. The building, a remarkable survivor, was still standing as late as 1954. During the course of renovations carried out that year, an old brass sundial was found mounted in the facade, bearing the inscription "William Thoms, 1829." A somewhat later advertise-

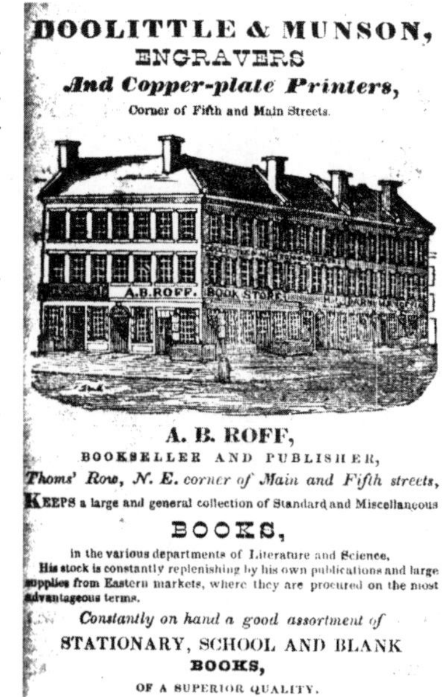

Fig. 2.10 Doolittle & Munson, / Engravers / and Copper-plate Printers, / Corner of Fifth and Main Streets.
Woodcut. 1 15/16 × 2 11/16 in (4.92 × 6.83 cm). *Cincinnati Directory Advertiser for 1831* (Cincinnati: printed and published by Robinson & Fairbank, 1831), preliminary page. The Public Library of Cincinnati and Hamilton County.

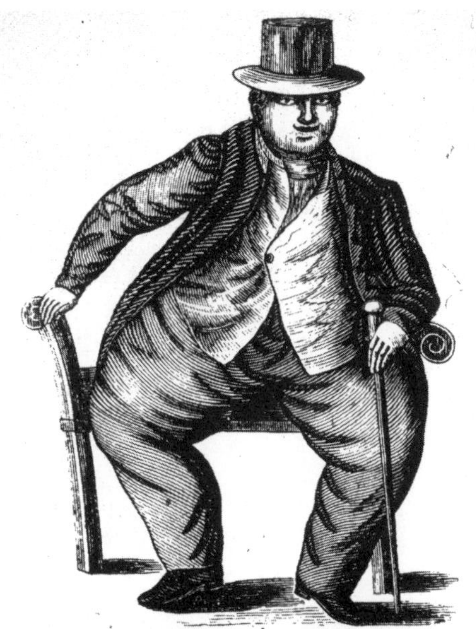

Fig. 2.11 Doolittle & Munson. / Engravers / and Map Publishers.
Engraving. 3 1/16 × 2 3/4 in (8.03 × 6.99 cm). *Cincinnati Business Directory for the Year 1844* (Cincinnati: R. P. Brooks, 1844), unpaged. Cincinnati Historical Society Library.

ment (fig. 2.11) was published when the firm had made a name for itself and could, perhaps, afford a lighter touch. One wonders if this could be a portrait of either Mr. Doolittle or Mr. Munson.

Comparing this eye-catching advertisement with the chaste and elegant *Topographical Map of the City of Cincinnati* confirms that Doolittle and Munson were all-purpose engravers: they could execute on demand either fine engravings on copperplate or much cruder, much cheaper engravings on wood. Examples of their "economy" views include four wood-engravings prepared for a children's periodical, the *Youth's Magazine*, published in Cincinnati in the mid-1830s. One view shows Christ Episcopal Church's new building on Fourth Street, completed in 1835. It stood until 1955 (fig. 2.12). The first building of the college that became the University of Cincinnati stood on the east side of Walnut Street, where the Mercantile Library Building is today (fig. 2.13). The handsome, neoclassical Lafayette and Franklin Bank was located on Third between Main and Walnut (fig. 2.14). Lane Theological Seminary in Walnut Hills, later a center of the abolitionist movement, was located off what is now Gilbert Avenue, north of Peebles Corner (fig. 2.15). This is a particularly interesting picture because Doolittle & Munson published another version of the same scene, a handsome copperplate engraving (fig. 2.16), and the two together illustrate the very different kinds of work the firm was capable of producing. The simple wood engraving was done in 1836 for the *Youth's Magazine*, while the copperplate view was engraved, as it states in the caption "for 'Cincinnati in 1841.'" The reference is to the first of Charles Cist's remarkable guides to the city, published successively in 1841, 1851, and 1859.

All but one of the illustrations in Cist's *Cincinnati in 1841* are the work of Doolittle & Munson. As befitted a major, published work, the plates were high-quality engravings on copper. The book's frontispiece is a lively view of the public landing (fig. 2.17), the center of Cincinnati's commerce, and always a favorite subject for artists. A little further on

Fig. 2.12 Christ's Church—Fourth Street.
Doolittle & Munson. Woodcut. 4⅛ × 3⅜ in (10.48 × 8.57 cm). *Youth's Magazine* 2, no. 17 (June 10, 1836), p. [257]. Cincinnati Historical Society Library.

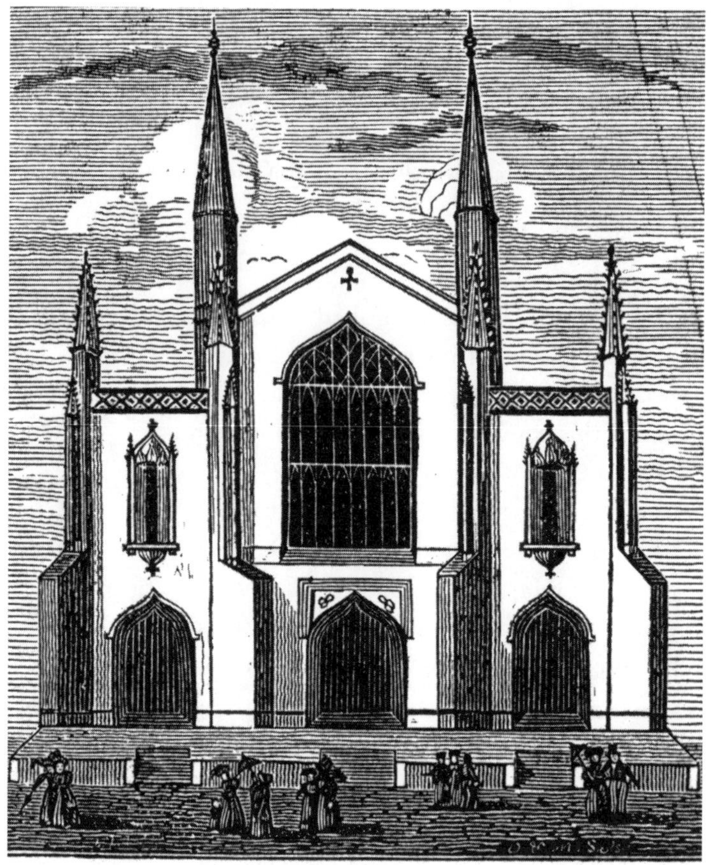

CHRIST'S CHURCH—FOURTH STREET.

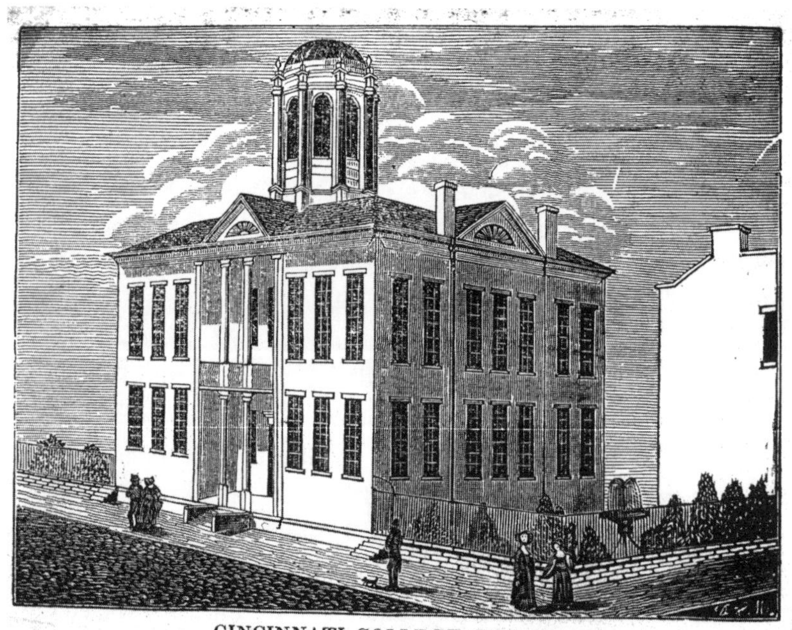

CINCINNATI COLLEGE EDIFICE.

Fig. 2.13 Cincinnati College Edifice.
Doolittle & Munson. Woodcut. 3 13/16 × 5 in (9.68 × 12.70 cm). *Youth's Magazine* 2, no. 23 (September 2, 1836), p. [353]. Cincinnati Historical Society Library.

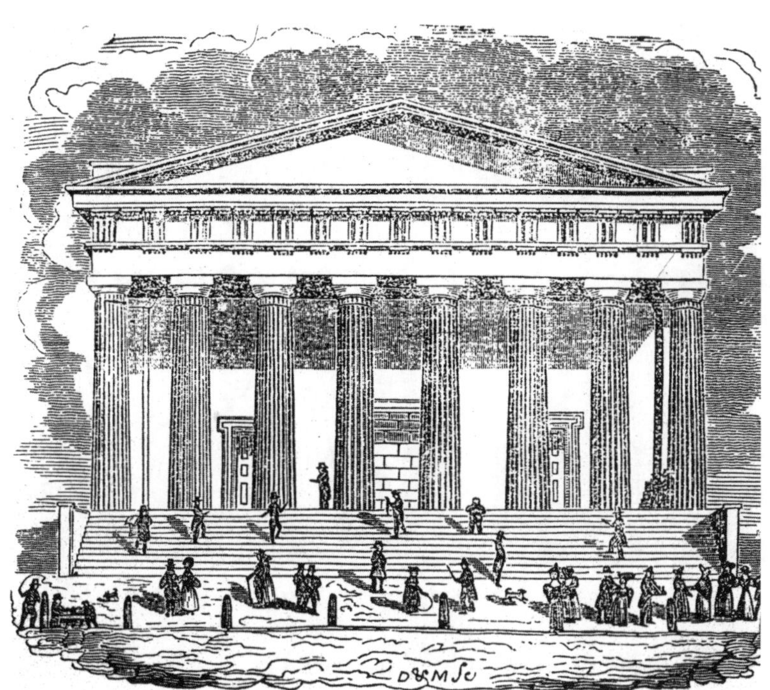

Fig. 2.14 Lafayette and Franklin Banks. (left)
Doolittle & Munson. Woodcut. $4\frac{1}{8} \times 4\frac{7}{8}$ in (10.48 × 12.38 cm). *Youth's Magazine* 2, no. 26 (October 14, 1836), p. [401]. Cincinnati Historical Society Library.

Fig. 2.15 Lane Seminary.—Walnut Hills, O. (below)
Doolittle & Munson. Woodcut. $3\frac{7}{8} \times 5\frac{9}{16}$ in (9.84 × 14.13 cm). *Youth's Magazine* 2, no. 24 (September 16, 1836), p. [369]. Cincinnati Historical Society Library.

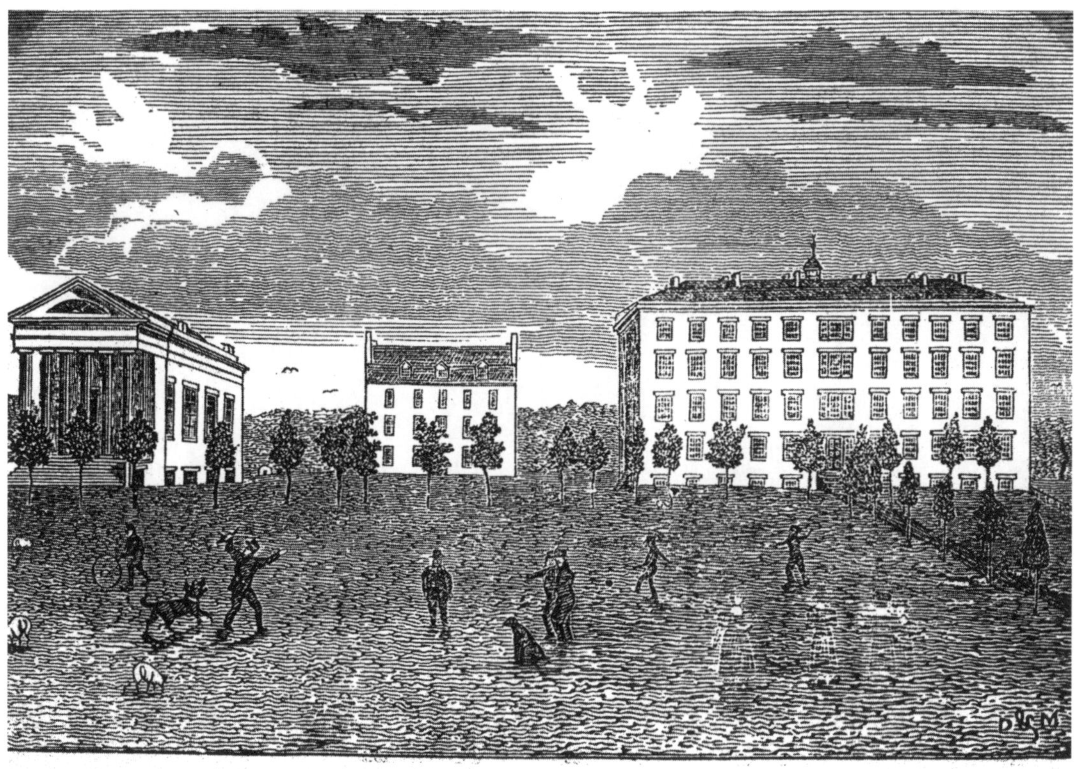

LANE SEMINARY.—WALNUT HILLS, O.

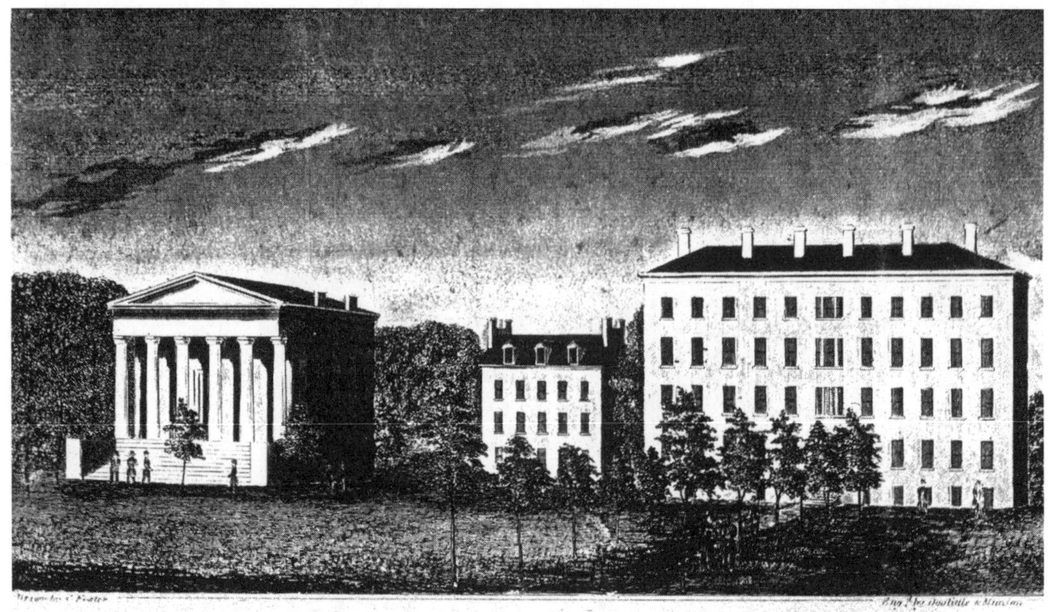

Fig. 2.16 Lane Theological Seminary, Walnut Hills. / Engraved for "Cincinnati in 1841."
Drawn by C. Foster; engraved by Doolittle & Munson. Engraving. 3 7⁄16 × 6 in (8.73 × 15.24 cm.) Charles Cist, *Cincinnati in 1841* (Cincinnati: printed and published for the author, 1841), facing p. 120. Archives and Rare Books Department, University of Cincinnati.

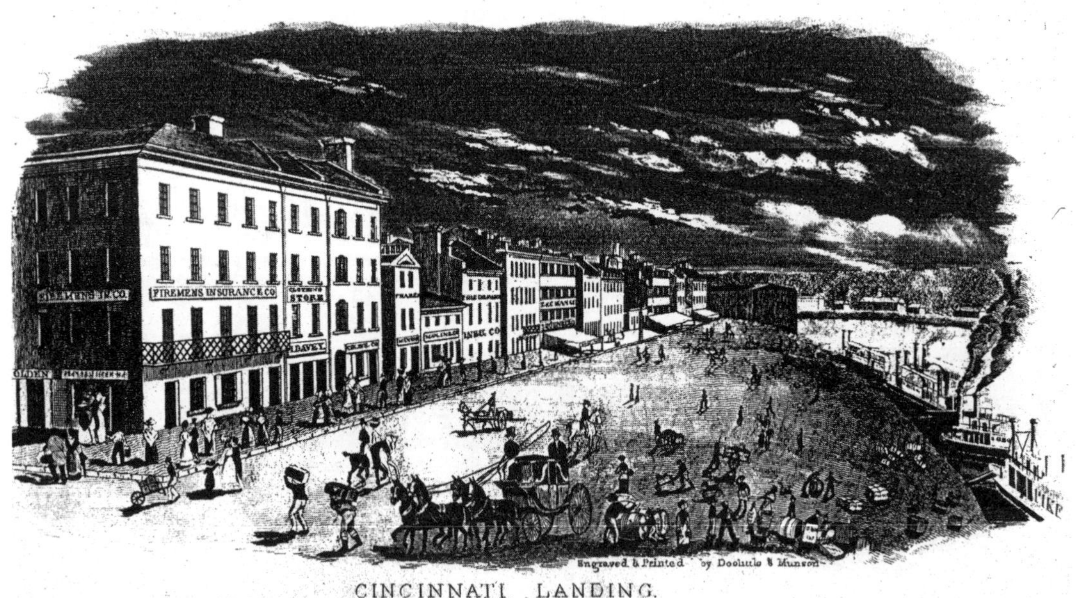

Fig. 2.17 Cincinnati Landing.
Engraved and printed by Doolittle & Munson. Engraving. 3 ¼ × 6 ½ in (8.26 × 16.51 cm). Charles Cist, *Cincinnati in 1841* (Cincinnati: printed and published for the author, 1841), frontispiece. Archives and Rare Books Department, University of Cincinnati.

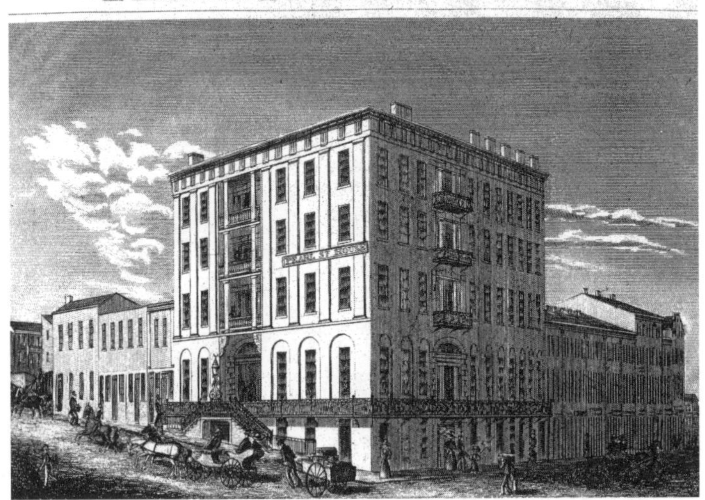

Fig. 2.18 Pearl Street House. / Cincinnati. Mrs. J. Goddard & F. M. Cockrell. Proprietors. Drawn and Engraved by Doolittle & Munson. Engraving. 3⅛ × 4½ in (7.94 × 11.43 cm). Charles Cist, *Cincinnati in 1841* (Cincinnati: printed and published for the author, 1841), facing p. 60. Cincinnati Historical Society Library.

there is a handsome advertisement for a recently opened hotel called the Pearl Street House, incorporating sophisticated blind arches, triglyphs, and ironwork balconies (fig. 2.18). There is an attractive plate bearing the caption "Post Office, Cincinnati, Third Street, between Walnut and Vine" (fig. 2.19). Because none of the buildings is identified as the Post Office, one is tempted to assume it is the elegant, pillared building in the center of the picture. The pillared building is, in fact, the residence of Samuel Foote, and the

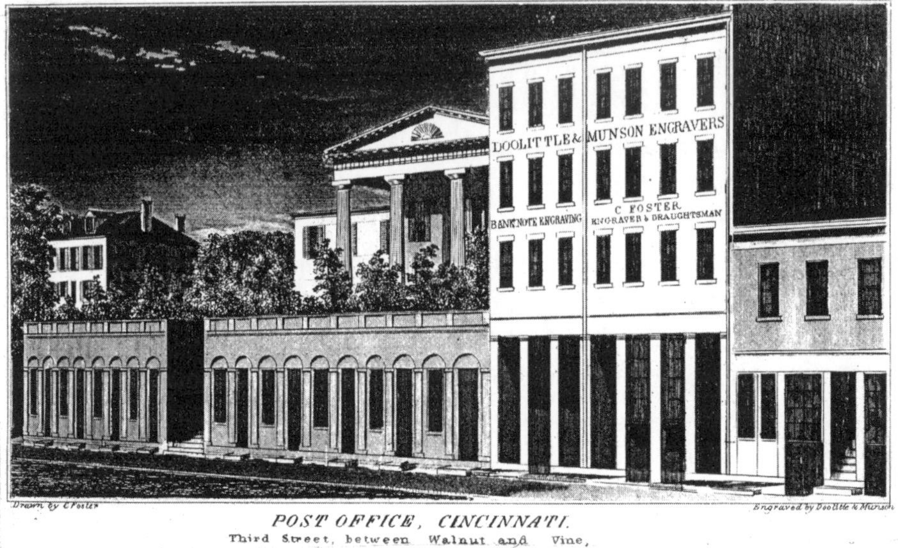

Fig. 2.19 Post Office, Cincinnati. / Third Street, between Walnut and Vine. Drawn by C. Foster; engraved by Doolittle & Munson. Engraving. 3⅜ × 6 in (8.57 × 15.24 cm). Charles Cist, *Cincinnati in 1841* (Cincinnati: printed and published for the author, 1841), facing p. 156. Archives and Rare Books Department, University of Cincinnati.

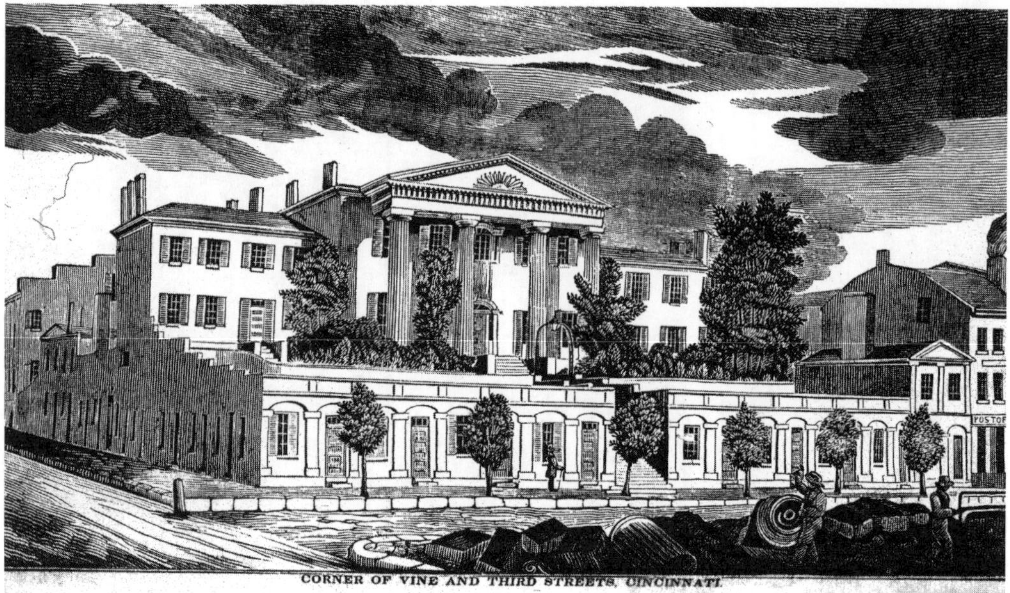

Fig. 2.20 Corner of Vine and Third Streets, Cincinnati.
Woodcut. 4½ × 7$^{15}/_{16}$ in (11.43 × 20.16 cm). *The Monthly Chronicle of Interesting and Useful Knowledge* 1, no. 5 (April 1839), facing p. 193. Cincinnati Historical Society Library.

row of little shops built at street level in front of it was known as Foote's Row. Doolittle and Munson, being shrewd businessmen, perhaps chose to depict the Post Office because it offered the opportunity to highlight their new offices on the third floor of the Odd Fellows Hall. The Post Office occupied the ground floor of that double building. The Odd Fellows themselves reserved the top floor for their meeting room. Confirmation can be found in a wood engraving of the same site, taken from a different perspective two years earlier, and published in the pages of *The Monthly Chronicle of Interesting and Useful Knowledge* (fig. 2.20). In the two years separating these views, Foote's Row lost the top part of its little pavilion on the east, and the building occupied by the post office expanded from a single building three stories high to a double building four stories high. Details of this kind may be of marginal interest to print collectors and connoisseurs, but they are useful to those who use prints to study urban development and growth. In the foreground is a construction site with one mason sawing a stone block, on the right, and another working on the base of a stone column.

This unsigned view of Foote's Row and the Post Office has an appealing vigor and vitality. Another woodcut that was very likely done by the same hand appeared in the same periodical just four months earlier and shows the magnificent building of the Ohio Life Insurance and Trust Company on the southwest corner of Third and Main Streets (fig. 2.21). Notice in particular the two totally out-of-scale horse-drawn vehicles in the left-hand lower corner of the picture. These two charming Cincinnati views are tentatively attrib-

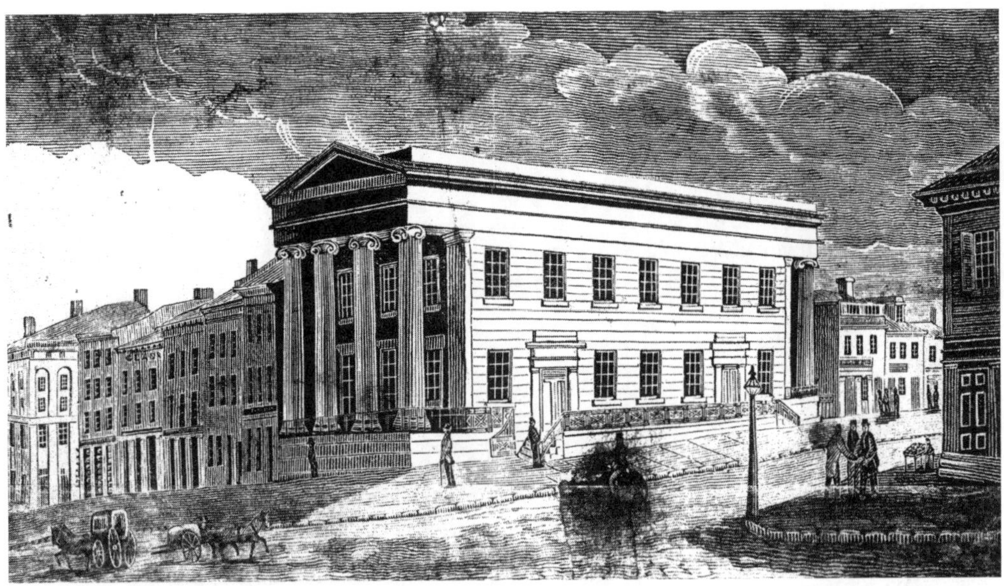

Fig. 2.21 [Ohio Life Insurance and Trust Co.—Main Street and Third]
Woodcut. 4 9/16 × 7 11/16 in (11.59 × 19.53 cm). *The Monthly Chronicle of Interesting and Useful Knowledge* 1, no. 1 (December 1838), opposite page [1]. Archives and Rare Books Department, University of Cincinnati.

uted to John H. Lovejoy, a wood engraver who worked for Doolittle & Munson in 1836–37 and then is listed as the proprietor of his own shop from 1840 to 1844. It is also suggested that Lovejoy engraved some of the cheap, wood-engraved views signed with the D & M (Doolittle & Munson) logo. The firm's proprietors, capable as they were of fine, copperplate engraving, would not waste their time on crude wood engravings if they had an employee like John Lovejoy who could do that kind of work for them. Support for this hypothesis is to be found in the signed work that Lovejoy produced after he went into business for himself. An advertisement for his own business, placed in the 1844 Cincinnati business directory, depicts "Serpent Charmers of Brazil" (fig. 2.22). Perhaps the cut was made to illustrate a geography book and was reused to demonstrate the proprietor's skill. It is eye-catching and exotic, but it is not in the same league as the fat man in the Doolittle & Munson advertisement, which is a skillful caricature and far more assured. This is a naive, childlike attempt at a serious illustration, which in its own way is every bit as appealing.

In the early 1840s John Lovejoy was also the joint proprietor of a weekly periodical called *The Elevator* (fig. 2.23), a journal of high moral tone devoted (in the words of its editors) "to the political, social, and intellectual elevation of the working classes." Each issue contained several simple woodcuts, unsigned, but presumably the work of John Lovejoy, that illustrated mechanical devices like pulleys and levers to help young workers and apprentices improve their technical skills and elevate themselves.

When his former bosses, Doolittle and Munson, first went into business, they

Fig. 2.22 Engravers. / Jno. H. Lovejoy, / Copper-Plate and Wood / Engraver & Printer, / N. W. Corner Sixth and Main Streets.
John H. Lovejoy. Engraving. 3 9/16 × 3 11/16 in (9.05 × 9.37 cm). *Kimball and James' Business Directory for the Mississippi Valley: 1844* (Cincinnati: printed by Kendall & Barnard, 1844), p. 111. The Public Library of Cincinnati and Hamilton County.

ENGRAVERS.

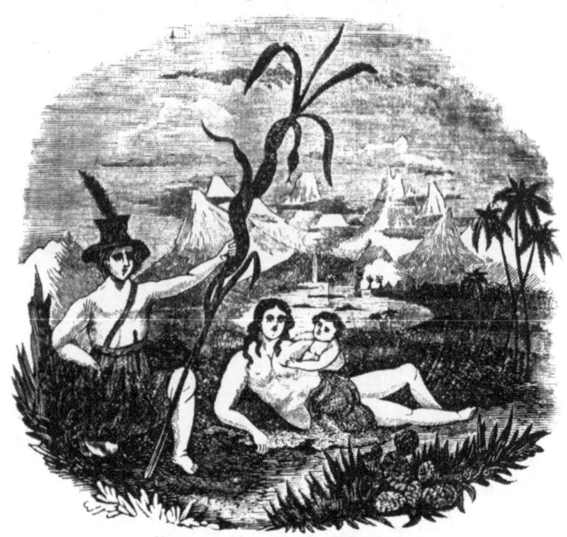

Serpent Charmers of Brazil.
Engraved by Jno. H. Lovejoy.

JNO. H. LOVEJOY,

COPPER-PLATE AND WOOD

ENGRAVER & PRINTER,

N. W. Corner Sixth and Main Streets.

☞ All orders in the above business, Seal Cutting, Bookbinders Ornaments, &c., promptly attended to, and neatly executed.

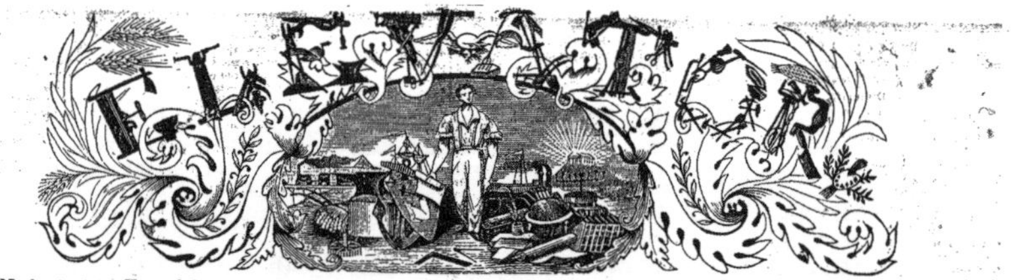

Devoted to Mechanic Arts, Natural Science, Agriculture, Biography, Literature, News, Inventions, and Political, Domestic and Social Economy.

VOL. I. PRESS ONWARD! NO. 5.

J. H. LOVEJOY, D. A. ROBERTSON, Publishers. CINCINNATI, SATURDAY, DECEMBER 18, 1841. Edited by D. A. ROBERTSON

PROSPECTUS OF THE ELEVATOR,

A weekly journal, published in the city of Cincinnati, and devoted to the Political, Social and Intellectual elevation of the Working Classes, wholly independent of existing political parties.

The chief design of the Elevator is to raise the entire base of society, by cultivating the mind, personal dignity, and political importance of the mass; not to depress or prejudice any useful or necessary class in the community.

Its cardinal principles will be those upon which all Workingmen, whether Farmers, Mechanics, or Laborers, fully agree; the first of which is, that all who live by toil, employers and employed, have one common interest; and that it is their duty to forget past differences, and unite as brethren for the purpose of promoting common views, and concerted political and social action upon all subjects concerning their general welfare.

In accordance with this design, the Elevator will open its columns to the investigation of the various questions of general interest which now divide and enfeeble the energies of the industrious classes. No exertion will be spared to unite all the sons of labor in one broad bond of brotherhood; to improve and concentrate their political views, by truth-searching enquiry; to elevate their social condition, by cultivating their personal dignity; and to stimulate and enlarge their minds, by furnishing them with cheap knowledge.

Each number will contain selected and original articles on the Natural Sciences, the Mechanic Arts, Agriculture, New Inventions, and Western Curios-

USEFUL SCIENCE RENDERED EASY.

HYDRAULICS.—No. III.

THE ARCHIMEDEAN SCREW.

ARCHITECTURE.

A portion of our coulumns will be devoted for several numbers, to the elements of Architecture. This, the first of the series, proposes only to explain architectural terms.

The following engraving of Corinthian architecture, will explain the terms applied to its several parts.

Definitions.—The front or *facade* of a building, made after the ancient models, or any portion of it, may present three parts, occupying different heights.

The *pedestal* is the lower part, usually supporting a column. The single pedestal is wanting in most antique structures, and its place supplied by a *stylobate*. The stylobate is either a platform with steps, or a continuous pedestal, supporting a row of columns. The lower part of a finished pedestal is called the *plinth*, the middle part is the *die*, and the upper part the *cornice* of the pedestal, or *surbase*.

The *column*, is the middle part situated upon the pedestal or stylobate. It is commonly detached from the wall, but is sometimes buried in it for half its diameter, and then said to be *engaged*. *Pilasters* are square or flat columns, attached to walls. The lower part of a column,

Fig. 2.23 *Elevator*
John H. Lovejoy. Woodcuts. Masthead: 2 1/4 × 7 1/4 in (5.72 × 18.42 cm); Archimedian Screw: 2 5/8 × 4 in (6.67 × 10.16 cm). Vol. 1, no. 5 (December 18, 1841), p. 1. The Public Library of Cincinnati and Hamilton County.

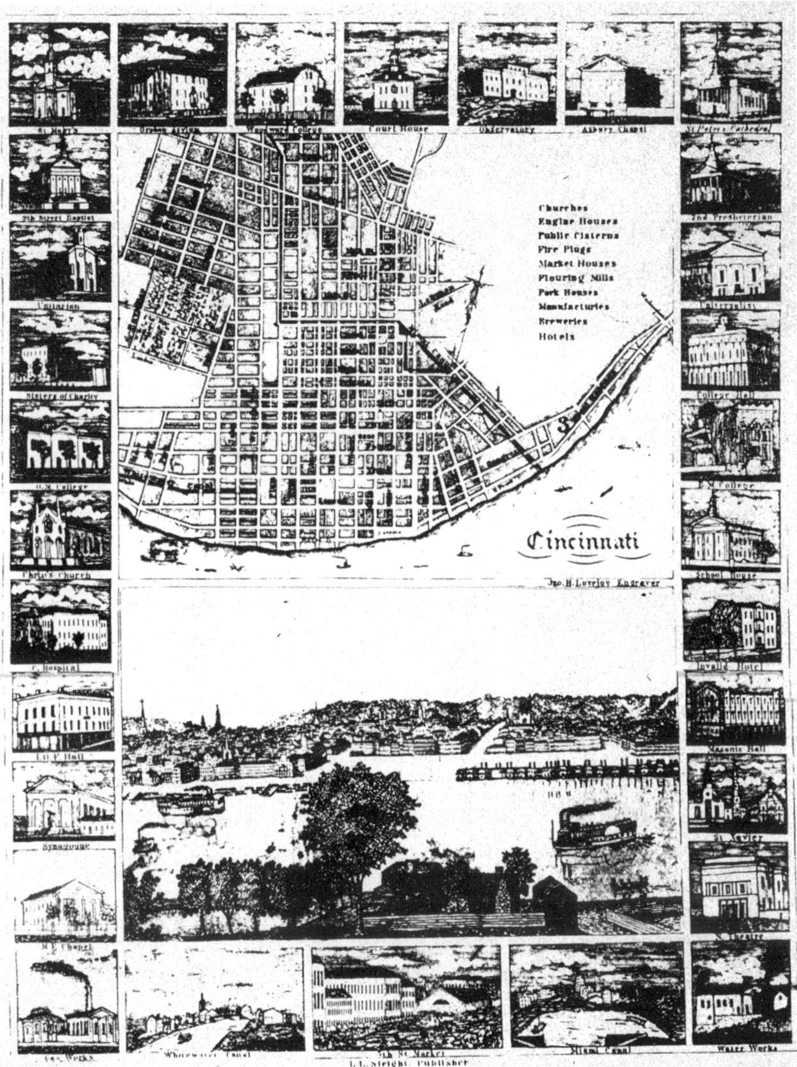

Fig. 2.24 Cincinnati [Map with frame of building vignettes]
John H. Lovejoy. Medium unknown. Size unknown. Cincinnati: John H. Lovejoy, 1840. Reproduced from photograph in Cincinnati Historical Society Library.

engraved an elegant map of Cincinnati surrounded by views. John Lovejoy in an endearing copycat move decided to publish a similar map when he first opened up a shop (fig. 2.24). The result is not elegant, but it is charming and of historical interest because of the number of the buildings he depicts. For example, the view of the Jewish synagogue on Main Street may be the only one that exists. What he lacked in the way of architectural draftsmanship, he made up for in the drama of his skies and cloudscapes.

When Lovejoy went into business for himself, Doolittle and Munson found themselves shorthanded and needed a new engraver to help with an increasing volume of business. The

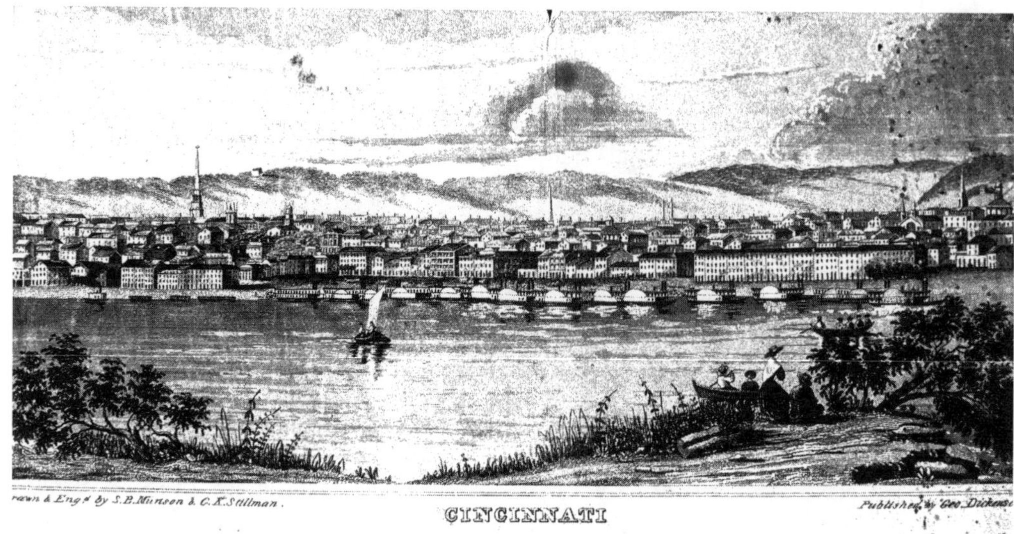

Fig. 2.25 Cincinnati. [View from Kentucky] [Letter sheet]
Drawn and engraved by S. B. Munson & G. K. Stillman. Engraving. n.d. 3¼ × 6$^{15}/_{16}$ in (8.26 × 17.62 cm). Cincinnati Historical Society Library.

person they hired sometime around 1840 was George K. Stillman, a young man in his early twenties who was a native of Boston and who in time also went into business for himself. To date there is only one known example of the work Stillman did when he was working for Doolittle & Munson. It's a view on the top of a letter sheet bearing the inscription "Drawn & Engd. by S. B. Munson & G. K. Stillman. Published by Geo. Dickinson" (fig. 2.25).

Letter sheets were commercially manufactured stationery: folded pieces of blank paper with an engraved view or decoration at the top of each folded sheet. The views were often city views. Letter sheets of this kind combined the advantages of a "wish you were here" postcard with the luxury of three and two-thirds pages of blank paper for the message. Our forefathers were great letter writers, and tended to go on and on, often running out of paper before they ran out of steam. So letter sheets enjoyed considerable popularity. George Magnus of New York was the best-known publisher of letter sheets, producing them with views of many American cities. The view at the top of Magnus's Cincinnati letter sheet is probably the most frequently encountered mid-nineteenth-century view of Cincinnati, which has been published as an illustration countless times (fig. 2.26).

But to return to the Munson/Stillman view, figure 2.27 shows another letter sheet illustrated with a slightly reworked version of the same plate. Munson and Stillman no longer get credit for having drawn and engraved it—they've been burnished right off the plate. Instead, we see the name of the new publisher: Derby & Bradley of 113 Main Street. That firm produced at least one other letter sheet design (fig. 2.28). Like the former, this one can be confidently dated 1846, not only because of the manuscript date on the letter, but because we know from city directories of the period that Derby & Bradley was in business only

Fig. 2.26 Birds-Eye View of Cincinnati. / in 1856. [Letter sheet]. George Magnus. Engraving. 3 9⁄16 × 7 1⁄4 in (9.05 × 18.42 cm). New York: George Mangus, 1850s. Cincinnati Historical Society Library.

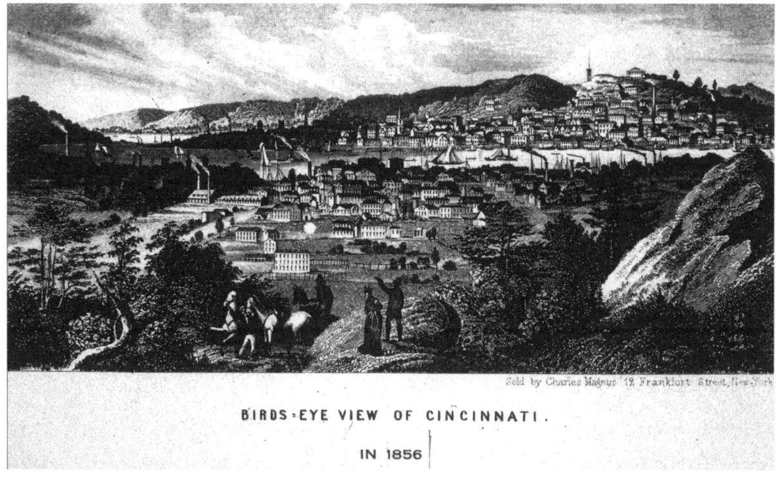

Fig. 2.27 Cincinnati. [View from Kentucky] [Letter sheet] Derby & Bradley. Engraving. 3 1⁄4 × 7 3⁄16 in (8.26 × 18.26 cm). Cincinnati: Derby & Bradley, ca. 1846. Cincinnati Historical Society Library.

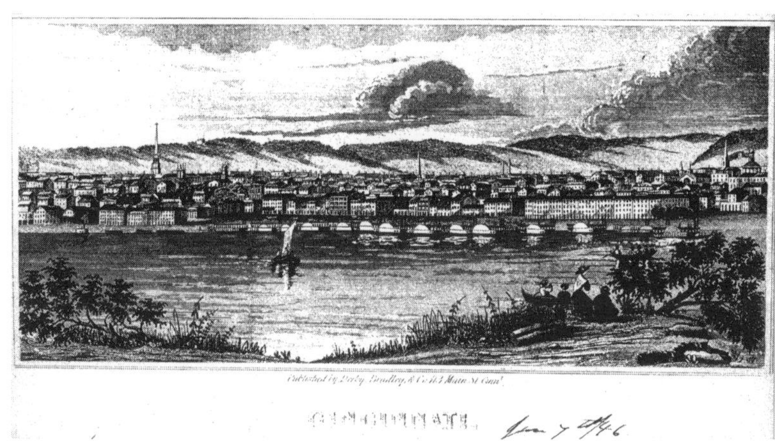

Fig. 2.28 Cincinnati. / from Mouth of Licking River Covington. [Letter sheet] Derby & Bradley. Engraving. 4 7⁄16 × 6 7⁄8 in (11.27 × 17.46 cm). Cincinnati: Derby & Bradley, 1846. Cincinnati Historical Society Library.

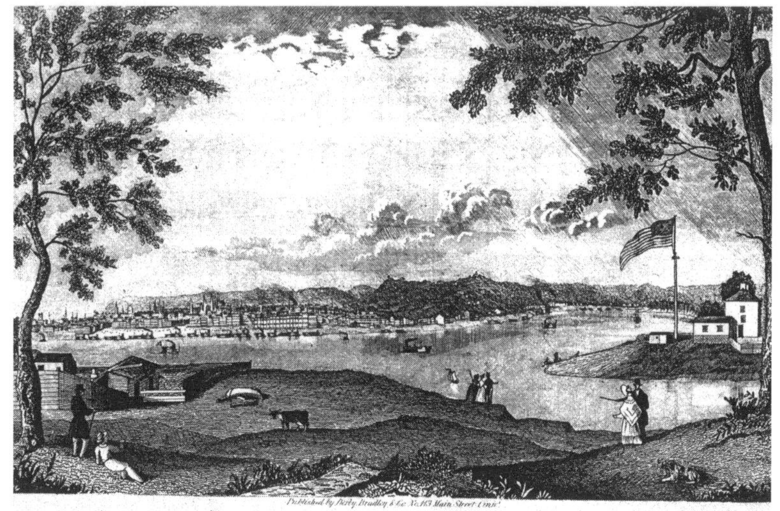

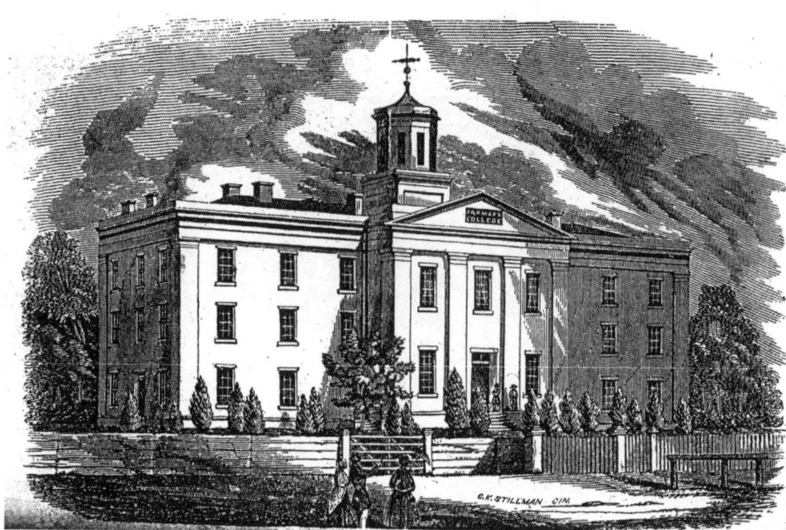

Fig. 2.29 Farmers College, Hamilton County, O. G. K. Stillman. Woodcut. $4 \times 5\frac{3}{4}$ in (10.16×14.61 cm). Charles Cist, *Cincinnati in 1851* (Cincinnati: Wm. H. Moore & Co., 1851), facing p. 359. Archives and Rare Books Department, University of Cincinnati.

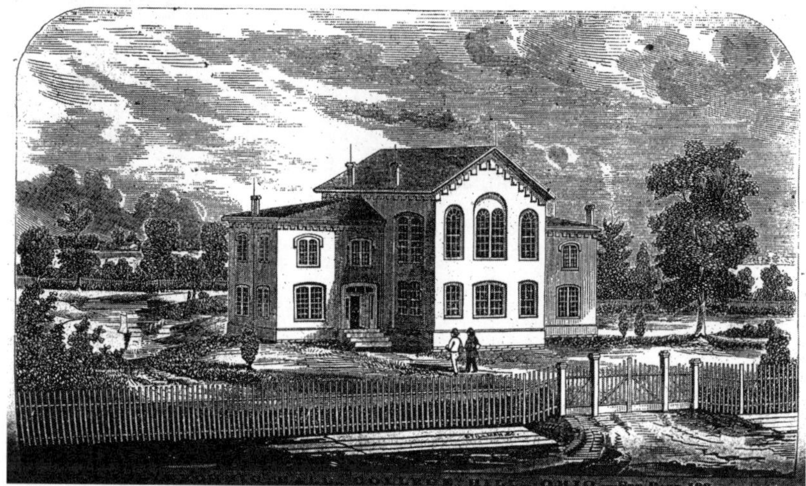

Fig. 2.30 Polytechnic Hall, College Hill, Ohio. G. K. Stillman. Woodcut. $3\frac{15}{16} \times 6\frac{1}{2}$ in (10×16.51 cm). *The Cincinnatus* (College Hill, Ohio) 2, no. 4 (April 1857), facing p. 145. Cincinnati Historical Society Library.

that one year. This view also shows the city from the Kentucky side of the river, but the artist has moved upstream a short distance, to the mouth of the Licking River. Across the Licking, on a site marked prominently with the American flag, stands the U.S. Arsenal, successor to Cincinnati's Fort Washington, and the military outpost commanded at one time by Capt. Jervis Cutler, whose pioneer view of Cincinnati was discussed above.

Stillman seems to have stayed with Doolittle & Munson until about 1850, when he set up shop on his own, taking on partners on two different occasions for brief periods. His view of the Farmer's College in suburban College Hill appeared in the new edition of Charles Cist's guide to Cincinnati, published in 1851 (fig. 2.29). The view was reissued six years later in a journal published by the Farmer's College itself, together with Stillman's view of another college building, the Polytechnic Hall (fig. 2.30). Both are straightforward, competent views.

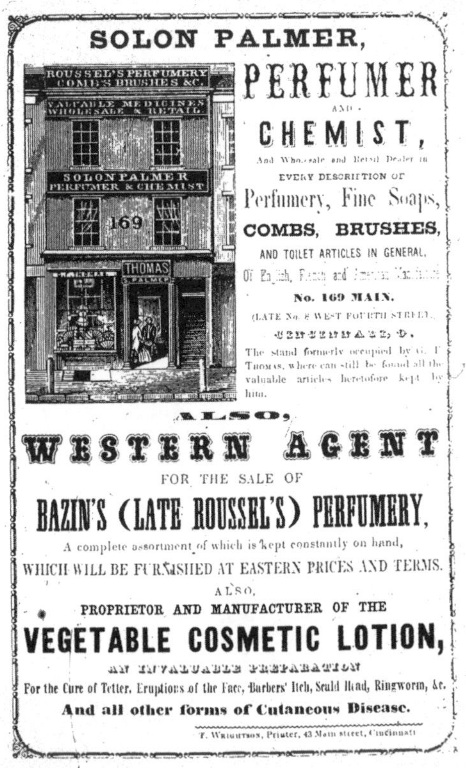

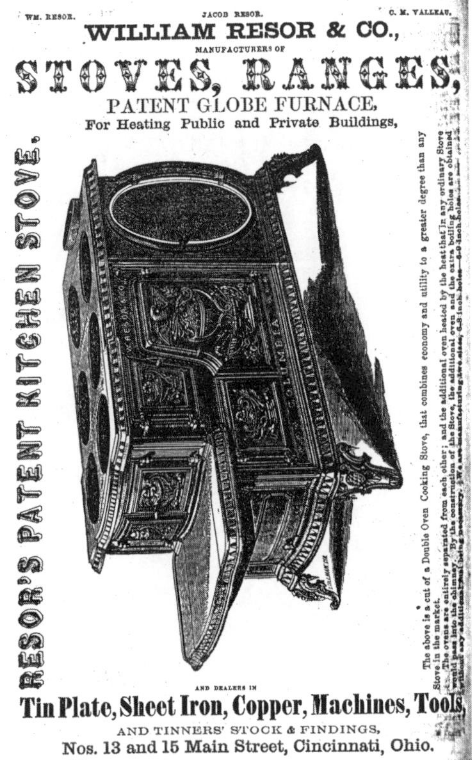

Fig. 2.31 Solon Palmer / Perfumer / and / Chemist . . . (left)
G. K. Stillman. Woodcut. 3⅛ × 1⅞ in (7.94 × 4.76 cm). *Williams' Cincinnati Directory . . . , 1851–1852* (Cincinnati: published by C. S. Williams, [ca. 1851]), inside front cover. Cincinnati Historical Society Library.

Fig. 2.32 William Resor & Co., / Manufacturer of / Stoves, Ranges, / Patent Globe Furnace, / For Heating Public and Private Buildings . . . (right)
G. K. Stillman. Woodcut. 3¾ × 5⅞ in (7.53 × 14.92 cm). *Williams' Cincinnati Directory . . . 1857* (Cincinnati: published by C. S. Williams, [ca. 1856]), p. 9116. Cincinnati Historical Society Library.

Like many local engravers, Stillman found a ready market for his cuts in Cincinnati's annual city directories. Two examples are the storefront of Solon Palmer, perfumer and chemist, and a highly accomplished woodcut of a Columbia stove manufactured by the Resor Company (figs. 2.31 and 2.32). Two fanciful advertisements for the C. D. Herrman Tea Dealer, signed by Stillman, appeared in the 1857 and 1858 city directories (figs. 2.33 and 2.34). The dates are important because C. D. Herrman was only in business for those two years. This makes it possible to date an attractive print of the Apollo Building, with Herrman Tea Dealer occupying a choice corner location at the northwest corner of Fifth and Walnut (fig. 2.35). That is pricey real estate today, being where the Fifth Third Tower now stands. Thanks to the information in the directory, the print can be precisely dated to 1857–58.

50 CINCINNATI ADVERTISEMENTS.

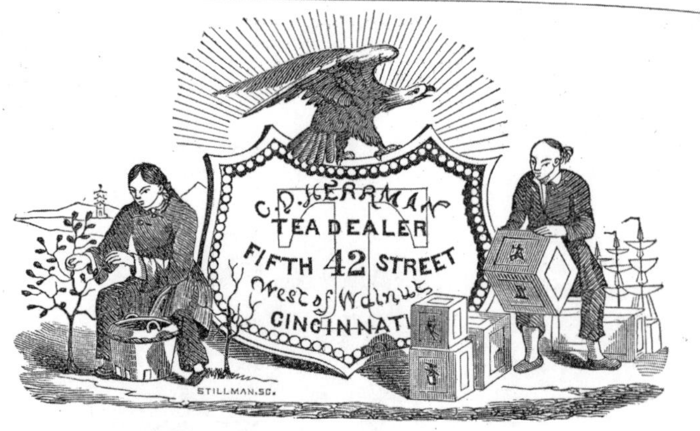

TEAS,

OF ALL DESCRIPTIONS AND QUALITIES,

AT THE LOWEST CASH PRICES.

Fig. 2.33 C. D. Herrman / Tea Dealer / 42 Fifth Street / West of Walnut / Cincinnati
G. K. Stillman. Woodcut. *Williams' Cincinnati Directory. . . 1857* (Cincinnati: published by C. S. Williams, [ca. 1856]), p. 50. The Public Library of Cincinnati and Hamilton County.

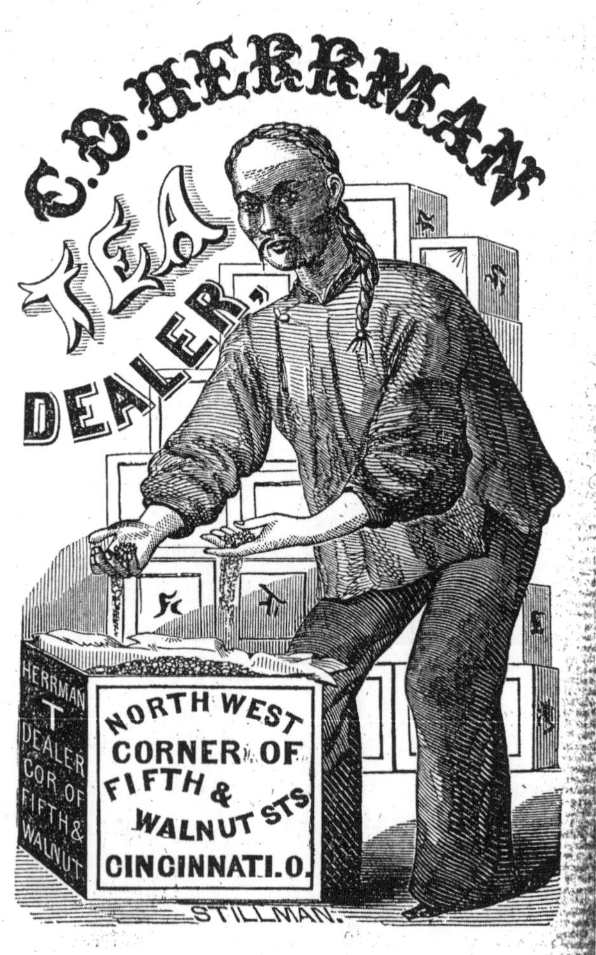

Fig. 2.34 C. D. Herrman / Tea / Dealer, / North-West / Corner of / Fifth & / Walnut Sts. / Cincinnati. O.
G. K. Stillman. Woodcut. 6⅞ × 4⅛ in (17.46 × 10.48 cm). *Williams' Cincinnati Directory . . . 1858* (Cincinnati: published by C. S. Williams, [ca. 1858]), p. [278]. The Public Library of Cincinnati and Hamilton County.

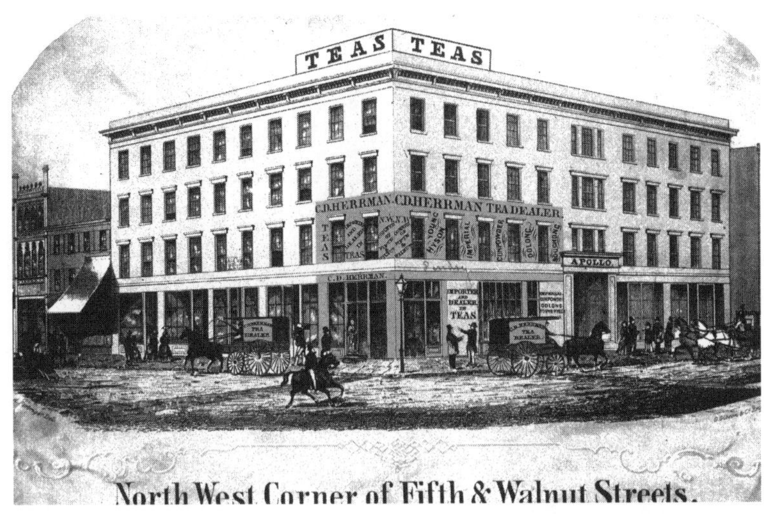

Fig. 2.35 [C. D. Herrman Tea Dealer] North West Corner of Fifth & Walnut Streets. [Apollo Building]
A. Forbriger. Engraving. 6 × 10½ in (15.24 × 26.67 cm). Cincinnati: G. Gibson & Co., 1857–58. Author's collection.

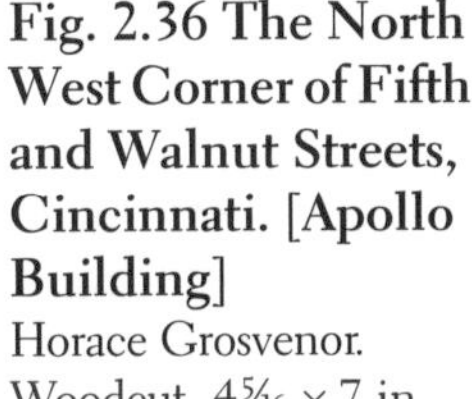

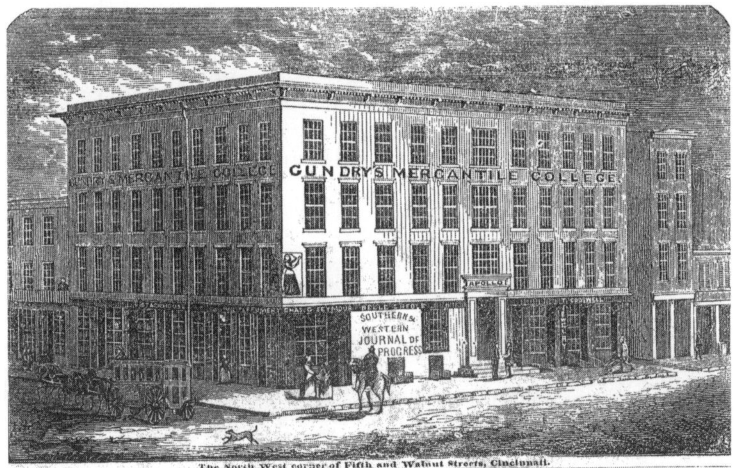

Fig. 2.36 The North West Corner of Fifth and Walnut Streets, Cincinnati. [Apollo Building]
Horace Grosvenor. Woodcut. 4$\frac{15}{16}$ × 7 in (12.54 × 17.78 cm). Richard S. Fisher, *The Progress of the Republic: Southern Edition* (Washington, D.C.: published by Wm. M. Morrison & Co., [1856]), unpaged. The Public Library of Cincinnati and Hamilton County.

There are two other views of the Apollo Building, one by Horace Grosvenor, the other by John Telfer (figs. 2.36 and 2.37). These views show that the building's long-term tenant was Gundry's Mercantile College. The corner location at street level apparently changed hands frequently, selling baking powder in 1853, perfume in 1854, and tea in 1857–58. The building later housed a gymnasium on one of its upper floors, a successful enterprise because it provided bathing facilities in the days before such amenities were commonly found in private houses.

John Telfer, who signed this view of the Apollo Building, continued to be active in Cincinnati for the whole of the 1850s, and, like many of the engravers of the day, he turned his hand to a variety of commissions. His own advertisement in the 1858 city directory—an assured piece of work—is very patriotic (fig. 2.38). Less successful is an advertisement for "fashionable and modern" furniture (fig. 2.39). Two portraits, published in a Cincinnati magazine, also lack the assurance one would expect (fig. 2.40). Maybe the

Fig. 2.37 Bishoprick's / Infallible / Baking Powder . . . [Apollo Building] John Telfer. Woodcut. 2⁵⁄₁₆ × 3 in (5.87 × 7.62 cm). *Williams' Cincinnati Directory. . . 1853* (Cincinnati: published by C. S. Williams, [ca. 1853]), p. 122. The Public Library of Cincinnati and Hamilton County.

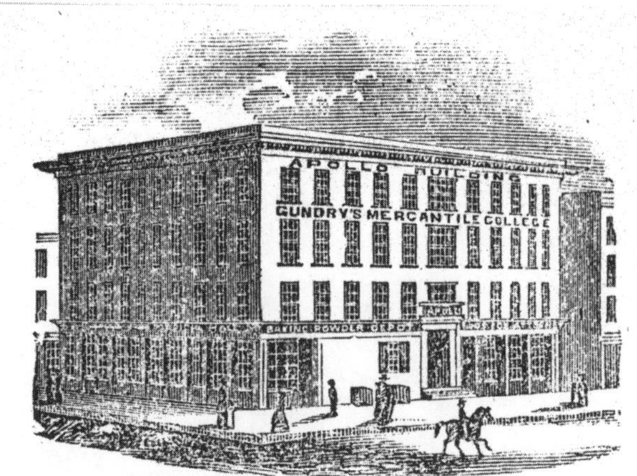

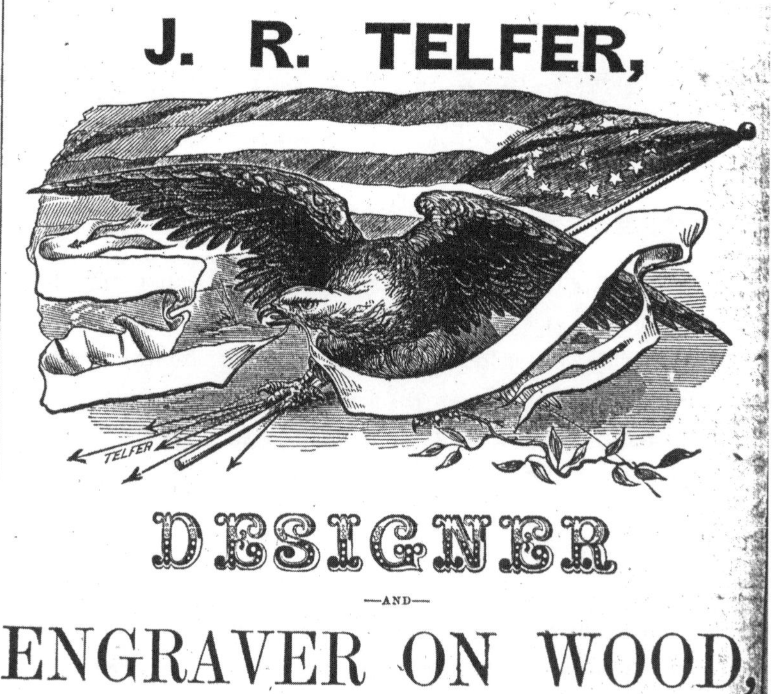

Fig. 2.38 J. R. Telfer, / Designer / and / Engraver on Wood, / No. 5 East Fourth Street, near Main. John Telfer. Woodcut. 2⅝ × 4¾ in (6.67 × 12.07 cm). *Williams' Cincinnati Directory. . . 1857* (Cincinnati: published by C. S. Williams, [ca. 1856]), p. 292. The Public Library of Cincinnati and Hamilton County.

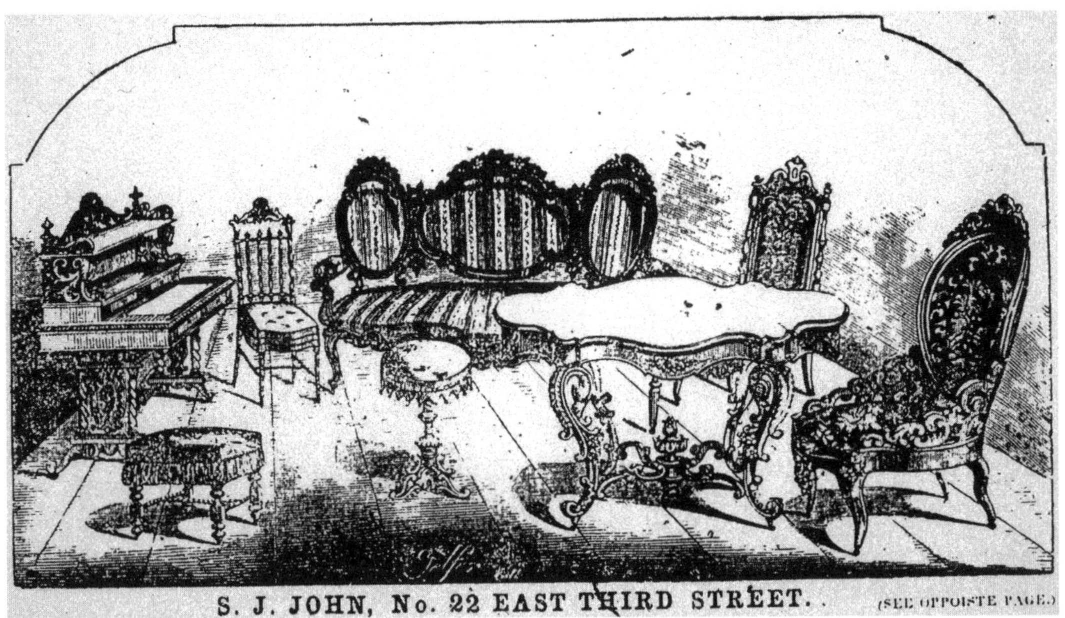

Fig. 2.39 S. J. John, No. 22 East Third Street.
John Telfer. Woodcut. 6 × 6 9/16 in (15.24 × 16.67 cm). *Cincinnati Business Mirror and City Advertiser, 1851–1852* (Cincinnati: A. Gray & Co., 1851), pp. 22–23. Cincinnati Historical Society Library.

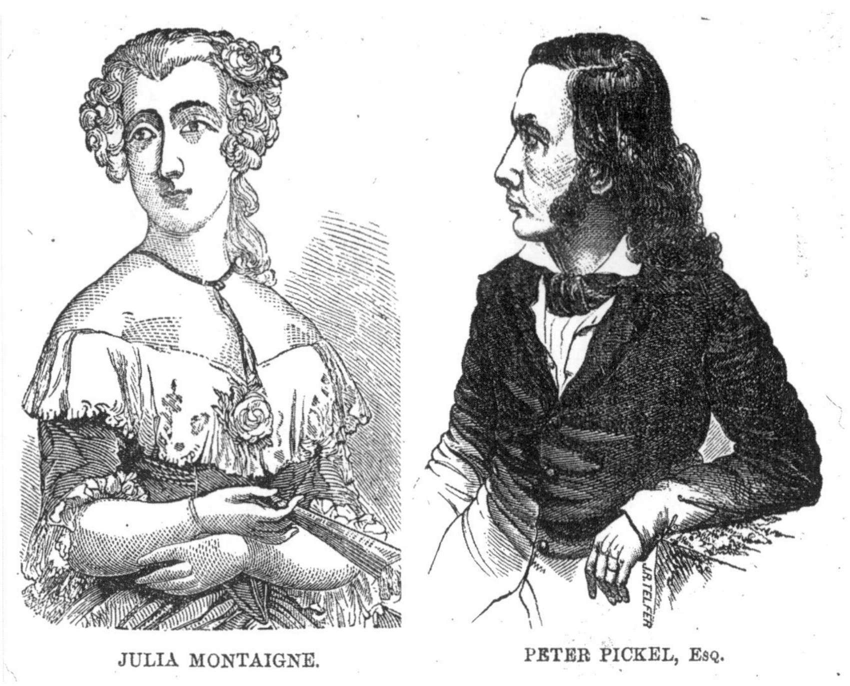

Fig. 2.40 Julia Montaigne. / Peter Pickel, [*sic*] Esq.
John Telfer. Woodcut. Julia Montaigne: 4 1/8 × 2 13/16 in (10.48 × 7.14 cm); Peter Pickel: 4 1/8 × 3 in (10.48 × 7.62 cm). J[ames] H. Kinkead, *Peter Pickle, Esqr.: The Philosopher* . . . (Cincinnati: A. Moore, publisher, n.d.), facing p. [1]. The Public Library of Cincinnati and Hamilton County.

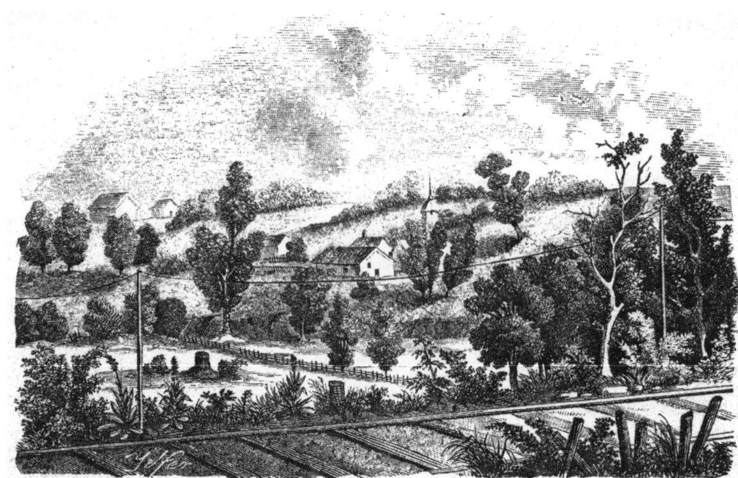

Fig. 2.41 View Near Milford. John Telfer. Lithograph. 3⅜ × 55⁄16 in (8.57 × 13.49 cm). *The Ohio Railroad Guide, Illustrated* (Columbus: Ohio State Journal Co., 1854), facing p. 21. The Public Library of Cincinnati and Hamilton County.

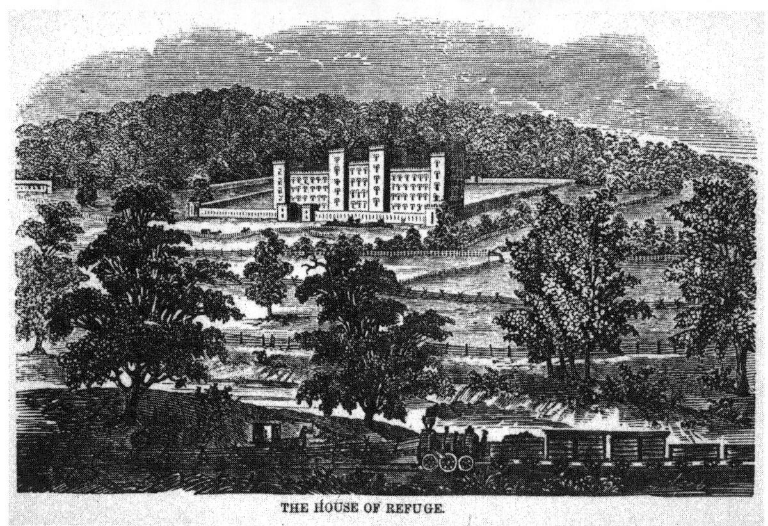

Fig. 2.42 The House of Refuge. [Near Cincinnati] John Telfer. Woodcut. 31⁄16 × 4¾ in (7.78 × 12.07 cm). *Moore's Western Lady's Book* (Cincinnati) 9, no. 4 (April 1854), frontispiece. Cincinnati Historical Society Library.

quality of his illustration varied in relation to the kind of publication in which it was to appear in and what the commission paid. Such was the case in Doolittle and Munson's work, and perhaps similar considerations account for the unevenness of Telfer's work. Certainly, these two views of places outside of Cincinnati, the village of Milford on the one hand and the House of Refuge on the other, display a high level of technical and artistic proficiency (figs. 2.41 and 2.42). The House of Refuge was a euphemism for a detention home for delinquents. Two even more successful efforts by Telfer were published in the *Western Horticultural Review* in 1851: one advertisement for Catawba wine produced at Yeatman's vineyard, showing the Yeatman house in the background; the other a wonderful gothic cottage, the residence of J. F. Meline on what is now Grandin Road in the attractive residential suburb of Hyde Park (figs. 2.43 and 2.44).

One more Cincinnati engraver warrants a preliminary introduction. Edward Henry Knight listed himself in the city directories not as an engraver but as a solicitor for patents

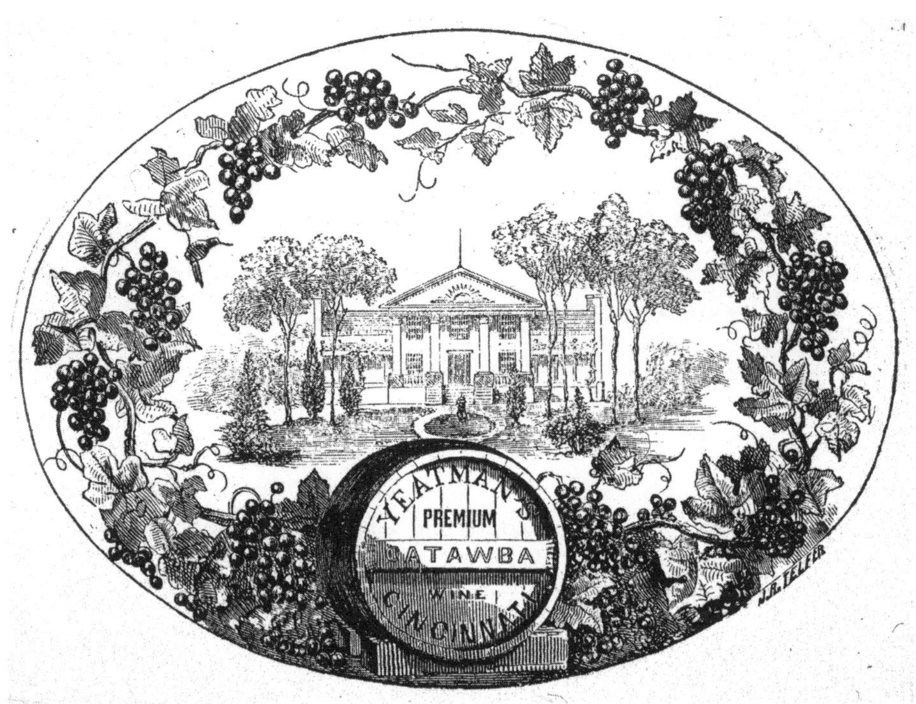

Fig. 2.43 Yeatman's / Premium Catawba / Wine, / Cincinnati [Residence of T. H. Yeatman].
John Telfer. Engraving. 3⅞ × 5¹⁄₁₆ in (9.84 × 12.86 cm). *Western Horticultural Review* (Cincinnati) 1, no. 7 (April 1851), facing p. [313]. Cincinnati Historical Society Library.

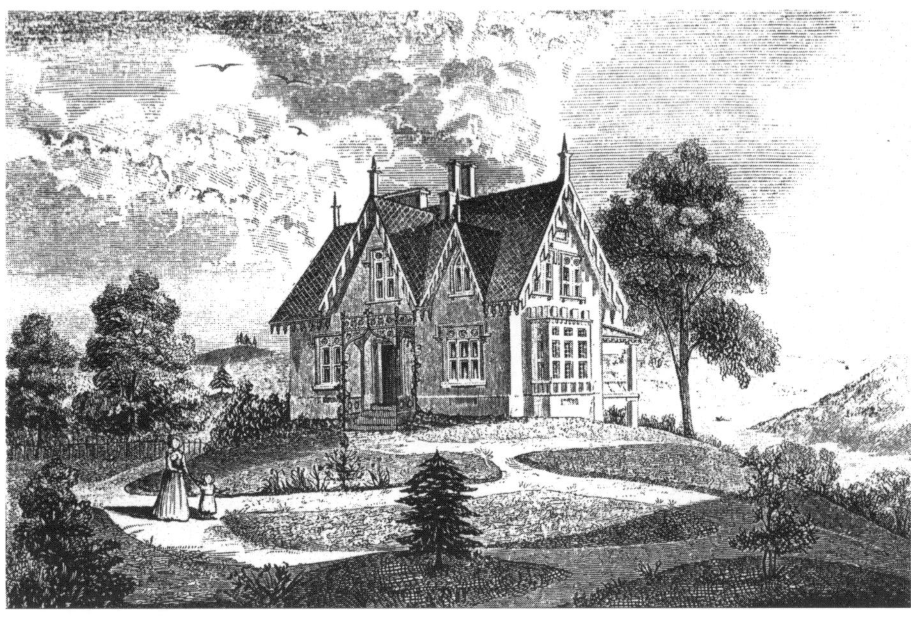

Fig. 2.44 [Residence of J. F. Meline]
John R. Telfer. Engraving. 4⅛ × 6 ¹⁄₁₆ in (10.48 × 15.40 cm). *Western Horticultural Review* (Cincinnati) 1, no. 8 (May 1851), facing p. [361]. Cincinnati Historical Society Library.

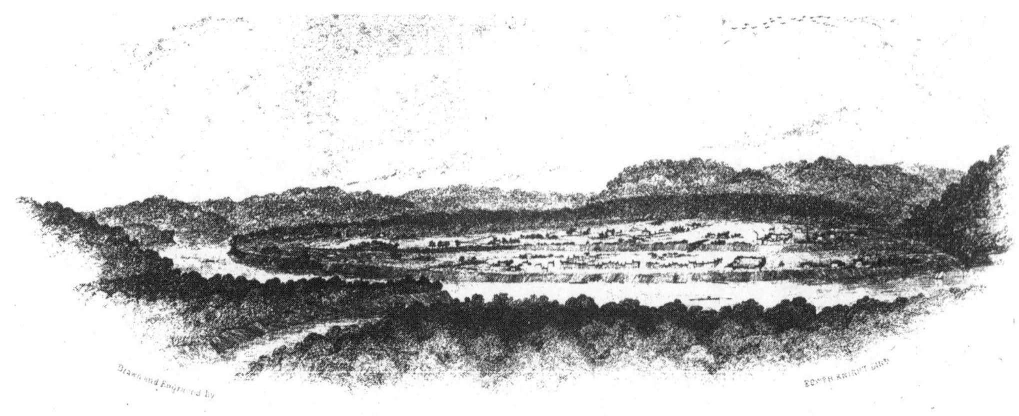

Fig. 2.45 Cincinnati in 1800. / Engraved for the *Gentleman's Magazine.*
Edward Henry Knight. Engraving. 3 7/8 × 6 13/16 in (9.84 × 17.30 cm). *The Gentleman's Magazine* (Cincinnati) 1, no. 1 (June 1848), frontispiece. Cincinnati Historical Society Library.

and a mechanical engineer. He was born in England in 1824 and settled in Cincinnati in 1845. Thus far only three signed Cincinnati engravings have been located: two views of Cincinnati, one of them a reconstruction of the settlement as it appeared in 1800 (fig. 2.45), the other a view of the city as he knew it in 1848 (fig. 2.46). Both were published in 1848 in a Cincinnati periodical called *The Gentleman's Magazine.* The third is a spirited view of the offices of the *Daily and Dollar Weekly,* presumably engraved as a letterhead or bill head (fig. 2.47). These meticulous renderings are the work of a young man only twenty-four years old.

Knight left Cincinnati probably around 1854, settling in Washington, D.C., where he was later employed by the U.S. Patent Office as the editor of its publications. An indefatigable worker, he compiled and in 1873 published a monumental, three-volume work called *The American Mechanical Dictionary.* In 1876 Knight was appointed commissioner in charge of the Patent Office exhibit at the Philadelphia Centennial Exhibition. His work there led to the publication of *A Study of the Savage Weapons at the Centennial Exhibition* (1879), which he not only wrote but also illustrated with 147 sketches. Having acquitted himself with distinction in Philadelphia, he was selected to serve as commissioner to the 1878 International Exposition in Paris and to supervise the publication of the official report, a work that extended to five volumes. The French recognized his contribution to the success of the exposition by later conferring on him membership in the Legion of Honor, making him the only Cincinnati engraver to be so honored. He had one further distinction—a distinction that was discovered only after his death. Edward Henry Knight had the heaviest brain on record in America at that time and the second heaviest on record in the world.

The story of Cincinnati's early engravers is not the story of one or two towering figures. There is no single artist who dominates the scene or, indeed, who made an enduring name

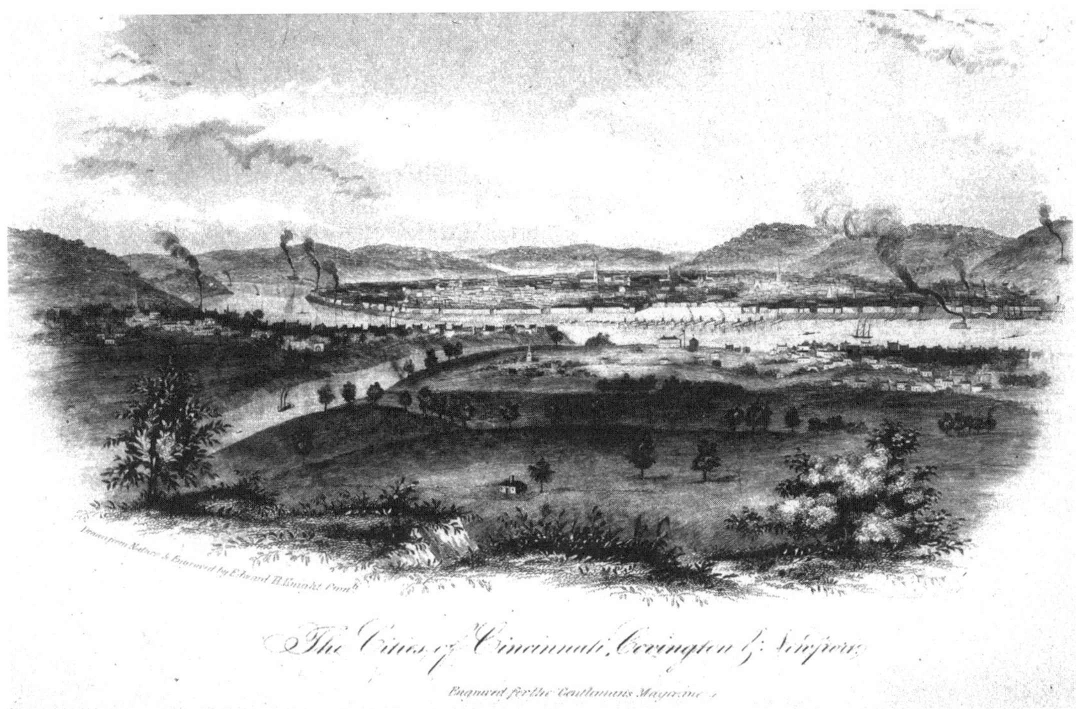

Fig. 2.46 The Cities of Cincinnati, Covington & Newport. / Engraved for the *Gentleman's Magazine*.
Edward Henry Knight. Engraving. 4⁵⁄₁₆ × 6¹³⁄₁₆ in (10.95 × 17.30 cm). *The Gentleman's Magazine* (Cincinnati) 1, no. 2 (July 1848), frontispiece. Cincinnati Historical Society Library.

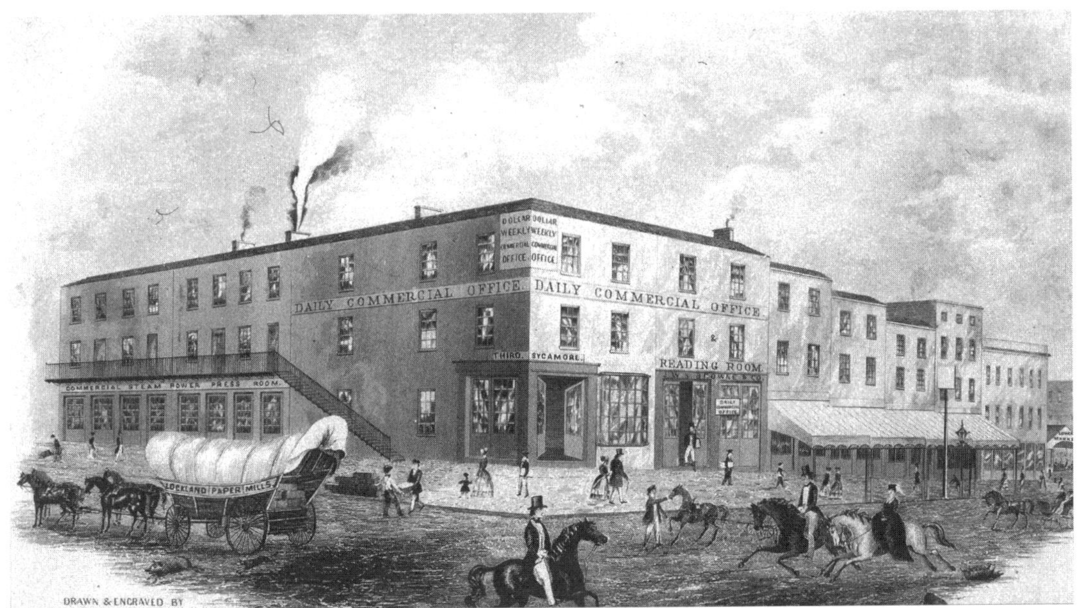

Fig. 2.47 [Daily and Dollar Weekly Commercial Office, Corner of Third & Sycamore, Cincinnati, O.] [Letterhead]
Edward Henry Knight. Engraving. 8⅜ × 9½ in (21.27 × 24.13 cm). Cincinnati Historical Society Library.

for himself. The story of engraving in early Cincinnati is the story of a great number of artists, artisans, and craftsmen, most of them identified by name only and varied in their skills and proficiency, who supplied Cincinnati's wide-ranging graphic needs. For fifty years, the first half of the nineteenth century, they provided an enormous quantity of illustrative material to a young, rapidly growing community, and by and large they did it well. The engravers reviewed here were selected because they are representative and because they are among the few who have left behind (in addition to their engravings) a handful of facts about their professional or personal lives. The others remain, for now, simply names in city directories or signatures along the bottom of cuts, advertisements, and views. In time, perhaps, more of them will achieve the recognition that is their due.

Notes

1. Samuel P. Hildreth, *Biographical and Historical Memoirs of the Early Pioneer Settlers of Ohio* . . . (Cincinnati: H. W. Derby, 1852), p. 420.

2. Benjamin Drake and E. D. Mansfield, *Cincinnati in 1826* (Cincinnati: Morgan, Lodge and Fisher, 1847), p. 29.

References

Cincinnati City Directories. Cincinnati: various publishers, 1819–60.

Hildreth, Samuel P. *Biographical and Historical Memoirs of the Early Pioneer Settlers of Ohio* . . . . Cincinnati: H. W. Derby, 1852.

Journal of Patent Office Society 14, no. 6 (June 1932): 484–85. Biography of Edward Henry Knight. CHS 051 P295 unb. per.

Knight, Edward Henry. Papers. Cincinnati Historical Society.

Sutton, Walter. *The Western Book Trade: Cincinnati as a Nineteenth-Century Publishing and Book-Trade Center*. Columbus: Ohio State University, 1961. Information on William Woodruff, p. 80; on Derby, Bradley and Co., pp. 134–37.

Chapter Three

Emil Klauprecht—Ohio Valley German American

Richard F. Askren
Indianapolis, Indiana

In his 1979 work on chromolithography in the United States, Peter C. Marzio states that "the 'Queen City' of Cincinnati, early a western outpost of commerce and culture, contributed a special impact on the democratic art. In a seemingly endless stream of prints springing from southwest Ohio, Americans found new directions for their taste in chromolithography."[1] Emil Klauprecht and the lithographic firm of Klauprecht & Menzel played an important role in establishing and maintaining this stream of art and culture in what had been wilderness only a few decades earlier.

Marzio provides a brief description of Klauprecht's life:

> The first Cincinnati lithograph was probably 'Galt House,' produced in 1836 by Emil Klauprecht [fig. 3.1]. Klauprecht was a German from Mainz, who is said to have sailed to America in 1832. It is not known where or how he learned the lithographic art. He arrived in Cincinnati in the mid-thirties, when the city was an optimistic upstart of about 34,000 inhabitants—within thirty years its population would increase sixfold. Throughout the 1840s Klauprecht worked in partnership with Adolph Menzel. In 1846–1847 they published a lithograph-illustrated German newspaper, *Fliegende Blätter.* By the mid-fifties Klauprecht's name disappeared from the ranks of lithographers in the city directories and found its way onto the mastheads of several German-language newspapers, including the *Deutsche*

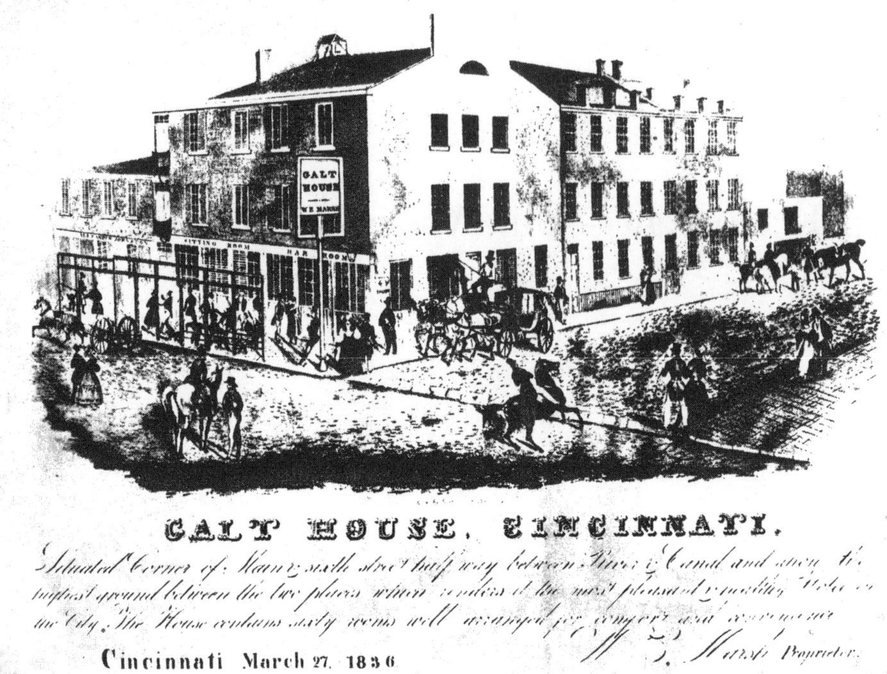

Fig. 3.1 Galt House, Cincinnati.
Klauprecht & Menzel. Lithograph. Size unknown. Cincinnati: Klauprecht & Menzel, 1836. Reproduced from photocopy. Cincinnati Historical Society Library.

> *Republikaner, Westliche Blätter,* and *Volksblatt.* In 1864 President Lincoln named Klauprecht American consul in Stuttgart, and he remained in his homeland the rest of his life.[2]

Building on Marzio's concise description, this essay examines Klauprecht's life and various literary and journalistic contributions and examines the *Fliegende Blätter.*

The Life of Emil Klauprecht

In September 1815, Emil Klauprecht (fig. 3.2) was born in Mainz, a German city whose residents were no strangers to the idea of being citizens rather than subjects. Under French occupation, they had come to understand the benefits of rights guaranteed by a constitution and the freedoms advocated by the French Revolution. In May 1832, thousands of liberals gathered at the Hambach Castle ruin not far from the home of young Klauprecht. Speakers from throughout Europe addressed the crowd, which Klauprecht later estimated at between 10,000 and 15,000. They called for a general uprising of the people and the unification of the German free states. The festival was forcefully broken up by government troops. Klauprecht witnessed this repression of his fellow Germans, some of whom were likely his friends and relatives. Fearing a revolution like that experi-

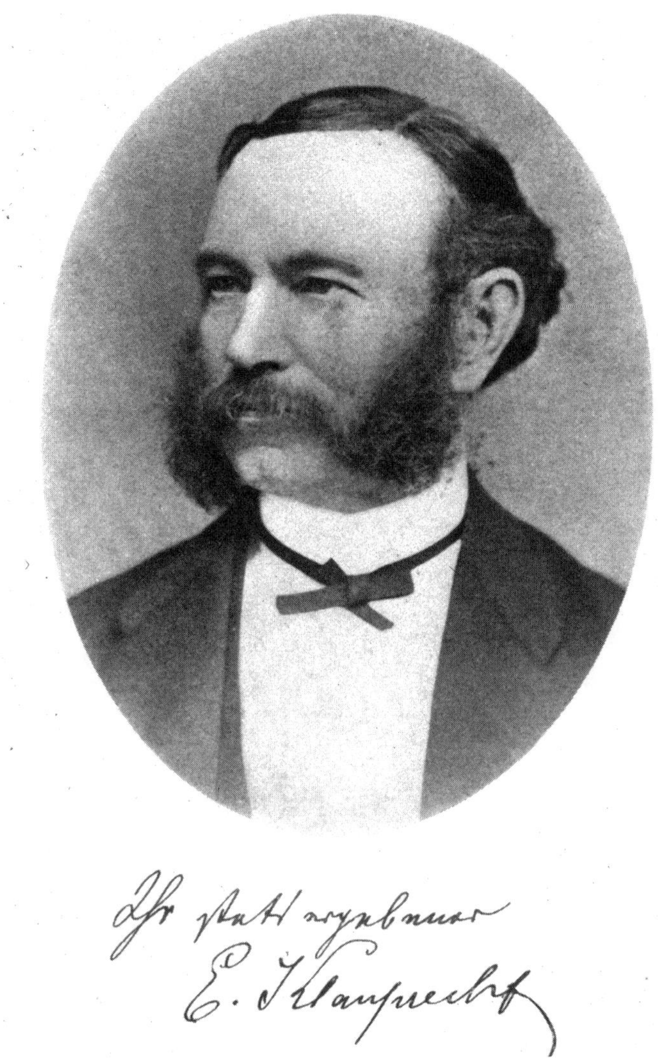

Fig. 3.2 Portrait of Emil Klauprecht (1815–1896)
Reproduced from photograph. Archives and Rare Books Department, University of Cincinnati.

enced in France only a few decades before, the German Confederation was quick to adopt energetic countermeasures. The Frankfurt Parliament adopted a resolution that banned gatherings of this sort and further limited civil rights. Prominent members of the republican opposition were exiled or imprisoned, while others were stripped of titles and prevented from continuing their livelihoods anywhere in Europe. Not long after the violent conclusion of the Hambach Rally, Emil Klauprecht left home, bound for America.

Coming to Cincinnati in the mid-1830s, Klauprecht quickly became a leading member of the city's German American community. He and Adolph Menzel established one of the first lithographic firms in the Ohio Valley and the first in Cincinnati, with offices at Fifth

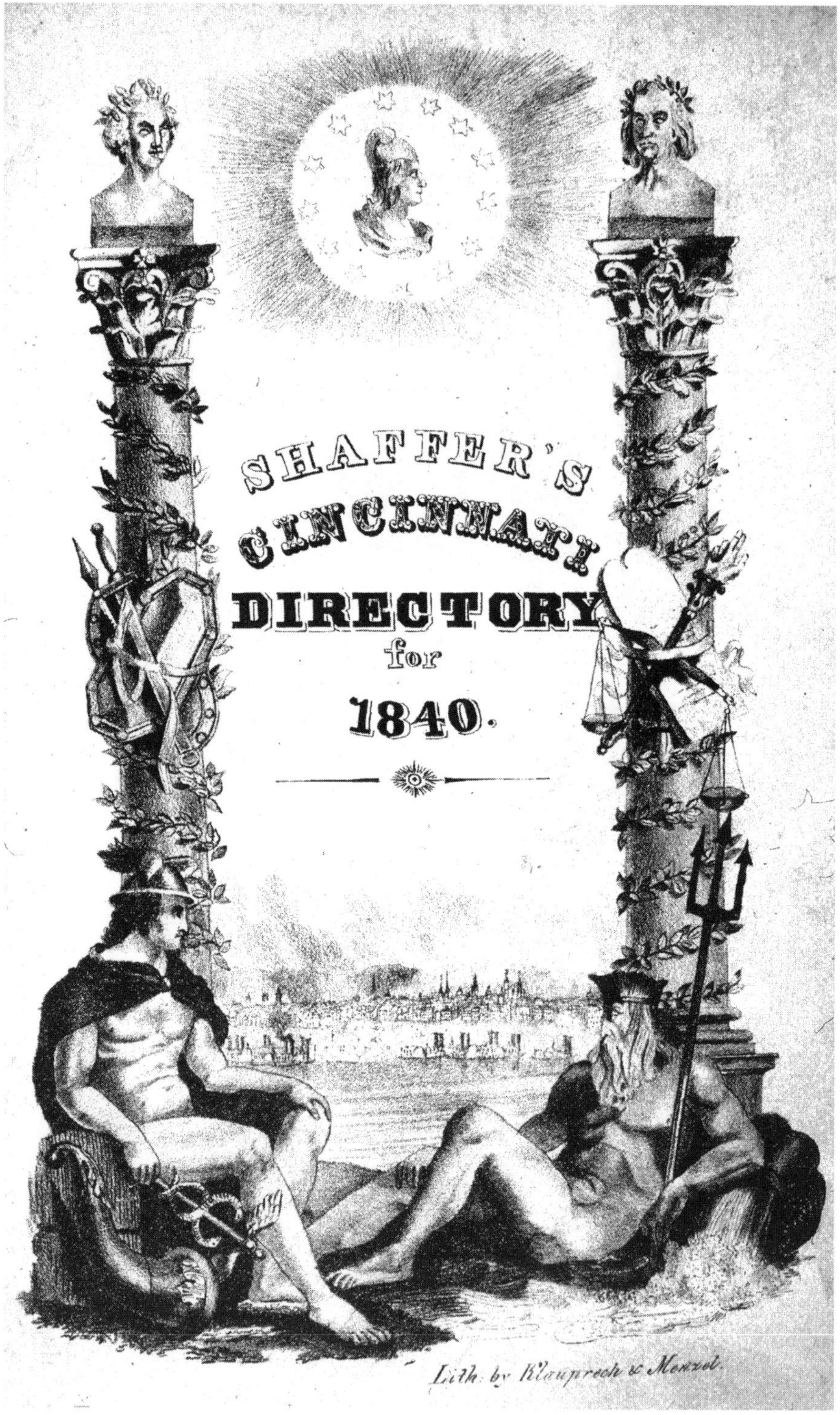

Fig. 3.3 Title Page. ***Shaffer's Cincinnati Directory for 1840.***
Klauprecht & Menzel. Lithograph. 7.75 × 5 in (19.69 × 12.7 cm). David Henry Shaffer, *Shaffer's Cincinnati Directory for 1840* (Cincinnati: printed by J. B. & R. P. Donough, no. 106 Main Street, 1840), title page. Archives and Rare Books Department, University of Cincinnati.

and Vine Streets. In addition to providing lithography for such publications as *Shaffer's Cincinnati Directory for 1840* (figs. 3.3 and 3.4), Klauprecht and Menzel published the *Fliegende Blätter* in the period 1846–47. It was a small-format weekly newspaper containing commentary on contemporary issues, literary works by respected authors, historical articles that focused on the German element in the Ohio Valley, and excellent lithographs often related to important current events. Although Klauprecht continued in the lithographic business with his partner, Adolph Menzel, after the termination of the *Fliegende Blätter*, Klauprecht also became editor of *Der Deutsche Republikaner*, the daily Whig German American newspaper of Cincinnati, and made it one of the leading newspapers in the city.

By the time Klauprecht assumed the editorship of the *Republikaner*, an emotionally charged situation was clearly building in the Cincinnati German American newspaper community. As a writer of political polemics, Klauprecht had few peers, and along the lines of personal attacks, even fewer. In the *Republikaner*, Klauprecht included many poems and stories, but also powerful satirical essays, making life miserable for his political rivals. This satire had been revealed earlier in the *Fliegende Blätter*, but his efforts in the *Republikaner* intensely angered his political rivals and led to open violence. Among these rivals were Heinrich Rodter and Dr. Wilhelm Albers, editors of the Democratic paper *Democratisches*

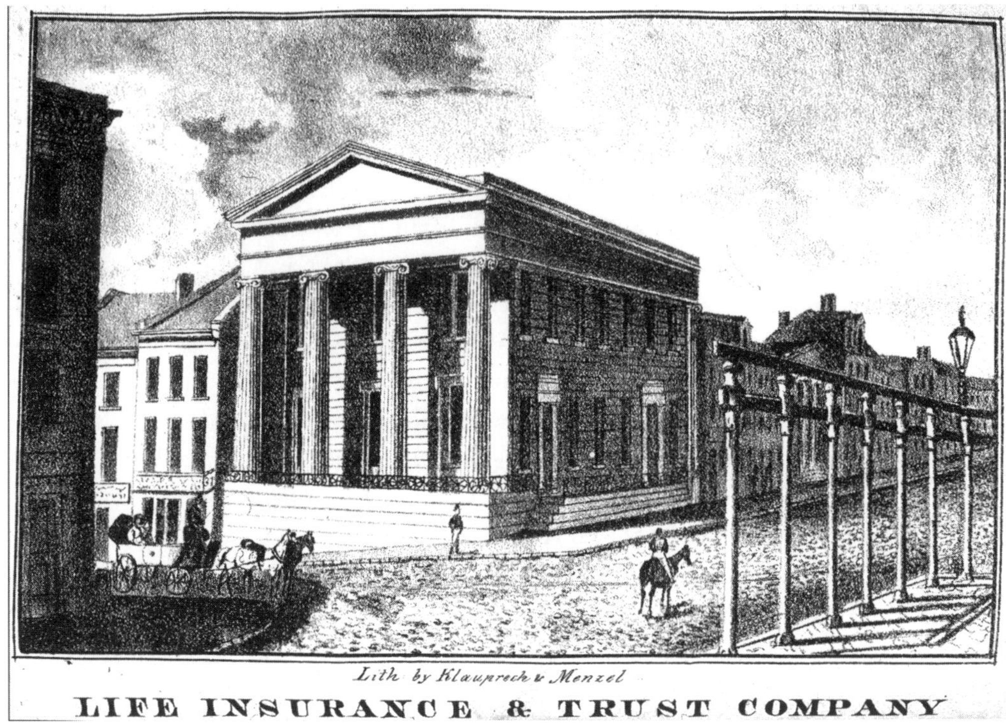

Fig. 3.4 Life Insurance & Trust Company
Klauprecht & Menzel. Lithograph. 7.75 × 5 in (19.69 × 12.7 cm). David Henry Shaffer, *Shaffer's Cincinnati Directory for 1840* (Cincinnati: printed by J. B. & R. P. Donough, no. 106 Main Street, 1840), facing p. 306. Archives and Rare Books Department, University of Cincinnati.

Tagesblatt, the leading adversary of the *Republikaner.* The exchanges between the two papers became increasingly vicious and escalated to the September 16, 1852, shooting of Albers by Klauprecht after Albers allegedly slandered Klauprecht's wife and mother-in-law in the *Tagesblatt.* Although he was tried, convicted, and received a prison sentence, Klauprecht was pardoned by the governor of Ohio after a great public protest against the sentence.

Nearly a year before the Albers shooting, Klauprecht began publishing the *Westliche Blätter* in association with Fenner von Vennerburg. First appearing October 19, 1851, this publication closely resembled the *Fliegende Blätter.* The *Westliche Blätter* presented serial novellas as well as both local and world news in brief and, like the *Fliegende Blätter,* contained no advertising. Some issues contained book reviews and news of the theater in Cincinnati. The *Westliche Blätter,* however, contained no lithographs and appeared on Sunday instead of Saturday. Perhaps because it did not contain the extensive number of lithographs it could be offered at the lower subscription price of $1.50 per year. Two of Klauprecht's novellas appeared in the *Westliche Blätter,* as well as his play. In the final issue, number 52, dated October 10, 1852, a small statement appeared that identified it as the last issue and informed subscribers who had paid beyond that time that they would be refunded any balance. Insufficient support was stated as the reason for discontinuation of the paper. Klauprecht resumed the editorship of the *Republikaner* and continued in that capacity for four years, after which he left to become editor of the *Tägliches Cincinnati Volksblatt*, the major German American newspaper in the Ohio Valley region. From 1856 to 1864, Klauprecht edited the *Volksblatt*, an influential newspaper with a national readership, leaving to accept his appointment by Abraham Lincoln as U.S. consul to Stuttgart. Upon completion of his duties as consul, Klauprecht remained in Europe the rest of his life. He continued his contact with Cincinnatian Heinrich Rattermann, contributing items for publication in Rattermann's journal, *Deutsche Pionier.* Emil Klauprecht died in 1896 in Vienna.

Klauprecht's literary publications included one of the first urban mystery novels: *Cincinnati: Or, Mysteries of the West*, published in 1855. His two historical novellas, *From the Diary of a Traveler in Texas* and *Mississippi Water and Ohio Wine*, dealt with the experiences of German Americans in the New World. They were published in the *Westliche Blätter* along with his play, a three-act farce entitled *The Song Festival on Bald Hill: Or, the White and Red Roses: A Picture Gallery from the German Life in Cincinnati.* His major historical work, *German Chronicle in the History of the Ohio Valley and Its Capital City Cincinnati in Particular,* was a narrative of the German American experience. He is also remembered among the German American community as an organizer of the first large German American singing festival in Cincinnati, which led to the foundation of the German Choral Society of North America.

The *Fliegende Blätter*

The rate of German immigration to the United States grew dramatically in the 1830s and 1840s. One role of the German American press was to provide assistance to the new arriv-

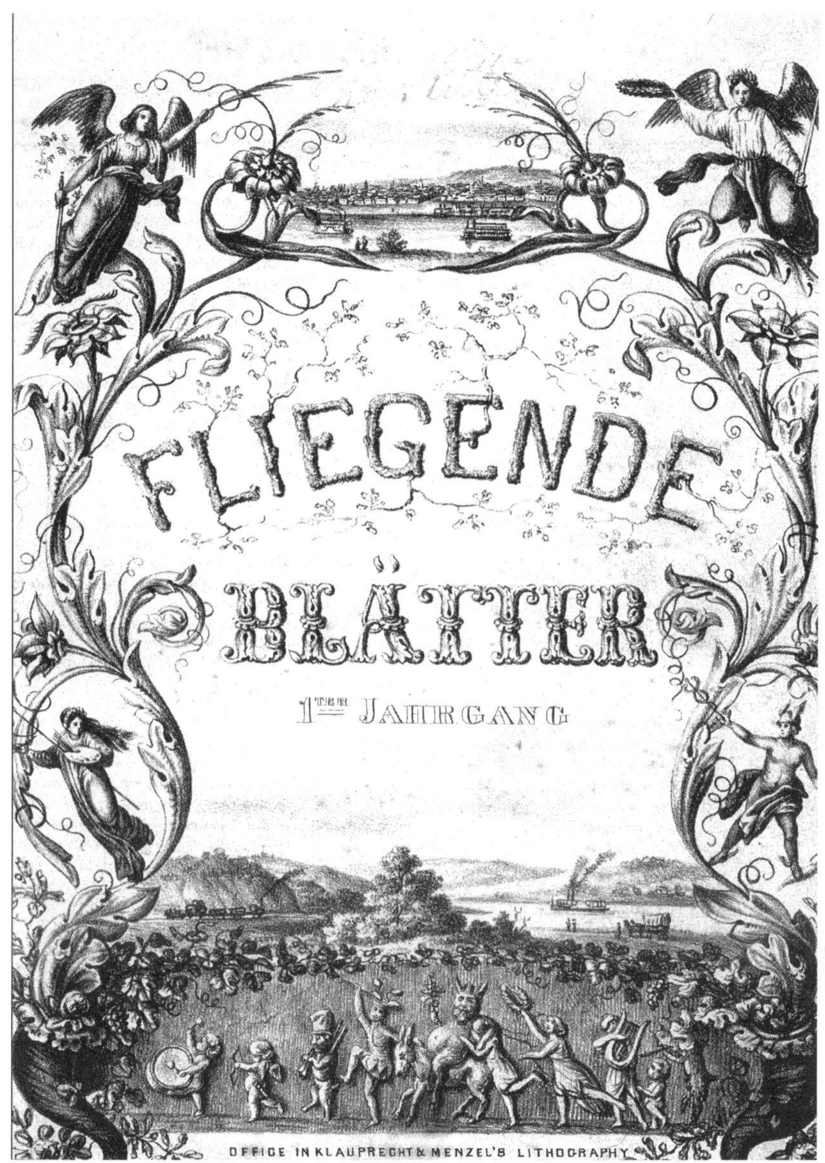

Fig. 3.5 Title Page. *Fliegende Blätter* 1ter Jahrgang
Klauprecht & Menzel. Lithograph. 10.4 × 7.9 in (26.5 × 20.0 cm). *Fliegende Blätter* 1, no. 1 (August 17, 1846), p. 1. Cincinnati Historical Society Library.

als in making their way in this new land as well as cultural continuity with their German origins. The *Fliegende Blätter* served this twofold mission. It was published by Klauprecht & Menzel Lithography between August 1846 and October 1847 from their offices on the southwest corner of Fifth and Vine Streets (fig. 3.5).

Early issues were sixteen pages in length and included lithographs in the pagination. Closing numbers were eight pages long and plates were inserted. The first issue contained

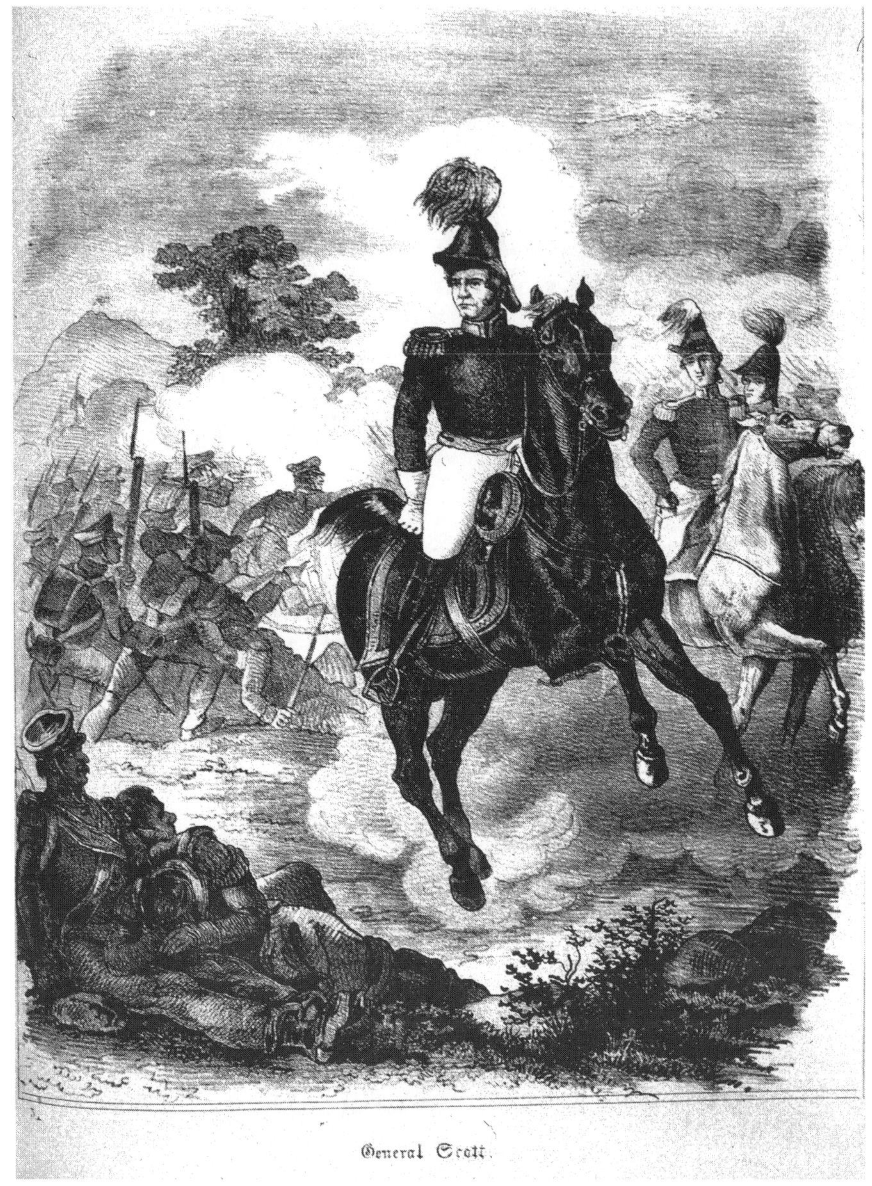

Fig. 3.6 General Scott

Klauprecht & Menzel. Lithograph. 11.2 × 8.6 in (28.5 × 22 cm). *Fliegende Blätter* 1, no. 34 (May 22, 1847), facing p. 136. Cincinnati Historical Society Library.

four pages of lithographs. By the end of the run, individual issues which did contain images usually included only one inserted leaf. Some of these were, however, elaborate foldouts. There are ninety-eight pages containing approximately 175 images. A checklist of the images appears as appendix B.

Textual contents dealt with national and international affairs, culture, and literature with an emphasis on topics of interest to the German American readership. In addition

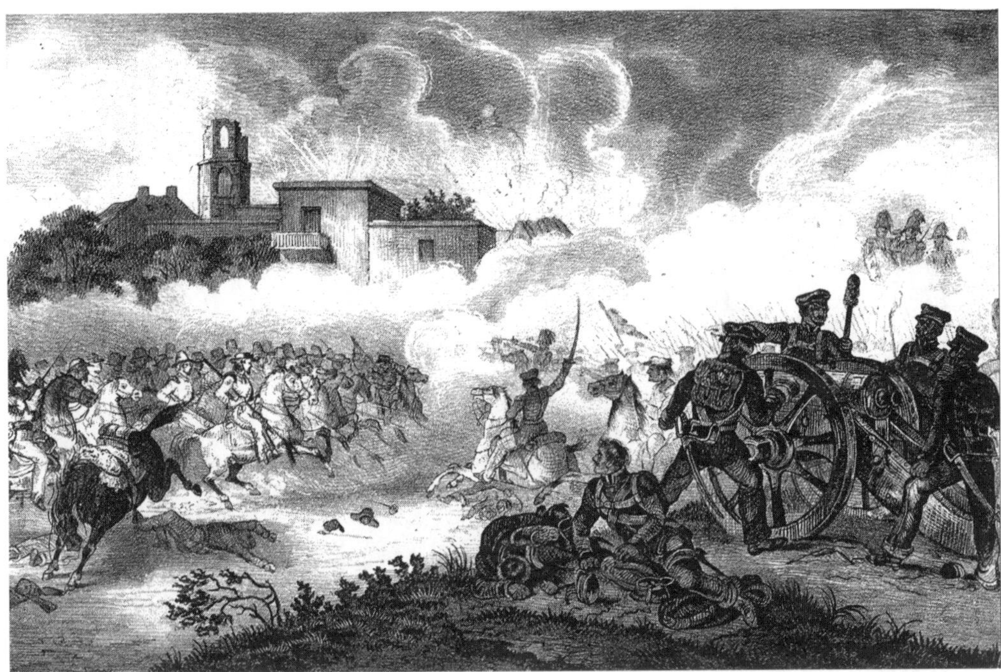

Fig. 3.7 Schlacht bei Buena Vista.
Klauprecht & Menzel. Lithograph. 8.6 × 11.2 in (22 × 28.5 cm). *Fliegende Blätter* 1, no. 27 (April 3, 1847), facing p. 80. Cincinnati Historical Society Library.

to the prospectus, the first issue included articles on the tariff and German patriotic societies; the first installment of a serialized novella by Eugène Sue entitled *Der Weibliche Blaubart oder Der Teufelsberg*; paragraphs describing each of four lithographs included; and a section of short reports dealing with the Mexican War, the Transcontinental Railroad, a French railroad wreck, a matador's conquest, and French, German, and Russian political and diplomatic developments.

A wide variety of lithograph images appeared in the journal. The title page of the first issue is highly decorated with scenes of Cincinnati and mythological figures. Only one lithograph is signed. The rubric "C. Menzel" appears on a large foldout entitled "The Blind Violinist." Some lithographs depicted current events, particularly the Mexican War. German Americans were especially interested in the conflict because of the large German population in Texas. There are portraits of Generals Zachary Taylor and Winfield Scott (fig. 3.6) and three panoramas of key battles: Battle of Buena Vista (fig. 3.7), Battle of Palo Alto, and Battle of Resaca de la Palma. The last two are foldout images measuring over 53 cm in width.

As expected, there is a variety of German scenes and landscapes (fig. 3.8), but only one view of Cincinnati (fig. 3.9). Portraits of contemporary royalty as well as literary and academic figures also appeared in the illustrative material, along with several caricatures offering biting social commentary (fig. 3.10). A lithograph depicting the 1832 rally at Hambach Castle (fig. 3.11), at which Klauprecht was an eyewitness, served as a reminder

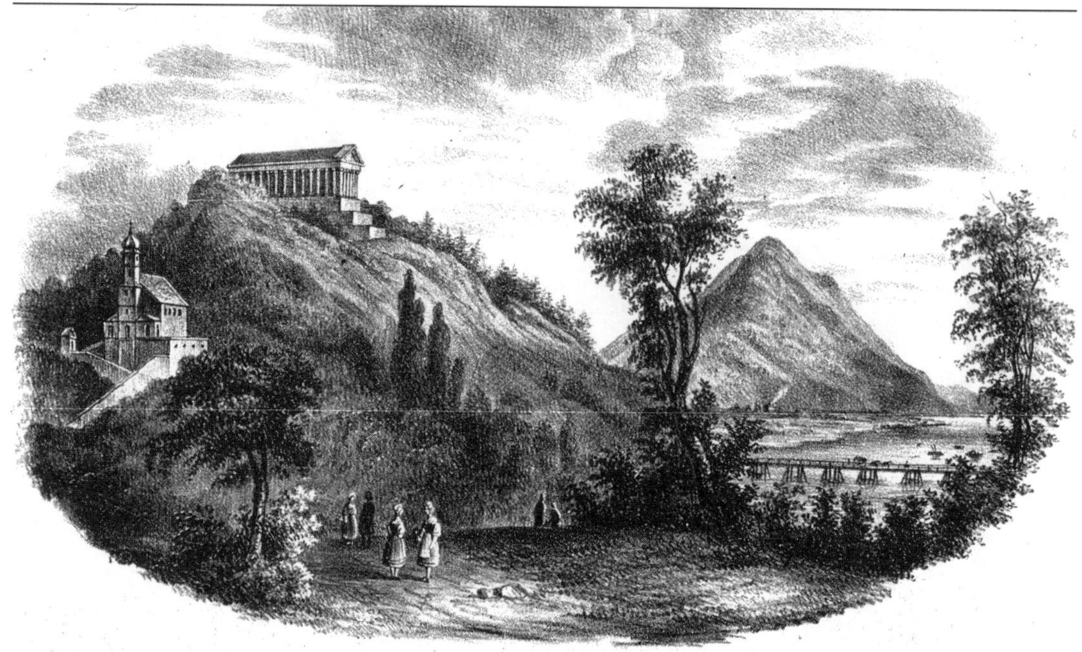

Fig. 3.8 Walhalla bey Regensburg
Klauprecht & Menzel. Lithograph. 7.9 × 10.4 in (20 × 26.5 cm). *Fliegende Blätter* 1, no. 8 (October 3, 1846), p. 125. Cincinnati Historical Society Library.

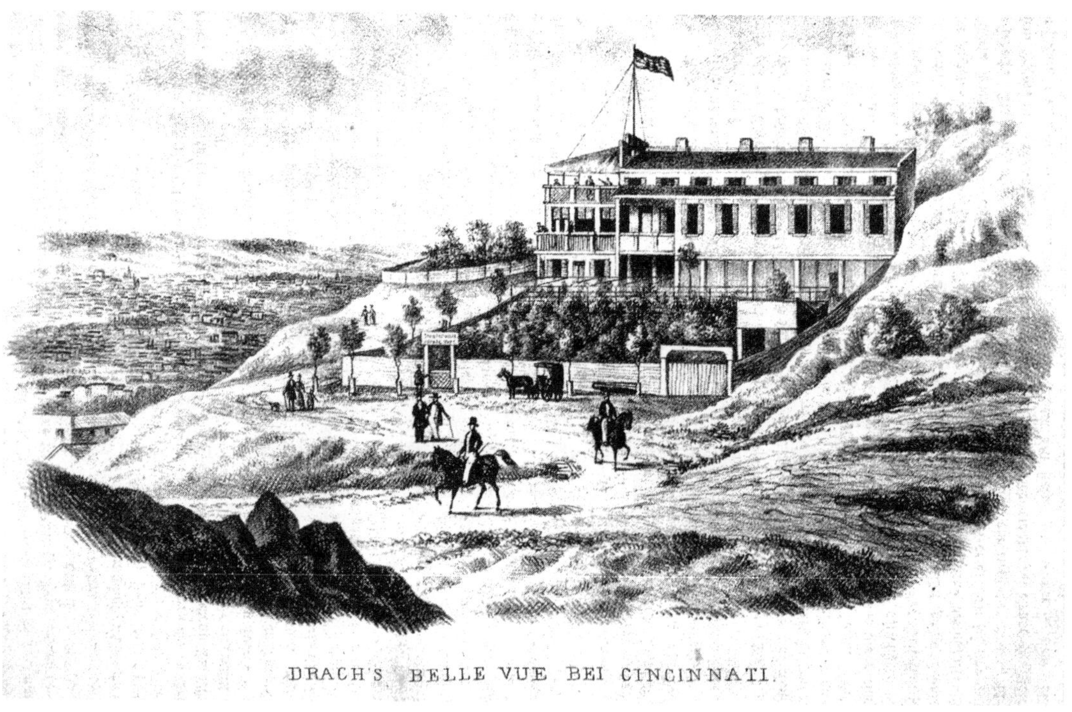

Fig. 3.9 Drach's Belle Vue bei Cincinnati
Klauprecht & Menzel. Lithograph. 7.9 × 10.4 in (20 × 26.5 cm). *Fliegende Blätter* 1, no. 1 (August 17, 1846), p. 12. Cincinnati Historical Society Library.

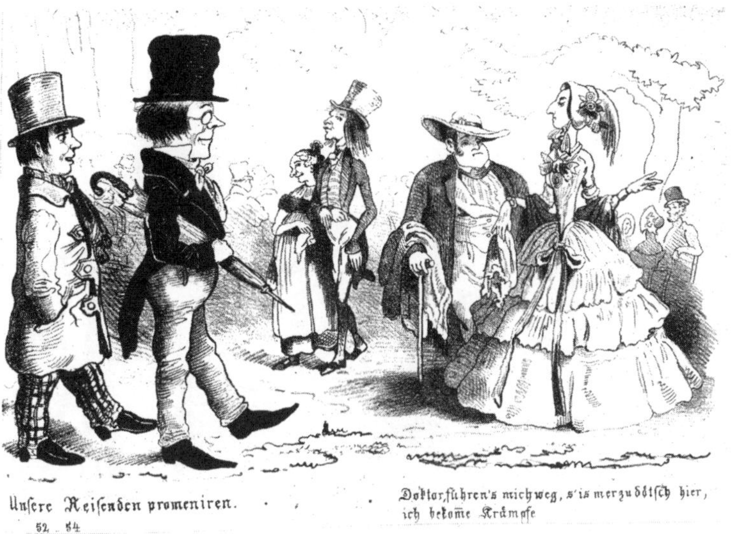

Fig. 3.10 New York
Klauprecht & Menzel. Lithograph. 11.2 × 8.6 in (28.5 × 22 cm). *Fliegende Blätter* 1, no. 35 (May 29, 1847), facing p. 140. Cincinnati Historical Society Library.

and restatement of the liberal politics of some of the German emigrants of the period. An elegant lithograph of Lola Montez (fig. 3.12) highlighted German American interest in the open liaison of King Ludwig I of Bavaria with the Irish dancer. Some images were described in short paragraphs of the journal, while others served to illustrate lengthy articles.

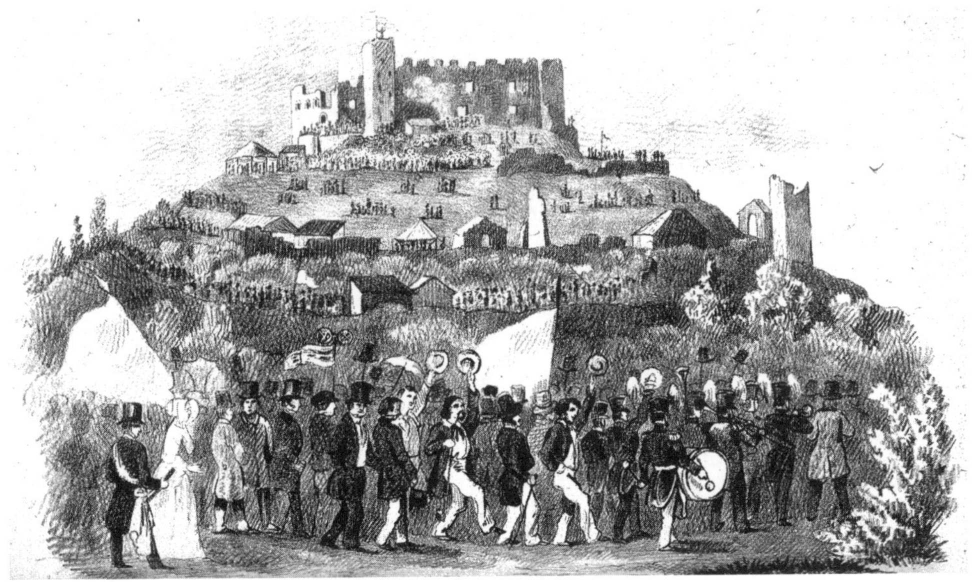

Fig. 3.11 Hambacher Fest.
Klauprecht & Menzel. Lithograph. 7.9 × 10.4 in (20 × 26.5 cm). *Fliegende Blätter* 1, no. 11 (October 24, 1846), facing p. 165. Cincinnati Historical Society Library.

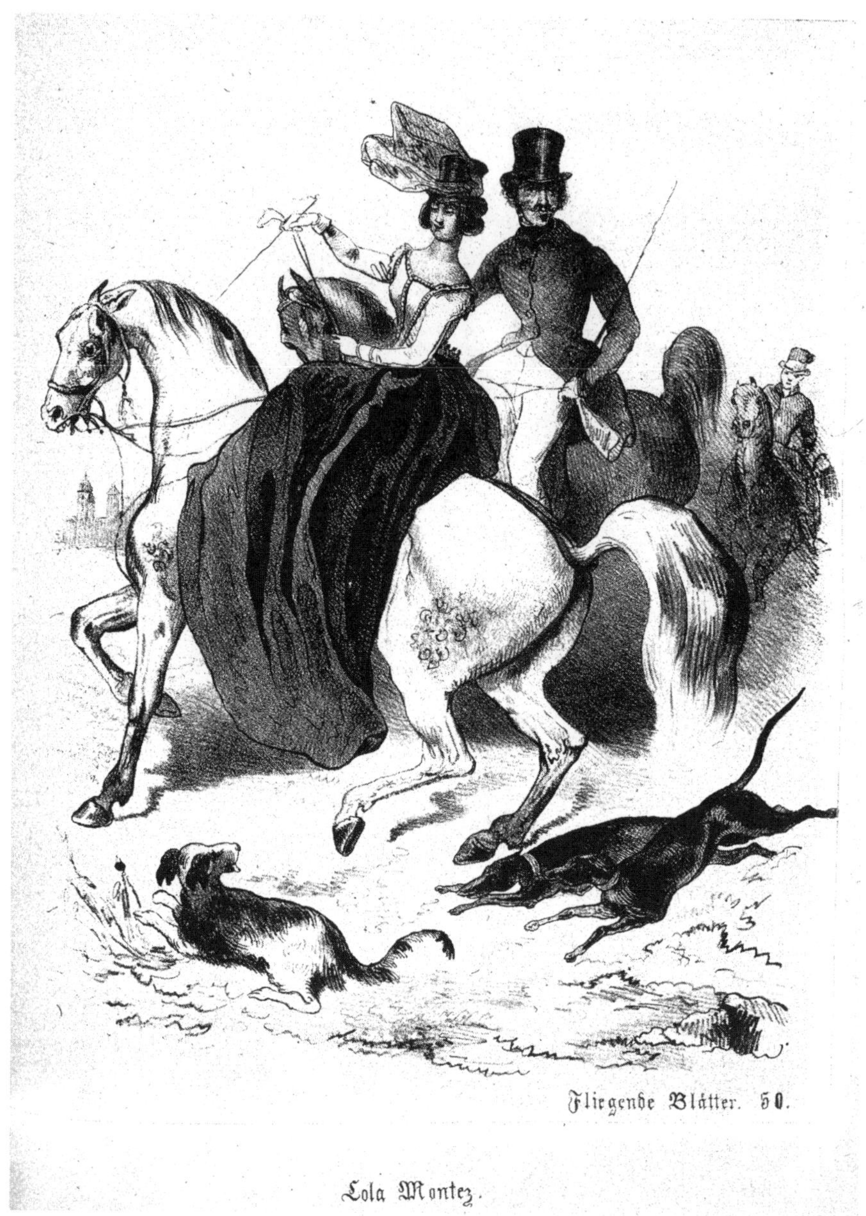

Fig. 3.12 Lola Montez.
Klauprecht & Menzel. Lithograph. 11.2 × 8.6 in (28.5 × 22 cm). *Fliegende Blätter* 1, no. 33 (May 13, 1847), facing p. 124. Cincinnati Historical Society Library.

There are copies of the works of other artists. "Wettrennen von Sioux Indianern" (fig. 3.13) is a reproduction of Karl Bodmer's "Horseracing of the Sioux Indians [at Fort Pierre]," which appeared as Vignette XXX in the atlas to accompany Maximilian zu Wied's *Travels in the Interior of North America, 1832–1834*. The portrait of Keokuk and his son (fig. 3.14) is a reproduction of plate 61 from volume 2 of the three-volume *History of the Indian Tribes*

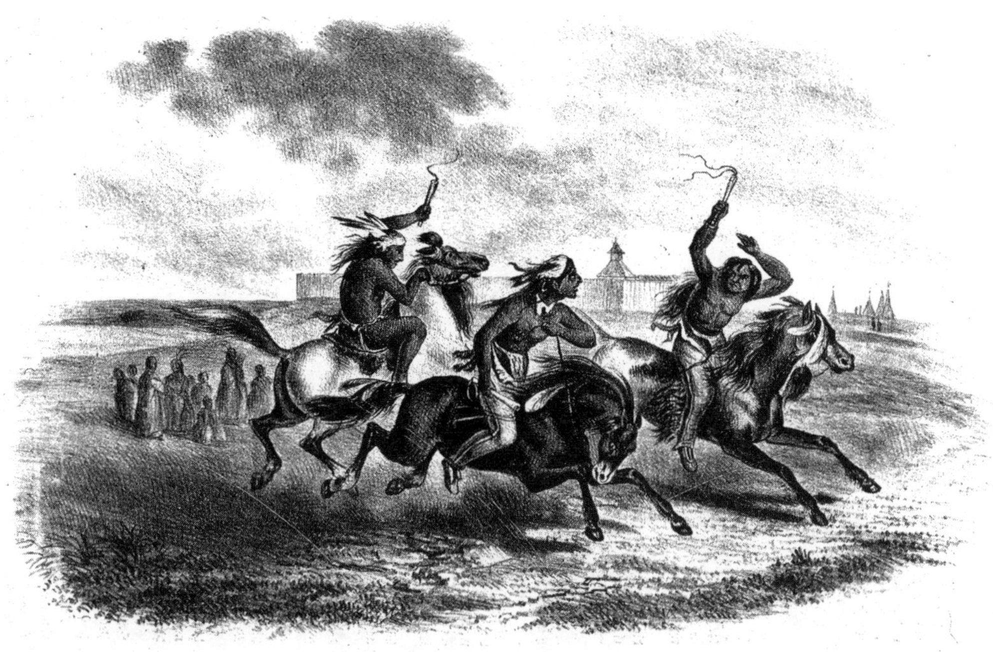

Fig. 3.13 Wettrennen von Sioux Indianern
Klauprecht & Menzel. Lithograph. 7.9 × 10.4 in (20 × 26.5 cm). *Fliegende Blätter* 1, no. 9 (October 10, 1846), p. 133. Cincinnati Historical Society Library.

of North America, by Thomas L. McKenney and James Hall, first published in Philadelphia from 1838 to 1844. Both of these images are reversed from the originals. Other images, yet to be identified, are no doubt reproductions of the work of other artists.

The reasons for the discontinuation of the *Fliegende Blätter* after just over a year have to do with economics and the sociological makeup of the nineteenth-century German immigrants. Most German Americans were not escapees of European tyranny like Klauprecht and others who came to this country after the revolutions of the thirties and were known as the Dreissiger or Thirtyers. Also unlike the Thirtyers, most immigrants were not highly educated. They came to better themselves financially, working in hard, dirty jobs in a strange land, attempting to master a new language and strange customs. Their needs were more practical than literary. Furthermore, the publication was expensive—five dollars per year and fifteen cents per copy—in comparison with other general rather than literary journals. Financial support from subscriptions did not warrant continued publication, and Klauprecht did not permit advertising in the paper.

Although the *Fliegende Blätter* was not a commercial success, it is an important document of the time. Besides serving as a platform for Klauprecht's ideas, it focused on issues of individual freedom as well as national and international affairs. As revolutions broke out in Europe, such topics were of immediate concern to German Americans with family and

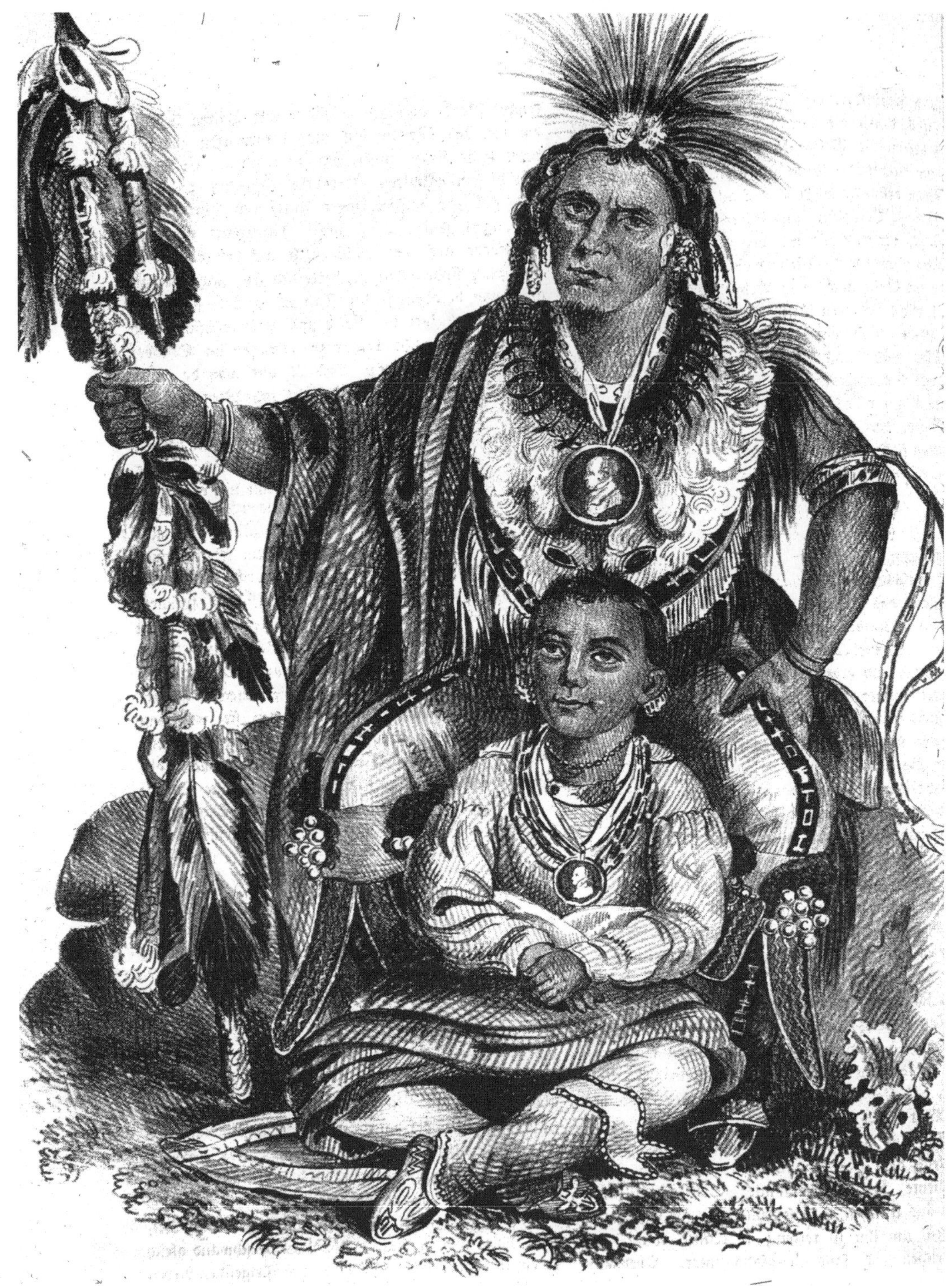

Fig. 3.14 Keokuk.

Klauprecht & Menzel. Lithograph. 10.4 × 7.9 in (26.5 × 20.0 cm). *Fliegende Blätter* 1, no. 4 (September 5, 1846), p. 52. Cincinnati Historical Society Library.

friends remaining in Europe. It offered practical advice to the new Americans on a variety of topics. And it provided cultural exposure and instruction in publishing serialized novellas and other literary offerings as well as historical accounts such as that of David Zeisberger, Ohio Valley missionary. The *Fliegende Blätter* was also an early, important, and rich source of lithographic images of a wide range of subjects designed for the people—a fine example of the democratic art in nineteenth-century Cincinnati.

Notes

1. Peter C. Marzio, *The Democratic Art: Pictures for a Nineteenth-Century America: Chromolithography, 1840–1900* (Boston: D. R. Godine, 1979), p. 130.
2. Ibid., p. 131.

References

Arndt, Karl J. R., and May E. Olson. *The German Language Press of the Americas.* 3d ed. Munich: Verlag Dokumentation, 1976.

Askren, Richard F. "The Life and Works of Emil Klauprecht: A German-American Author in the Ohio Valley." Master's thesis, University of Cincinnati, 1996.

Fliegende Blätter. Cincinnati: E. Klauprecht, 1846–47.

Groen, Henry John. "A History of the German-American Newspapers of Cincinnati before 1860." Ph.D. diss., Ohio State University, 1944.

Marzio, Peter C. *The Democratic Art: Pictures for a Nineteenth-Century America: Chromolithography, 1840–1900.* Boston: D. R. Godine, 1979.

Chapter Four

The Curious Case of the Hydra-Headed Stones

Ehrgott, Forbriger & Co.'s Civil War Portraits

Christopher W. Lane
Christopher W. Lane, Co-Owner
The Philadelphia Print Shop, Ltd.

In the midst of the Civil War, the Cincinnati lithographic publishing firm of Ehrgott, Forbriger & Co. produced a series of more than seventy portraits of federal and state government officials and Union military and naval officers.[1] These lithographs feature full-figure images of political and military individuals in settings appropriate to their professions. These prints are of particular interest because the facial portrait of each of the prints was based on a life photograph, yet portraits of different individuals share the same bodies and the same background images. This use of common backgrounds for portraits of different individuals is especially interesting for these Ehrgott, Forbriger & Co. prints because in some cases the prints were issued bound together into portfolios where this repetition of background is glaringly obvious. A study of the nature of these prints and these portfolios, along with a consideration of the context in which they were issued, helps shed light on print publishing and on the interests and expectations of the print-buying public in mid-nineteenth-century America.

Ehrgott, Forbriger & Co.

From the 1820s to 1840s, lithographic print publishers became well established in most large eastern cities in the United States, particularly Boston, Philadelphia, and New York. These firms offered quick and relatively inexpensive production of advertising, book and magazine illustration, music sheets, maps, financial documents, and popular prints intended for framing. The growing populations and economies of cities farther west soon created enough of a market for new lithographic firms to be started west of the Appalachians. Cincinnati was one of the first western cities to develop its own thriving lithographic industry. In 1859 Charles Cist wrote that from one lithographer with an output of $4,000 in 1840, Cincinnati then had six lithographic firms, employing sixty-six workers and producing a product worth $165,000.[2] One of the leading Cincinnati firms when Cist wrote, and the firm which produced the lithographs Cist used to illustrate his volume, was Ehrgott & Forbriger.

This firm was established in 1856 by Peter E. Ehrgott and Adolphus F. Forbriger, "one a practical lithographer, the other an excellent artist."[3] Around 1860 the name of the firm was changed to Ehrgott, Forbriger & Co., which it remained until 1869 when Adolphus Forbriger died.[4] In November of that year, Adolph K. Krebs joined as partner in the firm, and the name was changed to Ehrgott & Krebs. This version of the business lasted until 1874, when Ehrgott withdrew, leading to the formation of the Krebs Lithographic Company.

Ehrgott and Forbriger ran one of the most ambitious and creative lithographic firms in the Midwest. For example, they introduced the first steam press west of New York City in 1868. Their output was typical of American lithographic firms. As listed on a calendar they issued in 1863, Ehrgott, Forbriger & Co. produced "Show Cards, Music Titles, Portraits, Diplomas, Commercial Work, Labels of Every Description." Cist carried the following write-up on the firm in 1859:

> Ehrgott & Forbriger, practical lithographists [*sic*], Carlisle Block, south-west corner Fourth and Walnut streets, are prepared to execute in the very best style every species of work on stone, plain and in colors, as landscapes, portraits, show cards, diplomas, music titles, book illustrations, maps, bonds, checks, drafts, notes, bill and letter heads, cards, labels, machines, etc. etc.
>
> The establishment of Messrs. Ehrgott & Forbriger is in a great state of completeness, and those who may require lithographic work cannot do better than give them a trial. They guarantee their work to be equal to any executed in the country, and at the most reasonable cost. They are experienced workmen, and strive to excel in their department.[5]

Only slightly more than two hundred different publications made by Ehrgott & Forbriger have been identified, which must be a small portion of their total production.[6] Thus, it is difficult to draw firm conclusions about the history of the firm's output, though trends can be noted in those prints so far identified. Excluding ephemeral publications, intended to be used and then discarded, it seems reasonable to assume that the body of surviving Ehrgott & Forbriger prints is somewhat representative of their overall output, and so an analysis of trends within these prints can support some plausible speculation on the history of the firm.

There are very few recorded Ehrgott & Forbriger prints from before the Civil War, but it seems fairly certain that at that time Ehrgott & Forbriger was a typical local lithographic firm involved primarily with job printing. Based on the type of work known to have been done by other lithographic firms of the period,[7] together with the listing of items given by Charles Cist in 1859—show cards, diplomas, bonds, checks, drafts, notes, bill and letterheads, cards, and labels—it was almost certainly these job lot items that comprised the core of the firm's output prior to the Civil War. Also, the pre-1861 examples of Ehrgott & Forbriger prints of the other types mentioned by Cist, namely landscapes, portraits, music titles, and maps, were also all commissioned by other firms, not produced by Ehrgott & Forbriger on speculation.

As best as can be ascertained, Ehrgott & Forbriger continued to turn out these sorts of prints throughout its existence. Excluding Civil War prints, almost all recorded Ehrgott & Forbriger lithographs were either produced for another publisher or were commissioned advertisements, certificates, and other job lot prints. It was during the Civil War, however, that Ehrgott & Forbriger issued most of their prints. Only about 5 percent of dateable Ehrgott & Forbriger lithographs were published prior to the war and about a third afterwards; the rest were issued between 1861 and 1865. It seems obvious that the Civil War was good for Ehrgott & Forbriger's business. The apparent boom in the firm's print production during the war years was clearly based upon midwestern patriotic sentiment, for almost all Ehrgott & Forbriger's prints known to have been issued during the Civil War were related to that conflict and all of this output was pro-Union.

Besides the apparent significant increase in the output of Ehrgott & Forbriger during the Civil War, the nature of the firm's production also changed at this time. Many of the prints published between 1861 and 1865 were not typical job lot prints—advertisements, tickets, and so forth—but were prints produced for stock and intended to be sold to the general public. Among these sorts of stock prints were portraits, political cartoons, soldier's memorials, battle scenes, and camp scenes; some of these prints were separately issued, ready to be framed, and some were included in bound portfolios. Some, and possibly most, of these prints may still have been commissioned from Ehrgott & Forbriger by other businesses or individuals, but most of the Ehrgott & Forbriger prints from this period were not ephemeral in intent, but rather were designed to be viewed or hung in offices and homes by a public intensely interested in the events, politics, and personages of the Civil War.

Harold Holzer, in his article on portraits of Lincoln, notes that prior to the war there seems to have been a dearth of Lincoln prints issued in Ohio, and he suggests that "it may be conjectured that Ohio's print-buying public was well supplied during these periods with the products of nationally distributed East Coast firms such as Currier & Ives."[8] This may be the same reason that, prior to the war, Ehrgott & Forbriger did not try to break into the "frameable print" market, which was dominated by Currier & Ives and other East Coast firms. That type of print publishing was primarily speculative rather than job printing, and Ehrgott & Forbriger likely did not feel the potential rewards were great enough to compensate for the financial risks involved.

Holzer goes on to speculate that "only after the war had begun and Ohio had sent volunteers, signaling a strong and highly personal stake in the conflict, did regional artists finally begin portraying the commander in chief."[9] Similarly, it was likely the midwestern public's intense, personal concern with the Civil War that created a large potential market for speculative prints that in turn led Ehrgott & Forbriger to produce a substantial body of such images. In that endeavor, Ehrgott & Forbriger had two advantages over their larger competitors to the east: they could easily tailor their output to the local market and they did not suffer from the same distribution problems faced by the East Coast publishers.

Ehrgott & Forbriger had lower costs selling their prints in the Midwest, and they could much more easily judge local interests. This allowed the firm to issue prints which would have appeal mostly within the Cincinnati or midwestern region; many of the Ehrgott & Forbriger Civil War prints were of midwestern events and scenes or were portraits of midwestern figures. This was something a firm such as Currier & Ives was unlikely to do. Besides this, the problem of distribution of prints during the war was a positive boon to Ehrgott & Forbriger's business. Not only were long-distance distribution costs considerably more, but unlike the situation with prewar genre prints, images related to the Civil War needed to be timely in arriving at their market, and Ehrgott & Forbriger had easier and quicker access to the markets in Ohio, Kentucky, and elsewhere in the Midwest.

For these reasons, Ehrgott & Forbriger's print business blossomed during the Civil War years. Approximately two-thirds of the dateable Ehrgott & Forbriger prints were issued between 1861 and 1865, and even if we assume that none of the undated prints by the firm were issued during this period, still more than half the known prints by Ehrgott & Forbriger were produced during the Civil War. Almost all of these prints were related to the Civil War.[10] If we include in this category music sheets with a military or patriotic theme and prints such as those relating to Lincoln's signing the Emancipation Proclamation or obsequies after his assassination, then only about 10 percent of the Ehrgott & Forbriger prints dated during the war years are not related to the Civil War. Of these Civil War prints, more than half were individual portraits of politicians and military or naval officers.

Civil War Portraits

Almost all of the portraits that Ehrgott & Forbriger issued are of a recognizable type.[11] These are vertical portraits of a person shown full figure and put into an obviously stylized setting related to his profession. Political figures (fig. 4.1) are shown sitting by a covered table and holding a pen to a document that lies upon the table. The room in which the figures sit has a globe, a wall map of the United States, and a bust of George Washington, while through an archway can be seen a large mass of troops engaged in battle. Military figures (fig. 4.2) are shown in full uniform either on or next to a horse, often with troops or junior staff in the background. Naval figures (fig. 4.3) are also drawn in full uniform, each shown standing on the deck of a ship, either an ironclad or a regular naval vessel.

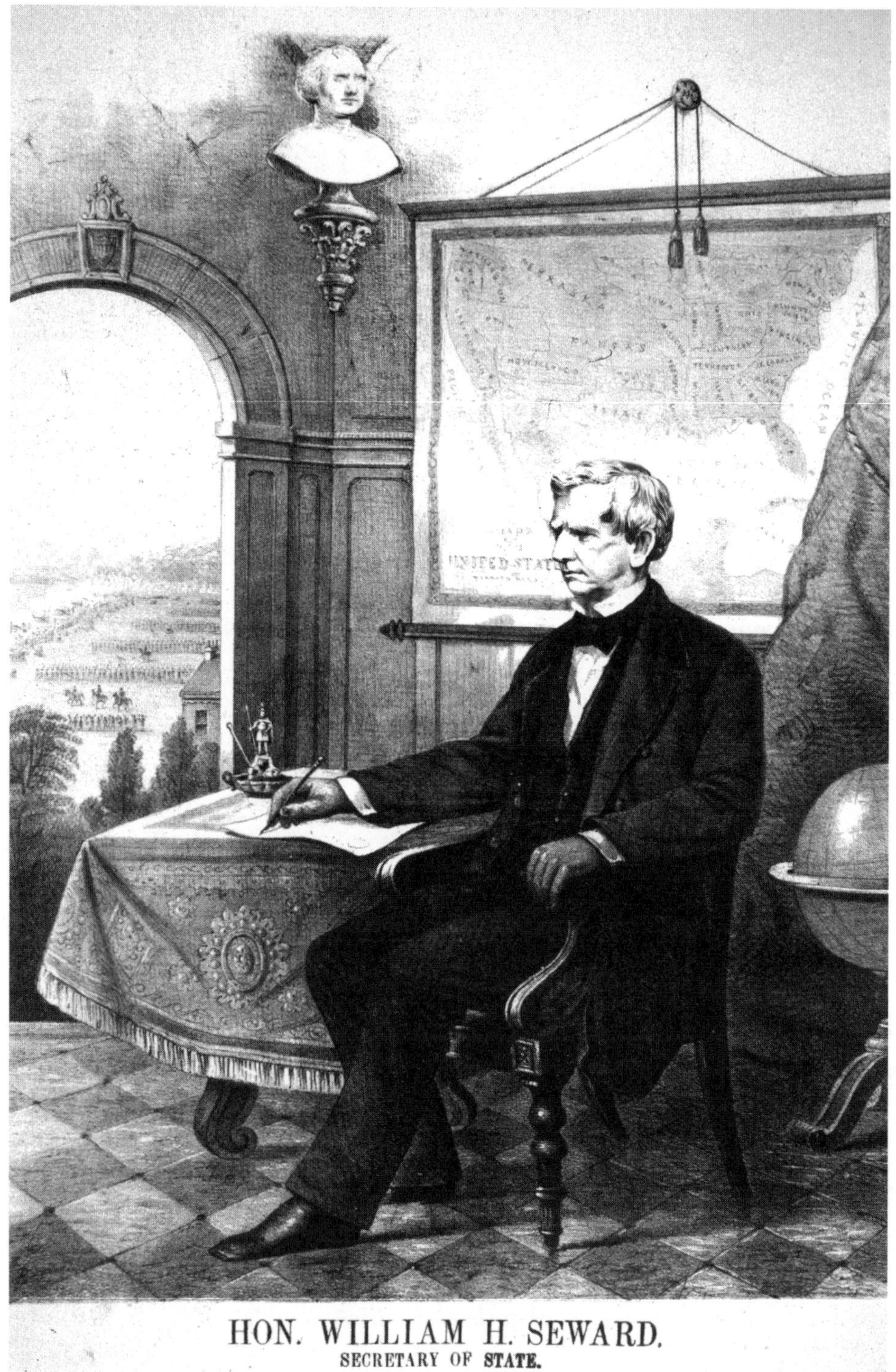

Fig. 4.1 Hon. William H. Seward. / Secretary of State.
Lithograph. Small folio: 13 × 10 in (33 × 25.4 cm). Cincinnati: Ehrgott & Forbriger, 1862–64. The Philadelphia Print Shop, Ltd. Background P.

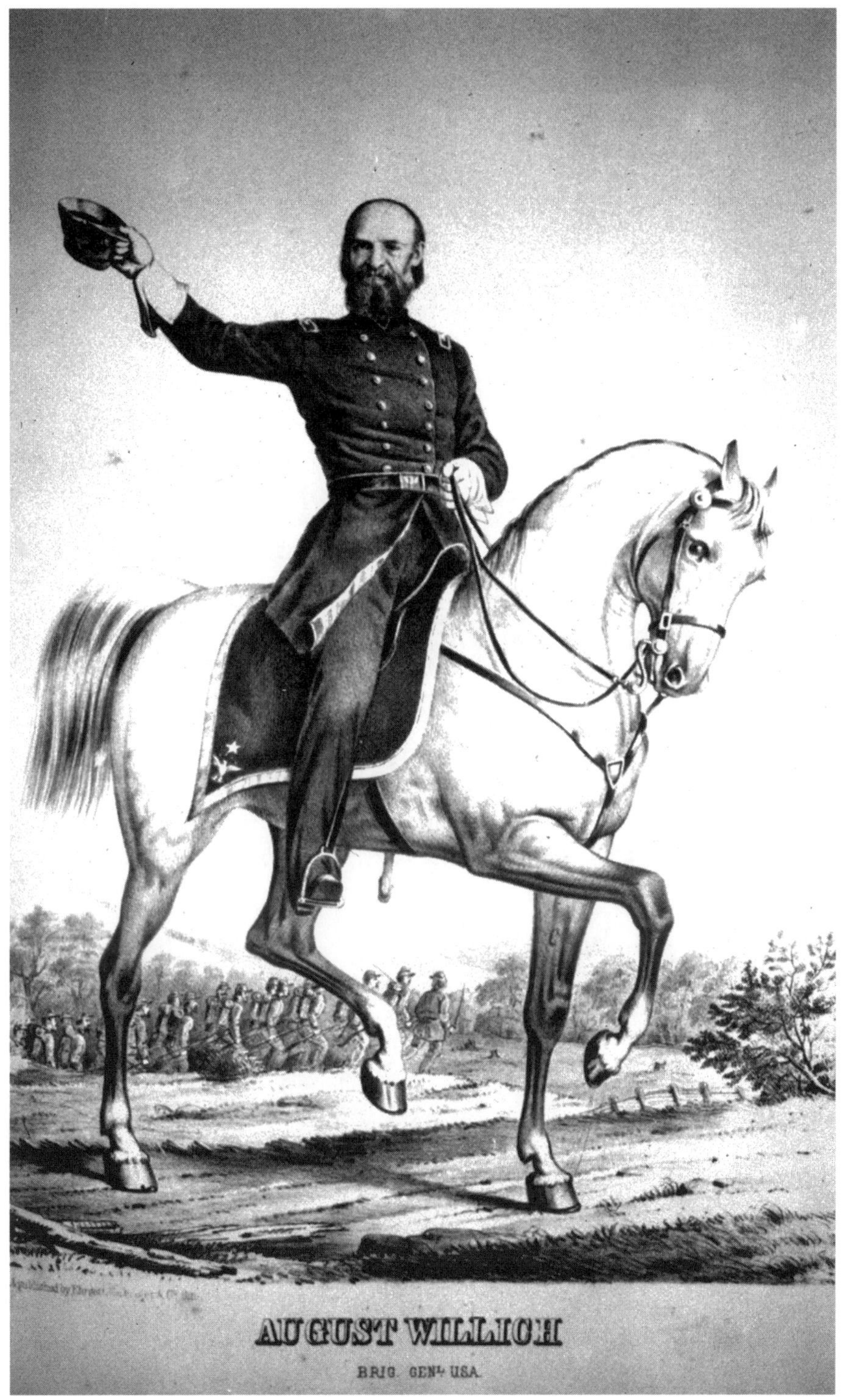

Fig. 4.2 August Willich / Brig. Gen[l]. U.S.A.
Lithograph. Small folio: 13 × 10 in (33 × 25.4 cm). Cincinnati: Ehrgott & Forbriger, 1862–64. The Philadelphia Print Shop, Ltd. Background S5b.

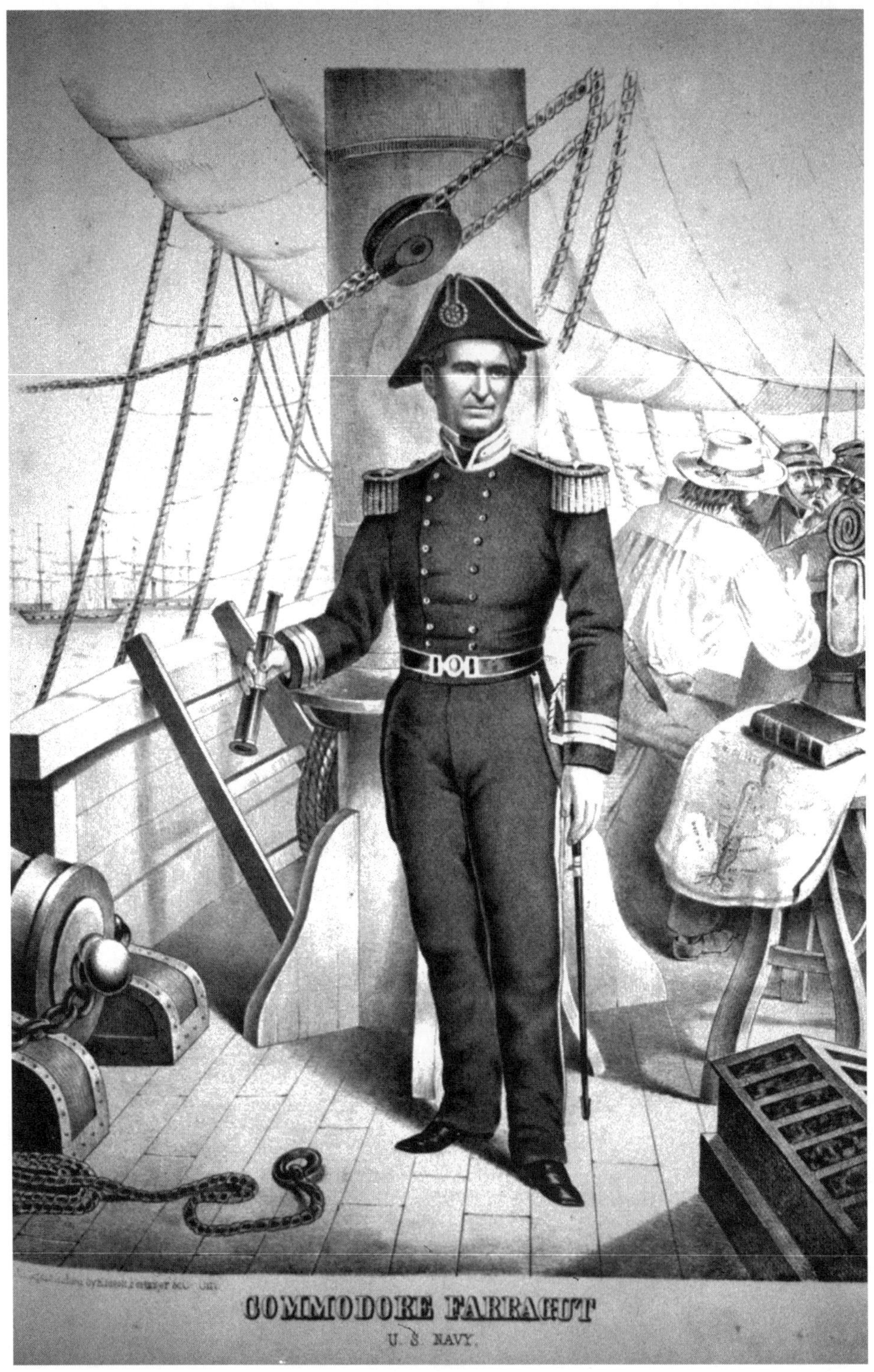

Fig. 4.3 Commodore Farragut / U.S. Navy.
Lithograph. Small folio: 13 × 10 in (33 × 25.4 cm). Cincinnati: Ehrgott & Forbriger, 1862–64. The Philadelphia Print Shop, Ltd. Background N5.

This particular style of lithographic portrait print was not an invention of Ehrgott & Forbriger.[12] There are quite a number of Civil War portraits by other lithographic publishers that are of the same type. Without making a comprehensive search, the author has identified about a dozen Currier & Ives Civil War prints from the same mold (fig. 4.4), two by Hartford publisher E. B. & E. C. Kellogg, and two similar images by fellow Cincinnati lithographer Gibson & Co. Perhaps the earliest Civil War portraits of this type are those from a series of at least ten prints by J. H. Bufford of Boston, which are dated around 1861. David Tatham calls the use of this stylized form of portrait "a tried and true formula" that was "used extensively in the 1850s by British lithographic artists such as John Brandard."[13] Even before that, Currier & Ives were issuing similar portraits of Mexican War heroes such as Winfield Scott and Samuel Ringgold, and about 1833 Risso & Browne issued a portrait of Andrew Jackson of just the same sort.

While the type of stylized lithographic portrait used by Ehrgott & Forbriger was not uncommon, the actual series of these portraits they produced is unusual on a number of counts. Just the total number of Ehrgott & Forbriger Civil War portraits of this type is exceptional. Ehrgott & Forbriger issued portraits of sixty-nine different political, naval, and military figures,[14] while the largest group of this sort of Civil War portrait issued by any other lithographer probably numbers less than a third of this figure. Equally unusual is the fact that many of the Ehrgott & Forbriger portraits of different individuals used the same backgrounds; a single background was used for all of the portraits of politicians, just five backgrounds were used for eight naval images, and only twenty-seven distinct backgrounds are found in more than twice as many military portraits. Finally, and equally unusual, the Ehrgott & Forbriger prints appear to have been sold in bound portfolios. We will consider each of these aspects of these prints in turn.

The Ehrgott & Forbriger Portraits

For the Ehrgott & Forbriger portraits of the sort under consideration, a total of sixty-nine different individuals[15] are pictured in seventy-nine different prints.[16] This includes nine politicians, eight naval figures, and fifty-two soldiers depicted in sixty-two prints. The politicians portrayed are President Lincoln; the secretaries of state, war, the navy and the treasury; the governor of Indiana; two different governors of Ohio; and the military governor of Tennessee. The naval figures include John L. Worden, commander of the *Monitor,* along with seven commodores and admirals. Among the soldiers, five colonels are pictured, the rest being generals.

Ehrgott & Forbriger selected the subjects for their prints either from those figures who were nationally famous or from those with a local connection. The president and important members of his cabinet were included and so were midwestern governors. Figures who achieved national notoriety early in the war—such as E. E. Ellsworth, the dashing martyr; Nathaniel Lyon, "the North's first military hero"; and John L. Worden, captain of the

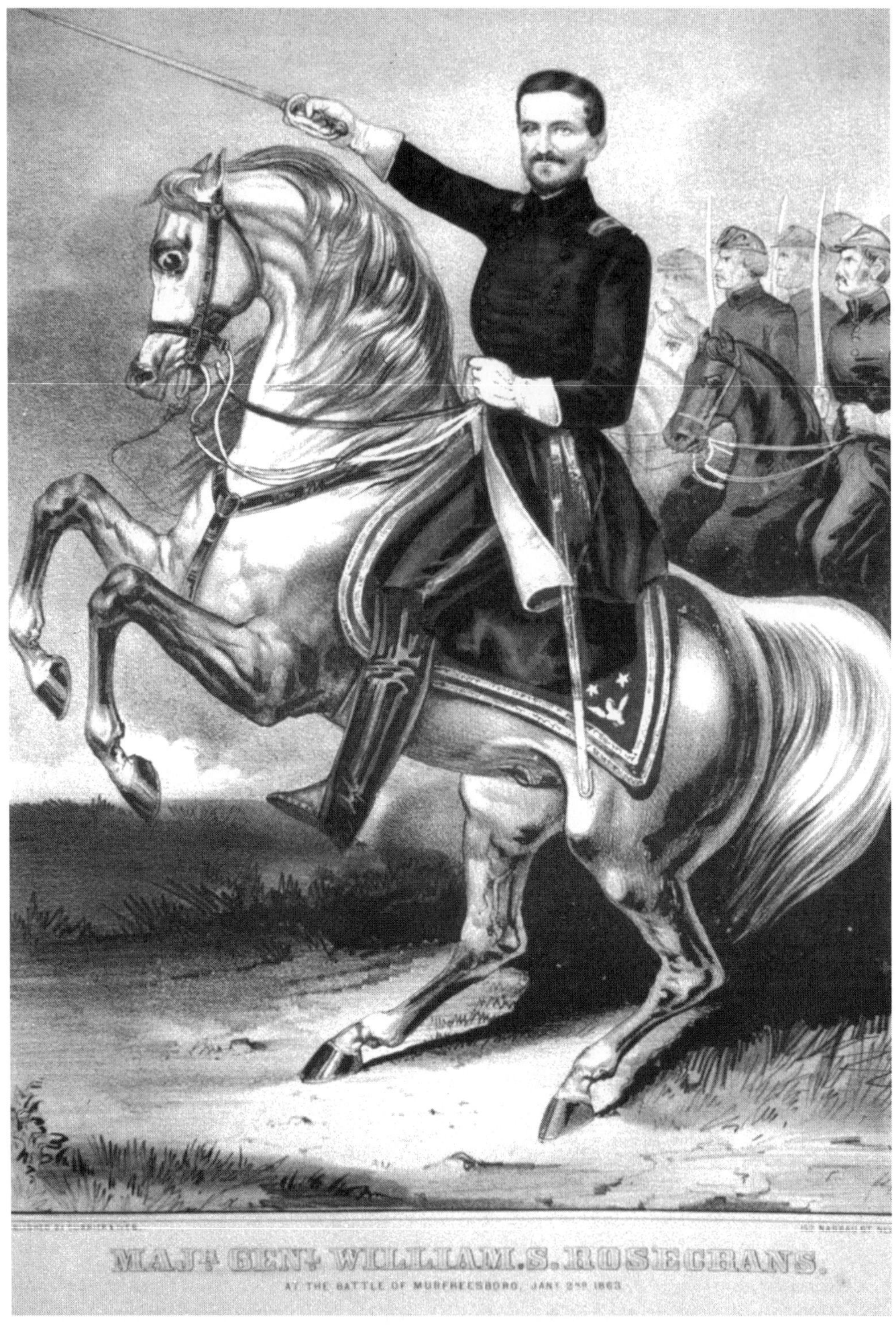

Fig. 4.4 Maj^{r}. Genl. William S. Rosecrans. / at the Battle of Murfreesboro [*sic*] Jany. 2nd. 1863.

Lithograph. Small folio. New York: Currier & Ives, 1863. The Philadelphia Print Shop, Ltd. Conningham: 3929.

Monitor—were well represented, as were top commanders such as George B. McClellan, Henry W. Halleck, and John E. Wool. Also depicted in Ehrgott & Forbriger prints were those involved in military actions of importance, such as A. H. Foote, U. S. Grant, and J. A. McClernand after the campaign of Forts Henry and Donelson and the battle of Shiloh.

A good number of the figures portrayed by Ehrgott & Forbriger had a local connection, many being native Ohio sons. Among other Ohioans were W. H. Lytle, Alexander and Robert McCook, Robert Schenck, and Minor Millikin, all better known in their home state than nationally. There was also a significant representation of Germans among the figures depicted by Ehrgott & Forbriger, inspired by the strong German presence in Cincinnati and elsewhere in the Midwest. Individuals with a German connection included Louis Blenker, who commanded three German brigades, and John C. Fremont, influential in the German American community, as well as P. J. Osterhaus, Franz Sigel, Carl Schurz, and August Willich.

As they are undated, it is difficult to determine exactly when these prints were issued. The only date that appears on any of the prints is August 10, 1861, given as the day Nathaniel Lyon was killed, but other dateable events are indicated by the rank or political office mentioned in the title of the print. The date on which a soldier or sailor achieved a rank or on which a politician was elected or appointed to a position gives the earliest possible date of publication for any print mentioning that rank or position. Most of the military figures in the Ehrgott & Forbriger series achieved the ranks cited in 1862, and both Andrew Johnson and E. M. Stanton were appointed to their given positions in that same year. There is nothing to indicate any of the prints were issued earlier than 1862, so this probably was when the Ehrgott & Forbriger series was started.

These prints were not all produced at one time, for Ehrgott & Forbriger continued to issue new prints—both variations on previous prints and new images—at least through late 1863 or early 1864. Franz Sigel, for instance, appeared first as a brigadier general; then, after his promotion to major general on March 21, 1862, the same image was reissued with its title changed to indicate the new rank. John L. Worden is first named as the commander of the *Monitor* and a later version of the same print names him as commander of the *Montauk*, Worden's ship during the blockade of the Atlantic coast in early 1863. At first the governor of Ohio was shown as David Tod, but later Ehrgott & Forbriger issued a print of John Brough as the governor, a position to which he was elected in the autumn of 1863.

The evidence is that Ehrgott & Forbriger issued their prints as the war went on, modifying their output according to the interests of their local market. They responded to the course of battles, promotions, and appointments, bringing out new or modified images as the news demanded. One example of this process can be seen in the two different Ehrgott & Forbriger prints of U. S. Grant. Both prints show him with the rank of major general, but the images of Grant are quite different. The first (fig. 4.5), which likely was issued shortly after his successes at Forts Henry and Donelson, shows Grant as a rather wild-looking figure leading his men into battle on foot. The later print (fig. 4.6), almost certainly issued after

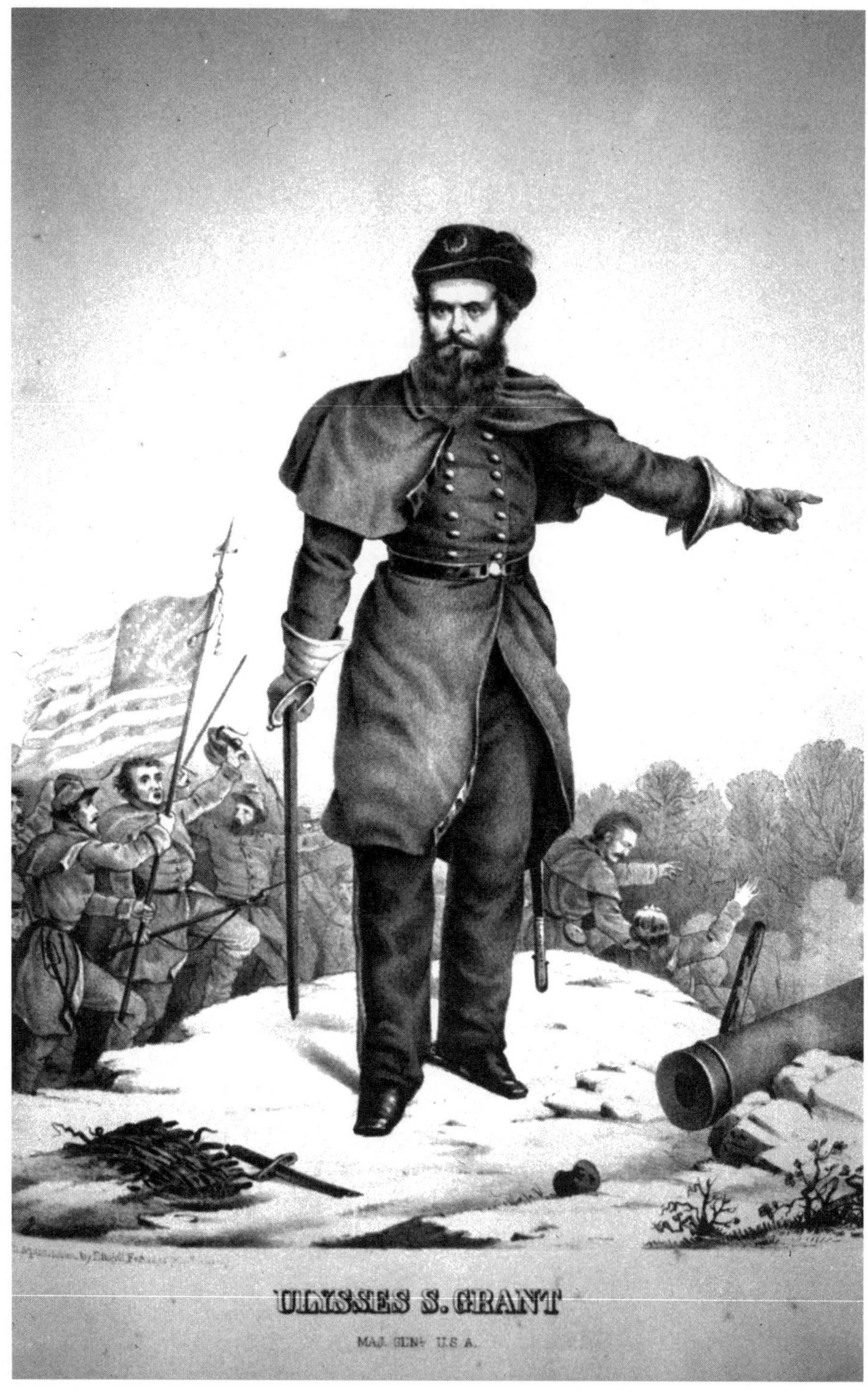

Fig. 4.5 Ulysses S. Grant / Maj. Genl. U.S.A.
Lithograph. Small folio: 13 × 10 in (33 × 25.4 cm). Cincinnati: Ehrgott & Forbriger, 1862–64. The Philadelphia Print Shop, Ltd. Background S11.

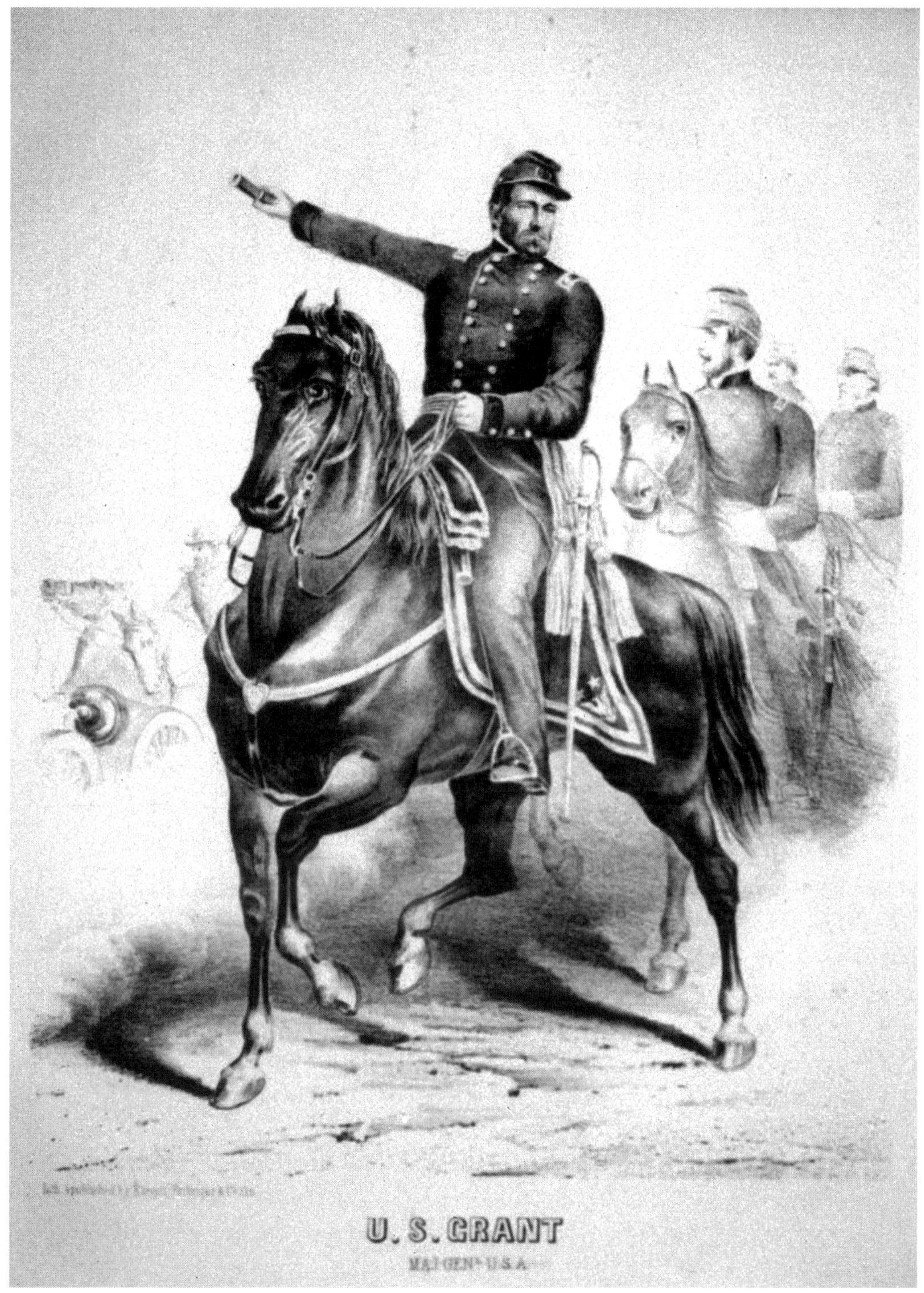

Fig. 4.6 U.S. Grant / Maj. Genl. U.S.A.
Lithograph. Small folio: 13 × 10 in (33 × 25.4 cm). Cincinnati: Ehrgott & Forbriger, 1862–64. The Philadelphia Print Shop, Ltd. Background S14a.

Grant was promoted to a more senior position, depicts a composed commander sitting astride his steed with a staff of junior officers behind.

Grant was not the only individual of whom Ehrgott & Forbriger produced two quite distinct portraits. Seven other soldiers are portrayed in two different renderings, and another, S. P. Heintzelman, had three distinct portraits made of him by Ehrgott & Forbriger. In none of these cases was it a change in rank or position that caused the new image to be made, so it seems likely that the original lithographic stones must no longer have been available when Ehrgott & Forbriger wanted to issue a print of the soldier in question, thus necessitating that they create a whole new image.

The history of the Ehrgott & Forbriger Civil War portraits, then, is one of a lithographic firm taking advantage of a local market demand for prints of individuals "in the news." The demand for portraits of newsworthy figures was huge in the 1860s, and Ehrgott & Forbriger met this demand with attractive and inexpensive lithographic prints which they were able to keep timely by issuing variations or new images as circumstances demanded. Ehrgott & Forbriger's need to be able to produce new images in this series as quickly and inexpensively as possible was obvious, and the solution they came up with was to create new prints by reusing the background images of previously issued prints. This solution had been used many times before but never quite to the extent that Ehrgott & Forbriger used it.

Hydra-Headed Stones

Ehrgott & Forbriger's Civil War portraits not only used stylized backgrounds, but in many cases reused the same background, including the same body, for prints of different figures, with the prints differing only by a changed title and head. Each of the political images shows an accurate image of the subject's countenance, but all nine have the same background (figs. 4.7 and 4.8). Of the eight naval portraits, four of the officers share an identical background, and another, interestingly, shares his background with a military officer.[17] Among the sixty-one other military prints, there are only twenty-seven different backgrounds. Thirteen of the backgrounds appear in only one print each; four backgrounds were used for two portraits each; three backgrounds were used for three portraits each; six backgrounds were used for four portraits each; and one background appeared behind the faces of seven different individuals.

It is not an uncommon thing for printmakers to have created a "new" portrait by taking an already existing portrait and putting onto it a new head. As Kaplan notes, George S. Layard, in his *Catalogue Raisonné of Engraved British Portraits from Altered Plates*, recorded 118 European portraits altered into 130 new prints, and many other examples have been recorded for European and American prints.[18] The reason for this practice is quite obviously the time and expense saved. To create a new print, by engraving or lithography, was time consuming and expensive. It was much more efficient to simply remove the old head from the plate or stone and draw in a new visage. Given the marketing needs of

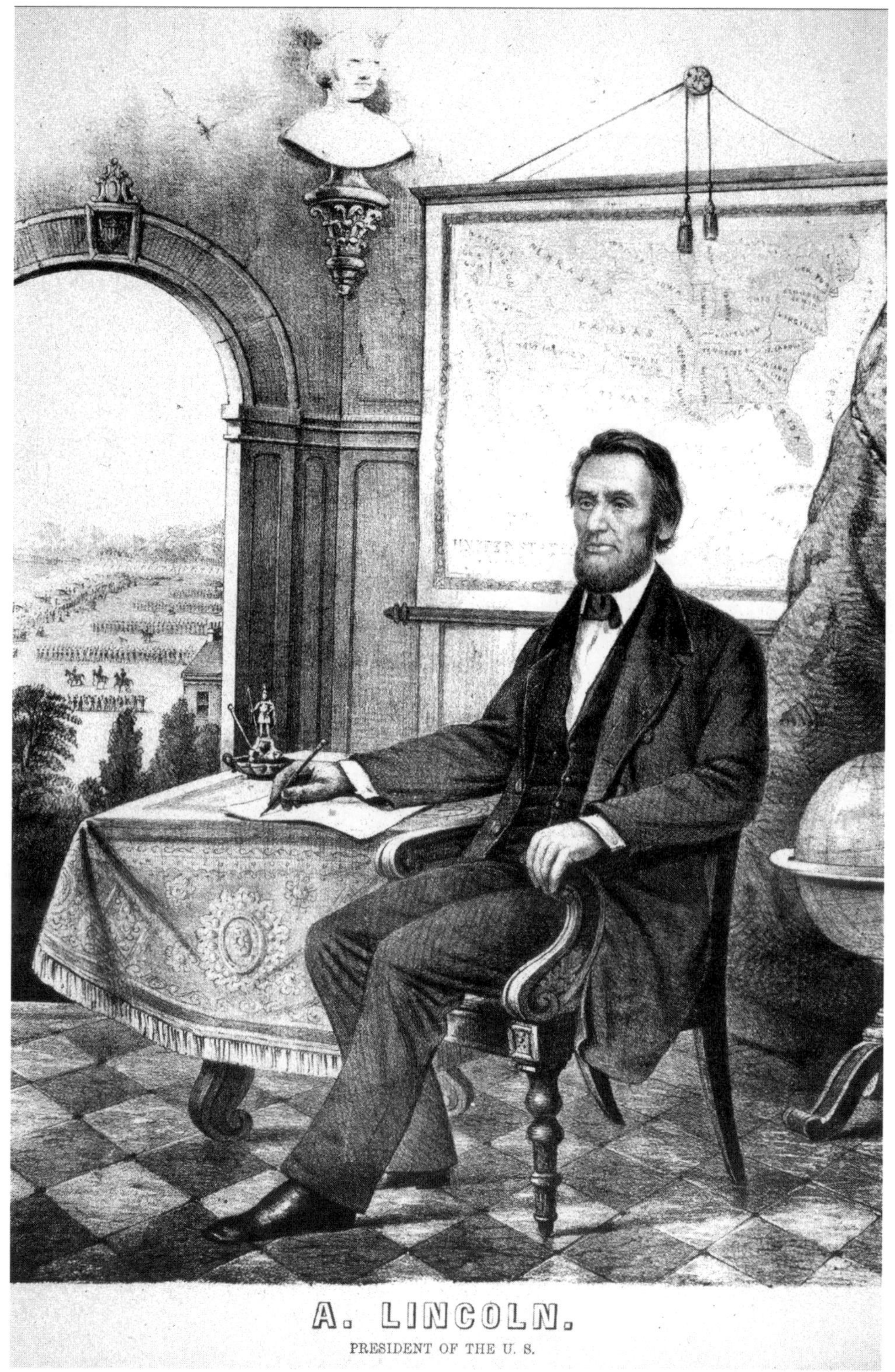

Fig. 4.7 A. Lincoln. / President of the U.S.
Lithograph. Small folio: 13 × 10 in (33 × 25.4 cm). Cincinnati: Ehrgott & Forbriger, 1862–64. The Philadelphia Print Shop, Ltd. Background P.

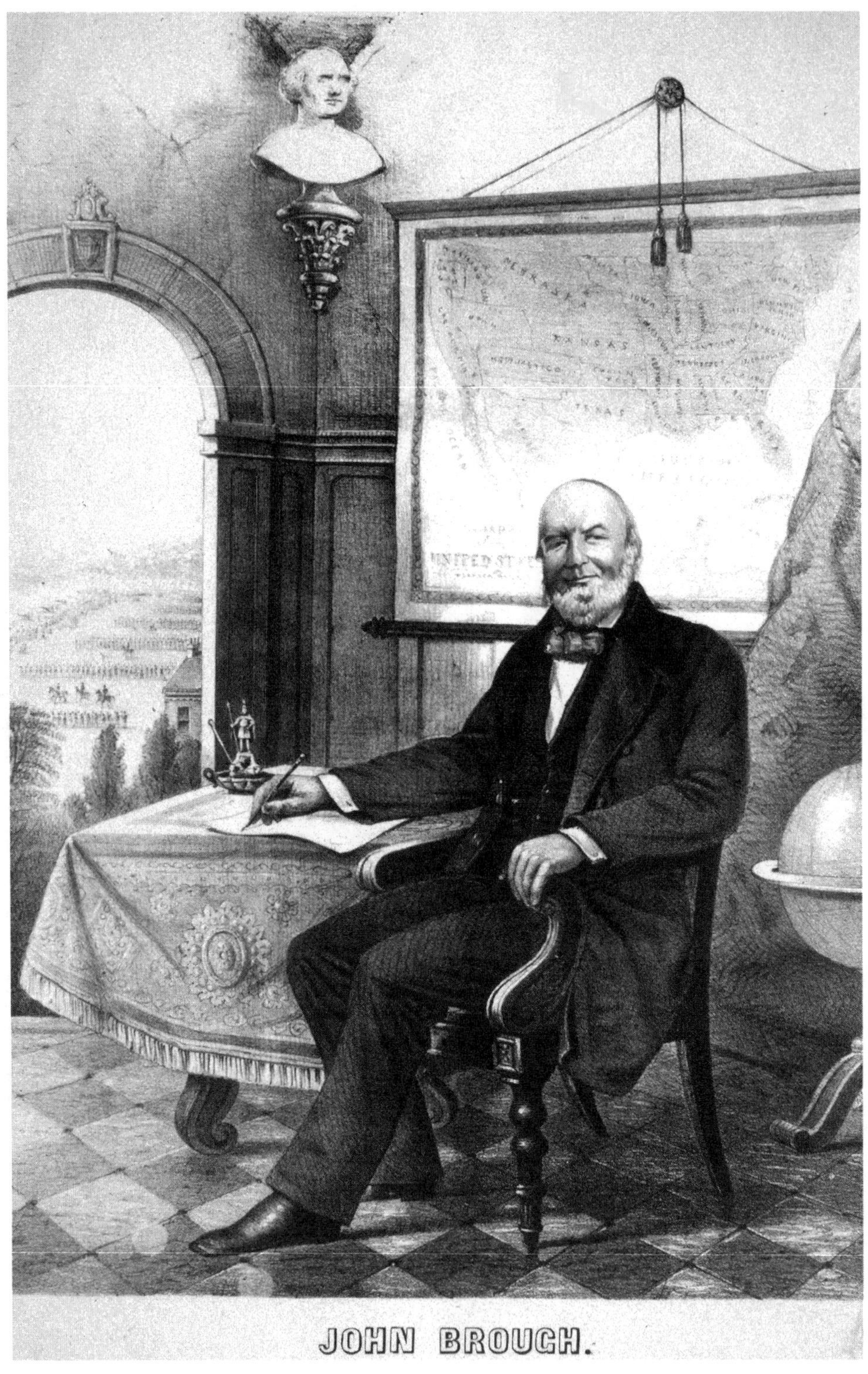

Fig. 4.8 John Brough. / Governor of Ohio.
Lithograph. Small folio: 13 × 10 in (33 × 25.4 cm). Cincinnati: Ehrgott & Forbriger, 1862–64. The Philadelphia Print Shop, Ltd. Background P.

Ehrgott & Forbriger relative to these Civil War portraits, it is not surprising that they would use this expedient process. Many printmakers other than Ehrgott & Forbriger had done it before, though certainly none to such an obvious and extended degree.

The backgrounds, including the bodies of the figures portrayed, are so stylized and so obviously reused for different portraits, that this aspect of the prints cannot be thought to represent accurate portrayals of the individuals in real settings. However the heads are accurate images of the subjects, for the countenances of these politicians, soldiers, and sailors clearly come from contemporary photographs (figs. 4.9 and 4.10). There were plenty of photographic images for Ehrgott & Forbriger to use, for cartes de visite were ubiquitous at the time the firm was producing these prints. The Civil War created a huge market for photographic portraits of important political, military, and naval figures, and this demand was met by thousands of cartes de visite of almost every figure of note. Photographic firms compiled libraries of negatives from which people could order, and cartes de visite were shipped all around the country.[19] It is usually impossible to establish which specific photograph was used for any individual print, for the different photographs often look very much alike, but a comparison of photographs and the Ehrgott & Forbriger prints makes it obvious that the heads of these portraits were taken directly from photographic sources.

The use of photographic images by lithographic publishers was quite common. Francis D'Avignon translated Mathew Brady's daguerreotypes into lithographs for the 1850 *Gallery of Illustrious Americans*, as well as producing a whole oeuvre of lithographic portraits based on photographs.[20] William Darrah lists seven companies making lithographic copies of cartes de visite by late 1862,[21] and the Civil War lithographic portraits by Joseph E. Baker, published by J. H. Bufford around 1861, are specifically attributed as being copied from photographs. Like Ehrgott & Forbriger, Currier & Ives also placed photographically derived heads into stylized backgrounds for some of their Civil War prints. The 1862 Currier & Ives print "The Storming of Fort Donelson, Tenn."[22] shows a scene drawn much like their other Civil War battle images, but the figure of U. S. Grant has a head which is clearly based on a photographic source. Two Currier & Ives group portraits, "Grant and His Generals"[23] and "Champions of the Union,"[24] also obviously used photographs for the faces of the generals depicted.

It seems likely that there was some sort of mechanical process by which a photographic portrait could be transferred to a lithographic stone, rather than always having to copy the photographs freehand. Grant's head in "The Storming of Fort Donelson, Tenn." stands out as being drawn differently from the rest of the print (fig. 4.11). It has an obvious photographic appearance which contrasts with the freehand drawing of the rest of the print.[25] Certainly many lithographs based on photographs were drawn freehand, but the large number of photograph-based prints, many with multiple heads, and the "photographic" appearance of many of these portraits seem to suggest not all were drawn that way. To duplicate freehand so many photographs so closely would have been very time consuming and likely not cost effective.

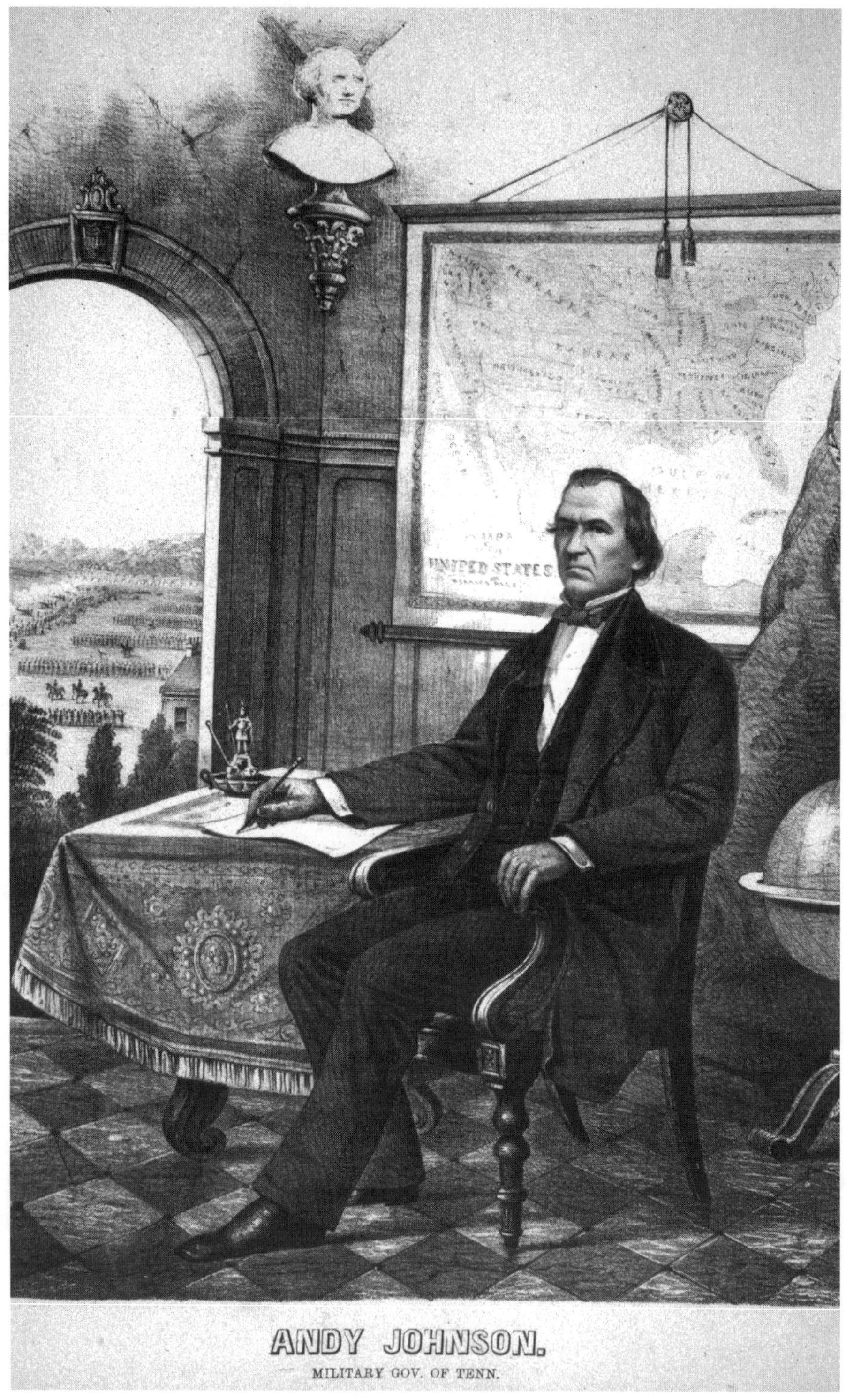

Fig. 4.9 Andy Johnson. / Military Gov. of Tenn.
Lithograph. Small folio: 13 × 10 in (33 × 25.4 cm). Cincinnati: Ehrgott & Forbriger, 1862–64. The Philadelphia Print Shop, Ltd. Background P.

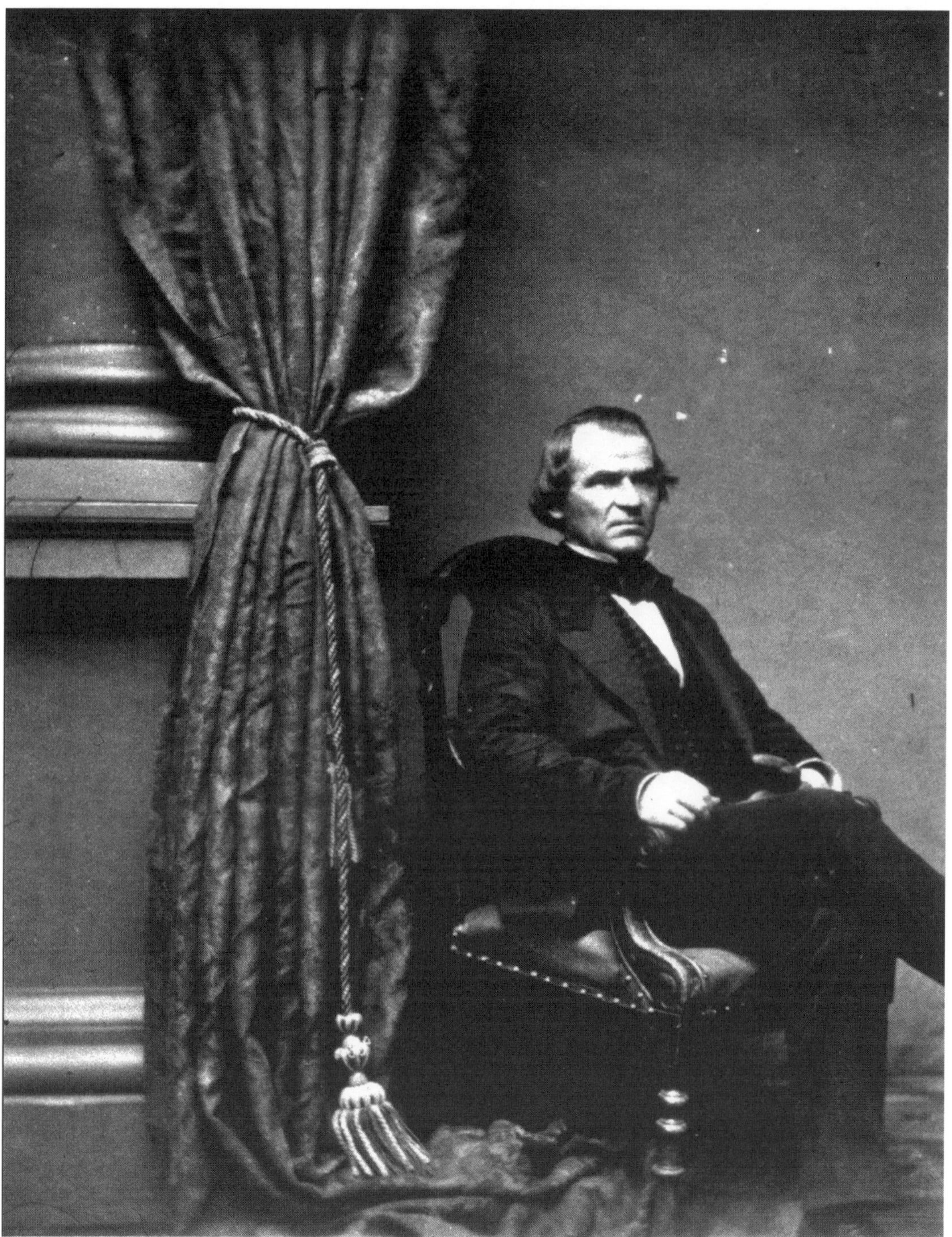

Fig. 4.10 [Andrew Johnson, 1808–1875]
Mathew Brady Studio. Print from Collodian Glass-Plate Negative. Negative: 3 15/16 × 3 3/16 in (10 × 8.1 cm). 1866. NPG.81.M10–M12. National Portrait Gallery, Smithsonian Institution.

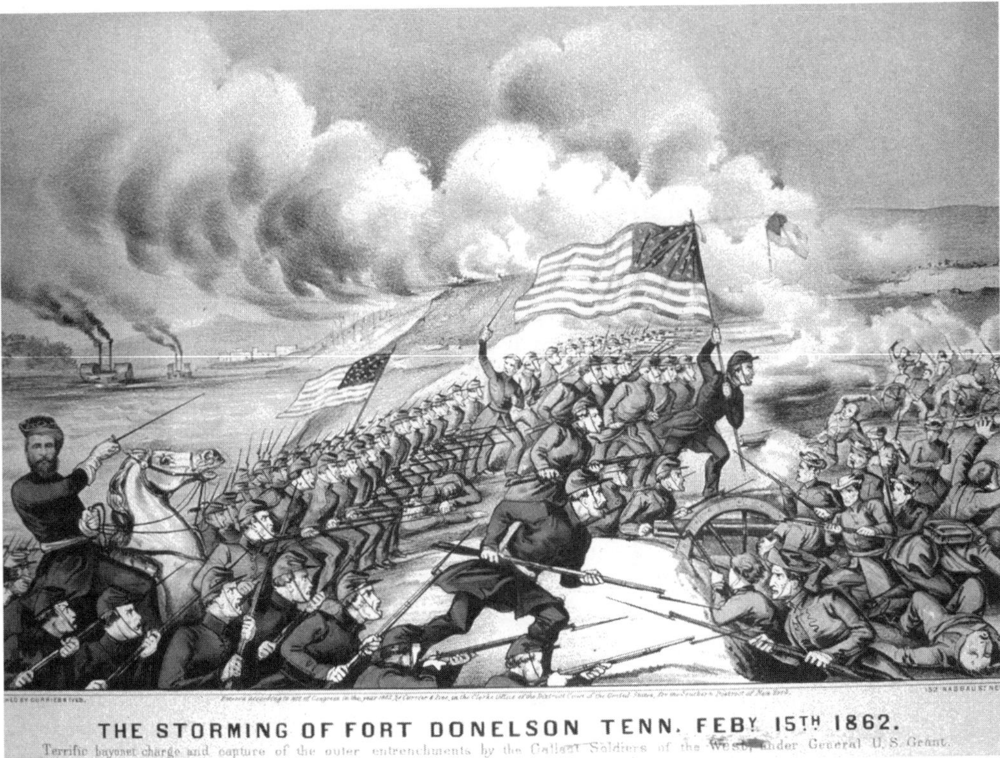

Fig. 4.11 The Storming of Fort Donelson Tenn. Feby. 15th 1862.
Lithograph. Small folio. New York: Currier & Ives, 1862. The Philadelphia Print Shop, Ltd. Previously unrecorded.

Some sort of mechanical process is indicated also by a previously unrecorded variant of Currier & Ives's "Champions of the Union." The first version of this print (fig. 4.12), dated 1861, shows a group of twenty-five generals, and the second version (fig. 4.13), also dated 1861, shows thirty-four generals, with the nine extra portraits added as a back row behind the original twenty-five. These new, photograph-derived portraits were, in effect, "dropped into" the original image. To do this freehand would probably have been more time consuming and costly than would be warranted just to add nine extra generals to the print. Though the process by which photographic images were transferred to lithographic stones is not recorded, William Darrah suggests that at least some lithographic reproductions of photographs were made by using a camera lucida, and this procedure certainly seems to be a likely candidate.[26]

Stylized Backgrounds

By whatever process, Ehrgott & Forbriger produced seventy-nine portrait prints of sixty-nine different individuals involved in the Northern cause during the Civil War. While the faces of each of these individual portraits are quite distinct, and accurately based on

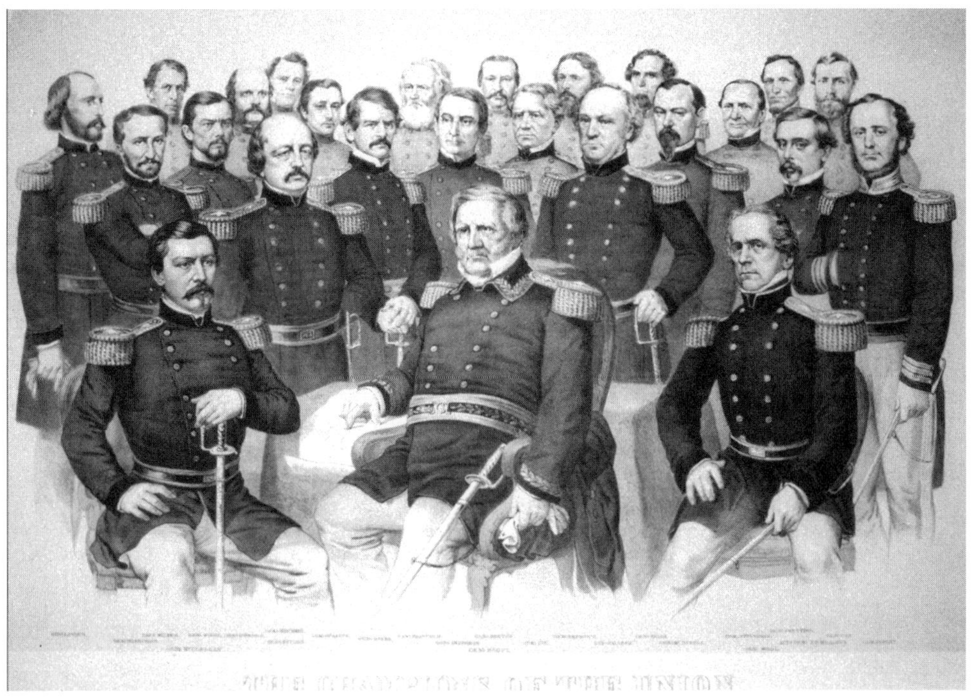

Fig. 4.12 The Champions of the Union.
Lithograph. Medium folio: 14⅛ × 19⅞ in (35.88 × 50.48 cm). New York: Currier & Ives, 1861. The Philadelphia Print Shop, Ltd. Conningham: 993.

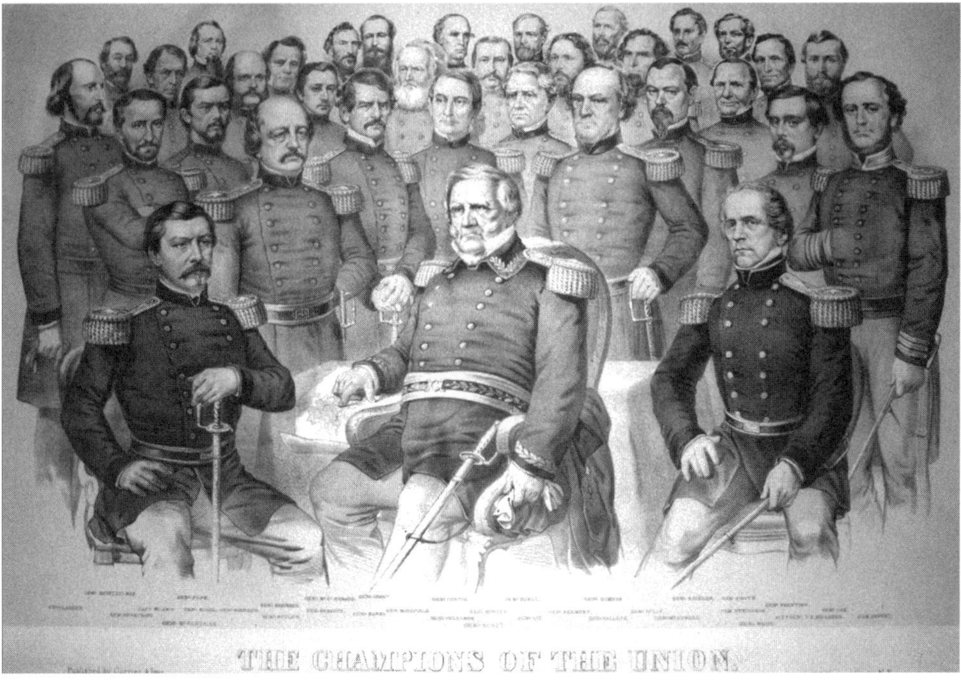

Fig. 4.13 The Champions of the Union.
Lithograph. Medium folio: 14⅛ × 19⅞ in (35.88 × 50.48 cm). New York: Currier & Ives, 1861. The Philadelphia Print Shop, Ltd. Previously unrecorded.

photographs, Ehrgott & Forbriger clearly did not try to make the backgrounds of the prints different or accurate. For their seventy-nine portraits there are only thirty-three distinct backgrounds, with almost half of the backgrounds being used for more than one individual. The background for the politicians was used nine times, another background appears behind seven different generals, and fourteen other backgrounds were used for between two and four portraits each.[27]

The reuse of the backgrounds is even more extensive than it appears at first, for quite a number of the backgrounds were closely copied from other backgrounds, with only moderate changes. The charging infantry behind the horse in one background becomes a cavalry troop; a small hill disappears to be replaced by a bush; or a dark horse becomes a dappled gray. If all the backgrounds derived from each other are grouped together, then there are only fifteen distinct groups. Two of the background groups have two variants each; three of the background groups have three variants each; and one background group has five distinct variations.

The evolution of the S4 group of backgrounds is typical.[28] The first version in this background group is S4a, in which a uniformed figure is mounted on a standing horse (fig. 4.14). Behind this figure, on the right, is a seaside fort and a lighthouse, while out at sea are shown a paddlewheel steamship and a fleet of other ships in the distance. This background was used to create another version, S4b (fig. 4.15), which includes the same mounted figure on the same horse, but with an extensively reworked image behind this figure. The seaside scene has now become riparian. The fort from S4a has been changed into a hill, with the lighthouse turned into a vaguely shaped building on top of the hill. A row of tents and trees replaces the paddlewheeler on the left, and an ironclad is drawn sailing along the river. In the distance the masts of the ships from S4a are still faintly visible; this looks rather strange, though perhaps the ships might be docked at a distant town along the river.

The third variant in this group, S4c (fig. 4.16), has exactly the same horse and rider, but the rest of the background has now been completely redrawn. The foreground is no longer flat, and a tree stump, stones, and plants have been added. Behind the rider is now a formation of troops marching in rank in front of a rail fence. Though the image surrounding the main figure is very different, background S4c was derived from S4a, for not only are the rider and horse identical, but a shadowy shape can be seen in S4c of the hat of General Wool, the person pictured in S4a. This ghost image and the masts, which don't really belong in background S4b, are but two of the many interesting features one can find through a close examination of the Ehrgott & Forbriger backgrounds.

Other ghost images can be found, for instance in background S6b, where the faint outline of a bugler's horse from S6a can still be seen, even though the bugler and his mount are not supposed to be part of the image. In backgrounds S13a and S13b, charging troops are drawn at the left, and these are replaced by cavalry in S13c. However, just below the horses in S13c one can still see a faint image of the legs of the troops from the earlier variants. The most humorous result of the background modifications appears in S14c. In

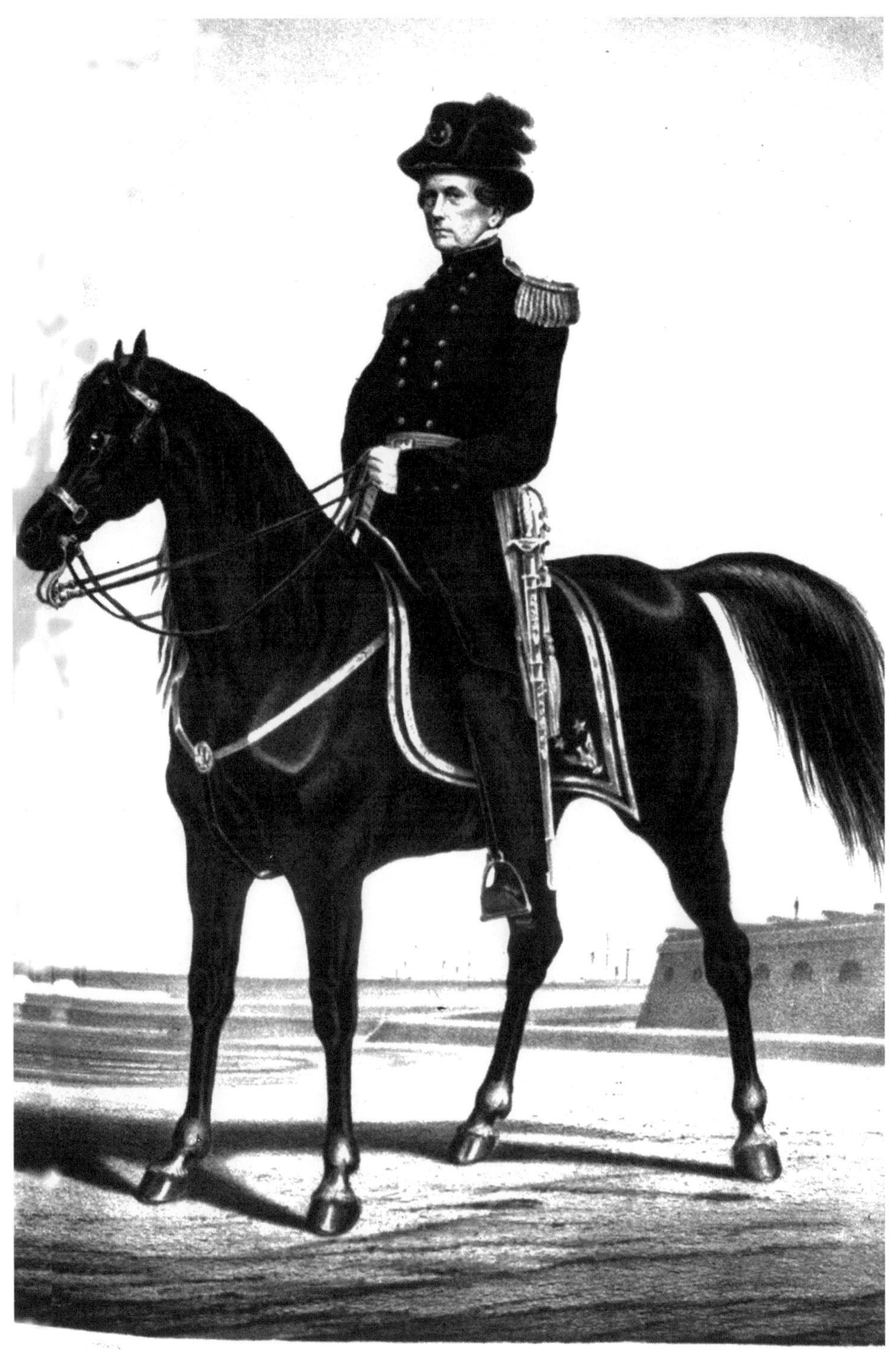

Fig. 4.14 John E. Wool. / Maj. Genl. U.S.A.
Lithograph. Small folio: 13 × 10 in (33 × 25.4 cm). Cincinnati: Ehrgott & Forbriger, 1862–64. The Philadelphia Print Shop, Ltd. Background S4a.

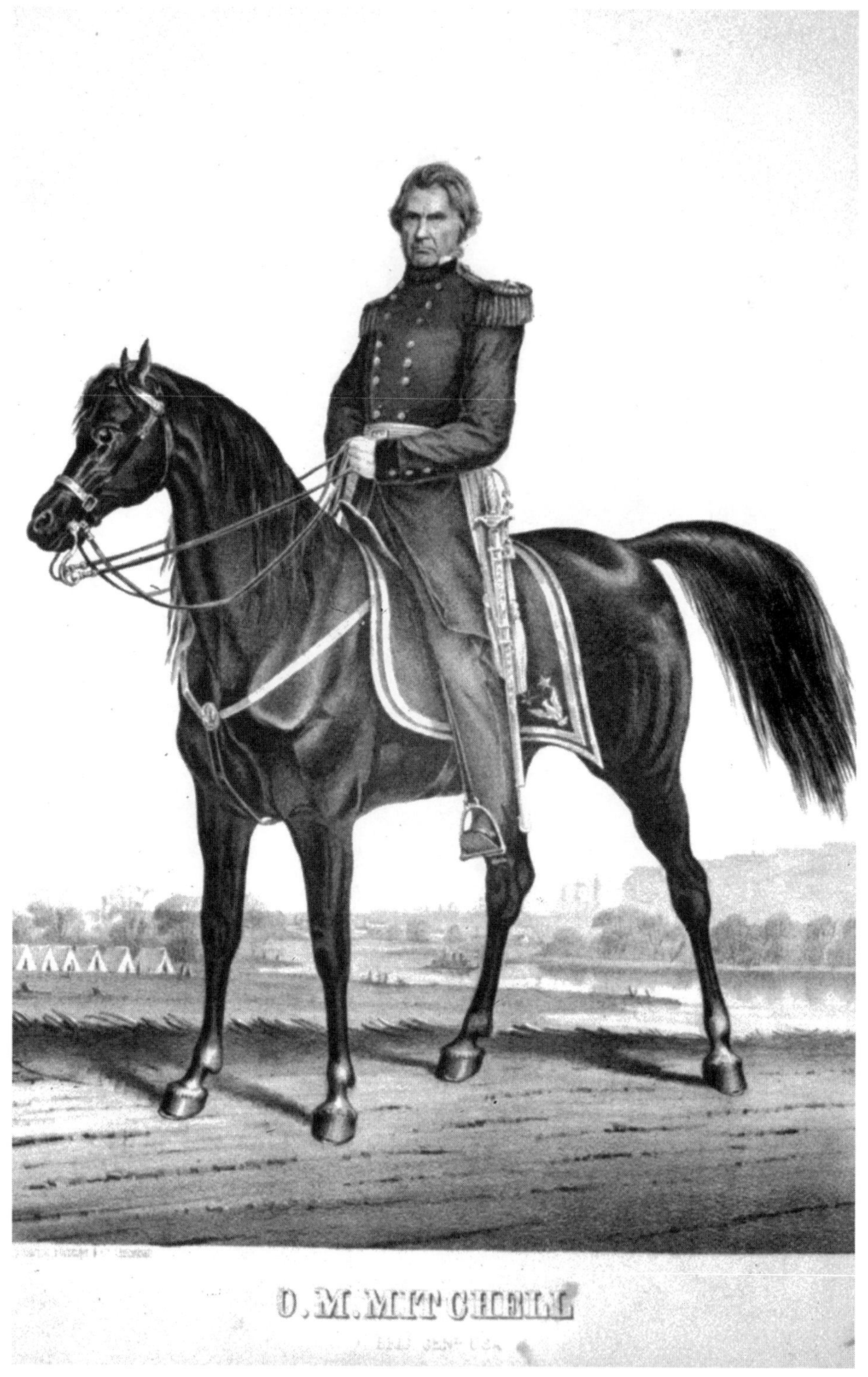

Fig. 4.15 O. M. Mitchell [*sic*] / Brig. Gen[l]. U.S.A.
Lithograph. Small folio: 13 × 10 in (33 × 25.4 cm). Cincinnati: Ehrgott & Forbriger, 1862–64. The Philadelphia Print Shop, Ltd. Background S4b.

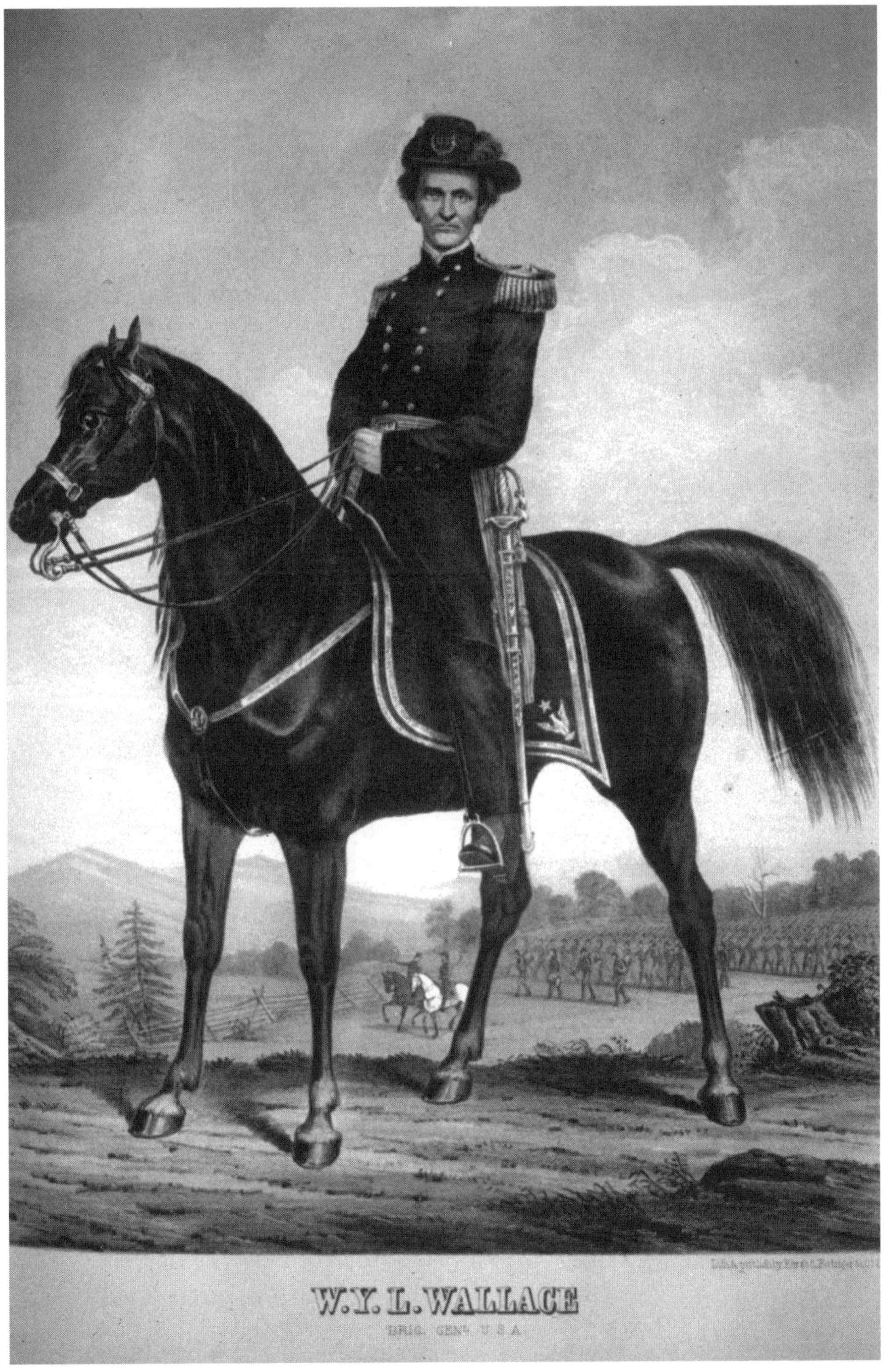

Fig. 4.16 W. Y. L. Wallace / Brig. Genl. U.S.A.
Lithograph. Small folio: 13 × 10 in (33 × 25.4 cm). Cincinnati: Ehrgott & Forbriger, 1862–64. The Philadelphia Print Shop, Ltd. Background S4c.

the previous two variants of this background, a group of mounted officers is drawn at the right behind the main figure. In S14a (fig. 4.17), this group starts out with four officers, the hindmost of which disappears from wear in some of the later portraits using this background. In S14b the back two officers of this group are eliminated completely and the heads of the front two are redrawn. By S14c (fig. 4.18), all of the officers on the right are gone, but the front legs of the lead horse of this group still appear under the belly of the main figure's mount. This makes it look like this horse has six legs, for there is nothing in this image to explain these two extra appendages left over from the earlier variants.

This close examination of the Ehrgott & Forbriger backgrounds leads to the conclusion that the different prints sharing backgrounds or with background variants were printed from different stones; that is, they were not just later states printed from the same stone after it was modified. When a rough temporal sequence of the impressions of the prints is made, this shows that it is very unlikely that all of the examples of one image were made before the publication of the other prints with the same or variant backgrounds.[29] This means that stones for different prints with the same or a variant background must have existed at the same time. Furthermore, in background group S3, at least three of the variants were modified directly from S3a; that is, all of S3b, S3c, and S3d are modifications of S3a, not from each other. This would be impossible if the stone for S3a were itself modified to make the variants. These two arguments show that at least some different prints with the same or variant backgrounds were printed from different stones, not from the same stone modified over time.

The visual evidence of the prints further indicates that this process involved the actual transfer of images from one stone to another, probably with the use of transfer paper. The bodies and horses of the main figures in the different variants are not just copies but are identical, excepting wear. Also, the ghost images in some of the variants could only appear if the image were actually transferred, and this is further supported by the transference of blemishes, which are carried over from some of the images to their variants. For instance, in the print of John C. Frémont, one of the later portraits printed with background S3a, some blemishes are evident in the image next to the main horse's front left hoof. These blemishes are then transferred to the portrait of E. E. Ellsworth with background S3b and again to the image of B. F. Butler with background S3c.[30]

The transferred images were at some point in the process modified to create new portraits. In the case of a print with a new background variation, there was often fairly extensive modification involving a change in landscape and background figures. If the new print kept the same background, less extensive modifications were made, such as the altering of the number of stars on the saddle blanket or a changing of the object held in the hand of the main figure—for instance, from a brandished sword to a waved cap. And, of course, for every new portrait a new head was attached to the old body. If one looks very closely at the prints, one can usually see where the new visage was attached to the old body. For some prints, such as the politicians, the change is only from the neck up, with the entire

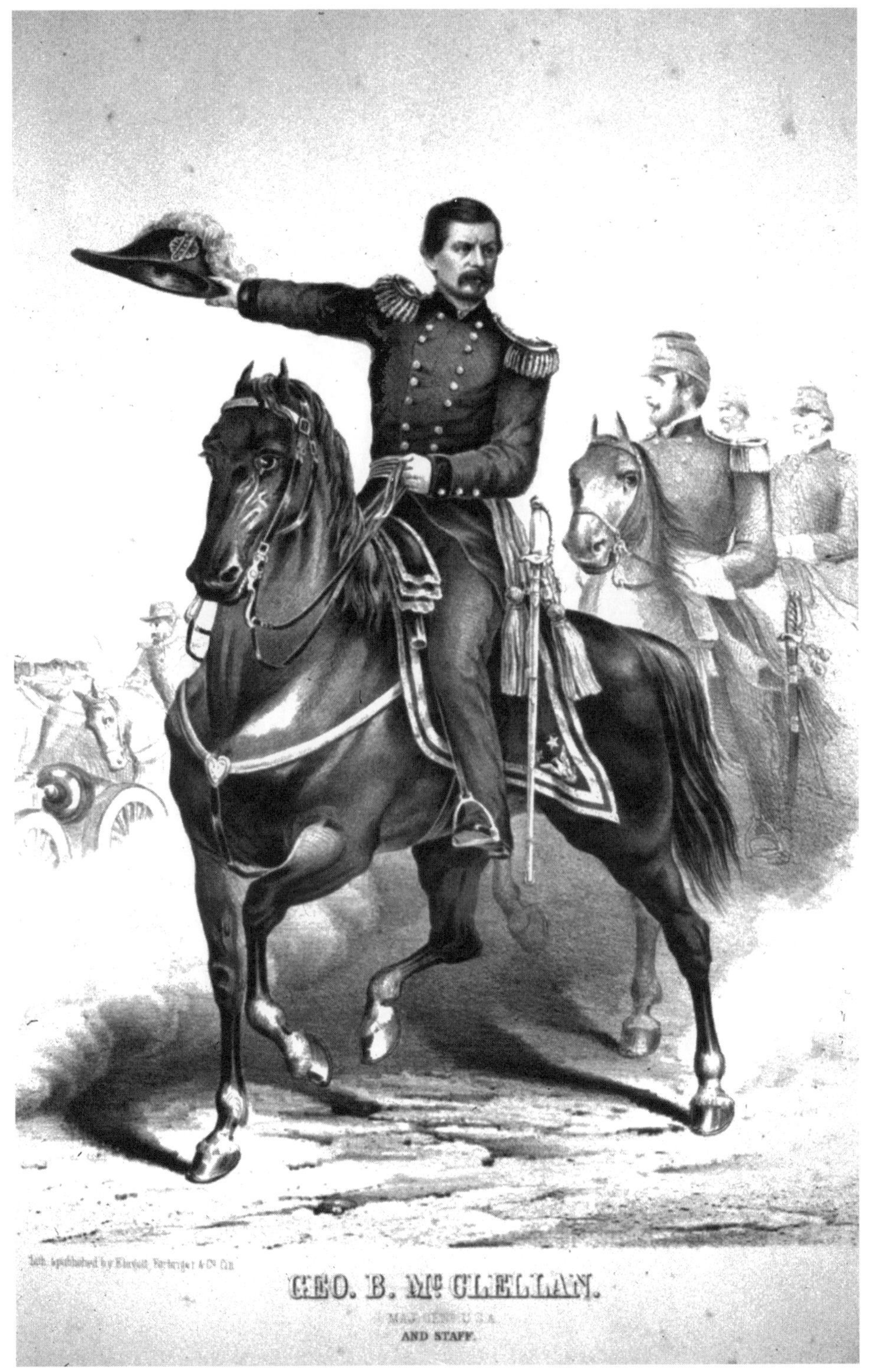

Fig. 4.17 Geo. B. McClellan. / Maj. Genl. U.S.A. / and Staff.
Lithograph. Small folio: 13 × 10 in (33 × 25.4 cm). Cincinnati: Ehrgott & Forbriger, 1862–64. The Philadelphia Print Shop, Ltd. Background S14a.

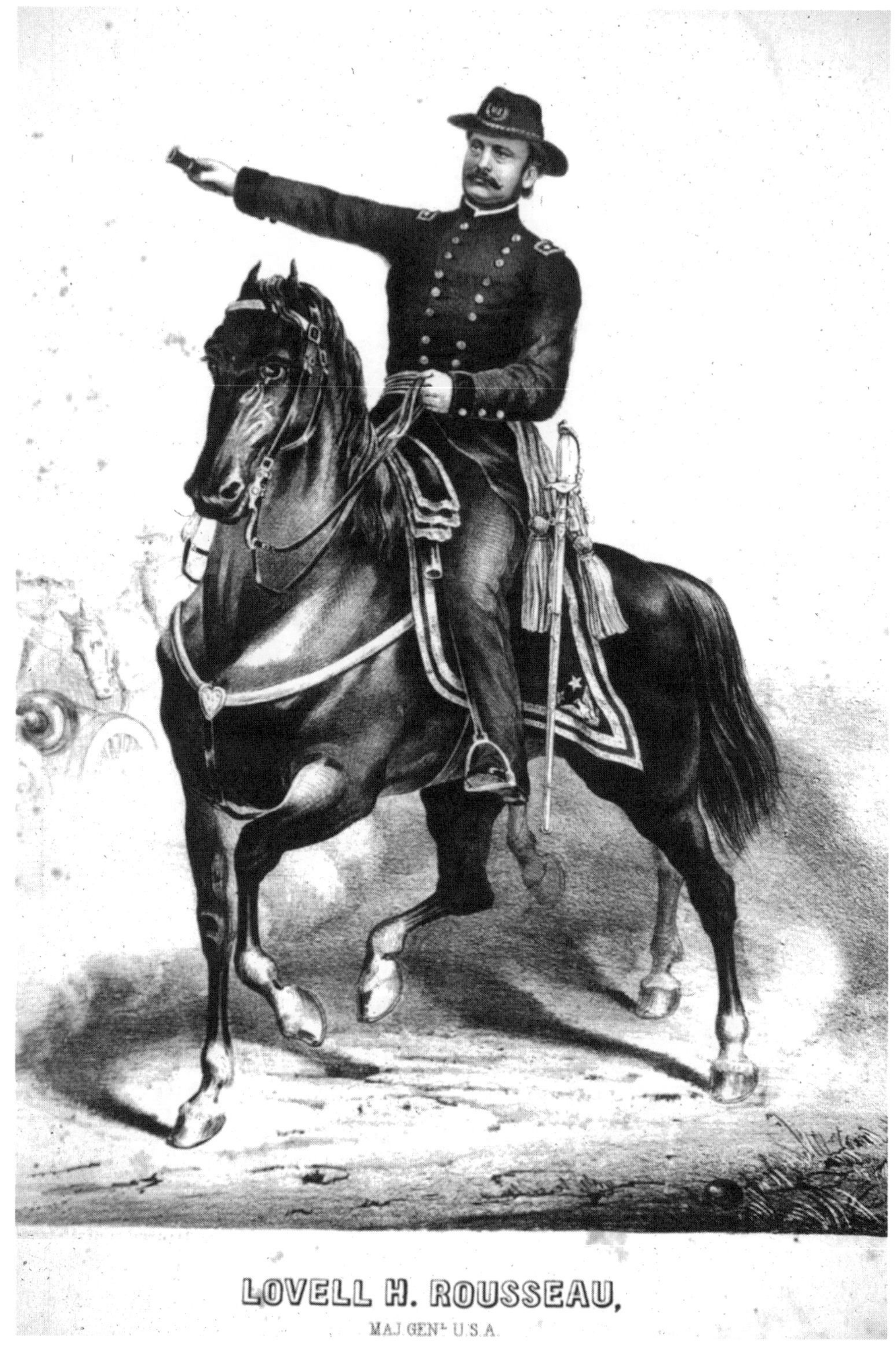

Fig. 4.18 Lovell H. Rousseau. / Maj. Gen[l]. U.S.A.
Lithograph. Small folio: 13 × 10 in (33 × 25.4 cm). Cincinnati: Ehrgott & Forbriger, 1862–64. Clements Library, University of Michigan. Background Sl4c.

body remaining the same from print to print. In other prints the changes sometimes extended about halfway down the torso, with even the arms being redrawn.

Portfolios

While other lithographic printmakers created Civil War portraits with obviously stylized backgrounds, none besides Ehrgott & Forbriger used exactly the same background for more than one such portrait. One might think that Ehrgott & Forbriger would try to hide the obvious recurrence of the backgrounds, but as their market region was relatively small and as they issued a large number of prints using the same backgrounds, this repetition must have been readily apparent to the print-buying public. Surprisingly, rather than hiding their reuse of backgrounds, they made this practice even more obvious by these prints being bound together and sold in portfolios, so that the reiteration was glaringly obvious.

Of the 263 individual examples of Ehrgott & Forbriger portrait prints that have been located, 153 were found as part of portfolios.[31] Four portfolios of Ehrgott & Forbriger portraits have been identified, each with approximately forty prints. Three of the four identified portfolios still have their original covers,[32] all of which have similar buckram boards. The earliest of the portfolios is bound with "Covert's Music Binder,"[33] where the boards are fastened by metal points that pass through the prints and are then bent to hold the portfolio together. The other two bound portfolios have almost identical covers, with the prints sewn into the binding, as was clearly done for the unbound portfolio. None of the portfolios has a title on the cover or spine, and none has a title page or a table of contents.

The nineteenth century was a period when people often collected prints or photographs and put them together into albums, so it would not be that surprising to find that someone had gathered a collection of Ehrgott & Forbriger prints and bound them into a portfolio. Indeed, the earliest of the portfolios was bound in "Covert's Music Binder," a cover intended for an album of music sheets, which could easily have been used by a collector to gather together a collection of portraits. The fact that four of the prints in the earliest portfolio were not by Ehrgott & Forbriger further supports the conjecture that it was a collector who put the prints together into the binder.

However, there is a uniformity and pattern to the four known portfolios that strongly suggests a single agent was responsible for their creation, rather than each portfolio being the product of an individual collector's actions. Not only is there a similarity in the manner in which the portfolios were bound, but there is a pattern to what prints were included and to their order within the portfolios. The earliest portfolio begins with a Currier & Ives portrait of George Washington, a print also included at the beginning of two of the other portfolios. Washington's portrait is followed in the earliest portfolio with a print by fellow Cincinnati lithographer Gibson & Co., of Winfield Scott,[34] the commander in chief of the U.S. Army at beginning of the Civil War. This portrait of Scott is included in all four portfolios and in a similar position of prominence[35]—that is, before all the other military figures of lesser seniority. The third print in the earliest portfolio is an Ehrgott & Forbriger portrait of George B. McClellan, the successor to Scott as head of the U.S. Army. Likewise, in the next two portfolios the portrait of McClellan follows that of Scott.[36] Interestingly, around the time the last portfolio was compiled it was U. S. Grant who was chief of the armies and it is his portrait which follows Scott in this portfolio.

In the earliest portfolio there is no discernible order to the rest of the prints, which include a mixture of naval and military figures. However, for the next two portfolios a new element was added: the inclusion of portraits of political figures. In both of these instances the political portraits were bound into the portfolios in front of the military and naval portraits. Both of these portfolios contain two members of Lincoln's cabinet (Salmon P. Chase, secretary of the Treasury, and E. M. Stanton, secretary of war) and the governors of Ohio (David Tod), Indiana (O. P. Morton), and Tennessee (Andy Johnson), with a portrait of Lincoln also included in one of these portfolios.

By the time the last portfolio was compiled the political representation was increased to include not only Lincoln, the two secretaries, and the three governors (though now John Brough was governor of Ohio), but also two other members of the cabinet, Secretary of State William Seward and Secretary of the U.S. Navy Gideon Welles. The order of the prints in this last portfolio is the most formalized. The portfolio opens with two Currier & Ives prints facing each other, the Washington portrait from the other portfolios, and an image of "The Star Spangled Banner." After Washington comes Lincoln, the members of his cabinet, and then the governors. As in the other portfolios, following the politicians are Scott and the chief of the armies, here U.S. Grant, after which come all the military figures and then all the naval figures at the end.

The uniformity in the external and internal character of these four portfolios makes it implausible that each was independently compiled by a different collector. It seems clear that a single agent was responsible for all four of these portfolios. It is possible that one collector compiled all four, but this seems improbable. It is possible that Ehrgott & Forbriger was the producer of these portfolios, but this too seems less than likely. Though an Ehrgott & Forbriger 1863 calendar is glued to the inside of one of the covers, there is no title page or any other indication that the firm published the portfolios, as one would expect if the firm itself were trying to market the prints in this manner.

It appears most likely that the portfolios were produced by someone who commissioned or simply acquired the prints from Ehrgott & Forbriger and then sold the portfolios to the general public.[37] This would explain the lack of any publisher information, as well as the inclusion in the portfolios of prints by other lithographers. The compiler and seller of these portfolios could have been a bookstore, a news agent, or, as hinted by the cover of the earliest of the portfolios, a music store. The portfolios might have been sold already bound or possibly they might have been put together on demand, with the purchaser selecting those figures to be included. The evolving nature of the portfolios, from a fairly loosely organized compilation of portraits to a more formal portfolio illustrating major

Union figures, suggests that the creation of these portfolios started off as a convenient sales technique which then grew and developed.

The Prints in Context

The Ehrgott & Forbriger portraits were very much part of a large corpus of similar portraits of Civil War figures that were flooding the market at the time. The largest number of Civil War portraits were card photographs, better known as cartes de visite. Introduced in the 1850s, cartes de visite were an immediate hit with the public. The phenomena was called cartomania or photomania, and in England alone 300 to 400 million cartes were sold every year from 1861 to 1867.[38] In the United States the market for cartes de visite really boomed with the advent of the Civil War. Their small size, accuracy of image, and wide accessibility made them the perfect keepsakes for families of soldiers. "Every boy called into the army wanted mementoes to leave the folks at home and it is more than likely that one or two similar mementoes went with him."[39] The ability of photographers to print many copies of the same image and the subsequent wide distribution of the cartes de visite led to their great popularity not only for images of family members but also for portraits of national figures of note.

> Negatives of individuals constantly in the public eye were in great demand by the large photographic houses, which printed card photographs in tremendous numbers from such negatives. The cards were then placed on sale at book stores, galleries, magazine shops—wherever the public passed by. It is difficult at the present day to realize the tremendous volume of business done; card photographs could be found "piled up by the bushel in the print stores, offered by the gross at book stands."[40]

The huge demand for portraits of Civil War notables, resulting from the spread of cartes de visite, created a booming market for other types of portraits, including steel engravings and lithographs. Steel-engraved portraits of generals, admirals, and politicians were issued in magazines as separate prints and in bound volumes. Similarly, lithographed portraits appeared in many formats, including the frameable lithographs by popular printmakers such as those discussed above.

The Ehrgott & Forbriger portraits, therefore, were but one small component of a huge body of Civil War portrait prints. They were, however, unique in a number of ways, most obviously in their extravagant reuse of backgrounds. This aspect of the Ehrgott & Forbriger prints has drawn some fairly stern admonitions from scholars. Milton Kaplan says, with particular reference to Ehrgott & Forbriger's prints, that the practice of placing different heads on the same body involves "unexpected liberties frequently . . . taken with portraits of prominent Americans,"[41] and he goes on to suggest that these "apparently documentary prints are not always what they claim to be."[42] Harold Holzer, speaking in particular of the practice of placing Lincoln's head on other bodies, comments that "these ungainly prints somehow enjoyed a substantial popularity, further evidence of the public's gullibility and naivete during the post-assassination Lincoln print boom," and he refers specifically to the head-switching practice of Ehrgott & Forbriger as a further egregious example of this "appalling" printmaking device.[43]

Ehrgott & Forbriger's blatant reuse of backgrounds and the marketing of these prints in portfolios where this duplication was particularly emphasized seems to demonstrate that this practice was not seen in such a negative light by the print-buying public during the Civil War. Indeed, if we look at the nature of portraits in the mid-nineteenth century we can see that the use of stylized backgrounds for portraits was the expected norm. For instance, folk painters of the nineteenth century often used standardized backgrounds for their portraits, and there is some evidence that these artists may have started with stock backgrounds already prepared so that the head of a sitter could simply be inserted.[44]

More closely related to the Ehrgott & Forbriger stylized backgrounds are those which appeared in the millions of cartes de visite issued during the Civil War. A typical carte de visite background used painted backdrops and stock props.

> The resulting "composition" was likely to show Joshua standing beside the always present column, his hand placed on a pedestal (which also carried as part of its burden an ornate urn or two), contemplating the ruins of Nineveh in the distance, while the Hudson rolled serenely on through the center of the picture. A curtain with tassels, an elaborate chair or two, and some fancy trellis work with artificial vines entwining it, completed the picture.[45]

This describes a background which is very similar to that which appears behind the political portraits by Ehrgott & Forbriger. In fact, the original inspiration of Ehrgott & Forbriger's political background was clearly a photograph, for the chair in which all the political figures sit is identical to that which can be seen in many Mathew Brady photographs.

There was no similar photographic inspiration for the military and naval backgrounds, but the principle is the same. Just as the elaborate formal backgrounds in the cartes de visite and in the Ehrgott & Forbriger political prints were not supposed to be realistic scenes from the sitters' lives, so the drawings of soldiers, ships, and battles in the backgrounds of Ehrgott & Forbriger's other prints were not intended to be taken as real life settings for the portraits. Nineteenth-century viewers were conditioned not to look at the backgrounds of portraits as being genuine but rather as stylized contexts for a countenance which they did expect to be realistic.

Just as they would not have been surprised or perturbed to see the same chair, table, column, curtain, bust, or other prop in many different cartes de visite, so too nineteenth-century viewers would not have been disconcerted or disappointed to see the same backgrounds repeated again and again in the Ehrgott & Forbriger prints. Nineteenth-century print buyers were not expecting to have portraits showing the subjects in life situations but were quite used to standardized backgrounds as long as the face was accurate. Ehrgott & Forbriger's portraits met this criterion perfectly well. Kaplan urges modern scholars to examine historic portraits carefully in order to separate fact from fiction, and this is a fair enough point. However, within the context of nineteenth-century portraiture it seems unfair to criticize Ehrgott & Forbriger for their reuse of the stylized backgrounds.

Looking at the Ehrgott & Forbriger prints within this context also helps explain why it made sense to have the portraits compiled into portfolios. The inspiration for these portrait portfolios was very likely the ubiquitous photograph album which made its appearance just at the beginning of the Civil War.

> As Lincoln was being nominated in Chicago, Queen Victoria began the custom of putting cartes de visite taken of herself and the royal family (by John J. E. Mayall) into a new style of photograph album designed specifically to house card photographs. This immediately sparked yet another new vogue; people everywhere began putting cartes de visite not only of their family and friends but also of celebrities into what became known as the "family album." Fifteen U.S. patents were issued for designs of carte de visite albums in the period 1861–65, most of them featuring recessed pockets in each leaf into which the card photographs could be inserted.[46]

People had not only family albums but also albums of photographs of particular topics, travel albums, and celebrity albums. These last were "collections of portraits of prominent persons—royalty, nobility, statesmen, military leaders, performers, literary figures, scientists, physicians, engineers, etc.,"[47] and these were almost certainly the inspiration for the production of the Ehrgott & Forbriger portfolios.

Conclusion

The Ehrgott & Forbriger Civil War portraits form one of the most engaging and fascinating series of American popular prints. One cannot help but be amused by the often crude grafting of heads onto bodies previously used for other countenances, and the complexity of this corpus of prints raises many interesting issues. These prints were very much a part of their time; their style, execution, and purpose are very similar to many other lithographed Civil War portraits. However, with the exuberant reuse of backgrounds and the existence of the portfolios, they are also unique within that same context.

No records or advertisements from the Ehrgott & Forbriger firm exist which help clarify matters, so all conclusions reached must come from the examination of the primary material of the prints themselves. A study of this material leads to some interesting but unanswered questions: how were the heads copied from photographs and applied to the stones? how were the backgrounds transferred and modified? and why and by whom were the portfolios produced? Some newly discovered Ehrgott & Forbriger prints, a further analysis of those already known, or comparisons with other nineteenth-century images might suggest some answers or open new questions. Whatever we learn, further study of these delightful American prints is well warranted.

Notes

1. The appropriateness of the allusion to Hydra for these prints was first noted by Harold Holzer in his article "Lincoln and the Ohio Printmakers," *Ohio History* 89 (autumn 1980): 415. These prints were also discussed in Milton Kaplan's "Heads of States," *Winterthur Portfolio 6* (Charlottesville: University Press of Virginia, 1970), pp. 143ff. It was this article that first attracted the author's attention to these prints. The author was assisted in his study by many persons and institutions, to all of whom he is grateful. In particular he would like to thank Donald H. Cresswell, Mary Ritzlin, and the staffs at the American Antiquarian Society; Cincinnati Art Museum; Cincinnati Historical Society Library; Cincinnati Public Library; Clements Library; Henry Ford Museum; Indiana University's Lilly Library; Library of Congress, Prints and Photographs; National Portrait Gallery; University of Cincinnati, Archives and Rare Books; and the University of Pennsylvania's Van Pelt Library, Rare Books.

2. Charles Cist, *Sketches and Statistics of Cincinnati in 1859* ([Cincinnati: printed and published for the author], 1859), p. 301.

3. Benjamin F. Klein, ed., *Lithography in Cincinnati*, pt. 1, *To the Advent of the Steam Press, 1836–68* (Cincinnati: Young and Klein, 1975–76).

4. For purposes of this paper, no distinction is made between prints produced by Ehrgott & Forbriger and those by Ehrgott, Forbriger & Co.

5. Cist, *Sketches*, p. 302.

6. The numbers and types of Ehrgott & Forbriger prints cited in this chapter are based on a listing compiled by the author as of October 1999. This list, with any subsequent updating, is posted on the Internet at http://www.philaprintshop.com/eflist.html. Categorizations are the author's own, and some of the attributions and dates are uncertain, so the figures used in this paper are not absolute; they should be understood as being made relative to this listing. It is likely that other Ehrgott & Forbriger prints will turn up over time, but it is unlikely that enough different prints will be discovered so as to affect significantly the conclusions drawn in this paper.

7. Most lithographic firms, at least before the Civil War, were primarily job printers. For example, cf. Sally Pierce and Catharina Slautterback, *Boston Lithography. 1825–1880: The Boston Athenaeum Collection* (Boston: Boston Athenaeum, 1991), pp. 6f. and 14.

8. Holzer, "Lincoln and the Ohio Printmakers," p. 403.

9. Ibid., p. 404.

10. Of known Ehrgott & Forbriger prints, the largest single type consists of Civil War prints. These include the seventy-nine portraits that are the subject of this article, twenty scenes in a portfolio by J. N. Roesler, and just over thirty other prints concerning the war or related topics. Music sheets make up the second most often issued type of Ehrgott & Forbriger print, with approximately seventy recorded examples. Ehrgott & Forbriger historical prints, advertisements, and views number under thirty examples of each type, and only a handful of their genre prints, calendars, ephemera, maps, and book illustrations are known.

11. Even counting group portraits and music sheets with portraits, there are less than ten known Ehrgott & Forbriger portrait prints that are not of the type described.

12. Similar stylized portraits have been around from the beginning of portrait prints, but this discussion concerns only lithographed, "popular" portraits like those issued by Ehrgott & Forbriger.

13. David Tatham, *The Lure of the Striped Pig. The Illustration of Popular Music in America, 1820–1870* (Barre, Mass.: Imprint Society, 1973), p. 136.

14. The numbers used in this chapter for the Ehrgott & Forbriger Civil War portraits are based on the listing of these prints in appendix C.

15. This assumes that "L. S. Rosseau" and "Lovell H. Rousseau" are different individuals.

16. This number does not include different states of prints where the variations are only in the title—for instance, for changes in rank or initials.

17. Brig. Gen. Thomas W. Sherman stands on the deck of the same ship and has the same body as Adm. Samuel F. Du Pont.

18. Milton Kaplan, "Heads of States," *Winterthur Portfolio 6* (Charlottesville: University Press of Virginia, 1970). For some other examples, cf. Noble E. Cunningham Jr., *Popular Images of the Presidency: From Washington to Lincoln* (Columbia: University of Missouri Press, 1991).

19. For instance, in November 1862, E. & H. T. Anthony issued a catalogue listing 2,000 portraits and 300 war scenes that could be ordered. William C. Darrah, *Cartes de Visite in Nineteenth Century Photography* (Gettysburg: W. C. Darrah, 1981), p. 49.

20. William F. Stapp, "Daguerreotypes onto Stone: The Life and Work of Francis D'Avignon," in Wendy Wick Reaves, ed., *American Portrait Prints* (Charlottesville: University Press of Virginia, 1984), pp. 194–231.

21. Ibid., p. 77.

22. "The Storming of Fort Donelson Tenn. Feb. 15th. 1862. Terrific bayonet charge and capture of the outer entrenchments by the Gallant Soldiers of the West, under General U.S. Grant." Currier & Ives, 1862. Small folio. Previously unrecorded.

23. Conningham, *Currier & Ives Prints* #2553.

24. Conningham, *Currier & Ives Prints* #993.

25. Compare this portrait of Grant, his face and hat, with the photograph on page 181 of Miller's *The Photographic History of the Civil War.* Note also that Grant's head is a bit too large for his body.

26. Darrah, *Cartes de Visite*, p. 77.

27. This reuse of the same stylized backgrounds for the Ehrgott & Forbriger portrait prints is well known and this topic was discussed in Milton Kaplan's article, "Heads of States," cited in note 1, and in Neely and Holzer's *The Union Image: Popular Prints of the Civil War North* (Chapel Hill & London: University of North Carolina Press, 2000). Kaplan based his analysis on twenty-eight Ehrgott & Forbriger prints in the Library of Congress, which he organized into nine different groups with shared backgrounds. Neely and Holzer based their analysis on the same twenty-eight prints plus an additional nineteen that they found at a book fair in Gettysburg. These authors had access to only a small percentage of the Ehrgott & Forbriger prints now recorded, and an analysis of the entire body of these prints shows that the reuse of the backgrounds is considerably more complex than these authors realized.

28. The identification of the backgrounds is based on the list in appendix D.

29. This sequence can be figured by a comparison of the variation in wear of different impressions of the same print, by an ordering of the changes in background features, and by a time frame determined by the dates of promotions, appointments, and elections.

30. The question of how the images were transferred is complicated by the existence of an unattributed music sheet entitled "En Avant!" (Illustrated in *The Lure of the Striped Pig*, p. 137.) This

1862 print, which obviously was lithographed by Ehrgott & Forbriger, shows Gen. George McClellan in a very similar setting to the Ehrgott & Forbriger military portraits. In fact, the body and horse are exact copies of those in background S10, except that they are approximately only two-thirds the size. Thus while either the image of the song sheet was copied from the image in background S10, or vice versa, the size difference means this could not have been done by a simple use of transfer paper.

31. There are characteristics of the collections of Ehrgott & Forbriger portraits in the Library of Congress (thirty-seven prints) and in the Clements Library (twenty prints), which make it plausible that each of these groups of prints also might once have been part of a portfolio. The portraits in each of these collections are physically very similar to each other and to the prints from the known portfolios in terms of size, paper condition, etc. The prints in the Clements Library were acquired together from one source at one time, but it has proved impossible to determine if these prints were originally part of a portfolio. In contrast, although the twenty Ehrgott & Forbriger prints in the Lilly Library are physically similar to each other and are all very early examples of Ehrgott & Forbriger's portraits, they are on a larger sized, untrimmed paper, indicating that they were never bound into a portfolio.

32. The fourth portfolio is missing its covers, but the prints still have the holes where they were sewn into a binding, and they have stains which, having passed through from print to print, match up when the prints are stacked together, proving that these prints were part of a bound portfolio.

33. A plausible order for when the portfolios were put together can be established by a comparison of the prints in each using changes in rank, wear to impressions, and the appearance and disappearance of different individuals—for instance, a change from Tod to Brough as governor of Ohio. The earliest portfolio was likely compiled in late 1862 or very early 1863; the next two within a short time of this, probably before June 1863; and the last either late 1863 or early 1864.

34. Ehrgott & Forbriger do not seem to have produced a portrait of either George Washington or Winfield Scott, for in all the portfolios the prints of these individuals are by Currier & Ives and Gibson & Co. respectively.

35. The portrait of Scott by Gibson & Co. from the last portfolio is actually a very slightly modified variant of the portrait which is included in the first three portfolios.

36. One of these portfolios is in the Cincinnati Historical Society Library. Some of the prints are currently missing from this portfolio, but the original card catalogue entry lists all the original prints in order. The portrait of McClellan is one of the prints missing, but here and elsewhere in this essay I will write as though all the prints were still with the portfolio.

37. There is another example of a portfolio containing Ehrgott & Forbriger prints that was produced by someone other than Ehrgott & Forbriger. This portfolio, *Album of the Campaign of 1861 in Western Virginia*, consists of twenty prints drawn and lithographed by J. N. Roesler but printed by Ehrgott & Forbriger. It was Roesler, not Ehrgott & Forbriger, who held the copyright to these prints and so was the portfolio's publisher. As with the Roesler portfolio, it is not unlikely that there was a close connection between Ehrgott & Forbriger and the compiler of these portrait portfolios.

38. Darrah, *Cartes de Visite*, p. 4.

39. Robert Taft, *Photography and the American Scene: A Social History, 1839–1889* (New York: Dover Publications, 1964), p. 149.

40. Ibid.

41. Kaplan, "Heads of States," p. 135.

42. Ibid., p. 149.

43. Holzer, "Lincoln and Ohio Printmakers," p. 415.

44. Robert C. H. Bishop, *The Borden Limner and His Contemporaries: An Exhibition* . . . (Ann Arbor: University of Michigan, 1975), pp. 72f.

45. Taft, *Photography*, p. 147.

46. William Welling, *Photography in America: The Formative Years, 1839–1900. A Documentary History* (New York: Crowell, 1978), p. 143.

47. Darrah, *Cartes de Visite*, p. 9.

References

Bishop, Robert C. H. *The Borden Limner and His Contemporaries: An Exhibition . . .* Ann Arbor: University of Michigan, 1975.

Cist, Charles. *Sketches and Statistics of Cincinnati in 1859.* [Cincinnati: printed and published for the author], 1859.

Cobb, Josephine. "Prints, the Camera, and Historical Accuracy." *American Printmaking before 1876: Fact, Fiction, and Fantasy*, pp. 1–10. Washington, D.C.: Library of Congress, 1975.

Cunningham, Noble E., Jr. *Popular Images of the Presidency: From Washington to Lincoln.* Columbia: University of Missouri Press, 1991.

Darrah, William C. *Cartes de Visite in Nineteenth Century Photography.* Gettysburg: W. C. Darrah, 1981.

Holzer, Harold. "Lincoln and the Ohio Printmakers." *Ohio History* 89, no. 4 (autumn 1980): 400 ff.

Kaplan, Milton. "Heads of States." *Winterthur Portfolio* 6, pp. 135–50. Charlottesville: University Press of Virginia, 1970.

Klein, Benjamin F., ed. *Lithography in Cincinnati.* Pt. 1, *To the Advent of the Steam Press, 1836–68.* Cincinnati: Young and Klein, 1975–76.

Levy, Lester S. *Picture the Songs: Lithographs from the Sheet Music of Nineteenth-Century America.* Baltimore: Johns Hopkins University Press, 1976.

Marzio, Peter C. *The Democratic Art: Pictures for a Nineteenth-Century America: Chromolithography, 1840–1900.* Boston: D. R. Godine, 1979.

Miller, Francis Trevelyan, ed. *The Photographic History of the Civil War in Ten Volumes.* New York: Review of Reviews Co, 1911.

Neely, Mark E., Jr., and Harold Holzer. *The Union Image. Popular Prints of the Civil War North.* Chapel Hill & London, University of North Carolina Press, 2000.

Peters, Harry T. *America on Stone: The Other Printmakers to the American People.* New York: Arno Press, 1976.

Pierce, Sally, and Catharina Slautterback. *Boston Lithography, 1825–1880: The Boston Athenaeum Collection.* Boston: Boston Athenaeum, 1991.

Reaves, Wendy Wick, ed. *American Portrait Prints.* Charlottesville: University Press of Virginia, 1984.

Taft, Robert. *Photography and the American Scene: A Social History, 1839–1889.* New York: Dover Publications, 1964.

Tatham, David. *The Lure of the Striped Pig: The Illustration of Popular Music in America, 1820–1870.* Barre, Mass.: Imprint Society, 1973.

Thomas, Dean S. *Civil War Commanders.* Gettysburg: Thomas Publications, 1986.

Welling, William. *Photography in America: The Formative Years, 1839–1900. A Documentary History.* New York: Crowell, 1978.

Chapter Five

Promotional Playing Cards

From Sultans to Salesmen, 1300–1900

Ronald Decker
Curator, Playing Card Museum
The U.S. Playing Card Company

The main areas open to promotional display have been the backs of the cards and, especially in America, the ace of spades. When the joker made its advent, it offered still more space for extraneous matter. The addition of the joker prompted some cardmakers to add other extra cards, sometimes promoting the manufacturer but sometimes his patron or client. To a lesser extent, messages have invaded the court figures and numerical cards. These areas of exploitation did not spring immediately from the minds of commercial designers, but emerged from an evolutionary process extending over centuries.

Muslim Artifacts

Sometime in the Middle Ages, Egyptian Muslims received playing cards, or at least the concept for them, from Asia.[1] Istanbul's Topkapi Sarayi has a deluxe pack of cards, large and lavish with gilding and delicate tracery. They were painted in Egypt for the ruling Mamelukes (1250–1517).[2] This is the oldest known deck that is substantially intact. It displays the structure of Muslim decks now known to be typical. Fifty-two cards are divided into four suits, with suit signs of scimitars, goblets, coins, and some sort of sticks (fig. 5.1). The suits in the Topkapi deck are named by Arabic calligraphy on the cards, but this is problematic because, except for "swords" *(suyuf)*, the writing does not yield exactly the right terms.[3] The

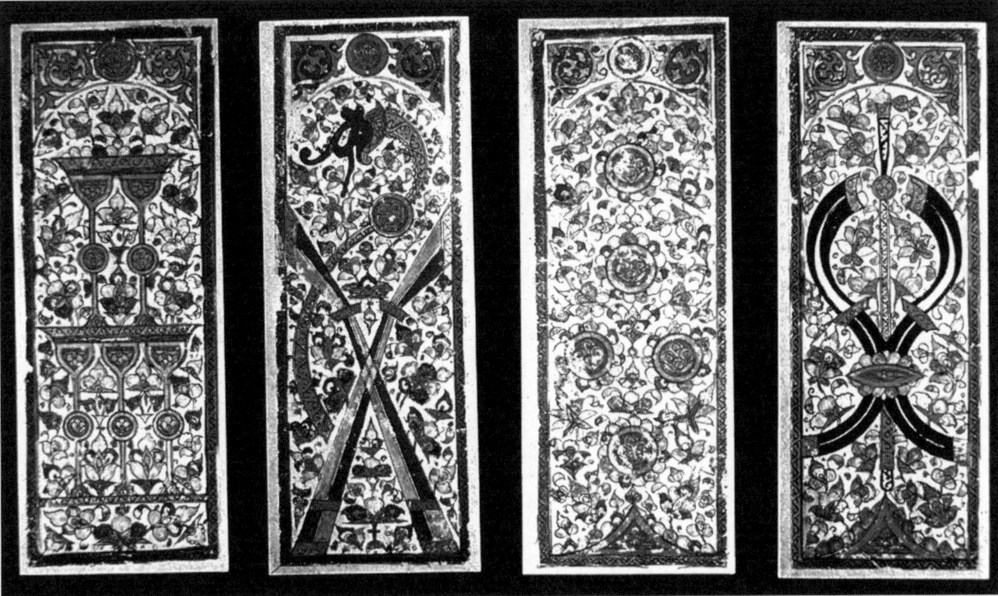

Fig. 5.1 Topkapi deck
Facsimile of card deck in Topkapi Sarayi, Istanbul, Turkey. Original ca. 1500; reprint, 1972. Author's collection.

inscriptions may be somewhat uninformed. These cards were made in Mameluke Cairo but possibly were taken to Ottoman Istanbul when the Turks conquered Egypt in 1517.[4] Perhaps, then, the inscriptions were added by new owners without a thorough understanding of Mameluke traditions. Each suit had a hierarchy of ten numerical cards plus three court cards. The courts in the Topkapi deck are named by their Arabic calligraphy: *malik* (commander), *na'ib malik* (lieutenant commander), and *thani na'ib* (second lieutenant).

Some Muslims almost certainly made decks with figural courts.[5] In this respect, the Topkapi pack is idiosyncratic. It is a makeshift deck amalgamated from several independent ones. Its peculiar court cards were previously aces and deuces, converted to their new ranks by the simple expedient of adding inscriptions but no figures. Oddly, not one of the authentic court cards was preserved by the redactor. Perhaps he deliberately removed the original courts from the Topkapi deck because the Koran discourages the use of representational art. This stricture was ignored by the Mamelukes but perhaps not by their Ottoman conquerors.

Muslims also produced cards by woodcut. Barcelona's Instituto Municipal de Historia has a mutilated leaf or sheet of twelve numerical cards (at an intermediate stage of manufacture, prior to their being cut apart). This was perhaps the work of Moorish craftsmen.[6] A few small fragments of numerical cards, either pen drawings or woodcut prints, have been preserved.[7] They deserve reexamination to establish their antiquity and possible clues about the diffusion of woodcuts in Islam. These examples confirm the wide currency of the suit signs occurring in the Topkapi pack.[8]

The symbolism of Muslim suit signs is still being debated. The possibility of mystical connotations was granted by Rudolph von Leyden. However, he believed more surely that those signs derived from the badges worn by the sultan's officers and their descendants.[9] The sultan certainly had his cupbearer, swordbearer, and polo master (relevant if the dragon-headed sticks are properly construed as polo mallets). But no coin emblem has been found among Mameluke badges. Moreover, the badges, which are of consistent form across many kinds of artifacts, are not precisely like those on the Mameluke cards. Despite these problems, it is reasonable to assume that the Topkapi deck, if only because of its refined style, meant to glorify the sultan or his court.

Cards in Christendom

Cards of the Muslim type arrived in Europe around 1350 and were imitated by the first cardmakers there. The Arabic term *na'ib* evolved into European terms for cards—that is, *naibi* in Italian and *naipes* in Spanish. Some Europeans knew that their models came from *Saracenia*, but Saracen symbolism was generally unfamiliar in Christendom. Whatever the intended nature of the stick emblem, it meant nothing to the Christians of Western Europe. That suit sign became the polished baton (in Italy and Portugal) or the rough cudgel (in Spain).[10] The court cards were still male: king, knight (or horseman), and knave (or valet or jack).[11] Given the tastes of aristocratic patrons, the first European cards undoubtedly were painted, but block printing was soon used for mass production. The Mediterranean paradigm for cards spread throughout Europe and, later, to the far-flung colonies of Spain and Portugal. Portuguese explorers and traders carried their cards as far as Japan, where variations survive.[12] Spanish contacts included American Indians: Apache cards, even in the early 1900s, followed Mexican models, generally faithful to the Spanish kind, which had descended from the Muslim world. Spanish suited cards are still made (fig. 5.2). They are widely available, having traveled in tandem with the Spanish language.

North of the Alps, early cardmakers experimented with a wide range of new card designs, with suit signs frequently based on natural forms or household objects. The Swiss settled on suits of bells, acorns, shields, and flowers,[13] while the Germans preferred bells, acorns, leaves, and hearts.[14] In about 1470, the French devised *carreaux, trefles, piques,* and *coeurs*, known respectively in English as diamonds, clubs, spades, and hearts.[15] These were not printed by woodblock but by stencil, far easier to make and use. Only the figures for the court cards needed to be reproduced by woodcut; even their costumes could be colored by stencil (fig. 5.3).

Several European countries had used the queen in special decks and for particular games.[16] The French permanently installed her in the standard fifty-two-card pack, eliminating the knight. The court figures were shown full length, but poses and costumes varied as different regions developed distinctive patterns. Another variation was in the identification of the figures.

In every region of France, exotic characters appeared as court cards. They suggest that the prototypes came from decks intended for educated players, literate and cosmopolitan. French

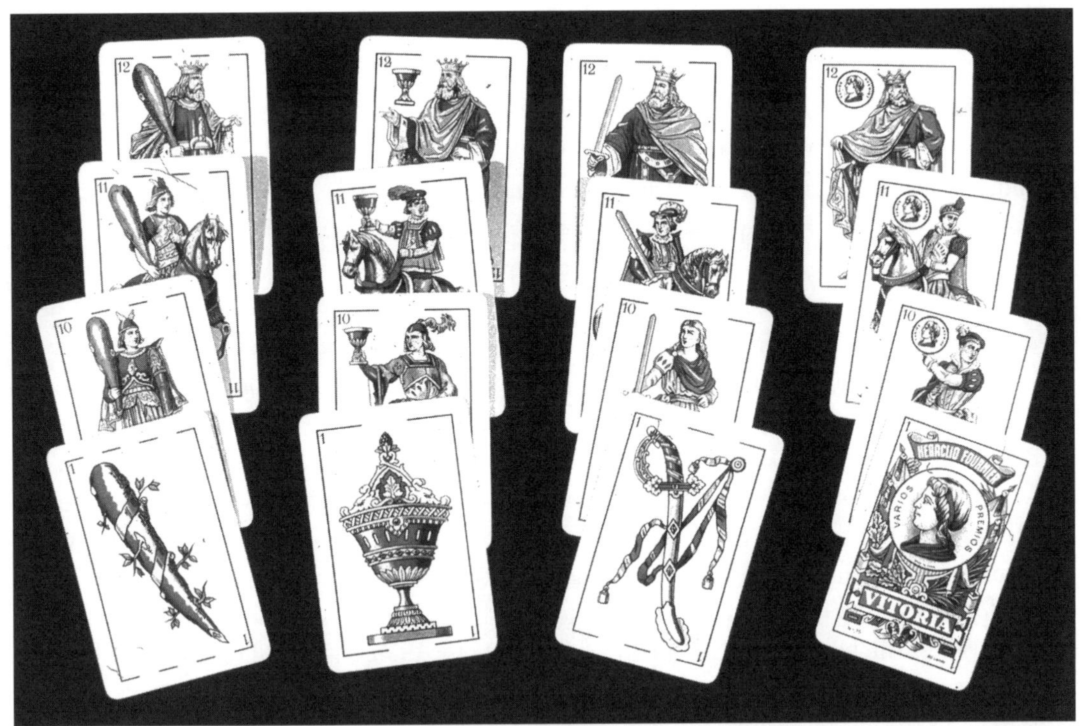

Fig. 5.2 Spanish suited cards
Fournier Company, Vitoria, Spain. 1995. The United States Playing Card Company Museum.

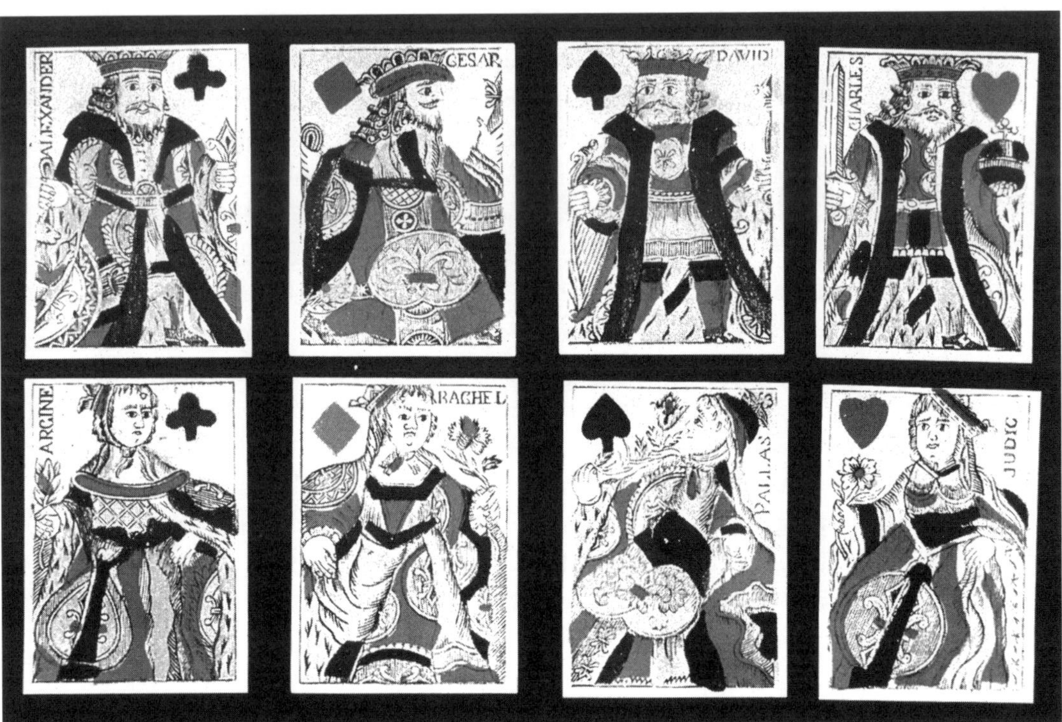

Fig. 5.3 French suited cards
Stenciled woodcuts. Facsimile of Danish deck. Original ca. 1800; reprint, 1976. The United States Playing Card Company Museum.

court cards seem to have been inspired by *les Neuf Preux* (the Nine Worthies). They exemplify three great "laws" or religions: Jewish (Joshua, David, Judas Maccabee), pagan (Hector, Alexander, Julius Caesar), Christian (Arthur, Charlemagne, Godfrey de Bouillon). The idea of the Worthies is credited to Jacques de Longuyon, author of the *Voeux du Payon* (1312). The heroes became familiar in paintings, sculptures, tapestries, and prints. The real mystery is why anyone forced three regimes into four card suits. Which of the nine Worthies deserved to be card kings? What female counterparts should be queens? Confusion was inevitable.

A good sampling of sixteenth-century Parisian cards can be found on a sheet by Guyon Guymier, one of several generations of Parisian cardmakers.[17] It never received its stenciled colors and therefore lacks suit signs. It accommodates eight figures (each appearing twice with slight variations). Their names are worked into the woodblock. Present are two queens (Rachel and Judith), who hold nondescript flowers, and six male figures. The men carry identifying attributes widely used in medieval art. Guymier's four kings are Alexander (his shield bearing his emblem, an enthroned lion holding a halberd), Caesar (with the imperial eagle on his shield), David (with a harp, appropriate for a psalmist), and Charles (holding a sword and a globe). This last ruler is understood as Charlemagne, emperor of the Holy Roman Empire (on his robe is a haloed eagle and the French *fleur-de-lys*). Guymier's remaining males are jacks: Hector of Troy (with a rampant lion embroidered on the back of his doublet) and Judas Maccabee (with two ravens embroidered on his doublet's chest).

Rouen, west of Paris, offered some of the alternative patterns for court cards. Their identities are largely obscure.[18] In its oldest known version, the kings of hearts, spades, diamonds, and clubs were Caesar, David, Charles, and Hector, respectively.

Another Rouennaise system of court cards was exported to England and, with minor adjustments, was adopted when cardmaking arose there. The names were eliminated from the courts, and their identities were forgotten by British viewers. Only the most alert would have noticed and recognized the heraldic clues that were still attached to the male court cards. In France, the Parisian pattern eventually prevailed and never lost its named courts.[19]

More questions remain for the iconographer. Did Christian cardmakers know any Mameluke symbolism? Did they invest any symbolism in the suit signs that became standard in Switzerland, Germany, and France? The relationships among the different sets of standard suit signs are unclear. The French *trefle* (trefoil) is perhaps the silhouette of the German acorn. The German leaf resembles the shape of the *pique*, or spade. At the same time, the word *spade*, pronounced as an Italian word, means "swords." The Italian baton or Spanish cudgel must somehow relate to the English club,[20] although its shape is that of the French *trefle*. Further research is obviously needed.

Proliferation in America

Cards traveled with British colonists, excepting the Puritans, who deplored gambling and frivolous play. During the more liberal eighteenth century, card playing became highly popular in colonial America. Players bought their decks from English firms.

In 1712 the British Stamp Office required that one of the cards in each pack should bear a tax stamp. The ace of spades was informally used; it became the official locus in 1765. On the standard English ace of spades, the suit sign was shown encircled by a beltlike garter, the emblem of the Royal Order of the Garter, sometimes complete with its motto, "*Honi soit qui mal y pense*" [Shamed be he who thinks evil of it]. Surmounting the garter was a royal crown. After the Revolutionary War, when American manufacturers arose, they sometimes copied the garter; but the despised crown was deposed by the American eagle.

The first U.S. card companies were in the industrial Northeast.[21] Cardmakers have yet to flourish in the South. American makers began with woodblocks. These survived for making cheaper brands throughout the nineteenth century, but metal engravings became common for better quality. As wood engraving and lithography developed, they too were used for card manufacture.

Even in the earliest examples, European cards generally have two or three layers of paper. The card faces were printed on lightweight sheets and then glued to heavier stock; often another thin layer was glued to the backs. The backs could be painted or decoratively printed or left blank, their usual condition on French and English cards. Blank backs invited secondary uses—all sorts of note taking, homemade flash cards for children, invitations, and calling cards. Such backs were also imprinted as announcements, tickets, and even official money when the government mint was inadequate. The first card catalog, actually made from playing cards with bibliographic data written on the backs, was invented by French librarians after the Revolution (the confiscation of church properties brought a huge influx of books into the government libraries).[22]

It was in the nineteenth century that card backs in Britain and America began routinely to carry some sort of printing. The cheaper cards were covered with asterisks, meanders, dots, or simple plaids on the reverse sides. Cards of higher quality were printed with commercial messages and images. They promoted tobacco, tonics, and household goods. During America's Civil War, Northern cardmakers designed decks celebrating the Union cause; decks had propagandistic courts and suit signs, and patriotic scenes and emblems graced the backs.

American manufacturers experimented with practical improvements on cards, such as rounded corners and refined finishes for improved handling and durability. The imagery changed drastically when cards became double-headed (either end could be uppermost). This incidentally destroyed the remaining clues about the identities of the Anglo-American court cards, for most of the old armorial bearings had resided in the bottom halves of the picture cards. The only distinguishing device to remain is the globe of Charlemagne (the king of clubs), because he happened to raise the emblem above waist level. The American impulse was toward modern efficiency, not ancient symbolism. Cardmakers now added indices, markings in each card's corners or margins, declaring its suit and rank. These "modern" features had occurred in Europe but were not promoted consistently and simultaneously as they were in America.

During this American ferment, the joker materialized. It was formerly thought to have evolved out of the tarot's "fool" card. But we now know that Americans were unacquainted with the tarot when the joker appeared. It seems to have had its origin in a special card used in a particular form of euchre. In this game, which began in Alsace-Lorraine, two jacks of the same color are designated as being especially powerful. When immigrants carried this game to America, they also brought some of their specialized terms, such as the German *Bauer* (jack). Euchre players still speak of their two highest cards as the left and the right Bauer, although the key word is envisioned as "bower." Americans added to the euchre deck an even higher card, the best bower or imperial bower or highest bower. According to the latest theory, this high card was called "the euchre card." This could have been mispronounced as "juker card," which could have become "joker card." Oddly, however, we have many old cards labeled as bower but not "juker" or even "euchre" card. Perhaps those transitional terms existed only in the speech of card players. But no nineteenth-century literature has been found to confirm this speculation. The very word *joker* naturally could have inspired designers to depict jesters, clowns, and other pranksters. Yet the best bowers and early jokers show much greater diversity—not only trickster types but also children, stage characters, animals, etc. Card players now were accustomed to seeing unique designs, not only for the aces of spades and the card backs but also for the best bowers and other extra cards. Advertisers exploited these areas in various combinations.

Cardmakers in Nineteenth-Century Cincinnati

This section briefly chronicles two nineteenth-century groups, the Longley family and the partnership of Russell and Morgan. The Longleys' story is fraught with gaps and misleading clues. The worst of the intricacies have been relegated to endnotes; they may prove useful for the next historian or antiquarian who wishes to improve the narrative.[23] The present author is in a relatively good position to consolidate scattered information about Russell and Morgan.

Of the seven sons of Mary and Abner Longley (1796–1879), five became Cincinnati publishers and printers. Of these, Servetus and Septimius maintained homes on farms on the east side of the Little Miami River near Foster's Crossing, about twenty miles northeast of Cincinnati. During the Civil War, the Longleys printed flags and decorative paper, the latter for lining trunks. In peacetime, the Longleys began to print playing cards under a confusing variety of company names, including Cincinnati Card and Longley & Bro. The latter referred specifically to Servetus and Septimius. Thanks to the generosity of Theodore Ashmead Langstroth II, the USPC Company Museum possesses some of the oldest surviving Longley cards.[24] A rare ace of spades gives the maker as "The Cincinnati Card Company, Longley and Bro. Manufacturers, No. 248 Walnut Street, Cincinnati, O." This dates the deck to about 1866.[25] The Longleys used some company names to express patriotism: American Card Company[26] and Eagle Card Company.[27] Less homespun was the choice "Paper Fabrique." Servetus founded that company in 1873 but sold it in 1874.[28] The new owners presumably continued to print cards.[29]

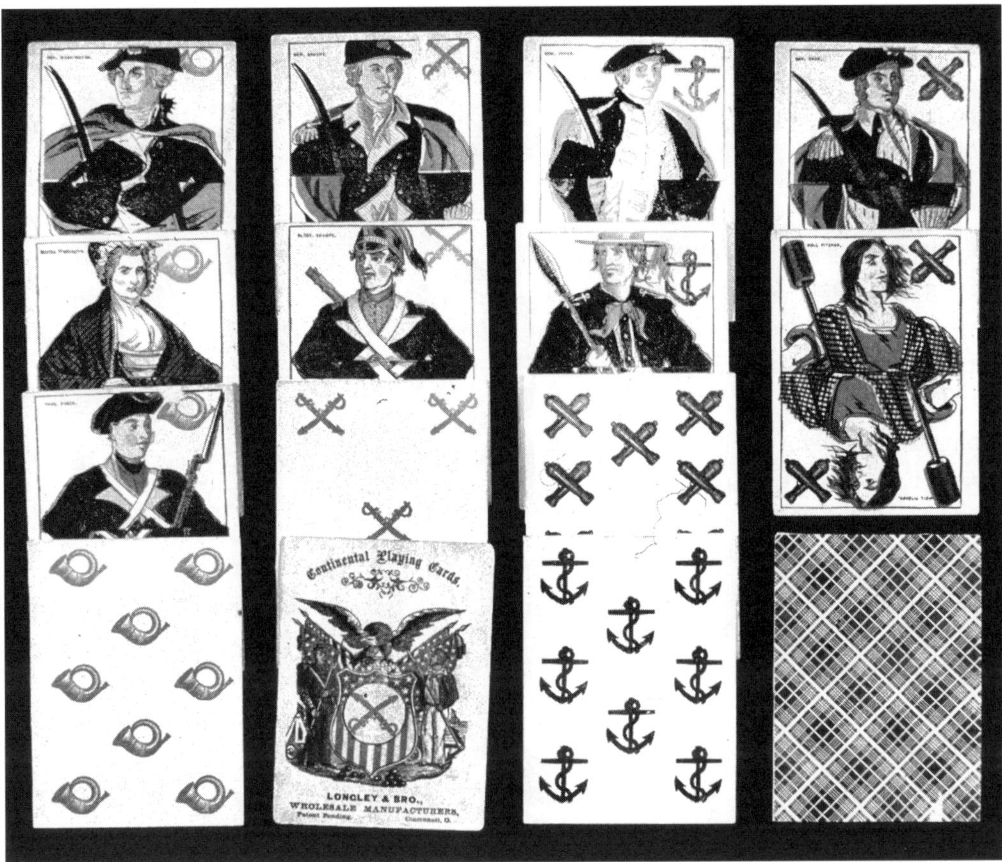

Fig. 5.4 Continental Playing Cards
Longley & Bro., Cincinnati, Ohio. Ca. 1876. The United States Playing Card Company Museum.

The Longleys made a nonstandard deck called Continental Playing Cards, intended to coordinate with the Philadelphia Centennial Exposition in 1876. This deck, like so many Longley projects, began well but ended poorly. It never went into full production, and no complete version is known. Langstroth possessed some of the Continental Cards (fig. 5.4), twenty-three of which are now in the USPC Company Museum. He also acquired more than seventy of the engraved copper plates for manufacturing this deck. He printed new impressions, which include two court cards otherwise unknown. The courts are as follows.

	Sabers (red)	**Cannons (black)**	**Bugles (red)**	**Anchors (black)**
K:	Gen. Greene	Gen. Knox	Gen. Washington	Com. Jones
Q:	Susan Bache	Moll Pitcher	Martha Washington	[missing]
J:	Sergt. Champe	Sergt. Jasper	Thos. Burch	[extant, but unlabeled]

One of Langstroth's prints preserves the layout for the blue coloration in the joker, its

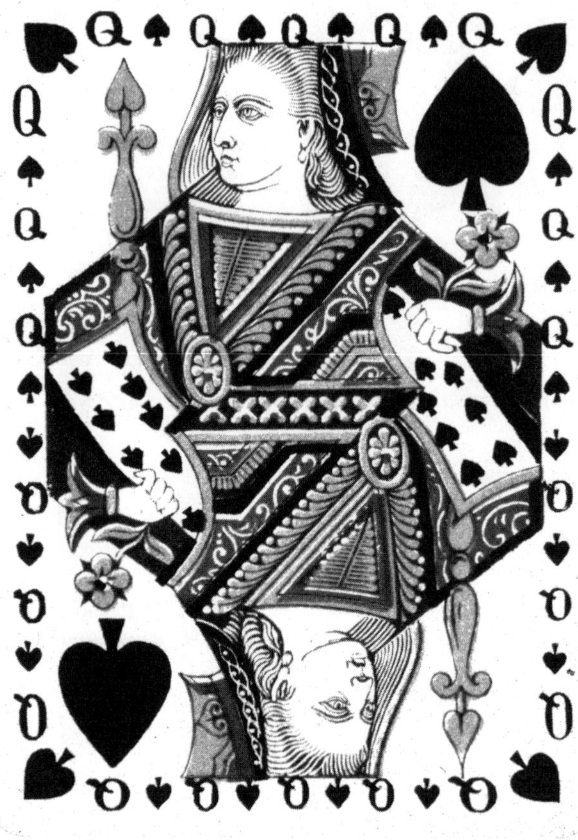

Fig. 5.5 Court card of "border index" deck
Paper Fabrique, Remington, Ohio. Ca. 1880. The United States Playing Card Company Museum.

only surviving manifestation: It depicts a flag-draped woman meant to personify Columbia. The card backs were printed in a blue plaid.

The Longleys made other notable jokers. One for the aforementioned Eagle Card Company must be among the oldest to be inscribed "The Joker" and to depict a jester in cap and bells.[30] Another Longley type of joker, known in variations, is the cardplaying man whose hair is braided in a single queue and whose jacket is embroidered in Chinese motifs. This type is sometimes labeled "Heathen Chinee" on the card. The reference is to Bret Harte's popular but mediocre poem "Plain Language from Truthful James" (1870), in which a Chinese gambler cheats by hiding cards in his voluminous sleeves.

In 1879 Servetus and Septimius reacquired Paper Fabrique and transferred it to Remington, midway between Cincinnati and Foster's Crossing. Production included the innovative "border index" cards, already patented in 1877.[31] The joker is double-ended and again represents a Chinese man holding cards. The court cards are also of interest, for they depict twelve members of royalty then reigning in Europe (fig. 5.5). Paper Fabrique closed in 1881.

Operations moved to Middletown, Ohio.[32] They continued as The Card Fabrique Company (1885–94) and The Globe Playing Card Company (1889–94).[33] These dates are approximate. It was not until 1887 that Card Fabrique was incorporated, with participation by Septimius, Servetus, and Servetus's son Herbert. Globe was formed by Servetus and William Hey Longley, Septimius's son. Overlapping production by the two companies is indicated by decks bearing both company names. Both firms presumably operated at the same Middletown plant. "Card Fabrique Co. Factory, Middletown" appears also in decks labeled "Union Club Card Company."[34] By 1890 the Longleys had departed, surrendering the business to backers. In the same year, at Basic City, Virginia, Servetus and his sons, Herbert and William S. Longley, founded another Paper Fabrique, the first card company in the South. The effort failed within the decade.[35] William Hey Longley achieved greater success at cardmaking: By 1891 he had organized the American Playing Card Company at Kalamazoo, Michigan.[36] He died in 1913, and his company disappeared a few years later. No Longley companies exist today.[37]

The United States Playing Card Company is a direct descendant of enterprises founded by Russell and Morgan. A. O. ("Pic") Russell was born in McConnellsville, Ohio, in 1826. At age eleven, he began to learn printing in newspaper workrooms. In adulthood, one of his positions was as supervisor of the Commercial Job Rooms of the *Cincinnati Enquirer.* (Large newspapers of the day often maintained a sideline in general printing.) Robert John Morgan was born in Bandon, County Cork, Ireland, in 1838. He embarked for the United States in his ninth year. An apprentice to the best printers in Cincinnati, he became a pressman at the *Enquirer,* where he met Russell.[38]

The *Enquirer* printed posters for the circus owned and managed by John Robinson and John Robinson Jr. In 1866 the job rooms suffered a fire, and the Robinsons' latest circus posters were destroyed. John Robinson Jr. decided to assume direct control over the printing of his advertising. He joined in a partnership with Pic Russell, Bob Morgan, and James M. Armstrong, a financial backer. In 1867 they bought the job printing operation from the *Enquirer.* The new business, called Russell, Morgan and Company, began with a dozen employees, chiefly making posters for stage productions and circuses. The factory was installed at 20 College Street but soon began to outgrow the space. A lot, fifty-three by ninety feet, was acquired on the east side of Race, opposite George Street. A new four-story building was completed and occupied by November of 1873.

In 1880 Russell persuaded his partners that the company should make playing cards. He wished to compete with northeastern cardmakers, already established for decades. The partnership added two stories to their factory and designed specialized machinery, including a card-punching machine that performed more rapidly and accurately than the old card-trimming devices. On June 28, 1881, the company began to print cards. Morgan handed Russell the first deck and said, "That pack of cards cost $35,000." The company, with about twenty employees, printed 1,600 packs per day. They made five brands of cards: Tigers, Sportsman's, Army, Navy, and Congress.

At the start of 1883, the firm became The Russell and Morgan Printing Company, quickly moving to a six-story building, 70 × 229 feet, newly built on Lock Street. Now in production were the company's Steamboat brand and, in 1883 or 1884, their Tourists brand. A single brand, Army and Navy, replaced the two separate lines for the armed services. Several new brands were introduced.[39] In 1885 the partners decided to challenge the Andrew Dougherty Company, cardmakers in New York. Dougherty's cards included a back design showing a stylish coach, called a tally-ho. "Tallyho" was the traditional call of fox hunters when giving chase. Dougherty was trying to appeal to such privileged sportsmen. Russell and Morgan wanted their new brand to have a name with mass appeal. August Berens, one of their printers, observed the growing number of cyclists. He

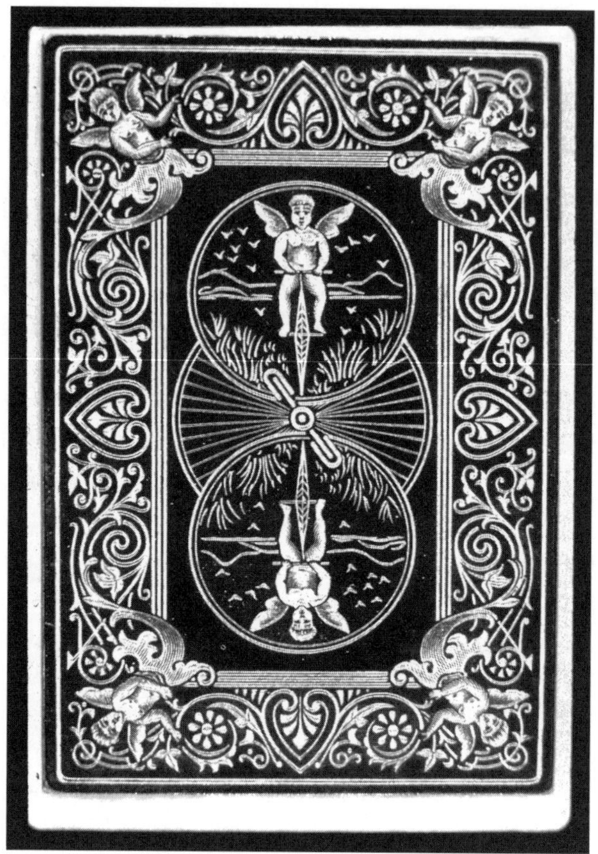

Fig. 5.6 Printing block for rider back Bicycle cards
The United States Playing Card Company, Cincinnati, Ohio. Ca. 1910. The United States Playing Card Company Museum.

recommended the name Bicycle. The best bower for the brand accordingly showed a high wheeler pedaled by a man in fashionable sportswear: knee socks, striped knee breeches, and a long-sleeved shirt with an ample bow tie. The first Bicycle back design included paper fans, each with a picture of a cyclist. (The fans apparently satisfied the popular taste for Japanese styles.) Other Bicycle jokers and back designs, having a variety of subjects, were steadily issued. This brand succeeded and became an American icon. The 1887 "rider back," depicting a cupid astride a two-wheeler, has never gone out of production (fig. 5.6). In 1887 about 530 employees produced 16,500 decks per day at Russell and Morgan Printing (fig. 5.7). The factory housed forty-six cylinder presses, four two-color presses, and an advanced five-color press designed and built by the Cincinnati Type Foundry.

All of the Russell and Morgan decks were advertised as "United States Playing Cards." The partners sometimes embellished their products with patriotic motifs. The ornate ace of spades includes Thomas Crawford's Statue of Freedom, which stands atop the capitol dome in Washington, D.C. (fig. 5.8).

John H. Frey was another Cincinnatian who succeeded in commercial printing. He consolidated his business with the New York firm of Hinds and Ketcham, printers of labels. By April 1891, the merger included Russell, Morgan and Company. The combined

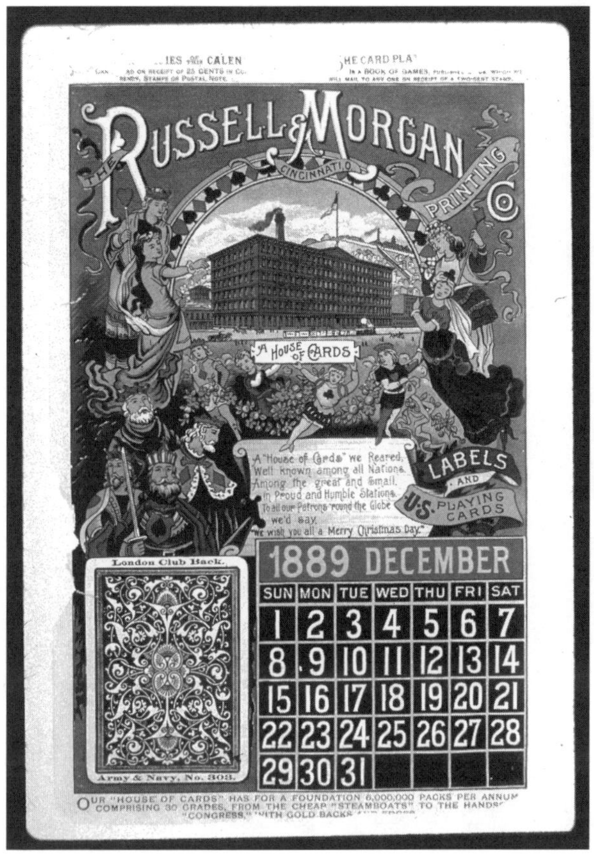

Fig. 5.7 Promotional calendar illustrating Russell and Morgan Printing Company building
Russell and Morgan Printing Company, Cincinnati, Ohio. 1889. The United States Playing Card Company Museum.

enterprise became The United States Printing Company. It promptly acquired National Card of Indianapolis.

When the directors of U.S. Printing learned that Perfection Card Company of New York was failing, they proposed to cooperate with their major competitors to buy and maintain Perfection. In the ensuing negotiations, U.S. Printing was offered not only the controlling interest in Perfection, but also Standard of Chicago and the prestigious New York Consolidated Card Company. This complex merger produced a new company, The United States Playing Card Company, on July 1, 1894. The printing company continued separately as U.S. Printing and Lithograph.

USPC acquired the rights to a plethora of brands belonging to its subsidiary companies. The famous Bee brand came from the New York Consolidated Card Company. The ace of spades shows bees surrounding a hive. This image has produced several unlikely fantasies to explain its possible symbolism. The present author suggests that the bee simply symbolized the spirit of cooperation, the spirit demonstrated by the original owners of the company when they agreed to consolidate.[40]

Shortly after 1900, the sister companies, The United States Playing Card Company and U.S. Printing and Lithograph, moved to attractive new buildings erected together in

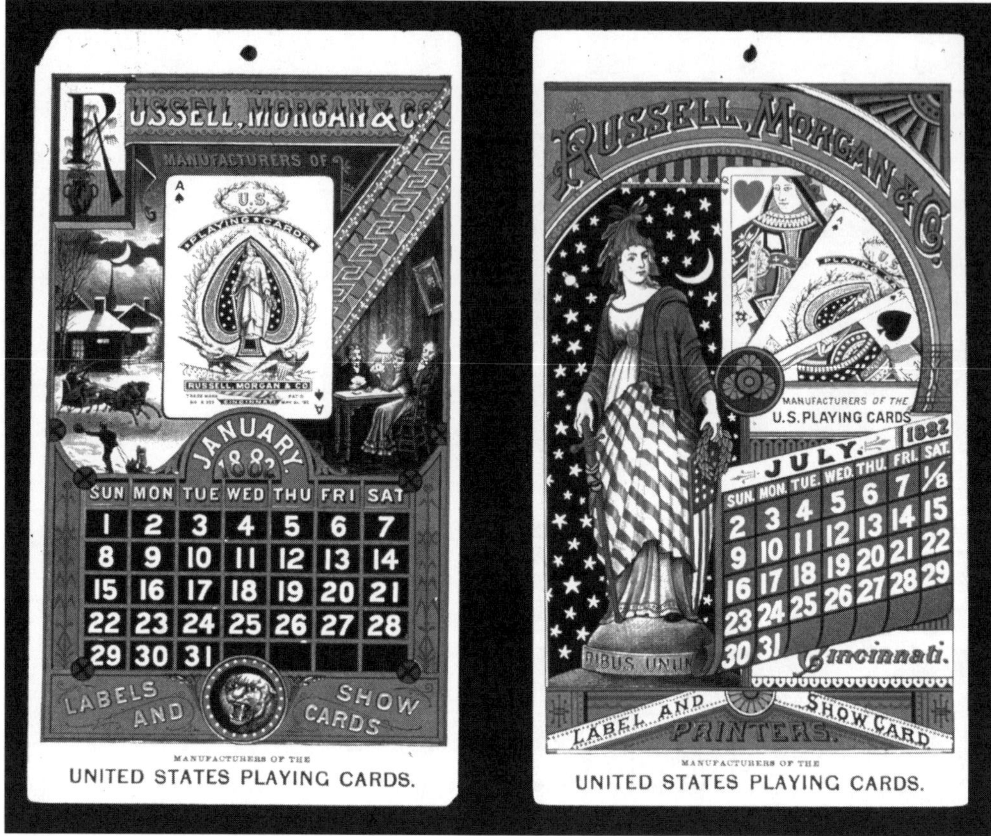

Fig. 5.8 Promotional calendar with illustration of Thomas Crawford's Statue of Freedom atop U.S. Capitol Dome

Russell and Morgan Printing Company, Cincinnati, Ohio. 1882. The United States Playing Card Company Museum.

suburban Norwood. The printing company has changed its name, but the USPC Co. continues as such. It is the largest playing card company in the world.

Customized Cards

Antique playing cards have become "collectible," and their study and conservation have engendered about a dozen specialized museums. Collectors and curators have begun to confront the problem of taxonomy. The late Gene Hochman, in *The Encyclopedia of American Playing Cards*, pragmatically recognized many groupings. For instance, some are based on physical form (such as odd shapes and sizes), some on nonstandard structure (such as unusual suit signs and/or courts). But he also noted that playing cards have acquired purposes beyond games, such as fortune-telling and creative imagery (novelties). Had he adopted our current theme of "promotional playing cards," many of his general divisions would have become subordinate themes. He identifies cards for expositions and world's fairs, tourist spots, railroads and steamship lines, entertainment and sports, war efforts, politics and patriotism, and organizations (he lists "Colleges and Universities" and "Unions and Company Organizations"). Another use—one of the most frequent—is advertising. Hochman lists seven categories, according to whether the advertising appears on

A the faces of all numerical cards and courts (many of his examples also have promotional back designs and jokers);
B certain faces but not the courts;
C all the backs and on the faces of the joker and of the ace of spades;
D all the backs and on the face of the ace of spades;
E all the backs of standard cards and on one or more special cards with additional information;
F the backs only (the most common form of advertising on cards).

Hochman also has a type G, "insert cards." Certain products—typically candy, gum, and tobacco—carried playing cards, generally only one inserted in the packaging of each item. Consumers were thus induced to buy more of the product in order to accumulate a full deck of cards. At least some of these usually refer to the brand name. Insert cards tended to have themes, such as animals, politicians, soldiers, and entertainers.

The following examples are decks printed by USPC. Most date slightly before 1900. Each represents a promotional type that became common thereafter.

Innovative decks were made to coordinate with industrial and cultural expositions. We have seen some of the cards that the Longleys planned for the 1876 centennial. In 1893 a deck was sold by G. W. Clark at Chicago's Columbian Exposition (fig. 5.9). The back design shows Columbus's arrival in the New World. The cards' fronts are late examples of "triplicate faces." They have three identifying zones—that is, the middle, with a large image, and two

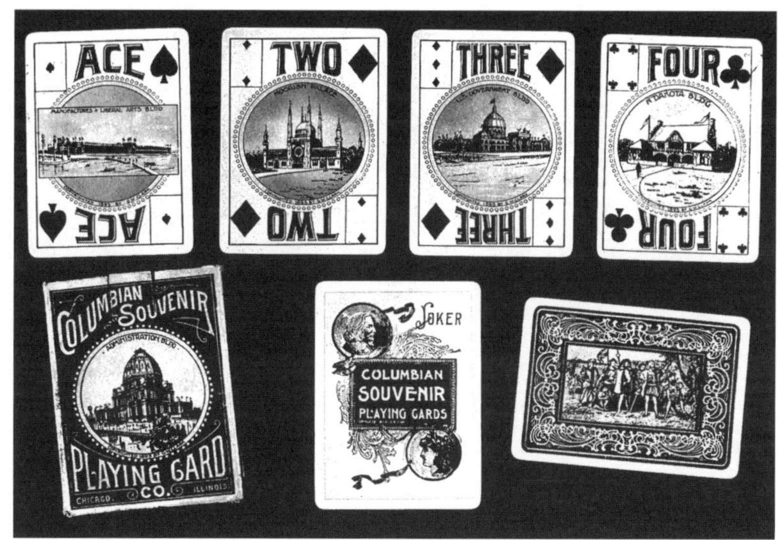

Fig. 5.9 Chicago Columbian Exposition cards
G. W. Clark, Chicago, 1893. The United States Playing Card Company Museum.

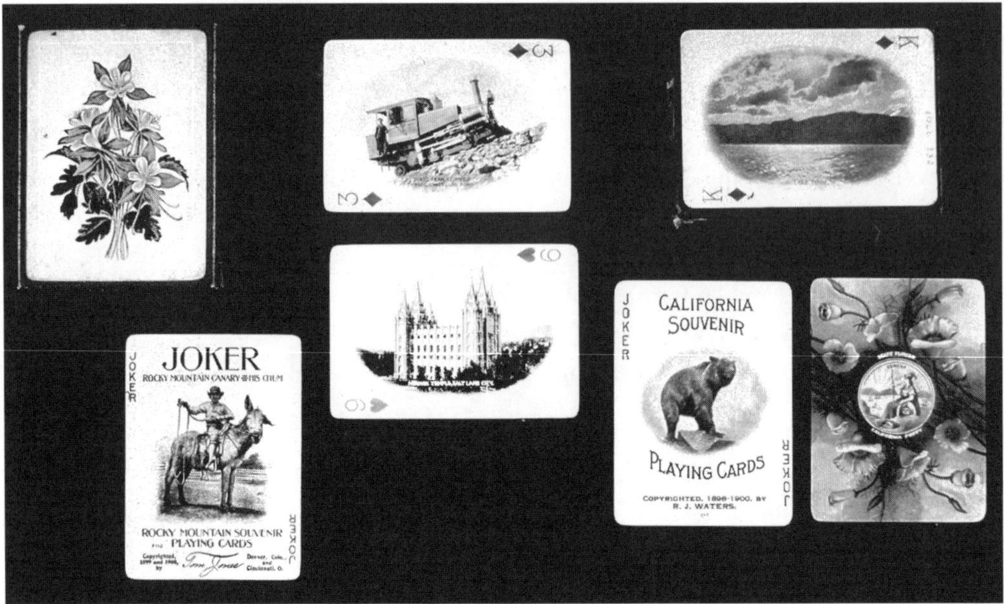

Fig. 5.10 California Souvenir Playing Cards
R. J. Waters, San Francisco. 1898. The United States Playing Card Company Museum.

diagonally opposite corners, each with a standard card in miniature. In Clark's deck, the central image is a pavilion at the fair.

Hochman's encyclopedia classifies Clark's Triplicates under "expositions." It uses "souvenirs" to cover more generalized scenic cards. This applies to the California Souvenir Playing Cards by R. J. Waters (fig. 5.10). The oval photographs were characteristic of such cards in the late 1800s. Cards printed by photolithography were still conservative in their color. Here it accents the card backs with the orange of the poppy, the state flower of California.

Also similar to souvenir cards in that period were railroad cards (fig. 5.11). Prosperous lines provided decks as courtesies to passengers, and each card captured an image that the travelers would have associated with their rail journey. The portrait head, depicting a native American (1899), occupies the backs of cards for the Choctaw railroad. This painting, which appears on other card backs by The United States Playing Card Company, is attributed to Matt Daly, a Cincinnati artist who worked for Rookwood Pottery and for the card company. He became USPC's art director in 1903. Other cards shown here have subtle colors and may date slightly after 1900.

The cards designed for Princeton University in 1896 are among the first made for college students and alumni (fig. 5.12). The graphics of course relate to scenes and motifs unique to the Princeton campus.[41] The copyright belonged to L. W. and H. N. Marshall. The same L. W. Marshall commissioned a comparable deck for Yale in the same year.

Brewers and tobacco companies were prominent among the early clients who commissioned special decks. Our sampling of tobacco advertising (fig. 5.13) belongs to Hochman's

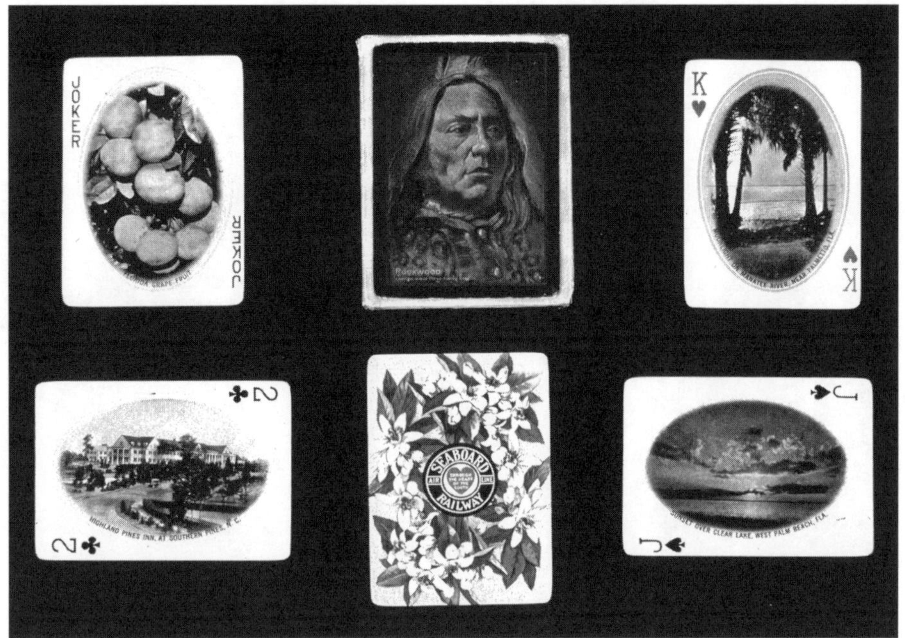

Fig. 5.11 Assortment of souvenir playing cards
The United States Playing Card Company, Cincinnati, Ohio. 1896. The United States Playing Card Company Museum.

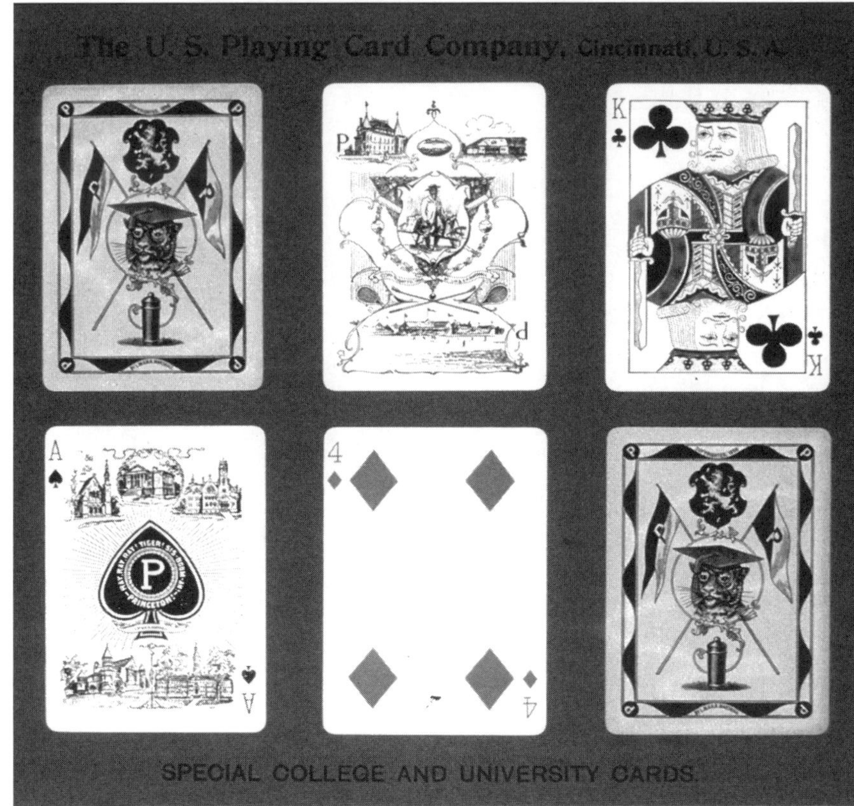

Fig. 5.12 Princeton University playing cards
The United States Playing Card Company, Cincinnati, Ohio. 1896. The United States Playing Card Company Museum.

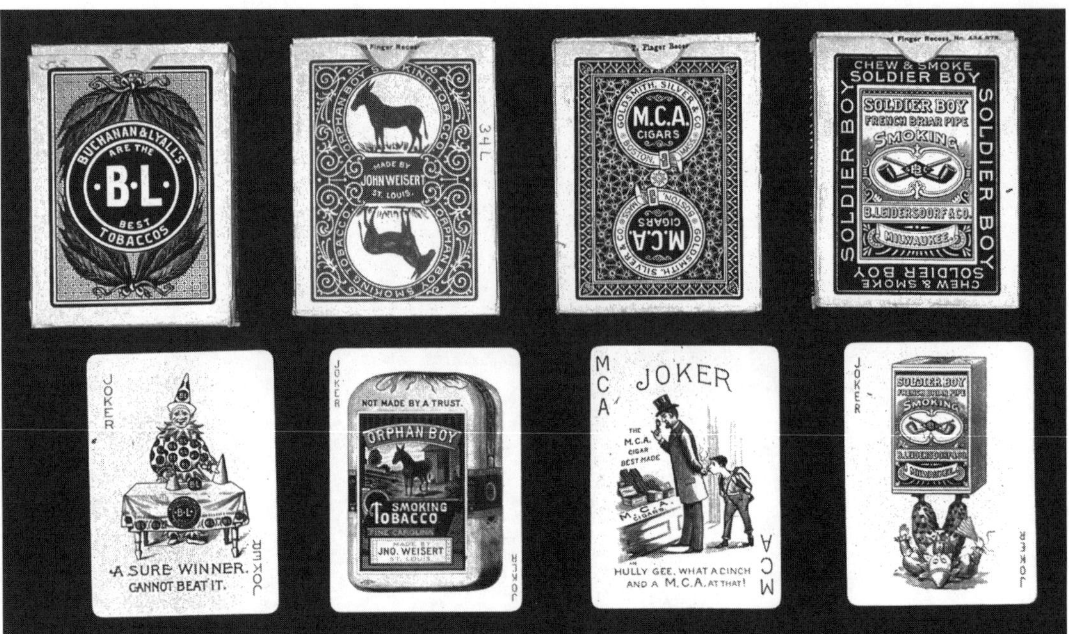

Fig. 5.13 Tobacco advertising cards
The United States Playing Card Company, Cincinnati, Ohio. Ca. 1900. The United States Playing Card Company Museum.

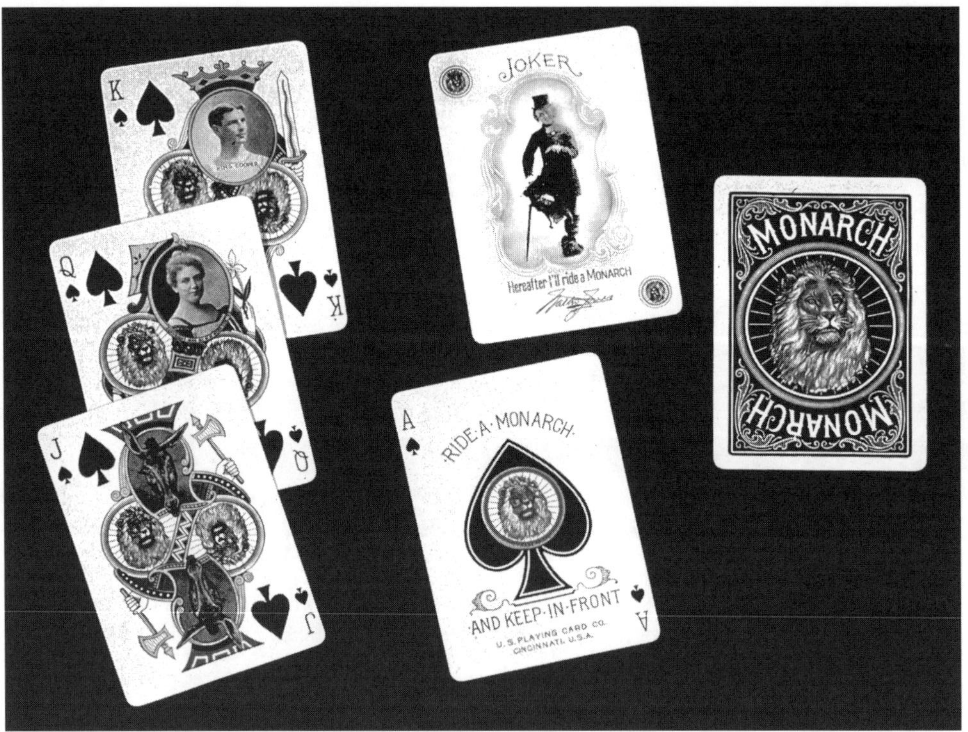

Fig. 5.14 Monarch Bicycle advertising deck
The United States Playing Card Company, Cincinnati, Ohio. 1895. The United States Playing Card Company Museum.

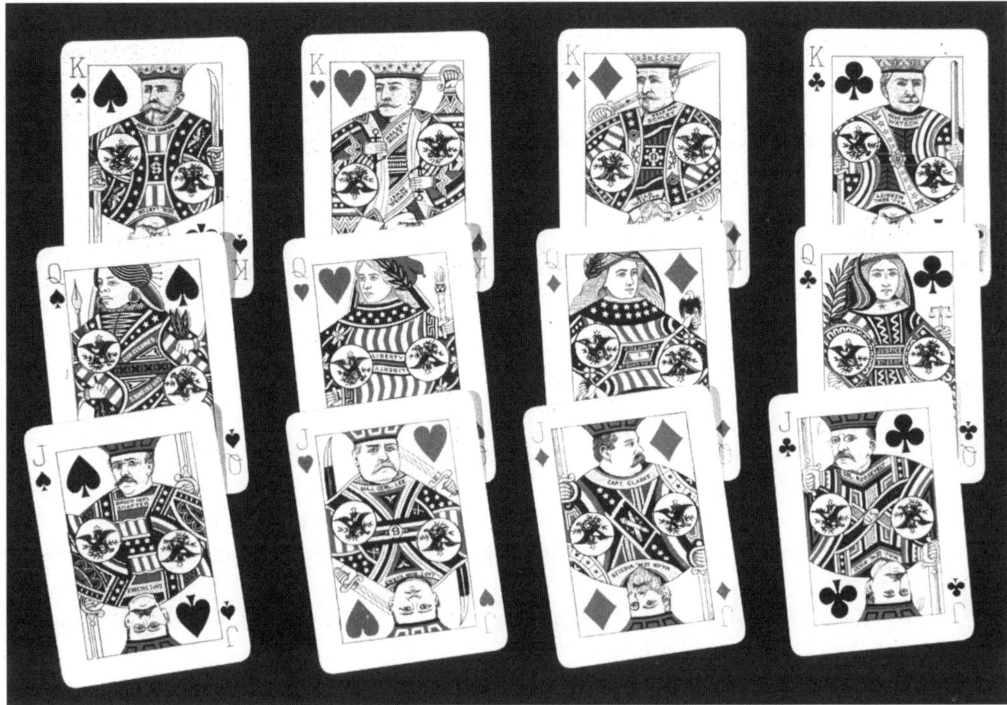

Fig. 5.15 Spanish-American War deck produced for Anheuser-Busch
The United States Playing Card Company, Cincinnati, Ohio. Ca. 1900. The United States Playing Card Company Museum.

category C. The illustration shows the jokers and the associated boxes (which reproduce the designs on the card backs). Tobacco advertising will become ever more collectible if the product finally is eradicated from America. Judging from the illustration, the designer for M.C.A. Cigar Company was amused, not horrified, by a boy's surreptitious smoking.

Two complex packs belong to Hochman's category A. The deck for Monarch Bicycle has advertisements on the card backs, the joker, and the ace of spades (fig. 5.14). The other card faces include the Monarch logo, a lion. Seemingly irrelevant figures appear in the other medallions. The jacks are jackasses while the queens and kings are actors. After the publication of this deck, in 1895, the idea of theatrical or "stage" decks flourished. The Monarch pack could be classified as advertising or as entertainment. Figure 5.15 shows the court cards in a Spanish-American War deck for Anheuser-Busch, the well-known brewers. Card faces have likenesses of military and political leaders. (Note Teddy Roosevelt on the jack of clubs.) References to the brewery appear on the deck's box, backs, joker, and all the numerical cards except the fours, each of which has an oval photo of a U.S. warship. This pack advertises but is a creative novelty too, while it also promotes patriotism. These cards are both elegant and practical, but their complexity suggests that no taxonomy for customized playing cards can be both elegant and practical.

Notes

1. Sources from China attest to playing cards there before 1000 A.D. See Michael Dummett, *The Game of Tarot* (London: Duckworth, 1980), p. 34. Chinese cards were of two types, paper dominoes and "money" cards. The latter are divided into suits, typically three or four of them, each with a hierarchy of emblematic cards; the suit signs allude to riches. However, the first Chinese cards have not survived, and scholars have not established the relationship between Chinese and Muslim cards. They may well have had a mutual ancestor in Central Asia.

2. See L. A. Mayer, "Mamluk Playing Cards," *Bulletin de l'Institute français d'archéologie orientale* 38 (1939): 113–18. Mayer erroneously counted five suits in the Topkapi pack. On this basis, Aurelia Books (Leuven, Belgium) published a flawed reproduction pack in 1972. For a better assessment, see M. Dummett and K. Abu-Deeb, "Some Remarks on Mamluk Playing Cards," *Journal of the Warburg and Courtauld Institutes* 36 (1973): 106–28.

3. Previous scholars give the cups as *tuman*, a word unknown in Arabic. The present author, while claiming no knowledge of Arabic, suggests that the calligraphy is erroneous or has been misread. The coins are labeled *darahim*, a silver currency; but the coins on the cards are golden, emphatically gilded. The sticks are labeled *jawkan*, polo sticks, but the implements are neither mallets nor canes but are bizarre in shape; some are angular and flared while others are sinuous and capped with a dragon head.

4. This is the opinion of Esin Atil, *Renaissance of Islam: Art of the Mamluks* (Washington, D.C.: Smithsonian Institution, 1981), p. 253.

5. This is a necessary hypothesis to account for the figural court cards in European and Indian decks, both having descended from Muslim prototypes.

6. See Simon Wintle, "A 'Moorish' Sheet of Playing-Cards," *Playing Card* 15, no. 4 (May 1987): 112–22.

7. One fragment is in the Benaki Museum, Athens, and four are in the private collection of Dr. Edmund de Unger. For sources of photographs and commentaries, see Michael Dummett, *The Game of Tarot*, p. 41.

8. However, they differ in form (for example, on the Barcelona sheet, the stick is a simple C-curve; contrast this with fig. 5.1).

9. Rudolph von Leyden, "Oriental Playing Cards: An Attempted Exploration of Relationships," *Journal of the Playing-Card Society* 4, no. 4 (May 1976): supplement 2, pp. 1–37.

10. The situation may be subtle. The so-called Portuguese pattern may actually preserve what had originated in Spain, while the so-called Spanish Pattern may actually preserve what had originated in France.

11. The term *jack* apparently meant "guy," as in jack-o'lantern and "jack of all trades."

12. See Sylvia Mann and Virginia Wayland, *The Dragons of Portugal* (Farnham, Surrey: Sandford, 1973).

13. See Detlef Hoffmann, *Schweizer Spielkarten 1: Die Anfänge im 15, und 16, Jahrhundert* (Schaffhausen: Museum zu Allerheiligen, 1998).

14. See Detlef Hoffmann, *Altdeutsche Spielkarten 1500–1650* (Nürnberg: Germanischen Nationalmuseum, 1993).

15. Regarding antique French cards, the standard authority is Henry-René d'Allemagne, *Les cartes à jouer du XIVe au XXe siècle* (Paris: Hachette, 1906).

16. A 1377 Swiss commentary on playing cards speaks of queens as variations within the male-dominated court cards. See Arne Jonsson, "Der *Ludus cartularum moralisatus* des Johannes von Rheinfelden," in Detlef Hoffmann, *Schweizer Spielkarten 1: Die Anfänge im 15, und 16, Jahrhundert* (Schaffhausen: Museum zu Allerheiligen, 1998), pp. 135–47. By 1425, the Italians had invented

the game of tarot and its distinctive pack, formed by expanding the standard Italian pack of fifty-two cards. The tarot's unique feature is a set of twenty-two allegorical cards (twenty-one trumps and a special card, the fool). In addition, each tarot suit was given a queen, ranking between the king and the knight.

17. The sheet is in the Musée Français de la Carte à Jouer, Issy les-Moulineaux (Inv. no. IS.30.1.54).

18. For an analysis of the set of court cards known as "Rouen I," see Ron Decker, "Who's Who in Court Cards," *Playing Card* 16, no. 3 (February 1988): 90–96.

19. The figures in the final version of the Paris pattern are:

	Hearts	Spades	Diamonds	Clubs
K	Charles	David	Caesar	Alexander
Q	Judith	Palas	Rachel	Argine
J	La Hire	Hogier	Hector	Lancelot

20. The use of the word *clubs* suggests that the first card players in England had used the archaic suit signs of cups, coins, swords, and sticks—the sticks being like the Spanish "cudgels." This type may have been imported from France (see note 10).

21. Regarding U.S. cards, the standard authority is Gene Hochman, *The Encyclopedia of American Playing Cards*, 6 vols. (Livingston, N.J.: author, 1976–82) (hereafter cited as Hochman, with year of volume).

22. See Judith Hopkins, "The 1791 French Cataloging Code and the Origins of the Card Catalog," *Libraries and Culture* 27, no. 4 (fall 1992): 378–404.

23. Our Longley chronicle derives from three archives in the USPC Company Museum: first, letters from Herbert Longley and from his relatives responding to inquiries by Louis Coffin, treasurer of the company, in 1939; second, albums compiled and annotated by Theodore Ashmead Langstroth II, a collector of print ephemera, in the 1960s; and third, an unpublished manuscript, "The Playing Card People" (ca. 1982) by Dick Race, games expert and *de facto* historian at the company.

24. Langstroth pursued the entire history of printmaking. The Public Library of Cincinnati and Hamilton County has many of his albums containing a wide range of prints, especially from early commercial printers in Cincinnati.

25. See time line in note 28.

26. This company is represented in Hochman 1980, p. 9, item U20. (In 1862 and 1863, another American Card Company, unrelated to the Longleys, made notable decks with Union army motifs. See Hochman 1976, p. 39, items W5, W6.) Two Longley decks in the USPC Company Museum have "American Card Company" appearing on identical aces of spades. One of these decks has its joker; the other has its wrapper. The wrapper bears a revenue stamp of five cents. Its penciled notation of 1862 has been accepted by Hochman and others, including Catherine Perry Hargrave, *A History of Playing Cards* (Boston and New York: Houghton Mifflin, 1930), p. 347. The wrapper says "Longley & Bro., . . . Cincinnati, Ohio." The aforementioned joker declares itself "Paper Fabrique Company's Highest Trump Card." The company name implies a date after 1873 (see note 28), possibly as late as 1881.

27. This company is represented in Hochman 1980, p. 10, items U22, U23, U24. Hochman, probably depending on Dick Race, says that The Eagle Card Co began in Cincinnati but moved to Middletown. That was where Eagle Cards disappeared around 1883. In effect, this company was absorbed into Card Fabrique (see text). Eagle, as in the case of American Card Company, apparently existed concurrently with other Longley companies in Ohio. In at least one brand, the ace of spades has the words "Eagle Cards" below the name "Paper Fabrique Company" (see note 31). Another Eagle Card Company was founded in Philadelphia in 1894, probably too late to be related to the Longleys.

28. Paper Fabrique was sold to Fuller and Hanna, who became president and secretary, respectively. They relocated (in 1874) to 13 East Third and later (in 1876) to 122 Main. According to Langstroth, the Longleys conducted business at the following locations:

1861: flag manufacturers at 164 Vine
1864: flag and card manufacturers at 143 Walnut
1866: card manufacturers at 248 Walnut
1868: card manufacturers at 216 Main
1871: card manufacturers at NE corner Sixth and Main
1873: Paper Fabrique Co., located as above
1874: Servetus Longley & Co., listed as makers of trunk paper at 135 Sycamore
1876: Servetus Longley & Co., listed as makers of flags and trunk paper, located as above
1879: Paper Fabrique, reacquired by Longleys, at 122 Main (but moved to Remington, Ohio, still with Fuller as president, Hanna as secretary)

29. An unattributed note in the USPC Company Museum says, "Paper Fabrique Co., Cincinnati, had a price list after Nov. 19, 1877." Can we assume that the list involved cards? The museum has an advertisement (January 1879) for Paper Fabrique at 122 Main Street, Cincinnati. Unfortunately, nothing indicates the owners, whether the Longleys or Fuller and Hanna (see further note 28).

30. The example in Hochman 1980, p. 10, item U22, illustrates an ace of spades that has the words "Samuel Cupples & Co., sole agents, St. Louis." This tells where the deck was sold but not where it originated. Cupples was a successful stationer and became a prominent citizen of St. Louis. The USPC Company Museum has one of Cupples's sample books for Eagle Cards. It displays no jokers; it gives no date or place of origin.

31. The ace of spades for the border index cards says "Paper Fabrique Company," underlined with the words "Eagle Cards." Note that the patent date falls in the period when Paper Fabrique was owned by Fuller and Hanna. This suggests that they had already made the same border index cards. An expertise in cardmaking is suggested by their maintaining their positions in the company when the Longleys reacquired it (see note 28).

32. The date of the move is uncertain. Hochman 1980, p. 9, following Dick Race, implies that Paper Fabrique began in Middletown in 1870. But this contradicts other authorities (notably Louis Coffin), who have the Longleys working in Cincinnati at that date, with mention of Middletown coming some ten years later. Card Fabrique and Globe occupied the old paper mill (no longer standing) at the southwest corner where the railroad crossed East Third (now Central Avenue). The railroad line was introduced in 1872 and encouraged a manufacturing area in Middletown's East End.

33. This Globe company was unrelated to Globe Playing Cards of Boston, copyright 1874.

34. See Hochman 1980, p. 75, item MSW55. Although probably unrelated to the Longleys, there was a Union Playing Card Company in New York (1886–94) and another in Chicago (1906).

35. In 1902 the same men helped found the New Chicago Playing Card Co. It operated at New Chicago, Indiana, but soon moved to Waukegan, Illinois, and closed in 1905.

36. He is said to have had help from Septimius, Servetus, and Servetus Jr. American Card Company of Kalamazoo sometimes used a pseudonym, The Detroit Card Company. Items from this APC Company have unexplained affinities with items from an earlier American Playing Card Company in New York, circa 1875 (see Hochman 1980, p. 72, item MSW22), and from Western Press in Chicago, circa 1910 (see Hochman 1980, p. 83, items MSW135, MSW136).

37. The designs and/or inscriptions on various card packages, jokers and aces of spades show that Longley enterprises at Middletown influenced the products of the companies named below. The following time line is informed by scattered notes by Louis Coffin. It suggests a definite continuity of ownership, probably by the Longleys' Middletown backers.

1890: The Longleys leave Middletown.
1894: Globe and Card Fabrique close in Middletown. Relocation by Longley backers could explain "New York & Chicago" printed on cards from Globe and Card Fabrique.
1897: Globe closes in Chicago.
1898–99: Chicago Card Company, 245 S. Jefferson St., briefly maintains Longley styles.

(A later Chicago Playing Card Company, 1039–47 West Thirty-fifth Street, appears to be a separate concern.) Hochman 1980, p. 75, flatly states that the Longleys moved to Chicago around 1890. However, a relocation by their former backers, who must have asserted their right to use "Card Fabrique" and "Globe," is more probable for two reasons. First, Herbert E. Longley and Col. F. F. Longley, the son of William Hey Longley, addressed Louis Coffin with letters about the Longley businesses. Neither correspondent mentioned Longleys in Chicago or New York. Second, we know that the year 1890 saw William Hey Longley moving to Michigan, while Servetus and two of his sons were setting up operations in Virginia. Another son, Franklin M. Longley, seems not to have pursued card making; he resided in Cincinnati and was known to Louis Coffin.

38. The biographical data are from "The Russell & Morgan Printing Co," *Superior Printer* 1, no. 2 (June 1887): 21–24. Much the same article appears in *British Printer* 8 (March/April 1899): 6ff.

39. According to Dick Race, the brands introduced in the era of The Russell & Morgan Printing Company were Capitol in 1885 (produced until 1928), Faro in 1887 (till 1900), Cabinet in 1888 (till 1930), Texan in 1889 (till about 1929 in the United States, but still available in Canada), and Skat in 1889 (till 1901). The last of these was available in standard Anglo-American faces or in German faces (i.e., having German suit signs and courts: *Koenig, Ober, Unter*). The company's advertising says that the German pattern—copied from cards by C. L. Wüst, a cardmaker in Frankfurt—was for "those Germans who have emigrated to this country to cast their lot with us, as Americans."

40. Lewis I. Cohen, an inventive and prosperous stationer in New York, ran a cardmaking business, where he trained his son Solomon and his nephews John M. Lawrence, Samuel Hart, and John J. Levy. When L. I. Cohen retired, he conferred his card firm to his son and Lawrence together. Hart and Levy had become cardmakers in Philadelphia and New York, respectively. On December 5, 1871, the firm of Lawrence and Cohen joined with Hart and Levy to form New York Consolidated Card Company.

41. The joker is especially noteworthy, as Hochman had failed to find it when he compiled his encyclopedia.

References

d'Allemagne, Henry-René. *Les cartes à jouer du XIVe au XXe siècle.* Paris: Hachette, 1906.

Atil, Esin. *Renaissance of Islam: Art of the Mamluks.* Washington, D.C.: Smithsonian Institution, 1981.

Decker, Ronald. "Who's Who in Court Cards." *Playing Card* 16, no. 3 (February 1988): 90–96.

Dummett, Michael. *The Game of Tarot.* London: Duckworth, 1980.

Dummett, Michael, and K. Abu-Deeb. "Some Remarks on Mamluk Playing Cards." *Journal of the Warburg and Courtauld Institutes* 36 (1973): 106–28.

Hargrave, Catherine Perry. *A History of Playing Cards.* Boston and New York: Houghton Mifflin, 1930.

Hochman, Gene. *The Encyclopedia of American Playing Cards.* 6 parts. Livingston, N.J.: author, 1976–82.

Hoffmann, Detlef. *Altdeutsche Spielkarten 1500–1650.* Nürnberg: Germanisches Nationalmuseum, 1993.

——. *Schweizer Spielkarten 1: Die Anfänge im 15, und 16, Jahrhundert.* Schaffhausen: Museum zu Allerheiligen, 1998.

Hopkins, Judith. "The 1791 French Cataloging Code and the Origins of the Card Catalog." *Libraries and Culture* 27, no. 4 (fall 1992): 378–404.

Leyden, Rudolph von. "Oriental Playing Cards: An Attempted Exploration of Relationships." *Journal of the Playing-Card Society* 4, no. 4 (May 1976): supplement 2, pp. 1–37.

Mann, Sylvia, and Virginia Wayland. *The Dragons of Portugal.* Farnham, Surrey: Sanford, 1973.

Mayer, L. A. "Mamluk Playing Cards." *Bulletin de l'Institut français d'archéologie orientale* 38 (1939): 113–18.

Race, Dick. "The Playing Card People." Unpublished manuscript, c. 1982.

[Russell & Morgan Printing Co]. *British Printer* 8 (March/April 1899): 6ff.

"The Russell & Morgan Printing Co." *Superior Printer* 1, no. 2 (June 1887): 21–24.

The United States Playing Card Company. Private Collection. Cincinnati, Ohio. (Referred to as USPC Company Museum.)

Wintle, Simon. "A 'Moorish' Sheet of Playing-Cards." *Playing Card* 15, no. 4 (May 1987): 112–22.

Chapter Six

The Smithsonian in Cincinnati

Exhibiting Prints at the Ohio Valley Centennial Exposition, 1888

Helena E. Wright
Curator, Graphic Arts Collection
National Museum of American History, Smithsonian Institution

In 1996 the Smithsonian Institution celebrated its 150th anniversary and the National Museum of American History mounted an exhibition marking 150 years of print collecting. A review of the collection—the oldest in the institution—indicated that some of the choicest prints, including a number of works by the old masters, had been purchased for two exhibitions: one at Cincinnati in 1888 (fig. 6.1) and the other at Chicago in 1893. The latter, the Columbian Exposition, was a major world's fair. But what was the Centennial Exposition of the Ohio Valley and Central States, and what did the Smithsonian's Graphic Arts exhibition there reveal about the role of prints in nineteenth-century America?

In 1888 the Smithsonian exhibited nearly one thousand prints at Cincinnati. Drawn from the Graphic Arts Section of the U.S. National Museum and from generous loans by artists and publishers, the exhibition presented both traditional media and the new photomechanical processes, everything from old master engravings to modern halftones and photogravures. Separate sections featured American wood engraving, spanning the nineteenth century from Alexander Anderson to *Harper's Magazine*, and American etching, including dozens of examples by women etchers of the period.

This exhibition reflects specific practices of print collecting and exhibiting typical of

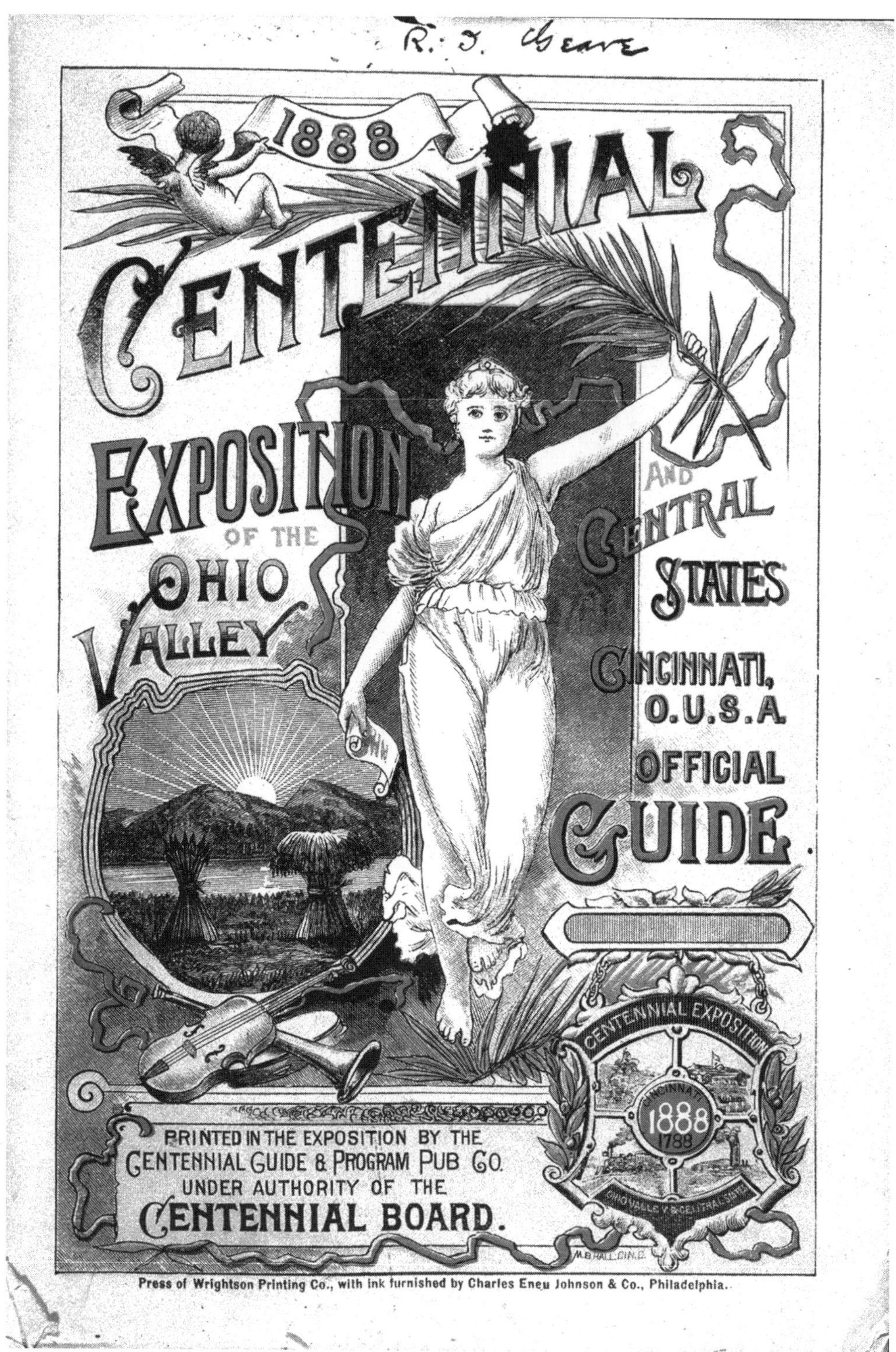

Fig. 6.1 ***1888 Centennial Exposition of the Ohio Valley and Central States, Cincinnati, O. U.S.A. Official Guide*** **[cover]**

M. B. Hall. Wood engraving, color. 1888. 9 × 6 in (22.7 × 15 cm) (sheet). Smithsonian Institution Archives. SI neg 99–4236.

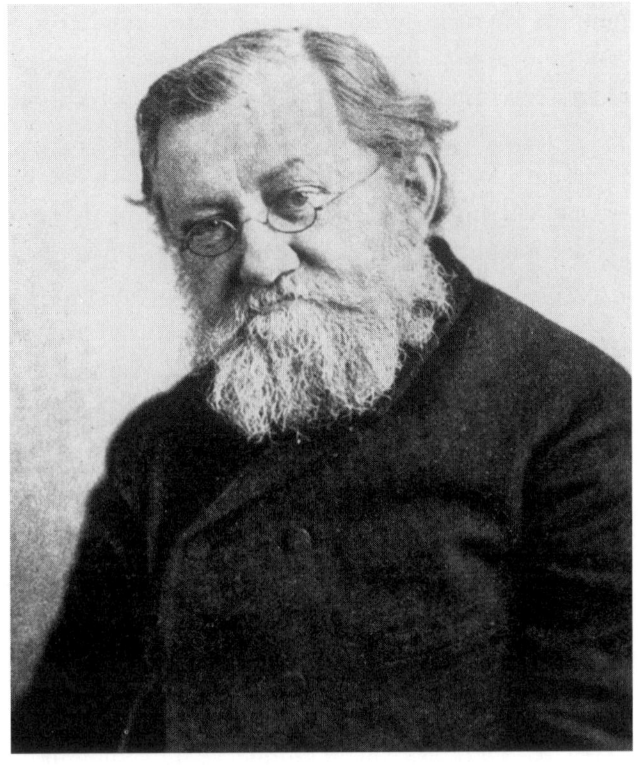

Fig. 6.2 Portrait of Sylvester R. Koehler
Halftone from a photograph. Ca. 1890. Graphic Arts Collection, National Museum of American History, Smithsonian Institution. SI neg 86–1071.

the time, as well as indicating a more general interest in art and cultural pursuits. The evidence suggests that there was a national audience for prints; a strong local audience for art (the Cincinnati Art Museum was formed in 1881 in part as a response to art shown at the series of industrial expositions there beginning in 1870); and, most importantly, a solid historical basis for today's decidedly visual culture.

Smithsonian Graphic Arts curator Sylvester R. Koehler's (fig. 6.2) organizing principle was to regard art as an industry and to explain how prints are made using examples from many periods and countries. Both for the temporary exhibition in Ohio and for the U.S. National Museum in Washington, Koehler wanted to show all the graphic processes then known, how they had evolved from drawing to photomechanical processes, and to present stages of work from the artist's original conception through plates to the finished print. Neither the subject of the picture nor the artist ranked first with Koehler, for "the technical process employed in the representation becomes the first thing to be considered, and the history of engraving consists in the records of the steps by which the various processes approached perfection."[1]

In choosing this rubric, he was following the scheme identified a generation before by George Perkins Marsh, Vermont congressman and Smithsonian regent, who sold his collection of engravings to the brand-new institution in 1849. Marsh had formed his collection to illustrate the history of engraving; when financial reverses necessitated its sale, he found a ready buyer in the Smithsonian. The purchase of the Marsh Collection (some thirteen hundred European engravings and three hundred reference works) helped the nascent Smithsonian to fulfill its congressional mandate to organize a library, museum, and gallery of art. As Assistant Secretary Charles Coffin Jewett noted in the *Annual Report* for 1850:

> Engraving seems to be the only branch of the fine arts which we can, for the present, cultivate. One good picture or statue would cost more than a large collection of prints. The formation of a gallery of the best paintings, is, in this country, almost hopeless. Engravings furnish us with translations, authentic and masterly, of the best creations of genius in painting and sculpture, the originals of which are utterly beyond our reach. Engraving, too, is more than a mere imitative art. The master's genius shines forth from some of the free and graceful etchings of Rembrandt almost as vividly as from his canvas.
>
> It can hardly be doubted, that, in no way, could this Institution, for the present, do so much for every department of the fine arts, without injury to other objects of its care, as by procuring a collection of engravings, so full and so well chosen as that which now adorns its Library.[2]

Jewett's remarks reflected a wider public attitude, and at about this time prints began to assume a national cultural importance. Specific engravings and chromolithographs were cited for their civilizing influence, providing moral uplift as well as training the eyes and minds of designers and consumers alike to "correctness of taste and refinement of thought."[3] Indeed, when the Marsh Collection had been in place for over a year, the interest it attracted was noted as coming "not from undiscriminating idlers, but from men of taste and particularly from artists."[4]

A belief in art as an agent of cultural improvement was widely shared by Americans through much of the nineteenth century, so it was not at all unusual for the National Museum to bring this didactic form of uplift to a broad audience as part of the federal government's section at the Cincinnati fair (fig. 6.3). Under the leadership of Smithsonian Assistant Secretary George Brown Goode, Koehler and his colleagues in the natural sciences consciously adopted a taxonomic model for exhibitions that presented developments from the simple to the complex. Koehler used examples of printmaking processes to illustrate chronological increments toward technical perfection. Taking this show on the road, so to speak, was seen as "making the work of the Museum known to the people of the Republic."[5]

Earlier in the century, mechanics' institutes and the Civil War sanitary commission fairs had offered Americans numerous opportunities to see works of art along with manufactured goods. By the 1870s industrial expositions in larger cities often showed inventions and products in combination with loan exhibitions of a more cultural nature. Paintings, drawings, and prints from private collectors, individual artists, and publishers were included in these fairs, mixing fine art, commercial art, and illustration in a truly multimedia approach.

The Cincinnati Industrial Exposition, styled as a "National Exhibition of Manufac-

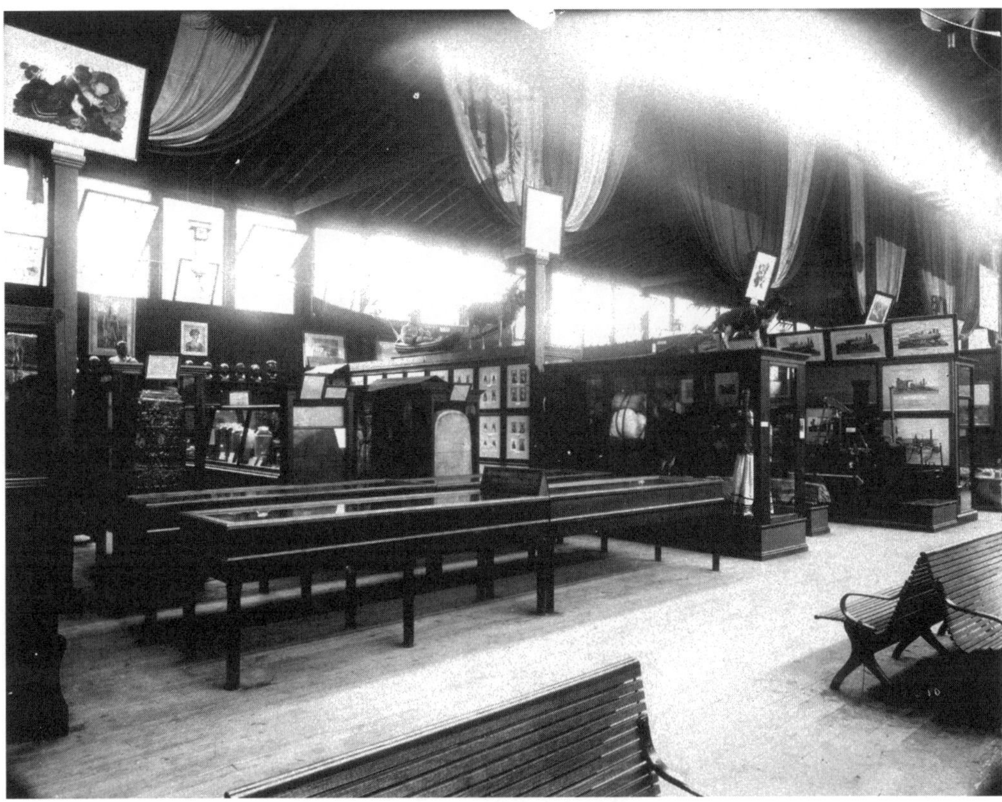

Fig. 6.3 Smithsonian Exhibition at the Ohio Valley Centennial Exposition, Cincinnati. Halftone from a photograph. S. R. Koehler, "Catalogue of the Contributions of the Section of Graphic Arts to the Ohio Valley Centennial Exposition, Cincinnati, 1888," *Proceedings of the U.S. National Museum* 10 (Washington, 1888). Smithsonian Institution Archives. SI neg 4470.

tures, Products, and the Arts," began in 1870 and flourished until 1888. Intended to promote restitution of the city's trade after the Civil War, the exhibitions built on the successful models of the antebellum mechanics' fairs with significant cultural components.[6] Art was included at most of these fairs, and prints were featured not only as current Cincinnati products, like the Strobridge Company's lithographs, but also from more distant firms like Prang & Company of Boston.

Beyond contemporary commercial productions like these lithographs, however, a rich and varied assemblage of prints appeared at the Cincinnati expositions and other similar fairs. Local lenders were represented, but many prints also came as traveling loan exhibitions drawn from private sources. Both Henry F. Sewall of New York and James L. Claghorn of Philadelphia lent portions of their print collections for national tours during the 1870s and 1880s. Claghorn, in particular, was a generous lender to the Cincinnati Industrial Expositions. Several hundred of his prints formed part of the exposition's art offerings in 1874, 1875, and 1879. In 1875 about 250 prints from the Claghorn Collection were shown in Cincinnati, "fine specimens of the etching needle and the burin from every great

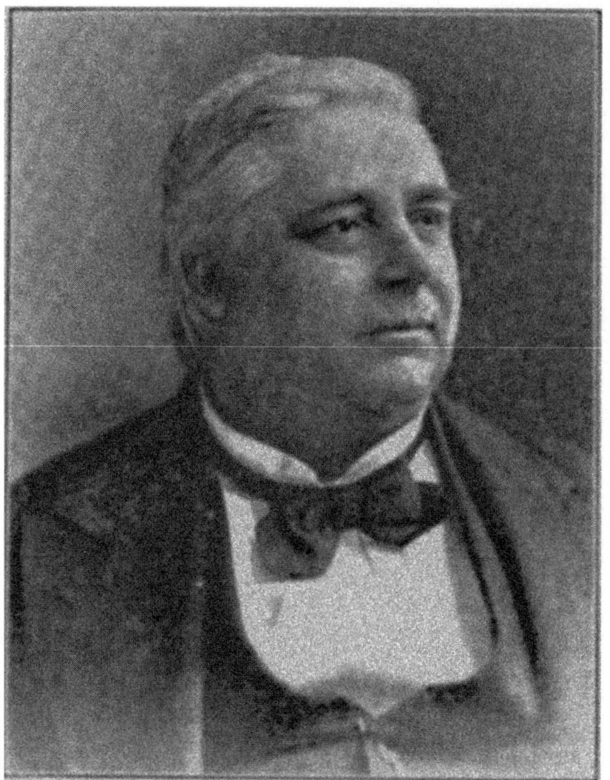

Fig. 6.4 James L. Claghorn
Halftone from photograph. N.d. 2 × 3 in (5 × 7.5 cm) (image). Theodore C. Knauff, *An Experiment in Training for the Useful and the Beautiful* (Philadelphia: School of Design for Women, 1922), p. 62. Graphic Arts Collection, National Museum of American History, Smithsonian Institution. SI neg 94–13560.

master since Duerer and Marc Antonio."[7] The 1879 catalog thanked him profusely for again placing "his plethoric portfolios at the disposal of the Art Committee."[8]

James Lawrence Claghorn (1817–1884) (fig. 6.4), a Philadelphia banker, was active on the boards of the Pennsylvania Academy of the Fine Arts, the Philadelphia School of Design for Women, and other arts organizations. His large personal fortune funded the formation of an important art collection—containing both paintings and engravings—that he had been acquiring since about 1840.

> Claghorn's collecting interests eventually settled on engravings and etchings, and after more than twenty years of collecting, he decided to sell his paintings for the stated purpose of turning full attention to the development and expansion of his already remarkable print collection. In 1877 his gallery of engravings was described as "one of the richest in America, and we believe it is his intention to make it rival the best European collection of this genre."[9]

Claghorn opened his home to art students and interested amateurs, allowing generous access to his private art gallery. He also initiated a series of public art receptions in

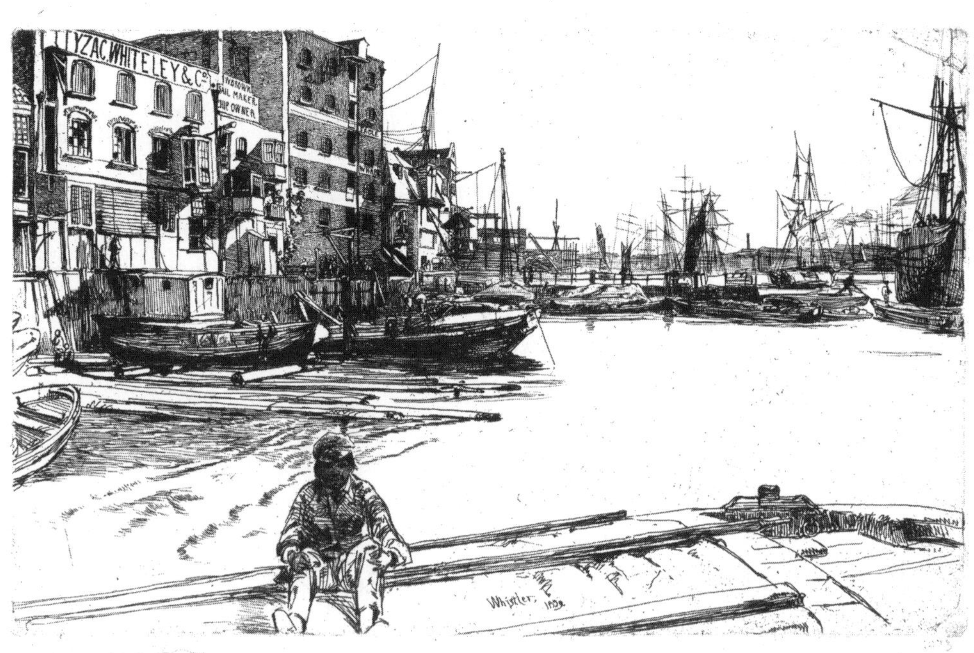

Fig. 6.5 Eagle Wharf
J. A. M. Whistler. Etching. 1859. 5.5 × 8.5 in (14 × 21.5 cm) (plate). Graphic Arts Collection, National Museum of American History, Smithsonian Institution. SI neg 99-4213.

Philadelphia.[10] In 1873 a selection of 231 engravings, etchings, and mezzotints from Claghorn's collection was presented at the Philadelphia Union League's Third Art Reception and traveled the following year to Boston, Brooklyn, and Cincinnati, where, it was said, "they attracted a great deal of attention."[11] The "'Extraordinary Claghorn Collection of prints'—chosen and arranged to illustrate the history of the art of engraving from Schongauer to Whistler, the most extensive and comprehensive exhibition of its kind ever before seen in America"—became known through exhibitions in Philadelphia and other cities like Cincinnati and through articles in the national press, especially genteel magazines like *Lippincott's*, *Appleton's Art Journal*, and *Harper's*.[12] The Claghorn Collection and its enthusiastic reception at Cincinnati and elsewhere represent the high level of interest in and regard for prints at a time when public exhibitions combined aspects of popular entertainment and educational opportunities (fig. 6.5).

For the Cincinnati expositions, Claghorn and other lenders—mostly Cincinnatians—showed primarily European prints; even Claghorn's Whistler etchings were identified as English.[13] A few contemporary American engravings by James Smillie, Robert Hinshelwood, and others were lent by Cincinnati's Western Methodist Book Concern for the 1875 exhibition, and more modern works were included among the commercial sections of the exposition.

Cincinnati Exposition art catalogs from the 1870s and early 1880s list the engravings and etchings alphabetically by graphic artist. Prints are noted as "original" or after a delineator, but "originals" were not segregated from reproductive works. Original and reproductive prints, both European and American, were held together in many collections. One of the critical points to understand about prints in this period is that audiences were open to all types of works; collections, exhibitions, and publications were inclusive, not hierarchical or restrictive. Fine art, commercial art, and popular graphic imagery were considered to be connected in a wide cultural field that recognized the instructive potential of any format (fig. 6.6). This assumption explains how these industrial exhibitions could include objects as diverse as "pork products displayed in every conceivable shape and form," together with prints.[14]

About this time, Joseph Maberly's manual, *The Print Collector,* first published in London in 1844, was reprinted in New York with an account of contemporary etching written by Robert Hoe Jr. A collector himself, Hoe noted that ten years earlier such a reprint would have proved a poor investment for booksellers, but by 1880 there was a great demand in the United States for trustworthy information on the subject. Exhibition visitors, who numbered half a million at Cincinnati in most years and one million in the final year of 1888, avidly sought instruction about how to reap the civilizing benefits of art. At the time, a good engraving was believed to be more beneficial than a bad painting. One art critic wrote:

> Hundreds of people who cannot, or who think they cannot, afford to buy original paintings, decorate their homes with engravings, and it is one of the commonplaces of art culture that a good engraving is far better worth having than a bad

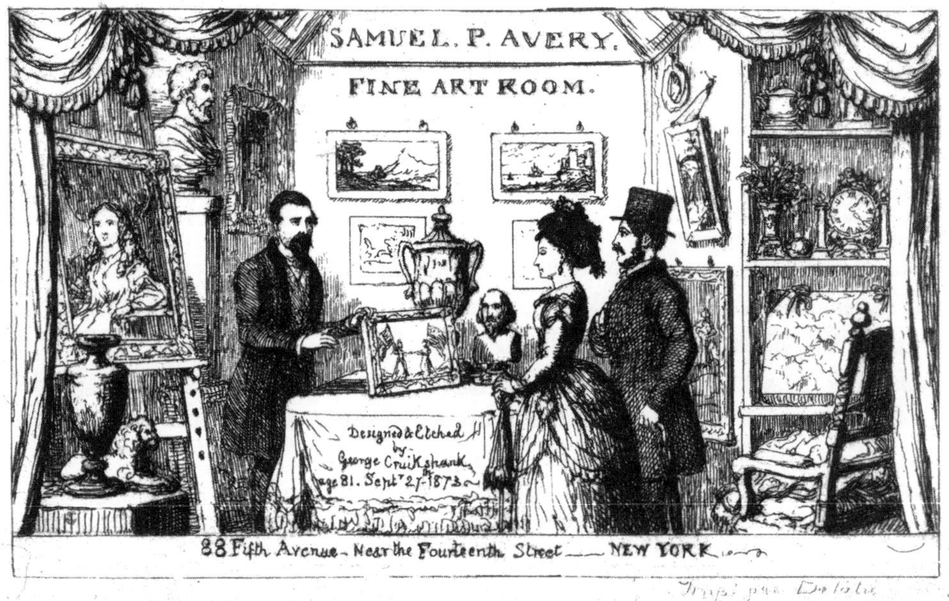

Fig. 6.6 Samuel P. Avery. / Fine Art Room. / 88 Fifth Avenue. Near the Fourteenth Street—New York

Designed and etched by George Cruikshank, age eighty-one. Etching. 1873. 2.3 × 3.75 in (6 × 9.5 cm) (image). GA 1439 SI neg 96–309.

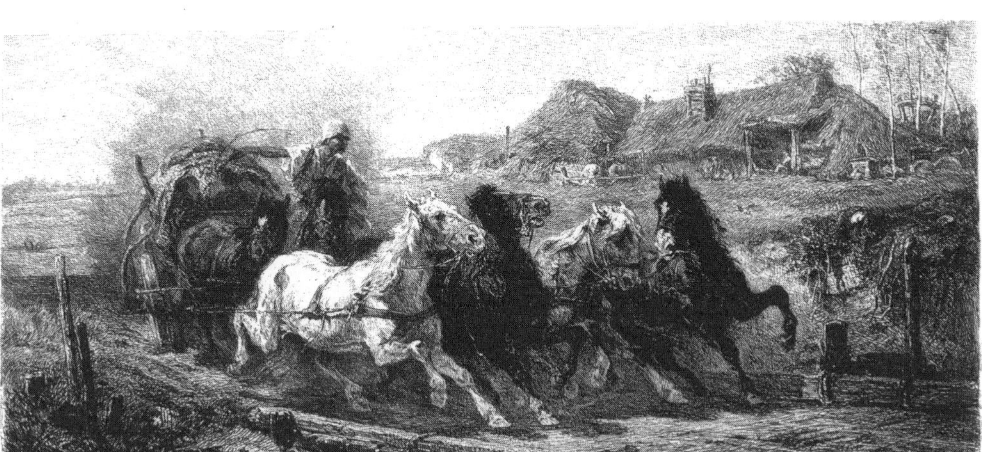

Fig. 6.7 The Wallachian Team
Wilhelm Unger after Adolf Schreyer. Etching. Ca. 1880. 7 × 9.25 in (17.5 × 23.5 cm) (plate). Graphic Arts Collection, National Museum of American History, Smithsonian Institution. SI neg 99–4223.

> painting. . . . It is impossible to overestimate the importance of an art like this, that finds its way into every household, and that exerts so potent an influence on the education of the taste of the masses.[15]

The Cincinnati Exposition art catalogs of the 1870s provided considerable information about the engravings, helping to inform visitors about what to look for in the prints. Typically an entry gave the artist's name, life dates, nationality, and his connection to master or pupil. There were descriptive passages telling the viewer something about him and what to look for in quotes taken from sources identified in the introduction.[16] The exhibition included engravers of all periods and countries, including the recent past and living artists. While Americans were but thinly represented in early years, their prints did include such diverse examples as Robert Hinshelwood's engraving after Eastman Johnson's *Pet Lamb* and Whistler's *Wapping Wharf*. Stylistic prejudices and period preferences are clear in the annotations: Bartolozzi was criticized for giving himself up to the "tasteless, weak, and stipple-like style which then was the rage in England," while those who showed the influence of Claude, like Jan Both and William Woollett, were highly praised. Rembrandt and Dürer were given their due, but in rather contained prose. Wilhelm Unger, although largely forgotten today, was praised as "one of the most talented and original of modern etchers" (fig. 6.7), while Whistler was not singled out for any annotation at all.[17]

Beyond Claghorn's generous loans, for the art exhibitions of the 1870s Cincinnati collectors had offered holdings that included an impressive array of old master prints and contemporary European works. In 1872 more than two hundred prints were shown, the majority from local men like William Henry Davis, M. F. Force, William Karrmann, and

George McLaughlin. Reproductive works were endorsed in the catalog: "A work of any of the great masters is better in an engraving by Longhi and Morghen than in any ordinary copy [that is, painted], and would probably cost more in the market.—Rosco."[18] William Henry Davis, a pork provision merchant, signed the introductory note and probably supplied the bibliographic and other references. For the 1872 exhibition, Davis and Karrmann lent a Mantegna apiece, as well as Dürers and Rembrandts, and a number of reproductive engravings. Karrmann, a pharmacist, assembled what was called "the finest collection of etchings west of the Alleghenies."[19]

In 1873 nearly four hundred prints were shown from the collections of Mrs. A. D. Bullock, Mrs. Thomas J. Biggs, James Le Boutillier, A. Douglass, William Henry Davis, William Karrmann, and George McLaughlin. A number were repeats from prints shown the previous year, but no American examples were included. Italian reproductive engraver Paolo Toschi, represented by a dozen works, was one of the most popular artists of the day. His prints after Raphael, Correggio, and other old masters offered Americans the opportunity to study reproductions of European paintings at home, whether or not they might someday make the Grand Tour to see the originals.[20]

The 1879 exposition included 342 prints, overwhelmingly European. Two engraved landscapes by Robert Hinshelwood included one original composition, *Natural Bridge, Virginia*, and a reproductive engraving, *Trenton Falls, New York*, after Kensett. Alfred Jones was represented by *The Image Breaker*, after Leutze, cited as "His best work. Proof before letters." Jones and Hinshelwood perhaps were known to Cincinnatians from their engravings for the American Art Union and for their plates in the Cincinnati-based periodical *The Ladies Repository*. James Smillie's etching, *Upper Ausable Lake, Adirondacks*, an "Original artist's proof on India paper," was another American print shown in 1879. An addenda to the catalog listed seven etchings (untitled) by Joseph Pennell, from the "Pen. School of Ind. Art," along with John Sartain's engraving of the Battle of Gettysburg. These American prints may have been included as part of the Claghorn loan of that year, as Claghorn's collection included a number of works by Sartain and other Philadelphia artists.

In 1880 many of the prints shown were lent by New York art dealers Frederick Keppel and Herman Wunderlich, and they were for sale. These included original etchings by contemporary artists such as Whistler, Haden, Tissot, Herkomer, Millet, Fortuny, Appian, Meryon, and Lalanne, and reproductive etchings by Rajon, Flameng, and others (fig. 6.8). Older prints by Visscher, Masson, Nanteuil, and Edelinck, also offered for sale by Keppel, were mixed in with the new works. Cincinnati must have been regarded as a good potential market for these European etchings just then coming into fashion.

Local collectors like F. E. Jones, Samuel C. Tatum, and Charles Wilby continued the practice of lending works into the 1880s. One A. Gunnison lent several Piranesis and a Dürer, among other old master prints. The McLaughlin family provided several prints: George lent works by Haden and Bartolozzi; James lent an architectural study; and Louise, a printmaker herself, showed a portrait etching (fig. 6.9).[21]

Fig. 6.8 Kilgaren Castle
Sir Francis Seymour Haden. Etching. 1864. 4.25 × 5.85 in (11 × 15 cm) (plate). Graphic Arts Collection, National Museum of American History, Smithsonian Institution. SI neg 99–4218.

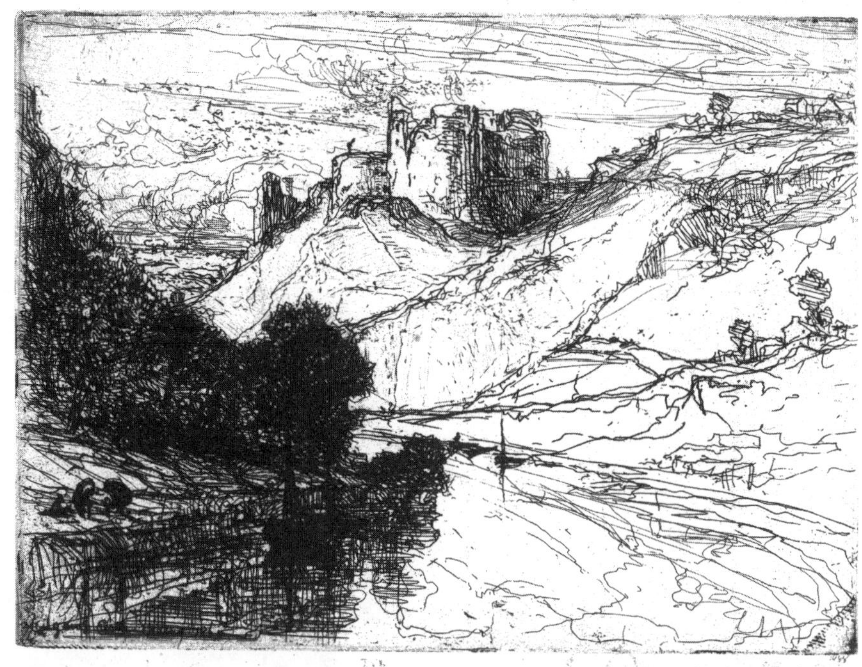

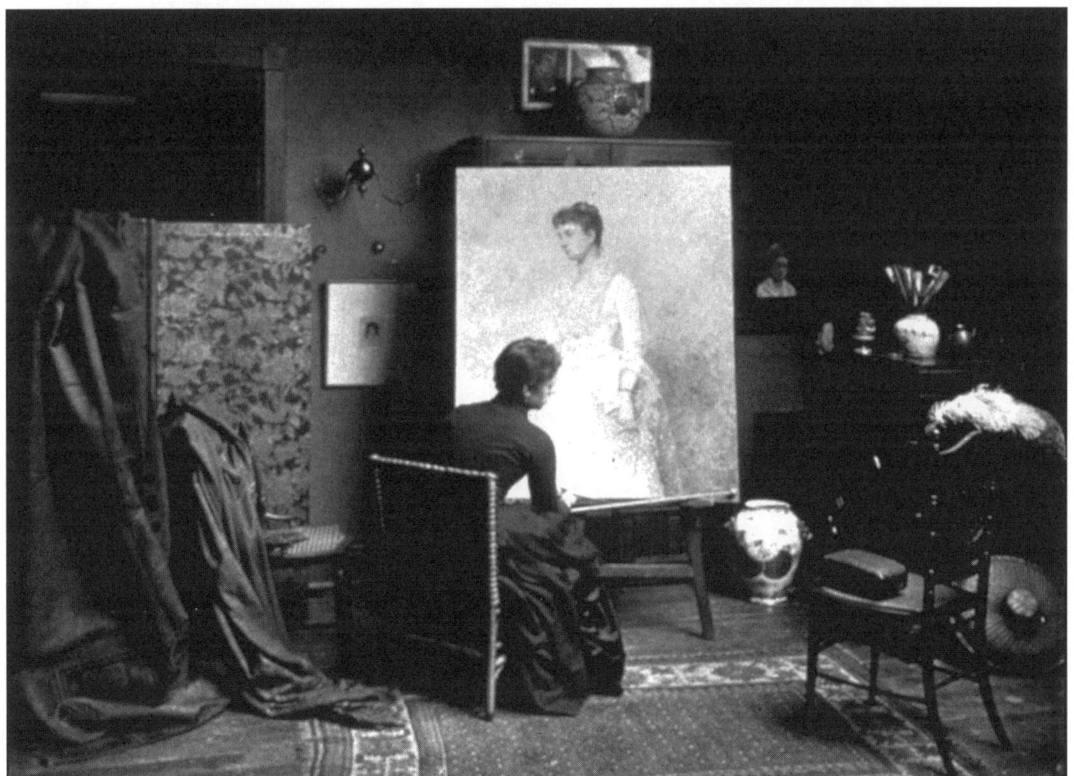

Fig. 6.9 Mary Louise McLaughlin in Her Studio
Photograph. n.d. 6 × 8 in (15.25 × 20.5 cm). Cincinnati Art Museum, Gift of Theodore A. Langstroth.

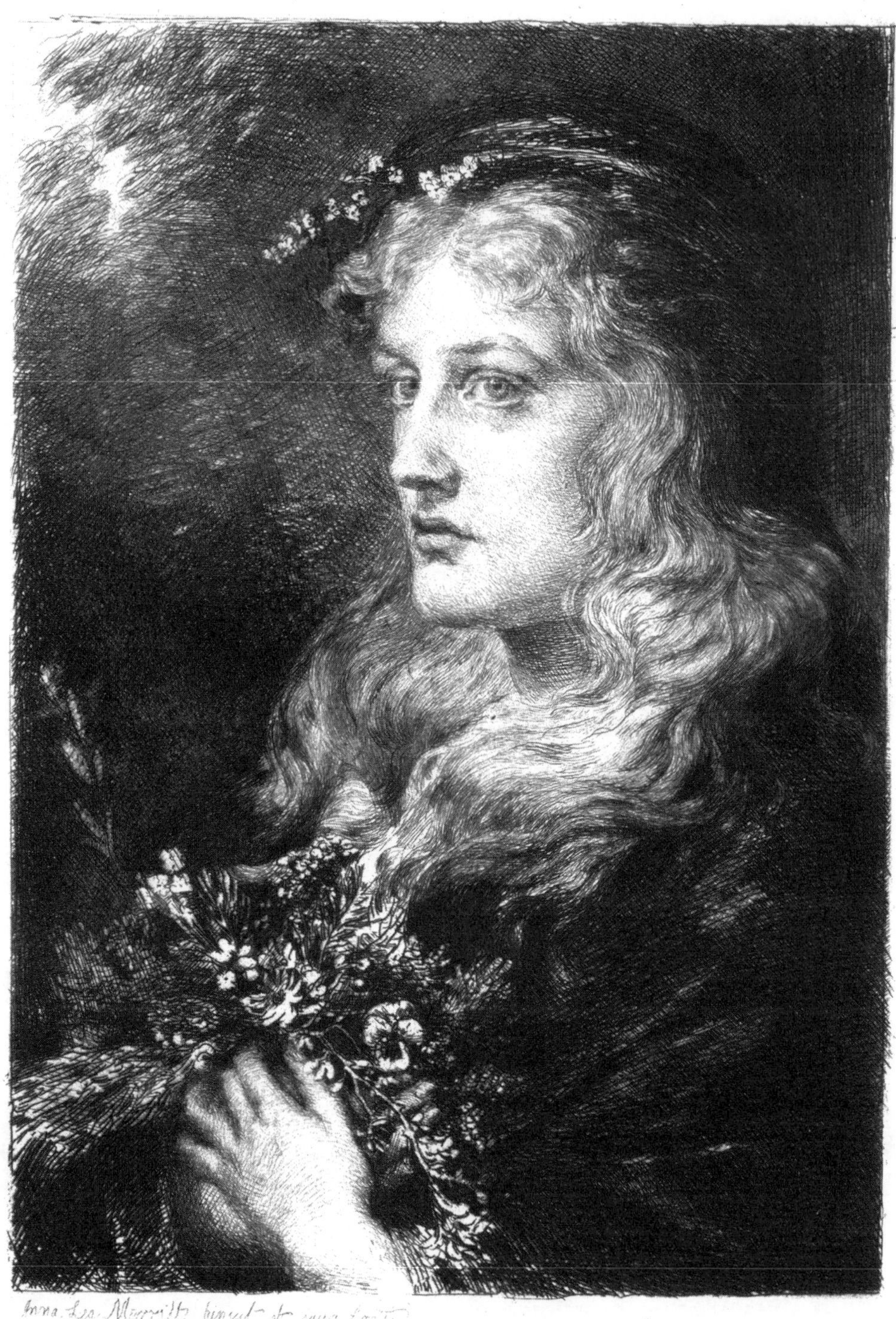

Fig. 6.10 Ophelia
Anna Lea Merritt. Etching. 1880. 8.75 × 6.75 in (22.5 × 17.5 cm) (plate). Graphic Arts Collection, National Museum of American History, Smithsonian Institution. SI neg 89–5622.

American prints made their debut in the 1880 exposition. Some seventeen etchings—offered for sale by the new *American Art Review*—included two images by Anna Lea Merritt (fig. 6.10) and others by Thomas Moran, Stephen Ferris, J. M. Falconer, and Samuel Colman. Whether instigated by Koehler, who was then the magazine's editor, or by his Cincinnati correspondent, George McLaughlin, an officer of the Cincinnati Etching Club and a generous lender to previous Cincinnati Exposition art shows, this selection prefigured the portion of Koehler's 1888 exhibition devoted to the work of contemporary American etchers.[22] Ten examples of preliminary drawings for printed illustrations, lent by Scribner's and other publishers, also anticipated the important contribution publishers would make to the 1888 exhibition, with its emphasis on process.

With the tutelage of these impressive loan exhibitions as precedent, Cincinnati exposition visitors in 1888 probably were not surprised to find Koehler's Smithsonian show very catholic in its content. Part of a larger government initiative that included fisheries, forestry, the army, and the navy (fig. 6.11), the Smithsonian's exhibits presented graphic arts and photography as separate sections, along with other subjects such as anthropology, ethnology, botany, and ornithology. Among the bird specimens, colored prints, including some plates from Julius Bien's chromolithographic edition of Audubon's *Birds of America* (1860), stood in for extinct species not available for exhibition.

The didactic mode is conveyed in Koehler's catalog of the Graphic Arts Section.[23] He worked very hard to pull together the nearly one thousand prints, proofs, plates, and blocks in a few short months, and, in fact, almost half the items were lent from his personal collection. He also persuaded other collectors like Samuel Putnam Avery of New York to lend prints, and he called upon artists and publishers to send individual works as well as significant groupings.

Koehler defined the scope of pictorial printing as needing only two "grand subdivisions," what he called the "older methods," those "involving only hand work or physical power," and "the modern processes based upon the chemical action of light." He divided the exhibition into four approximately equal sections, covering the traditional media and the photomechanical processes, plus American wood engraving (fig. 6.12) and American etching (fig. 6.13). He broke out these two special sections in recognition of the "American centennial celebration" the Cincinnati Exposition represented, stating:

> The wood engravers and etchers of the United States have done more than their share in calling the attention of the world to the art of their native or adopted country, and the exception made in their favor is a just recognition of the value of the work, and of its importance in the history of art in America.[24]

Koehler's career had prepared him well to serve as a national interpreter of prints and, more specifically, of American contributions to printmaking. Born in Germany in 1837, he came to the United States as a boy. He acquired direct technical experience as a

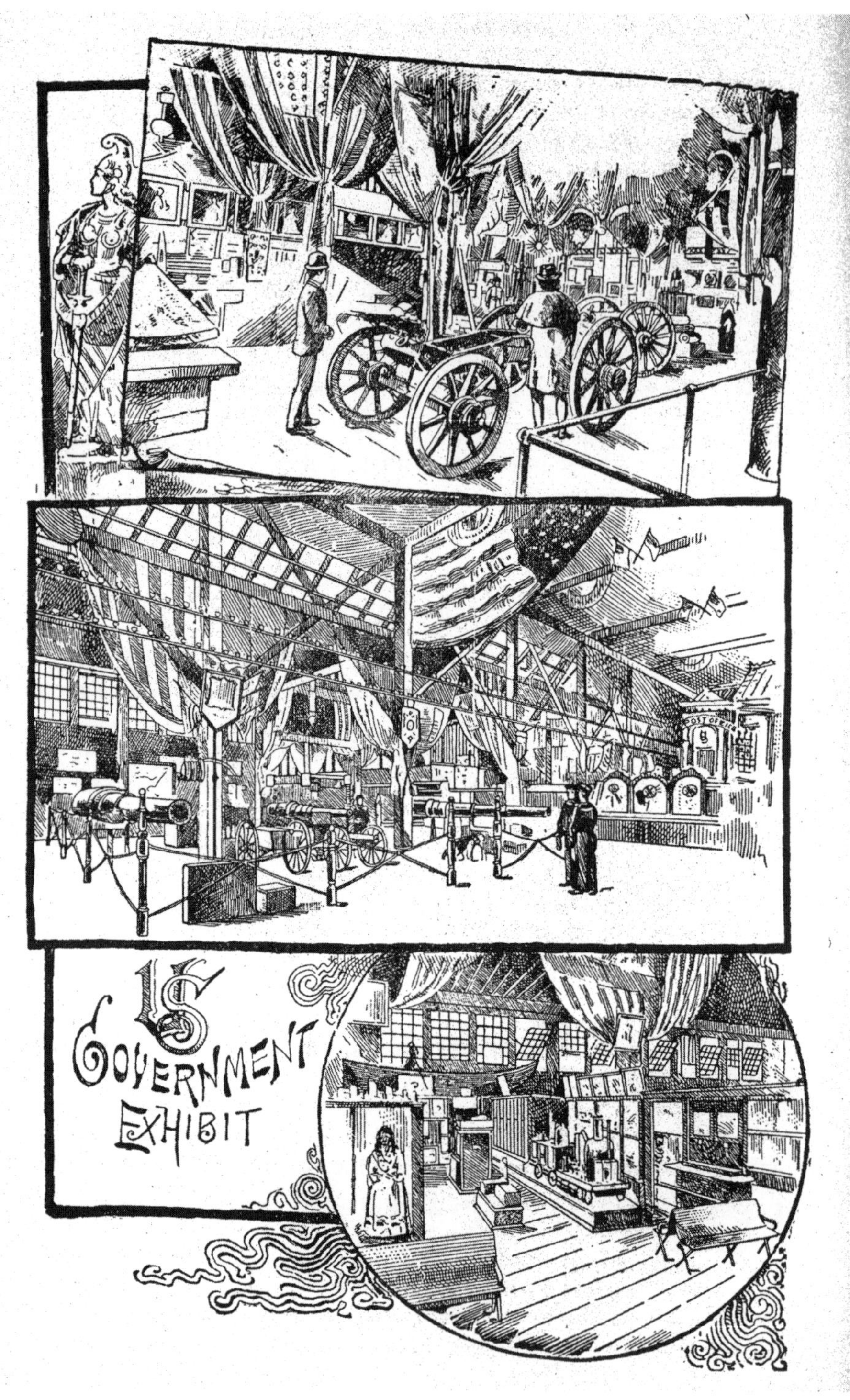

Fig. 6.11 1888 Centennial Exposition of the Ohio Valley and Central States, Cincinnati, O. U.S.A. Official Guide [U.S. government exhibit]
Line cut. 1888. 9 × 6 in (22.7 × 15 cm) (sheet). Smithsonian Institution Archives. SI neg 99–4235.

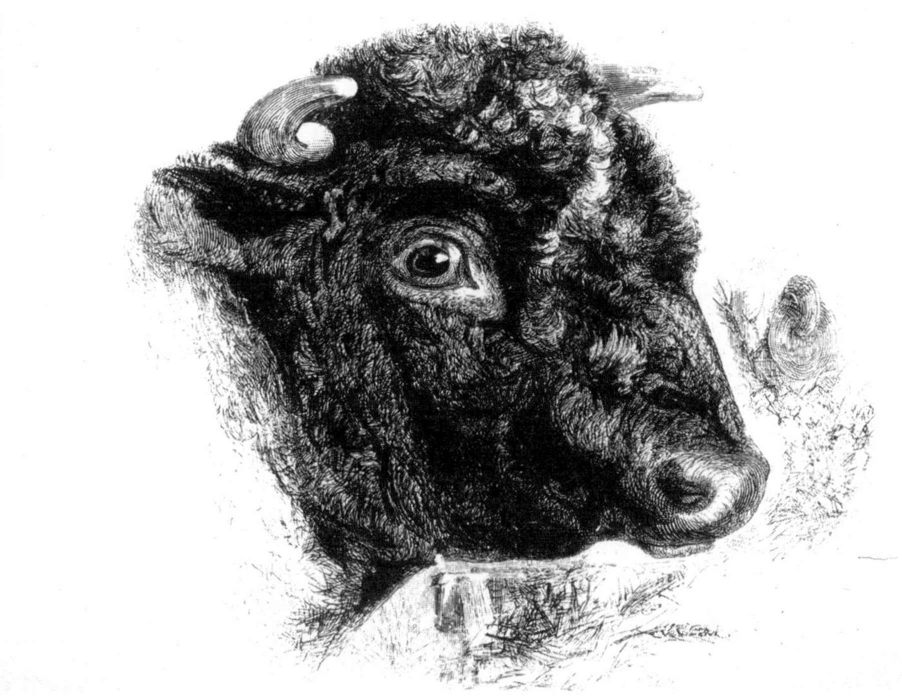

Fig. 6.12 Bull's Head
John Andrew, after Field. Wood engraving, knife proof. N.d. Size: 5.25 × 6.5 in (13 × 16.5 cm) (sheet). Graphic Arts Collection, National Museum of American History, Smithsonian Institution. SI neg 79–14337.

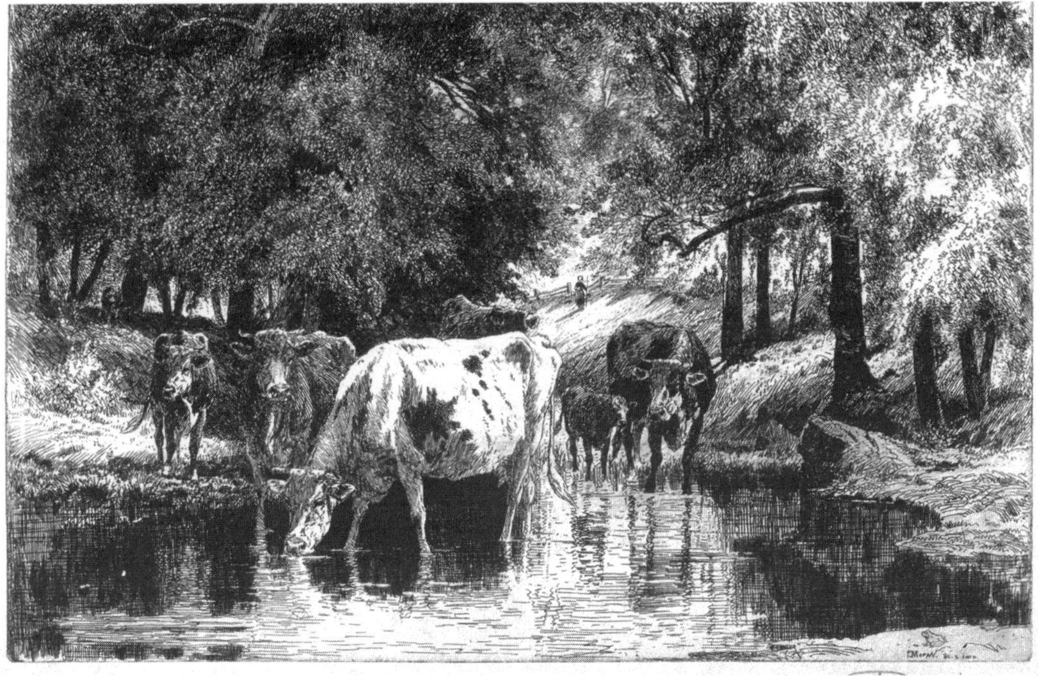

Fig. 6.13 The Pool
Peter Moran. Etching. 1884. 8 × 12 in (20 × 30 cm) (plate). Graphic Arts Collection, National Museum of American History, Smithsonian Institution. SI neg 99–4214.

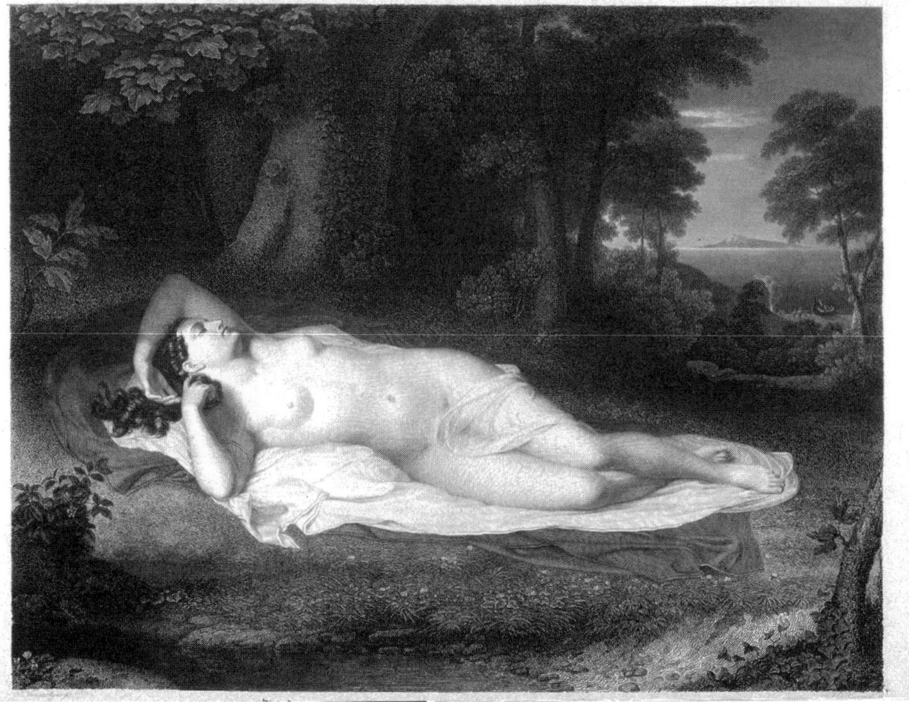

Fig. 6.14 Ariadne.
Published by A. B. Durand, New York. Hodgson, Boys & Graves, London, and Rittner & Goupil, Paris, 1835. Asher B. Durand after John Vanderlyn. Copper engraving. 1835. 17.5 × 20.85 in (44.5 × 53 cm) (plate). Graphic Arts Collection, National Museum of American History, Smithsonian Institution. SI neg 99–4227.

manager in the Boston lithographic firm of Louis Prang in the 1860s and 1870s, and he edited the influential, if short-lived, *American Art Review* from 1879 to 1881. He had compiled directories of art-related firms and had wide-ranging connections with both artists and the graphic arts industry. His publications in German and English established him as a scholar of international reputation.

In his monumental volume *Etching*, published in 1885, Koehler described the world's famous print collections, but he praised as most ambitious and "scientifically the most valuable and interesting" those collections formed with a historical scope, aiming to illustrate the development of printmaking from its invention to the present.[25] He followed this concept in shaping the Smithsonian's collection and permanent exhibition and for his print exhibit at the Cincinnati Exposition.

Twenty-four processes were represented in the first section, which was devoted to traditional handwork. About fifty specimens showed relief and intaglio engraving in wood and metal from Albrecht Dürer to Asher B. Durand, including the white line work of Thomas Bewick and modern French wood engraving after Gustave Doré. Durand's *Ariadne* (fig. 6.14), which Koehler called "the finest engraving of its size executed in America," had a screen to itself, next to Raphael's Sistine Madonna.[26] Another fifty examples of etching cov-

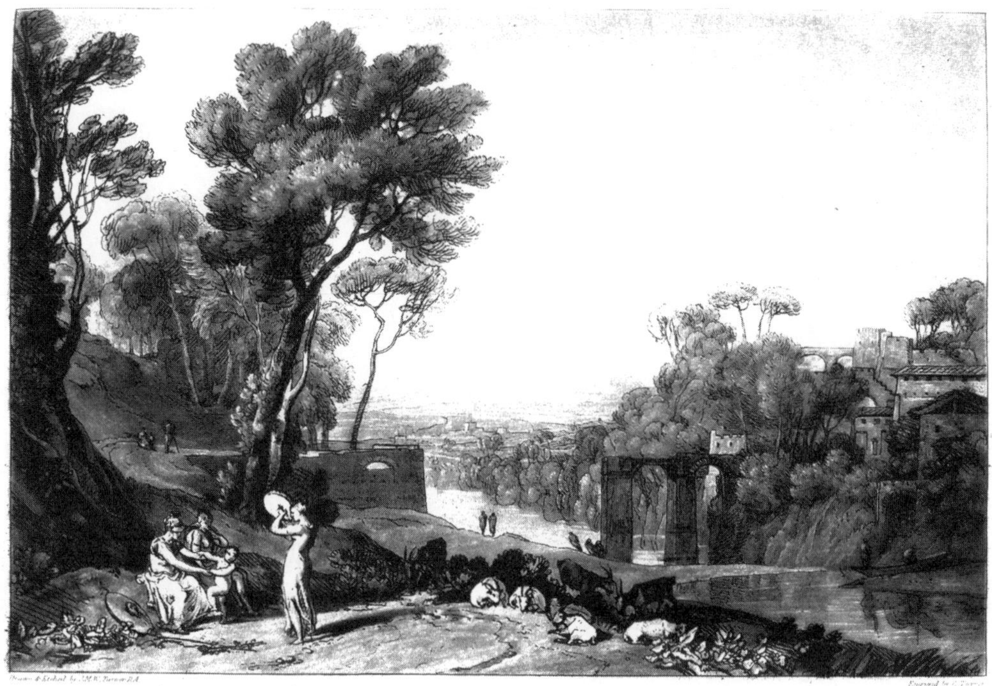

Fig. 6.15 The Woman and Tambourine (plate 3 from the *Liber Studiorum*)
J. M. W. Turner. Etching. Ca. 1806. 8.25 × 11.35 in (21 × 29 cm) (plate). Graphic Arts Collection, National Museum of American History, Smithsonian Institution. SI neg 99–4225.

ered the European history of the medium beginning with Hopfer and Dürer, continuing from Callot, Rembrandt, and Turner (fig. 6.15) to contemporary work, both reproductive and original, from artists like Lalanne, Jacquemart, and Unger.

Thanks to congressional support for the Smithsonian exhibition, Koehler was able to buy prints. He spent some $2,300 on 294 prints, mostly from New York City art dealers Keppel, Meder, and Wunderlich. (See appendix E.) Purchases for the permanent collection included Dürer's *St. Jerome* and *Death of the Virgin* (fig. 6.16), a fine impression of Rembrandt's *Christ Preaching* (fig. 6.17), and Muller's *Madonna di San Sisto*, a reproductive engraving after Raphael (fig. 6.18). This image was one of the cultural icons of the period, and the two pensive cherubim in the foreground have morphed into all kinds of twentieth-century imagery as well. Another impression of the Sistine Madonna had been lent by Cincinnati collector Louise Jones for the 1872 and 1873 exhibitions.[27]

Americans were only thinly represented in these sections, as they had their own areas coming up, which were dedicated to nineteenth-century wood engraving and etching. The mezzotint section, however, featured the work of Americans John Sartain (fig. 6.19) and Charles H. Moore, and the drypoint section included M. Louise McLaughlin of Cincinnati. Unfortunately, there are few title references, other than for the classic old master prints, so we don't know which of McLaughlin's works were chosen.

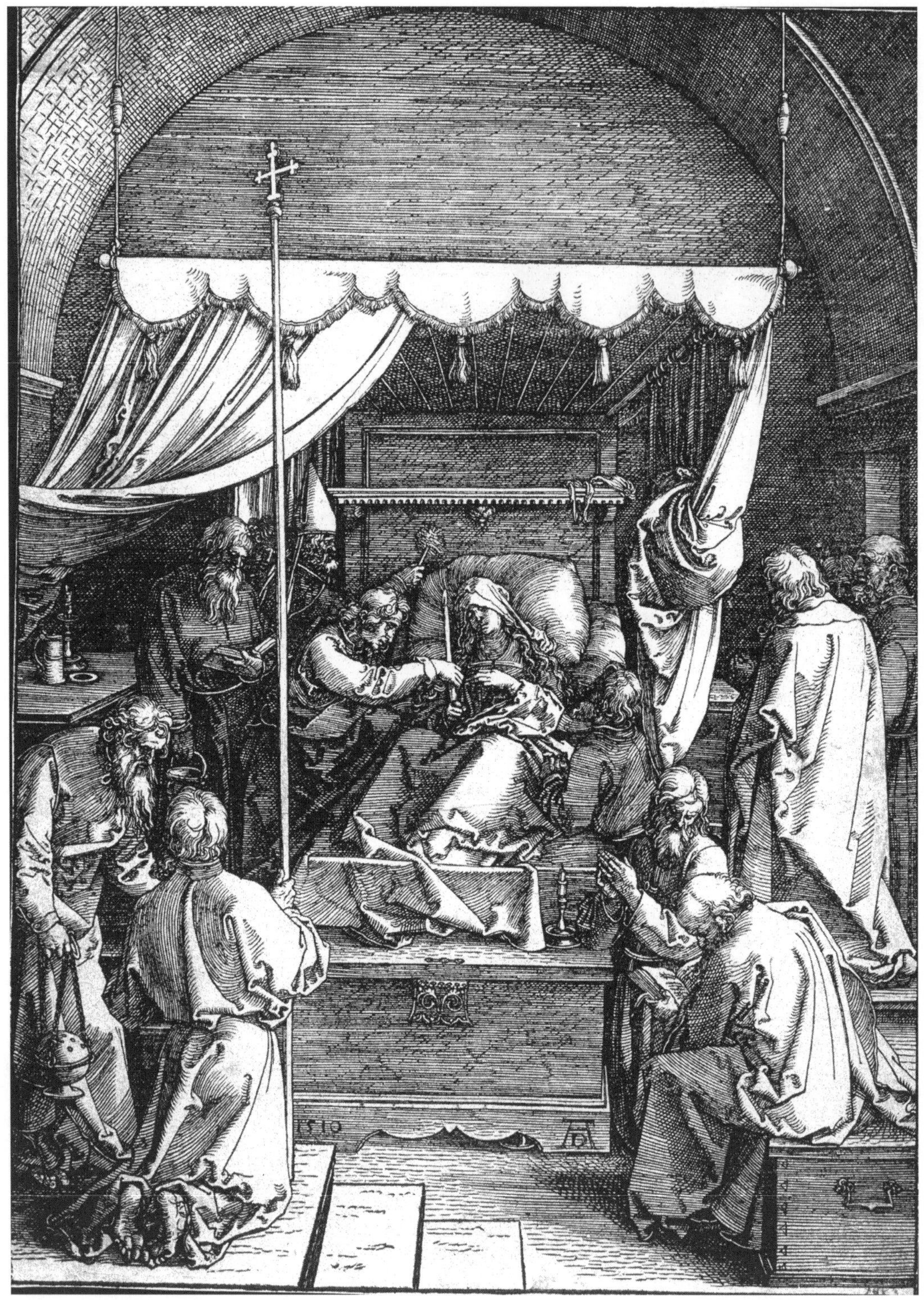

Fig. 6.16 Death of the Virgin
Albrecht Dürer. Woodcut. 1510. 11.5 × 8.12 in (29 × 21 cm) (trimmed). Graphic Arts Collection, National Museum of American History, Smithsonian Institution. SI neg 85–19679.

Fig. 6.17 Christ Preaching
Rembrandt van Rijn. Etching. Ca 1652. 6.25 × 8.25 in (16 × 21 cm) (trimmed). Graphic Arts Collection, National Museum of American History, Smithsonian Institution. SI 96–307.

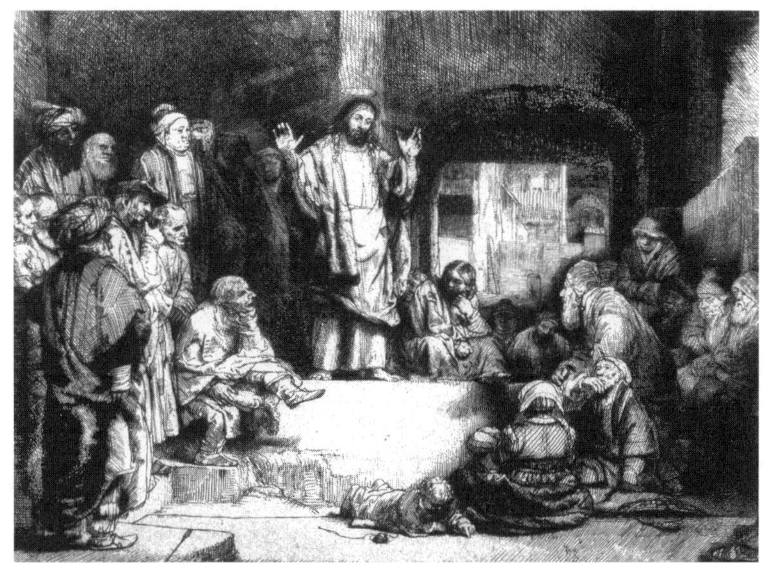

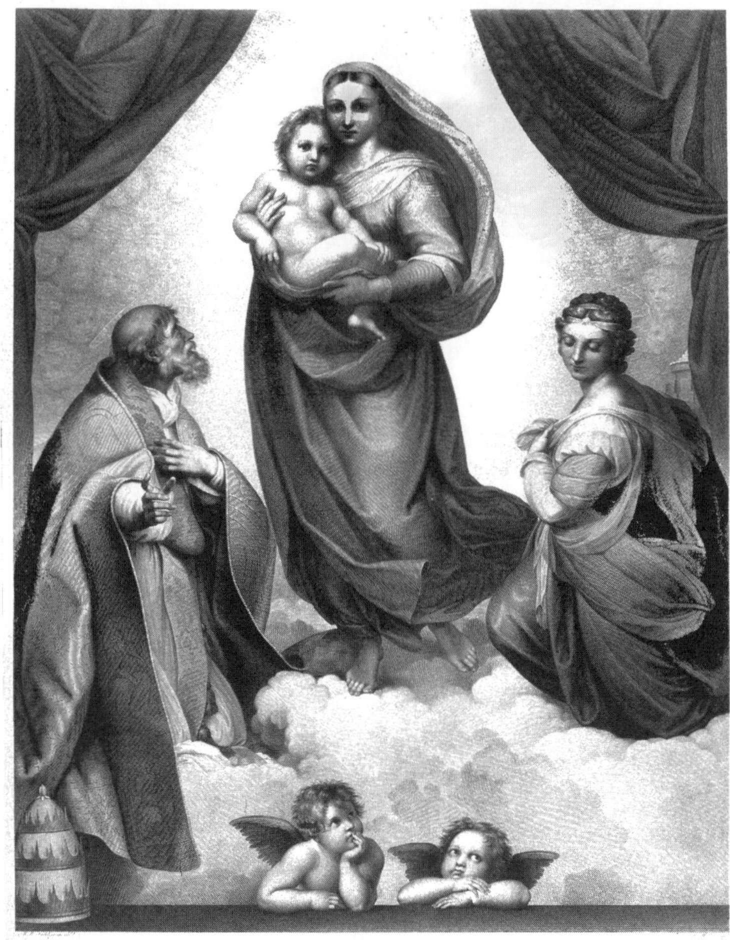

Fig. 6.18 La Madonna di S. Sisto di Rafaello. Della Reale Galleria di Dresda.
Friedrich Muller after Raphael. Engraving. Ca. 1810. 30 × 22 in (76.5 × 56 cm) (plate). Graphic Arts Collection, National Museum of American History, Smithsonian Institution. SI neg 99–4228.

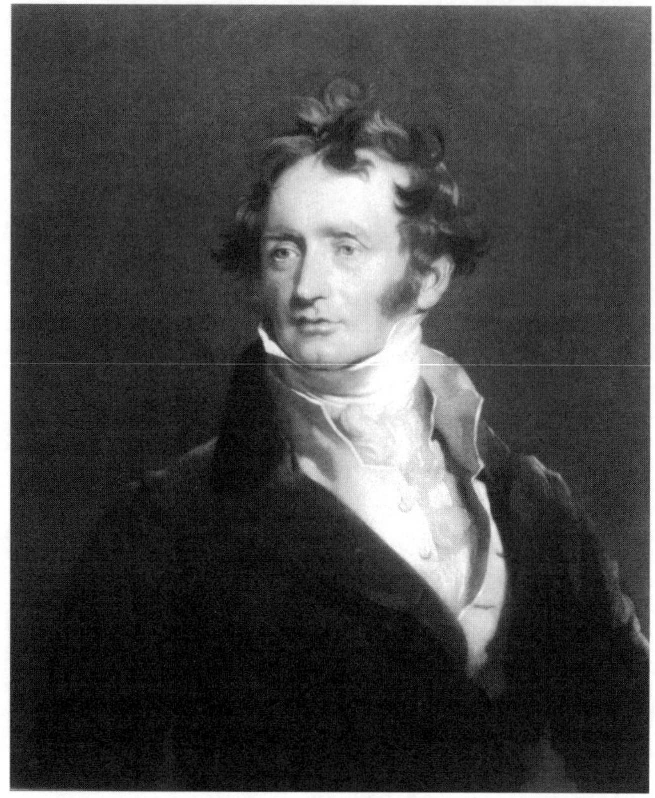

Fig. 6.19 Robert Gilmor, Esqr. of Baltimore
John Sartain after Sir Thomas Lawrence. Mezzotint. Ca. 1835. 12.5 × 8.75 in (32 × 22.5 cm) (plate). Graphic Arts Collection, National Museum of American History, Smithsonian Institution. SI neg 79–5334.

Only a handful of items represented the intaglio media of aquatint, crayon manner, and stipple, but nearly thirty prints showed various techniques—French, German, and English examples of ink, crayon, and lavis work—in the relatively new process of lithography. Drawn largely from the Prang gift to the Smithsonian a few years before, these lithographs are a reminder of Koehler's roots in that field. A dozen specialized processes, such as machine engraving, wax engraving, graphotype, and galvanography, represented more commercial methods of making blocks and prints, while *cliché-verre* and nature printing relied on simple contact printing by the sun.

In the photomechanical section, Koehler described the remarkable progress this new concept had made in the field of pictorial representation. "The block or plate which is to produce the print is wholly or partly the result of the chemical action of light," he said, while "the print itself is the product of the press, a mechanical contrivance."[28] The goal of many publishers at the time, both artistic and commercial, was to reduce the time involved in making a plate. Some contracts with engravers for the production of large prints after paintings (like James Smillie's effort on the engraving of Albert Bierstadt's *Rocky Mountains*) involved years of work.[29] Reproductive etchings were faster—and becoming more popular—than line engraving, but the possibility of producing a printing plate by means of photography, without the intervention of the engraver, was eagerly pursued. Koehler assembled more than three hundred examples to show three decades of experi-

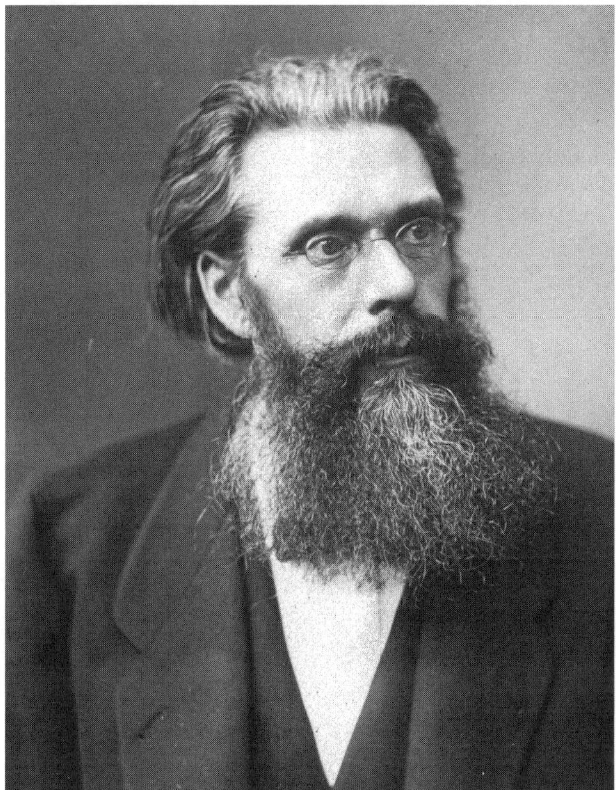

Fig. 6.20 John Walter Osborne Julius Ulke. Photograph. 1874. 4 × 2.5 in (10 × 6.5 cm). Graphic Arts Collection, National Museum of American History, Smithsonian Institution. SI neg 10626.

mentation in Europe and America to achieve photomechanical solutions in relief, intaglio, lithography, and collotype.

A number of the photomechanical prints came from the collection of John Walter Osborne (1828–1902) (fig. 6.20), donated to the Smithsonian only a few months before the Cincinnati Exposition opened. These items represented photoengraving, halftone, collotype, photogravure, and—Osborne's particular specialty—photolithography. In the catalog Koehler noted that "the specimens of early work, given to the National Museum by Mr. J. W. Osborne . . . lend to the exhibition something of an historical character."[30]

Osborne's gift encompassed many of the international experiments combining photography and printing that began in the 1850s. Beyond the items shown in Cincinnati, the collection included another one thousand specimens Osborne had acquired from nearly one hundred practitioners in Australia, England, France, Belgium, Germany, Canada, and the United States. Collectively, their contributions resulted in the explosive growth of printed pictures that created modern media. Individually, their achievements rank with some of the most beautiful aesthetic productions of the time.

Born in Ireland in 1828, Osborne moved to Australia as a young man.[31] In 1859, while employed by the surveyor general of Victoria in Melbourne, he developed and patented a photolithographic transfer method suitable for copying maps, then much in demand for land surveys and property development. For some time he had been following contemporary

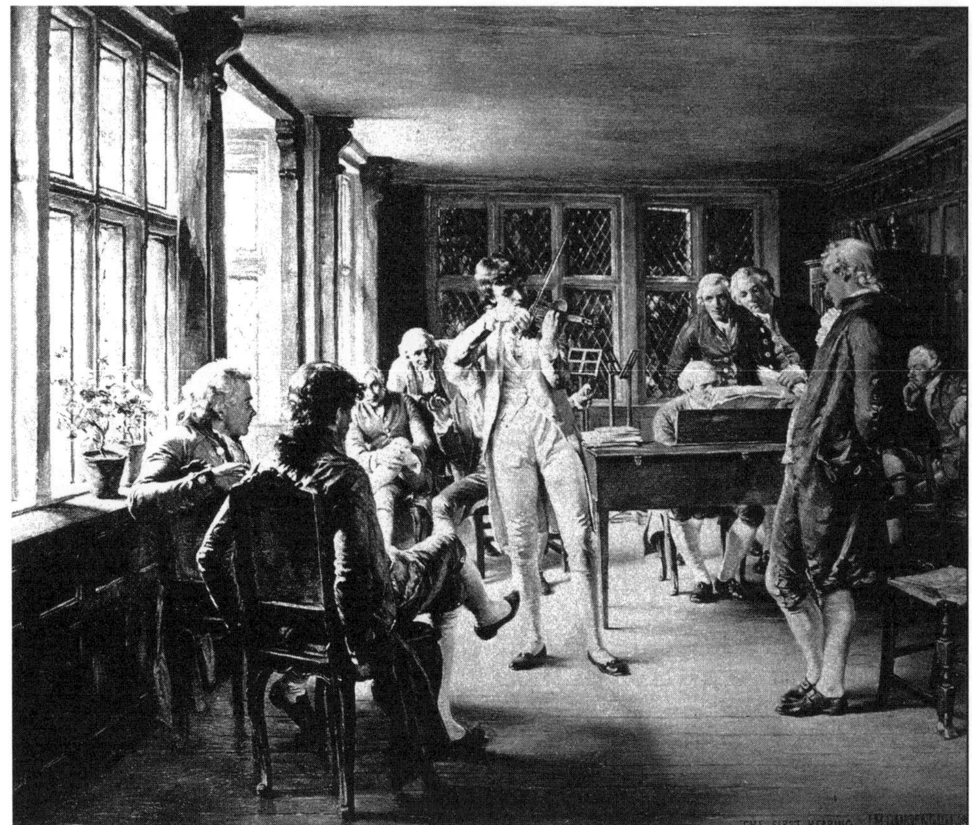

Fig. 6.21 The First Hearing
Forbes Lithographic Company, Boston, after I. M. Gaugengigl. Collotype. 1887. 7 × 8 in (17.5 × 20.5 cm) (image). Graphic Arts Collection, National Museum of American History, Smithsonian Institution. SI neg 99–4224.

discoveries in applying photographic science to the graphic arts, and in 1862 he took a leave of absence, traveling to Britain, where he visited the Crystal Palace Exhibition. He contacted Henry Fox Talbot and acquired examples of Talbot's photogravures, as well as works by other experimenters, that were shown at Cincinnati in 1888. Osborne came to the United States in 1864. He organized the American Photo-Lithographic Company in Brooklyn, New York, and later lived in Washington, D.C., where he seems to have served as a consultant for a number of government printing operations.[32]

Osborne's collection offered a rare contemporaneous assessment of a technology in the making. Its research value was recognized by Koehler, who noted that "already myths and false statements" cloud the beginnings of photomechanical work. "The difficulty of clearing it up and of illustrating [it] with authentic specimens grows from year to year."[33] Koehler's didactic purpose in presenting the history of photomechanics at Cincinnati is clear, and visitors to the exhibition must have absorbed a great deal of information about the rapidly changing images in their pictorial world.

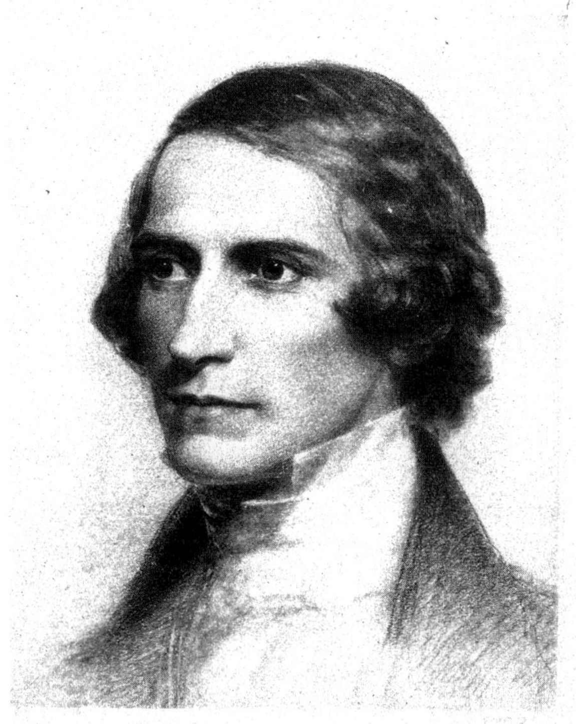

Fig. 6.22 Ephraim Peabody
Heliotype Printing Co. after Seth Cheney. Collotype. N.d. 3.25 × 2.5 in (8.5 × 6.5 cm) (image). Graphic Arts Collection, National Museum of American History, Smithsonian Institution. SI neg 99-4211.

Bostonian L. H. Bradford, one of the American pioneers of photolithography, was represented by several specimens.[34] The work of other Boston firms included Albertypes by the Forbes Lithographic Company (fig. 6.21), Heliotypes by James R. Osgood's Heliotype Printing Company (fig. 6.22), and Phototypes by the Boston Photogravure Company, all proprietary forms of collotype or gelatine printing, as were the Artotypes of Edward Bierstadt's New York firm. The examples showed how superbly the process presented portraits or objects directly from nature as well as reproductions from engravings and paintings.

Intaglio processes shown included the early photogravure efforts of Talbot, Pretsch, and Niepce de St. Victor, and work by Goupil of Paris, a publisher known for decades in the United States for its high-quality reproductions of paintings produced by the more traditional methods of engraving and lithography. Gebbie & Husson of Philadelphia (fig. 6.23) and the Photogravure Company of New York also were represented. Photomechanical relief methods in the exhibition included both line work and several experiments with halftone by the Moss Engraving Company, the Photo-Engraving Company (fig. 6.24), the Canadian Leggo Brothers, William Kurtz, and Frederic Ives, plus a number of other European and American firms.

The remaining two sections of the exhibition were divided equally between the American wood engravings and the American etchings, with about 250 examples of each process shown. Koehler's professional contacts and his publishing career had involved him in two important contemporary graphic movements: the etching revival and the "new school" of

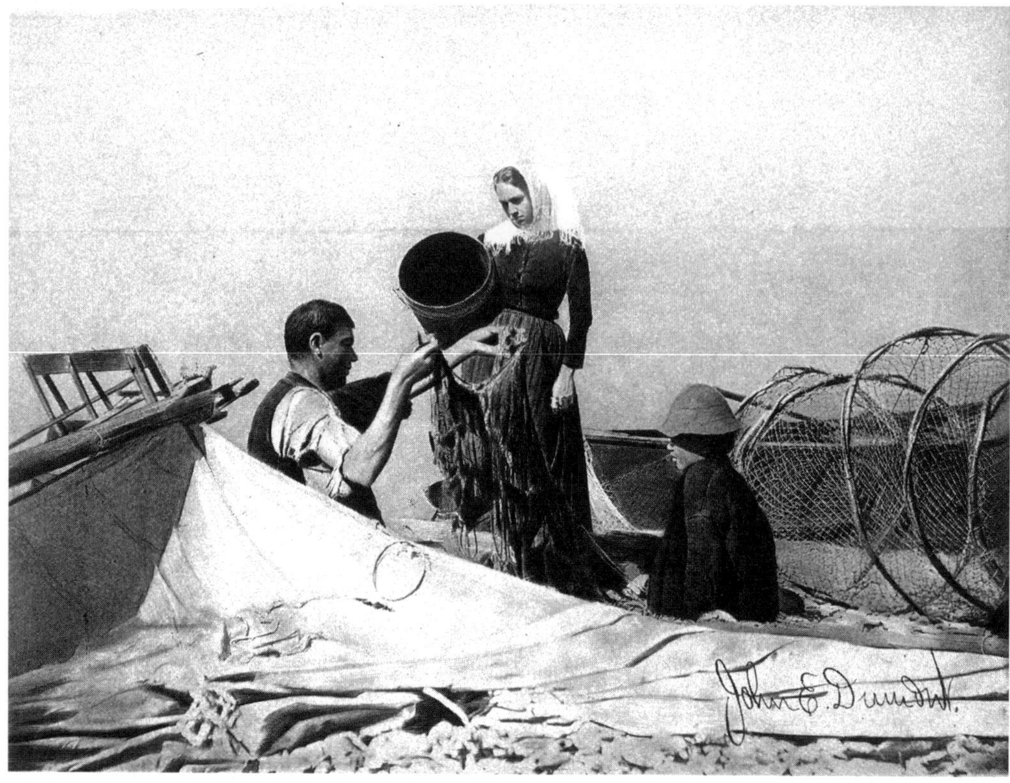

Fig. 6.23 Mending the Nets
Photogravure by the Gebbie & Husson Company Ltd. Philadelphia. From a Negative by John E. Dumont, Rochester, New York. Ca. 1885. 6.25 × 7.5 in (16 × 19 cm) (plate). Graphic Arts Collection, National Museum of American History, Smithsonian Institution. SI neg 99–4233.

wood engraving. Calling upon his colleagues in this active network, he persuaded artists and publishers to donate works to the National Museum and, for those not quite ready to give, to lend material for his exhibitions. Koehler served simultaneously as curator of prints for the U.S. National Museum and for Boston's Museum of Fine Arts, receiving his Boston appointment early in 1887, a few months after his Smithsonian position was established in December 1886. Commuting by train up and down the East Coast, he had the opportunity to cultivate collectors and artists in New York and Philadelphia as well as Washington and Boston, and he solicited important gifts and loans from these contacts.

The wood engraving section of the Cincinnati exhibit drew upon Koehler's knowledge of the process and its practitioners. Representing the importance of wood engraving in nineteenth-century visual culture, major collections of preliminary drawings, engraved wood blocks, and finished prints were acquired from publishers and from individual artists. Koehler gave a retrospective cast to the exhibition, beginning with the work of Dr. Alexander Anderson (1775–1870), the physician who has been called the father of wood engraving in America, even though as noted in the catalog, wood engraving was practiced here before Anderson's time.[35]

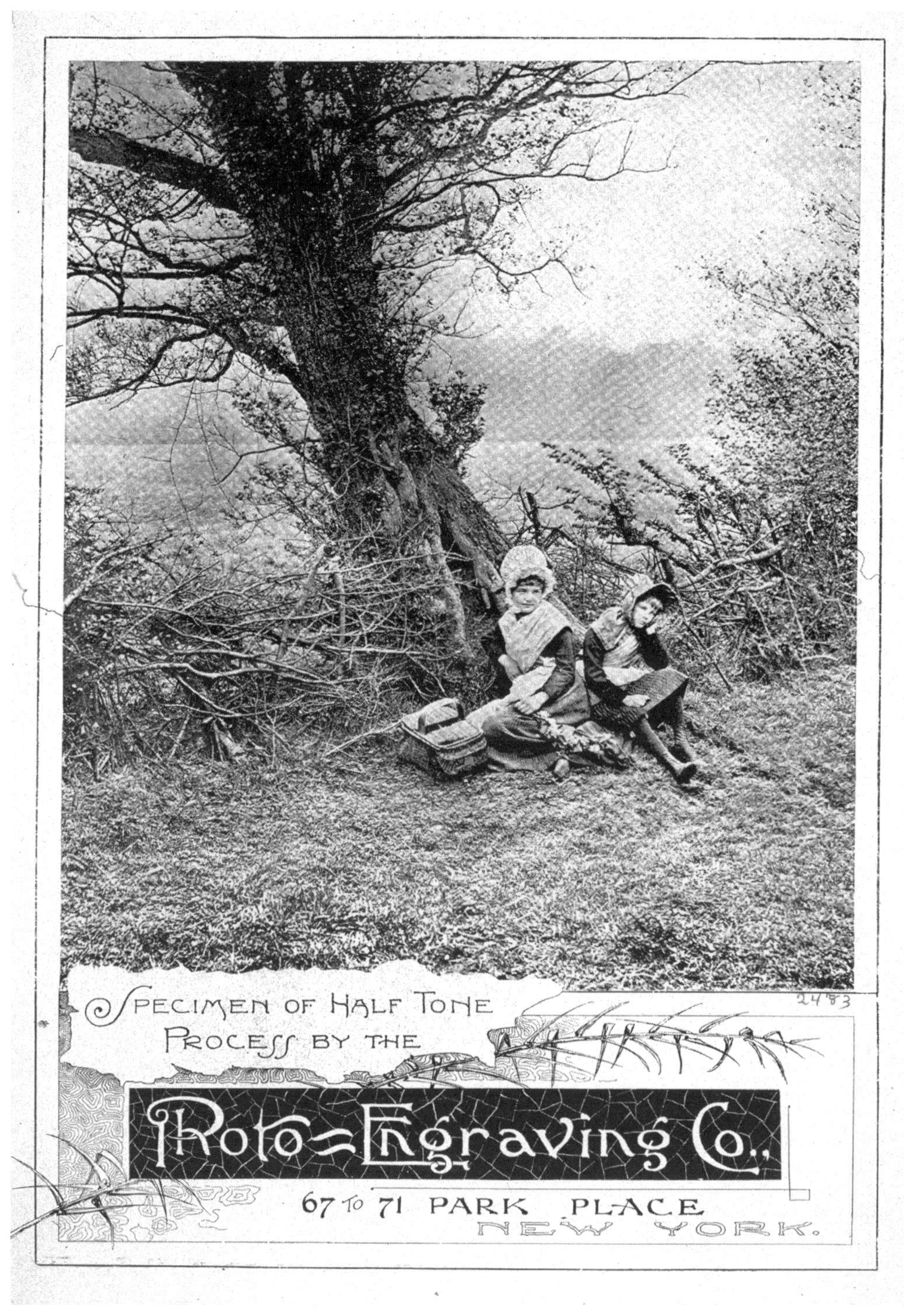

Fig. 6.24 Specimen of Half Tone / Process by the / Photo-Engraving Co.
Photo Engraving Co. From a photograph. Photomechanical halftone. Ca. 1885. 9 × 6 in (22.5 × 15 cm) (image). Graphic Arts Collection, National Museum of American History, Smithsonian Institution. SI neg 99–4221.

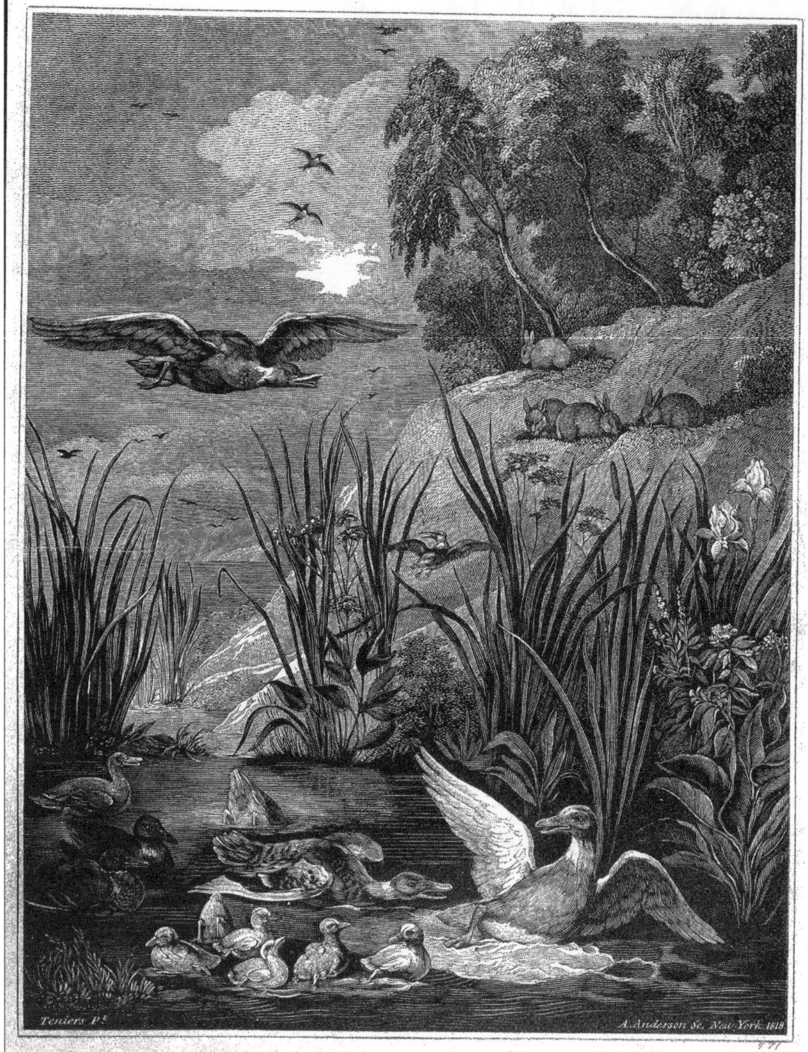

Fig. 6.25 Waterfowl
Alexander Anderson, after Teniers. Wood engraving. 1818. 11.75 × 9 in (30 × 22.5 cm) (image). Graphic Arts Collection, National Museum of American History, Smithsonian Institution. SI neg 79–14346.

The early nineteenth-century work exhibited included Anderson's *Waterfowl* after Teniers (fig. 6.25), engraved in 1818, and half a dozen of his pieces for the American Tract Society. Illustrations from other improving publications, *Harper's Illuminated Bible* (1843) and *Women of the Bible* (1868), by popular wood engravers such as John Andrew, J. W. Orr, Henry W. Herrick, and E. J. and J. H. E. Whitney, maintained a decorous tone.

Engravers of the new school marked what Koehler regarded as a new path, "attracting the attention, if not always the universal praise, of the world" for American efforts.[36] About ten of W. J. Linton's wood engravings were featured (fig. 6.26), along with half a dozen each

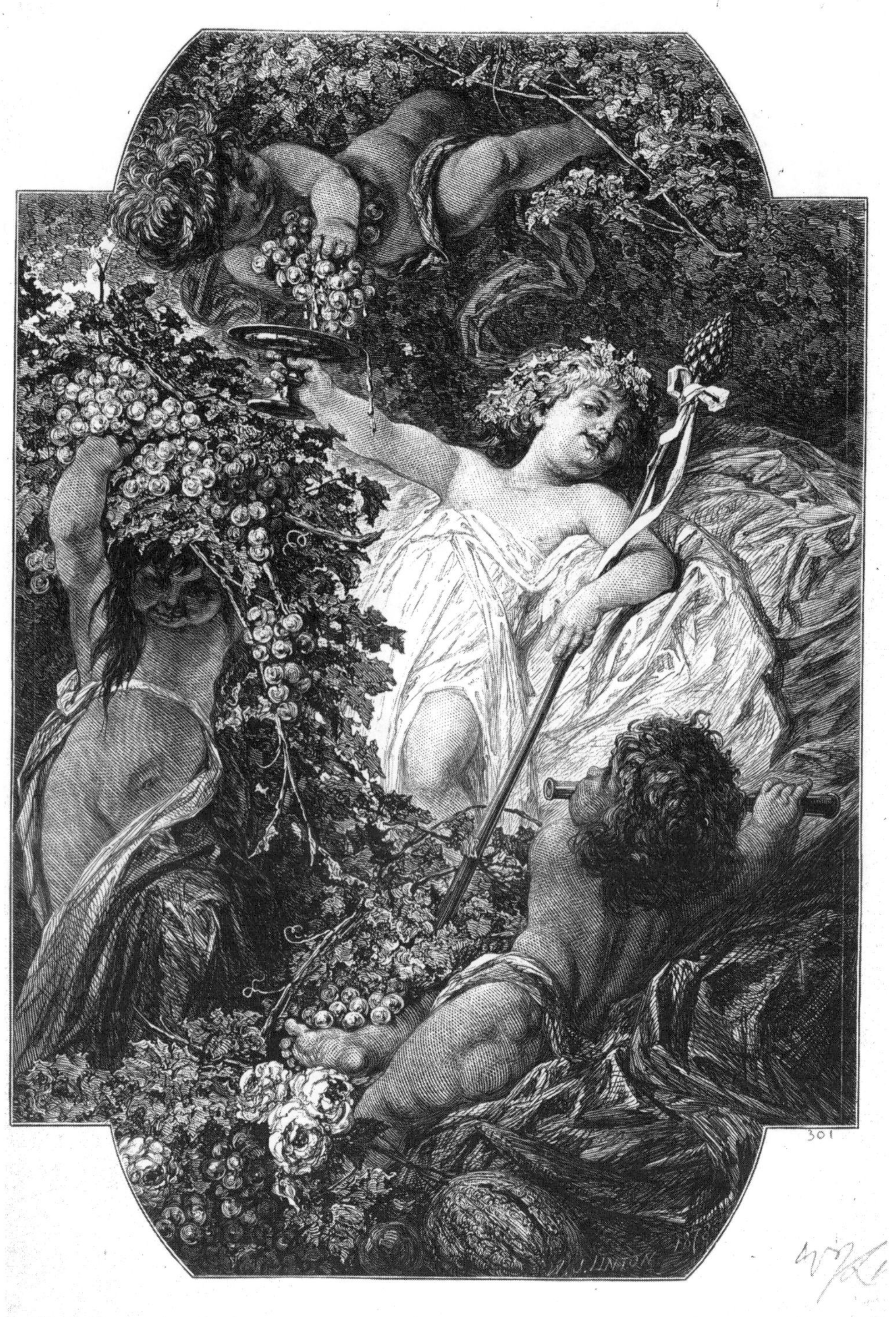

Fig. 6.26 The God of Wine
W. J. Linton, after F. Barth. Wood engraving. 1878. 9.25 × 6.25 in (23.5 × 16 cm) (image). Graphic Arts Collection, National Museum of American History, Smithsonian Institution. SI neg 99–4212.

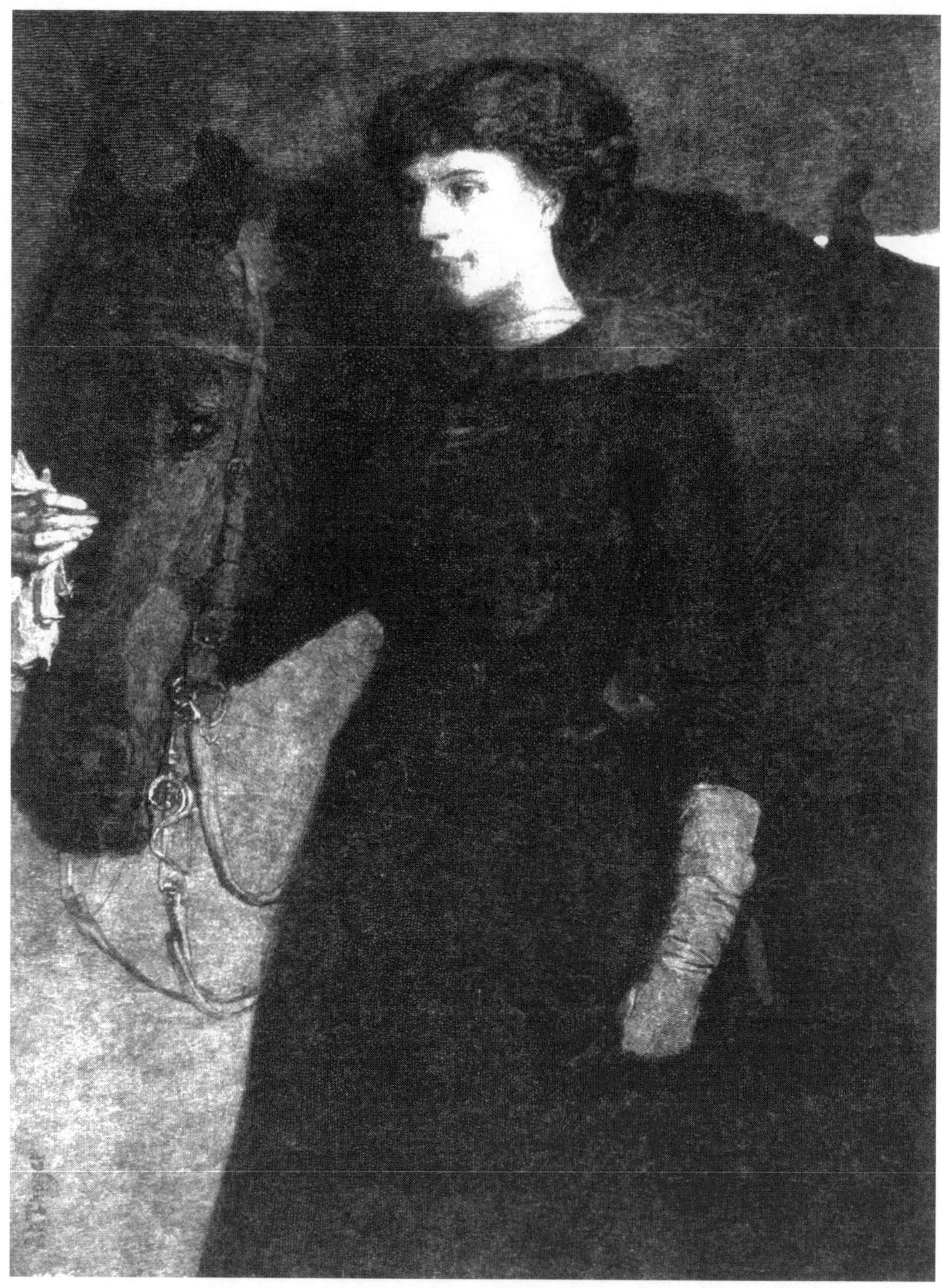

Fig. 6.27 Lady & Horse
Caroline Amelia Powell, after A. H. Thayer. Wood engraving. 1887. 9.125 × 6.75 in (23 × 17 cm) (image). Graphic Arts Collection, National Museum of American History, Smithsonian Institution. SI neg 94–13531.

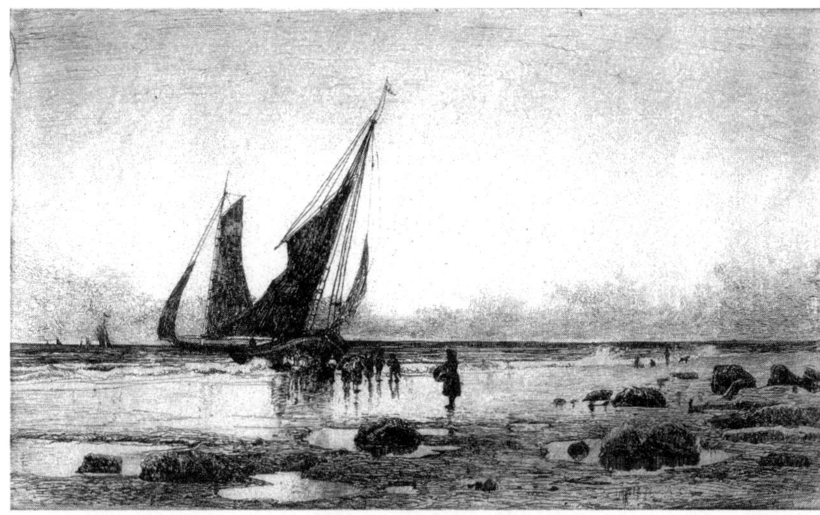

Fig. 6.28 Long Beach, York Harbor, Maine Emily Kelley Moran. Etching. 1883. 7.5 × 12 in (19 × 30.5 cm) (plate). Graphic Arts Collection, National Museum of American History, Smithsonian Institution. SI neg 94-13547.

by William B. Closson and Timothy Cole. The more commercial side of the business was represented by proofs borrowed from "the two leading magazines, *The Century* and *Harper's Monthly*," as well as from individual engravers and firms like Russell and Richardson of Boston. Individual proofs from *Engravings on Wood*, the special portfolio published by Harper's from members of the Society of American Wood Engravers, included works by a dozen men and the first woman member of the Society, Caroline Amelia Powell (fig. 6.27).

Prints by women artists also were featured in the section of the exhibition devoted to etching in the United States. Koehler championed artists who etched, and he had organized the first American exhibition devoted exclusively to women's artwork, *Women Etchers of America*, at the Boston Museum of Fine Arts in 1887. He included some fifty etchings by women at Cincinnati in 1888, one-fifth of the total 250 etchings shown. Most of them were borrowed from the artists, but he later added women's prints to the collections he curated in Washington and Boston. Koehler had introduced both etching and women printmakers to American audiences through his work as editor of the *American Art Review* between 1879 and 1881, and in his other publications that included original etchings.[37]

For the Cincinnati exhibition, Koehler borrowed eight etchings by Mary Cassatt from New York dealer-collector Samuel Putnam Avery, and he also tapped Cincinnati women etchers Mary Louise McLaughlin and Martha Scudder Twachtman for their work. McLaughlin had shown a portrait etching in the 1880 Cincinnati exhibition.[38] Unfortunately, neither the loan files nor the catalog entries identify these prints by name; we have only the artists' names and the number of their works exhibited, and most of the prints went back to the artists rather than entering the Smithsonian collection. Some women, like Philadelphians Emily Kelley Moran and Anna Lea Merritt, showed only a few images in any exhibitions, so we can be pretty confident that Moran's *Long Beach, York Harbor, Maine* (fig. 6.28) and Merritt's *Ophelia* (see fig. 6.10) would have been included. All of the women Koehler chose for Cincinnati had exhibited in the two shows held in Boston

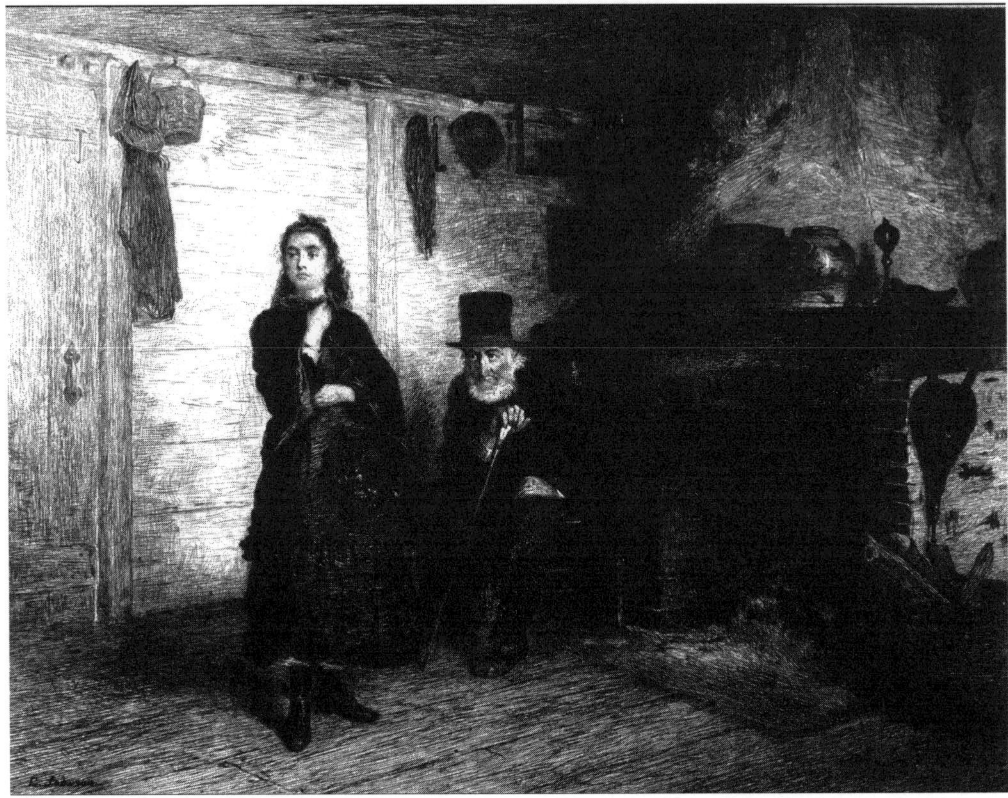

Fig. 6.29 The Reprimand
Walter Shirlaw after Eastman Johnson. Etching. Ca. 1880. 13 × 16 in (33 × 40.5 cm) (plate). Graphic Arts Collection, National Museum of American History, Smithsonian Institution. SI neg 99–4226.

and New York in 1887–88, reassembled so beautifully in Phyllis Peet's 1988 traveling exhibition, *American Women of the Etching Revival.*[39]

Nearly two hundred etchings by American men surrounded the screens holding the women's prints. Works by John Gadsby Chapman and George L. Brown, executed in Rome during the 1850s, opened the section, followed by dozens of examples from the male artists Koehler also had promoted in the *American Art Review* and his other works on etching. Among them were Samuel Colman, Henry Farrer, Stephen J. Ferris, R. Swain Gifford, Peter and Thomas Moran, J. C. Nicoll, and Stephen Parrish. Koehler featured Whistler's work, dating from 1859 and later, together with the younger artists whom he influenced, some with Cincinnati connections like Otto H. Bacher and Frank Duveneck. Reproductive etchings like Walter Shirlaw's *The Reprimand* after Eastman Johnson (fig. 6.29) were included alongside the original works, as a number of the etchers produced both types of prints.

In Koehler's interpretation for the Cincinnati exhibition, he identified etching as "specifically a painter's art," and he discriminated between the intentions of original work and smaller reproductive plates made early in the revival as inherently different from "the large plates of a more commercial character which have appeared lately."[40] He regarded American etching's popularity as a recent phenomenon he dated to the founding of the New York Etching Club in 1877 and the publication of his own *American Art Review* in 1879, and he linked it to the increase in the popular interest and acceptance of art. Even while he applauded this interest and encouraged its growth, however, in hindsight we must recognize that he was contributing to the rise of the cult of the original print and the decline of a more democratic and comprehensive regard for printed images. Koehler presented all four sections of his exhibition equally in 1888, but society's unqualified response to pictorial sources of any kind was nearing an end. The rapid rise of quickly produced but coarser forms of reproduction resulted in a hierarchical snobbery dividing images into categories of fine art, commercial art, and mass media. In the twentieth century, prints became ever more strictly demarcated as either artistic or commercial, with little understanding of the effort involved in reproductive engraving or its creative function as a translation to black and white of a painting's tonal range. Media that once had been accorded significant cultural and educational value went out of fashion. Didactic, inclusive exhibitions like the Cincinnati Fair of 1888 continued to be produced for a few more years, but art and illustration ultimately went their separate ways.

As the culmination of Cincinnati's industrial exposition program, the 1888 exhibit celebrated Cincinnati's centennial with participation by three cities, fifteen states, the federal government, and five foreign countries.[41] The Smithsonian exhibition of prints comprised a retrospective that was something of a watershed, looking backward to the beginning of printmaking in Europe and in America as well as forward to a new understanding of the parameters of art. Etchings and other original prints would take pride of place in a new century, even as popular imagery exploded into the mass media brought about by the photomechanical revolution. Visitors to the Smithsonian's exhibition in Cincinnati saw both together in 1888, the new visual world building on the graphic art of the past.

Notes

1. S. R. Koehler, *Etching: An Outline of Its Technical Processes and Its History, with Some Remarks on Collections and Collecting* (New York and London: Cassell & Co., 1885), p. 191.

2. Smithsonian Institution (SI), *Annual Report of the Board of Regents of the Smithsonian Institution for the Year 1850* (Washington, D.C.: Smithsonian Institution, 1851), p. 30.

3. Catharine Beecher and Harriet Beecher Stowe, *The American Woman's Home* (1869; reprint, Hartford, Conn.: Stowe-Day Foundation, 1975), p. 94. The Beecher sisters organized and taught at Cincinnati's Western Female Institute during the 1830s and 1840s; their father, Lyman Beecher, headed the Lane Theological Seminary there between 1832 and 1851. I am grateful to Philip Spiess for pointing out this connection.

4. SI, *Annual Report for 1850*, p. 29.

5. Goode's ideas about museum collections and exhibitions are elaborated in his essays. See Sally Gregory Kohlstedt, ed., *The Origins of Natural Science in America: The Essays of George Brown Goode* (Washington: Smithsonian Institution Press, 1992).

6. Philip D. Spiess II, "Exhibitions and Expositions in Nineteenth-century Cincinnati," *Cincinnati Historical Society Bulletin* 28, no. 3 (fall 1970): 171–73.

7. *Exhibition of Paintings, Engravings, Drawings, Aquarelles and Works of Household Art in the Cincinnati Industrial Exposition* (Cincinnati: Robert Clarke & Co., 1875). Copy in the Western Reserve Historical Society, Cleveland, and in the Cincinnati Art Museum (CAM).

8. *Catalogue of Paintings, Engravings, Sculpture, and Household Art in the Seventh Cincinnati Industrial Exposition, 1879* (Cincinnati: Press of R. Clarke & Co., 1879), p. 52. I am most grateful to Kristin L. Spangenberg, Curator of Prints, Drawings, and Photographs at the Cincinnati Art Museum, for her generous assistance in providing copies of several of these important catalogs.

9. Catherine Stover, "James L. Claghorn, Philadelphia Collector," *Archives of American Art Journal* 27, no. 4 (1987): 6, including quote from the *New York Herald Tribune*, April 9, 1877.

10. Stover, "James A. Claghorn," p. 6.

11. William J. Clark Jr., "Critical Notices," in *Exhibition of Prints (Claghorn Collection) under the Auspices of the Pennsylvania Academy of the Fine Arts* (Philadelphia, 1875), p. 14.

12. Stover, "James A. Claghorn," p. 7; see also Clark, "Critical Notices."

13. Cincinnati Exposition print catalog, 1875, p. 20.

14. Spiess, "Exhibitions and Expositions," p. 181.

15. Clark, "Critical Notices," p. 15.

16. Authors cited in the 1872 and 1873 Cincinnati Exposition print catalogs include G. K. Nagler's dictionaries of artists; Shearjashub Spooner's works on painters, engravers, sculptors, and architects; Louis Thies's catalog of Harvard's Gray Collection of Engravings, published in 1869; and Mrs. Jameson's commentaries on European painting.

17. Cincinnati Exposition print catalog, 1875.

18. Probably Thomas Roscoe's English translation of Luigi Lanzi, *History of Painting in Italy* (London: H. G. Bohn, 1847 and other editions). See *Official Catalogue of the Works of Painting, Sculpture, and Engraving Exhibited in the Art Department, 1872* (Cincinnati: Wrightson and Co., 1872), p. 28. Copy in CAM.

19. Joseph E. Holliday, "Collector's Choice of the Gilded Age," *Cincinnati Historical Society Bulletin* 28, no. 4 (1970): 310. The Davis and Karrmann collections are mentioned in J. R. W. Hitchcock, *Etching in America* (New York: White, Stokes, & Allen, 1886), pp. 52, 94–95, and with other local print collectors in James W. Dawson, *Picturesque Cincinnati* (Cincinnati: The John Shillito Company, 1883), pp. 10–11. I am most grateful to Philip Spiess for his help with Cincinnati references.

20. On the young Mary Cassatt's study of Claghorn's Toschi engravings, see Andrew J. Walker, "Mary Cassatt's Modern Education: The United States, France, Italy, and Spain, 1860–73," in *Mary Cassatt, Modern Woman* (Chicago: Art Institute with Harry N. Abrams, 1998), pp. 24–28. Walker clearly understands the importance of engraved copies for aspiring artists, especially in the United States.

21. *Catalogue of the Art Department of the Eighth Cincinnati Industrial Exposition* (Cincinnati: Press of Robert Clarke & Co., 1880). Copy in CAM. For the McLaughlin references, see pp. 63, 65, and 71.

22. On the Cincinnati Etching Club, see Henry Russell Wray, *A Review of Etching in the United States* (Philadelphia: Penfield, 1893), pp. 80–81.

23. Correspondence between Koehler and Goode indicates that the catalog was not published until after the exhibition closed, and there were difficulties in getting Koehler's text labels printed for the specimens on view. See Smithsonian Institution Archives, Record Unit 70, Box 27, Folder 7. A useful description of all the SI materials related to the 1888 Cincinnati Exposition is contained in the SI Archives Guide to Collections 12: *Exposition Records of the SI and the U.S. National Museum, 1867–1939*, by Joan Brownell, edited by James A. Steed (Washington, D.C.: Archives and Special Collections of the Smithsonian Institution, 1991), pp. 28–32.

24. S. R. Koehler, "Catalogue of the Contributions of the Section of Graphic Arts to the Ohio Valley Centennial Exposition, Cincinnati, 1888," *Proceedings of the U.S. National Museum*, 10 (Washington, D.C.: Smithsonian Institution, 1888): 704.

25. Koehler, *Etching*, p. 186.

26. Koehler, SI Cincinnati catalog, 1888, p. 708.

27. S. R. Koehler, "Report on the Section of Graphic Arts in the U.S. National Museum, 1889," in Smithsonian Institution, *Annual Report of the Board of Regents of the Smithsonian Institution for the Year Ending June 30, 1889. Report of the National Museum* (Washington, D.C.: Smithsonian Institution, 1891), pp. 302–3; for the Jones loan, see 1872 and 1873 Cincinnati Exposition print catalogs.

28. Koehler, SI Cincinnati catalog, 1888.

29. On Smillie's engraving, see Helena E. Wright, "Bierstadt and the Business of Printmaking," in *Albert Bierstadt: Art & Enterprise* (New York: Hudson Hills Press, 1990), pp. 272–73; and Brucia Witthoft, "The History of James Smillie's Engraving after Albert Bierstadt's *Rocky Mountains*," *American Art Journal* 19 (1987): 40–51.

30. Koehler, SI Cincinnati catalog, 1888, p. 725.

31. For details of his early life, see "Osborne, John Walter," *Australian Dictionary of Biography*, 5:375–76.

32. This chronology of Osborne's travels is drawn from his letter to G. Brown Goode, June 6, 1888, accompanying his gift (SI Accession File 23,199), and from his remarks in the *British Journal of Photography* 9, no. 176 (October 15, 1862): 387–89; and 9, no. 178 (November 15, 1862): 425–26.

33. S. R. Koehler to G. Brown Goode, October 1, 1891, Smithsonian Institution Archives, Division of Graphic Arts files, Record Unit 70, Box 39. Koehler urged the publication of a catalog of photomechanical examples, a goal he realized in 1892. See S. R. Koehler, *Exhibition Illustrating the Technical Methods of the Reproductive Arts from the XV Century to the Present Time, with Special Reference to the Photo-Mechanical Processes, January 8 to March 6, 1892* (Boston: Museum of Fine Arts, 1892). For this Boston exhibition, Koehler borrowed much of the photomechanical work from the U.S. National Museum, the majority of which came from the Osborne Collection.

34. See David Tatham, "The Photolithographs of L. H. Bradford," in James O'Gorman, ed., *Aspects of American Printmaking, 1800–1950* (Syracuse: Syracuse University Press, 1988), pp. 105–40, the publication of the Seventeenth North American Print Conference held in Boston in 1985.

35. Koehler, SI Cincinnati catalog, 1888, p. 718.

36. Ibid., p. 719.

37. See Clifford Ackley, "Sylvester Rosa Koehler and the American Etching Revival," *Art & Commerce: American Prints of the Nineteenth Century* (Boston: Museum of Fine Arts with University of Virginia Press, 1978), pp. 143–50, the publication of the Sixth North American Print Conference held in Boston in 1975.

38. Cincinnati Exposition print catalog, 1880, p. 65.

39. See Phyllis Peet, *American Women of the Etching Revival* (Atlanta: High Museum of Art, 1988).

40. Koehler, SI Cincinnati catalog, 1888, p. 721.

41. Spiess, "Exhibitions and Expositions," p. 186.

References

Ackley, Clifford. "Sylvester Rosa Koehler and the American Etching Revival." In *Art & Commerce: American Prints of the Nineteenth Century*, pp. 143–50. Boston: Museum of Fine Arts, 1978.

Australian Dictionary of Biography. Melbourne: Melbourne University Press, 1966–.

Beecher, Catharine, and Harriet Beecher Stowe. *The American Woman's Home*. 1869. Hartford, Conn.: Stowe-Day Foundation, 1975.

Brownell, Joan. *Guide to the Exposition Records of the Smithsonian Institution and the United States National Museum, 1867–1939.* Edited by James A. Steed. Washington, D.C.: Archives and Special Collections of the Smithsonian Institution, 1991.

Cincinnati Industrial Exposition. *Catalogue of the Art Department of the Eighth Cincinnati Industrial Exposition.* Cincinnati: Press of Robert Clarke & Co., 1880.

———. *Catalogue of Paintings, Engravings, Sculpture, and Household Art in the Seventh Cincinnati Industrial Exposition, 1879.* Cincinnati: Press of R. Clarke & Co., 1879.

———. *Exhibition of Paintings, Engravings, Drawings, Aquarelles, and Works of Household Art in the Cincinnati Industrial Exposition.* Cincinnati, 1873.

———. *Exhibition of Paintings, Engravings, Drawings, Aquarelles and Works of Household Art in the Cincinnati Industrial Exposition, 1875.* Cincinnati: Robert Clarke & Co., 1875.

———. *Official Catalogue of the Works of Painting, Sculpture and Engraving Exhibited in the Art Department.* Cincinnati: Wrightson and Co., 1872.

Clark, William, Jr. "Critical Notices," in William Spohn Baker. *Exhibition of Prints (Claghorn Collection) under the Auspices of the Pennsylvania Academy of the Fine Arts.* Philadelphia: Rue & Jones, 1875.

Dawson, James W. *Picturesque Cincinnati.* Cincinnati: John Shillito Company, 1883.

Hitchcock, J. R. W. *Etching in America, with Lists of American Etchers and Notable Collections of Prints.* New York: White, Stokes, & Allen, 1886.

Holliday, Joseph E. "Collector's Choice of the Gilded Age." *Cincinnati Historical Society Bulletin* 28, no. 4 (1970): 295–315.

Koehler, S. R. "Catalogue of the Contributions of the Section of Graphic Arts to the Ohio Valley Centennial Exposition, Cincinnati, 1888." *Proceedings of the U.S. National Museum* 10 (1888): 701–31.

———. *Etching. An Outline of Its Technical Processes and Its History, With Some Remarks on Collections and Collecting.* New York and London: Cassell & Co., Ltd., 1885.

———. *Exhibition Illustrating the Technical Methods of the Reproductive Arts from the XV Century to the Present Time, with Special Reference to the Photo-Mechanical Processes. January 8 to March 6, 1892.* Boston: Museum of Fine Arts, 1892.

———. "Report on the Section of Graphic Arts in the U.S. National Museum, 1889." *Annual Report of the Board of Regents of the Smithsonian Institution for the Year Ending June 30, 1889. Report of the National Museum*, pp. 301–15. Washington, D.C.: Smithsonian Institution, 1891.

Kohlstedt, Sally Gregory, ed. *The Origins of Natural Science in America: The Essays of George Brown Goode.* Washington, D.C.: Smithsonian Institution Press, 1992.

Lanzi, Luigi Antonio. *The History of Painting in Italy, from the Period of the Revival of the Fine Arts to the End of the Eighteenth Century.* Translated by Thomas Roscoe. London: H. G. Bohn, 1847.

Nagler, Georg Kaspar. *Die Monogrammisten und diejenigen bekannten und unbekannten Künstler aller Schulen . . . .* 5 vols. München: G. Franz, 1858–79.

Osborne, John Walter. [Remarks]. *British Journal of Photography* 9, no. 176 (October 15, 1862): 387–89, and 9, no. 178 (November 15, 1862): 425–26.

Peet, Phyllis. *American Women of the Etching Revival.* Atlanta: High Museum of Art, 1988.

Smithsonian Institution. *Annual Report of the Board of Regents of the Smithsonian Institution for the Year 1850.* Washington, D.C.: Smithsonian Institution, 1851.

Spiess, Philip D., II. "Exhibitions and Expositions in Nineteenth-Century Cincinnati." *Cincinnati Historical Society Bulletin* 28, no. 3 (fall 1970): 171–92.

Stover, Catherine. "James A. Claghorn, Philadelphia Collector." *Archives of American Art Journal* 27, no. 4 (1987): 4–8.

Tatham, David. "The Photolithographs of L. H. Bradford." In *Aspects of American Printmaking, 1800–1950*, ed. James O'Gorman, pp. 105–40. Syracuse: Syracuse University Press, 1988.

Thies, Louis, comp. *Catalogue of the Collection of Engravings Bequeathed to Harvard College by Francis Calley Gray.* Cambridge, Mass.: Welch, Bigelow, and Company, Printers to the University, 1869.

Walker, Andrew J. "Mary Cassatt's Modern Education: The United States, France, Italy, and Spain, 1860–73." In *Mary Cassatt, Modern Woman*, pp. 21–43. Chicago: Art Institute with Harry N. Abrams, 1998.

Witthoft, Brucia. "The History of James Smillie's Engraving after Albert Bierstadt's *Rocky Mountains.*" *American Art Journal* 19 (1987): 40–51.

Wray, Henry Russell. *A Review of Etching in the United States.* Philadelphia: Penfield, 1893.

Wright, Helena E. "Bierstadt and the Business of Printmaking." In *Albert Bierstadt: Art & Enterprise*, ed. Nancy K. Anderson, pp. 267–88. New York: Hudson Hills Press with the Brooklyn Museum, 1990.

Chapter Seven

Cincinnati Prints

A Checklist of Selected Materials in The Public Library of Cincinnati and Hamilton County

Judy Inwood and Sylvia V. Metzinger
The Public Library of Cincinnati and Hamilton County

In a series of exhibits in 1998 and 1999, The Public Library of Cincinnati and Hamilton County featured materials from its extensive holdings of prints in both the Rare Books and Special Collections Department and Art and Music Department. Because of the scope and depth of these holdings and the resulting exhibits, a checklist from these exhibits is offered as an introduction to this resource for researchers interested in the history of prints, Cincinnati printing, and Cincinnatiana.

Prints from two major collections of The Public Library of Cincinnati and Hamilton County have been included in this checklist. They are the Langstroth Collection and the Strobridge Collection.

Theodore Ashmead Langstroth II compiled scrapbooks of original manuscripts and printed and other materials on a multitude of topics. A large collection of these scrapbooks, along with other manuscript materials and artifacts, is among the holdings of the Art and Music Department of The Public Library of Cincinnati and Hamilton County. The collection is described in detail in John Fleishman, "The Labyrinthine World of the Scrapbook King, *Smithsonian* 22, no. 11 (1992): 78–87.

In 1960 the Strobridge Lithography Company of Cincinnati was sold and a donation of approximately 3,000 posters was divided between the Cincinnati Art Museum, the Cincinnati Historical Society, and The Public Library of Cincinnati and Hamilton County.

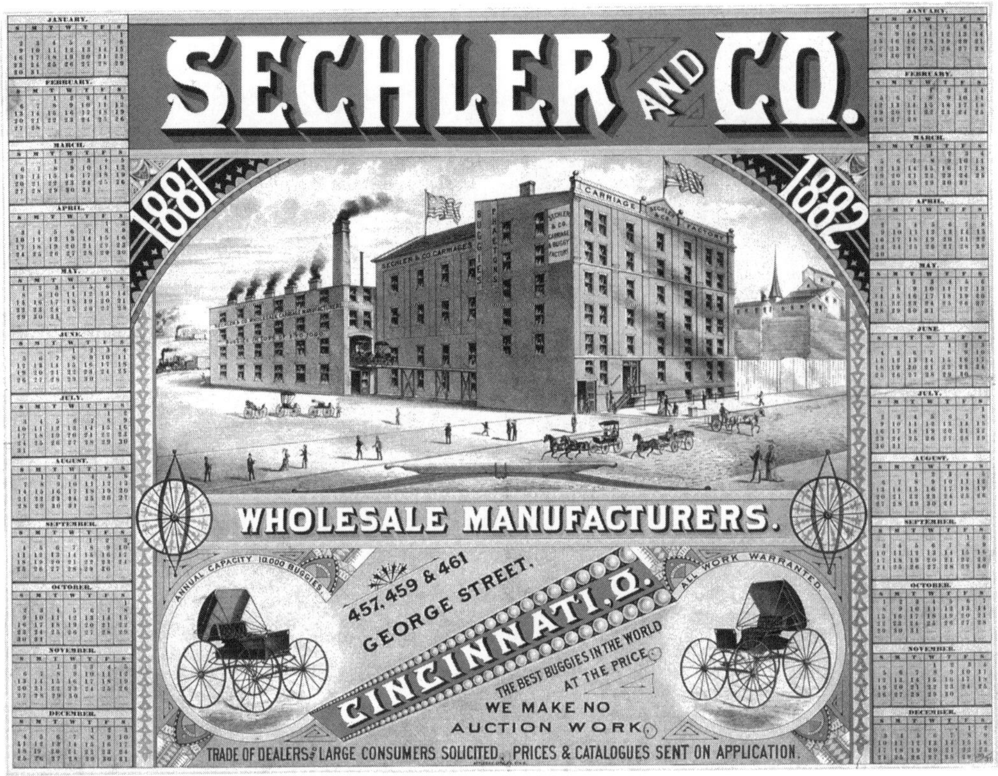

Fig. 7.1

The latter's Art and Music Department holds 1,035 posters printed in the late nineteenth and early twentieth centuries.

Attlesey Lithographing Company

[Man shot with arrows]

Lithograph. N.d. $10\frac{3}{8} \times 10\frac{5}{16}$ in (26.4 × 26.2 cm). Cincinnati, Attlesey Lith. Co. Langstroth Collection. Art and Music Department.

[Proof sheet for calendar 1881–82] Sechler and Co. / Wholesale Manufacturers. [of Buggies] / Cincinnati, O. (fig. 7.1)

Lithograph. 1881. $17\frac{3}{8} \times 22\frac{5}{16}$ in (44.1 × 56.7 cm). Cincinnati: Attlesey Lith. Co. Langstroth Collection. Art and Music Department.

[Tobacco advertisement] Chew / Monarch / Senour & Noonan / Covington, / Ky.

Lithographs: Black & white and colored. N.d. Each $14\frac{3}{16} \times 14\frac{3}{16}$ in (36 × 36 cm). Cincinnati: Attlesey Lith. & Prtg. Wks. Langstroth Collection. Art and Music Department.

[Woman on beach]

Lithograph. N.d. $10\frac{3}{16} \times 10\frac{3}{16}$ in (25.9 × 25.9 cm). Cincinnati: Attlesey Lith. Co. Langstroth Collection. Art and Music Department.

Ault and Wiborg

[Poster] (fig. 7.2)

12 × 9 in (30.5 × 22.9 cm). Poster Album. Cincinnati: Ault & Wiborg Co., [1902]. Unpaged. Rare Books and Special Collections Department.

John W. Browne

[Landscape]

Wood Cut. [1810]. Image: 2⅜ × 2⅞ in (6.0 × 7.3 cm). Sheet: 7¼ × 4½ in (18.4 × 11.4 cm). John W. Browne, *Browne's Western Calendar, or the Cincinnati Almanac* (Cincinnati: John W. Browne, [1810]). Cover—Title Page. Rare Books and Special Collections Department.

Burgheim

Map of / Cincinnati / And Suburbs / And Covington & Newport. / Bellevue, Dayton, Ludlow & Bromley, [Ky.].

Lithograph. 1884. 28 × 32½ in (71.1 × 82.6 cm). Cincinnati: M. & R. Burgheim. Rare Books and Special Collections Department.

Cincinnati Illustrated News

Supplement to the Cincinnati Illustrated News—Grand Exposition Number, August 21, 1886. / Cincinnati in 1886. / From Fountain Square, Looking North.

C. A. Fries, delineator. Engraving. 1886. Image: 22 × 40½ in (55.9 × 102.9 cm). Sheet: 32 × 44½ in (81.3 × 113.0 cm). Cincinnati: Cincinnati Illustrated News. Rare Books and Special Collections Department.

Supplement to the Cincinnati Illustrated News—Grand Holiday Number, Christmas 1886. / Cincinnati in 1886. / From Bellevue, Kentucky, Looking West.

Philip Barnard, delineator. Engraving. 1886. Image: 22 × 40½ in (55.9 × 102.9 cm). Sheet: 32 × 44½ in (81.3 × 113.0 cm). Cincinnati: Cincinnati Illustrated News. Rare Books and Special Collections Department.

Cincinnati Lithographic Company

The Cincinnati / Lithographic / Company.

Lithograph. N.d. At greatest extent: 9¼ × 12½ in (23.5 × 31.8 cm). Cincinnati: Cincinnati Lithographic Company. Langstroth Collection. Art and Music Department.

Cincinnatier Freie Presse Kompagnie

[Pigs]

Lithograph. [1896]. Image: 1.65 × 1.77 in (4.2 × 4.5 cm). Sheet: 9.96 × 6.5 in (25.3 × 16.5 cm). *Illustrierter Deutsch-Amerikanischer VolksKalendar* (Cincinnati: Cincinnatier Freie Presse Kompagnie, [1896]), p. 28. Rare Books and Special Collections Department.

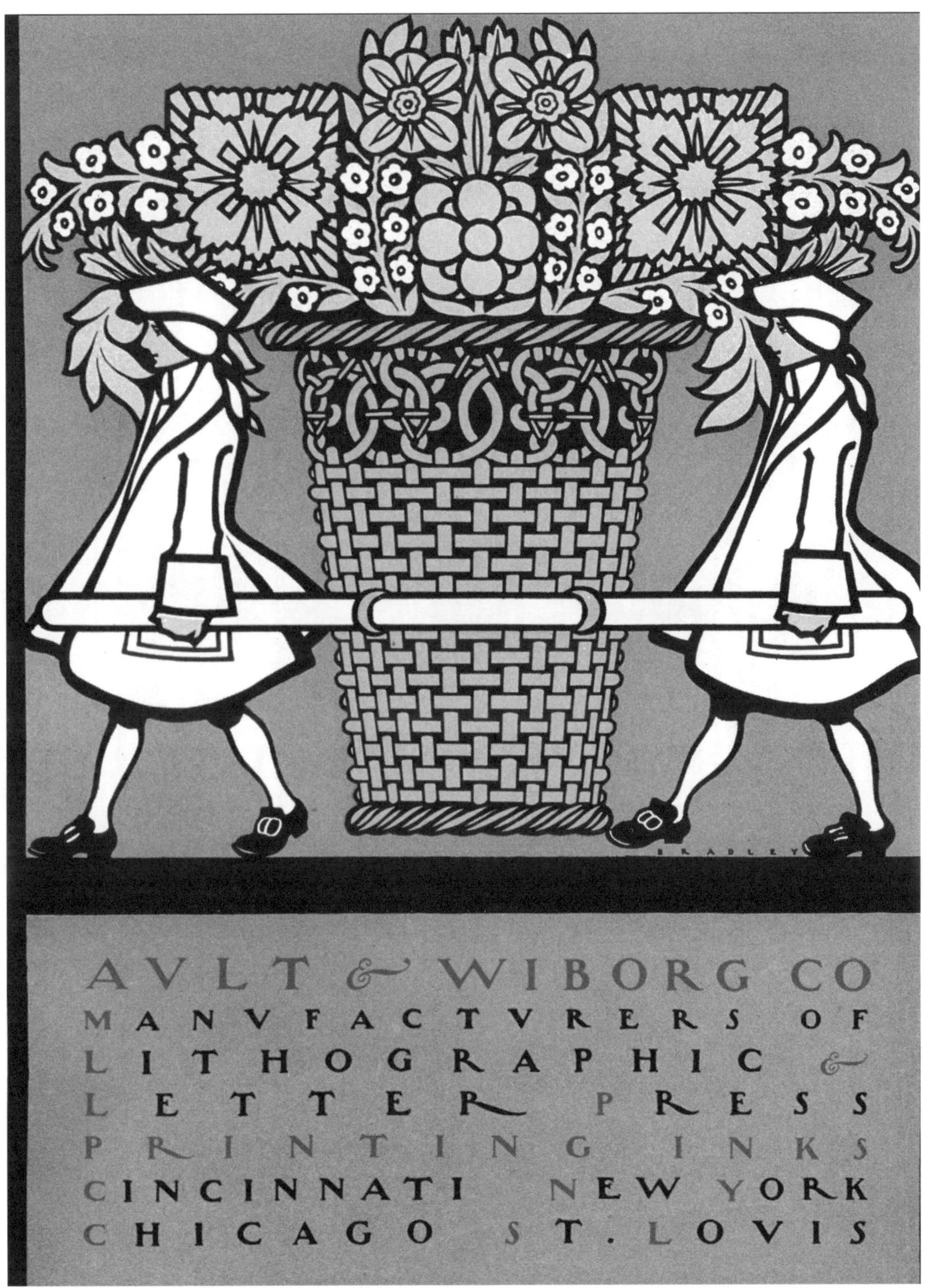
BRADLEY
AVLT & WIBORG CO
MANVFACTVRERS OF
LITHOGRAPHIC &
LETTER PRESS
PRINTING INKS
CINCINNATI NEW YORK
CHICAGO ST. LOVIS

Fig. 7.2

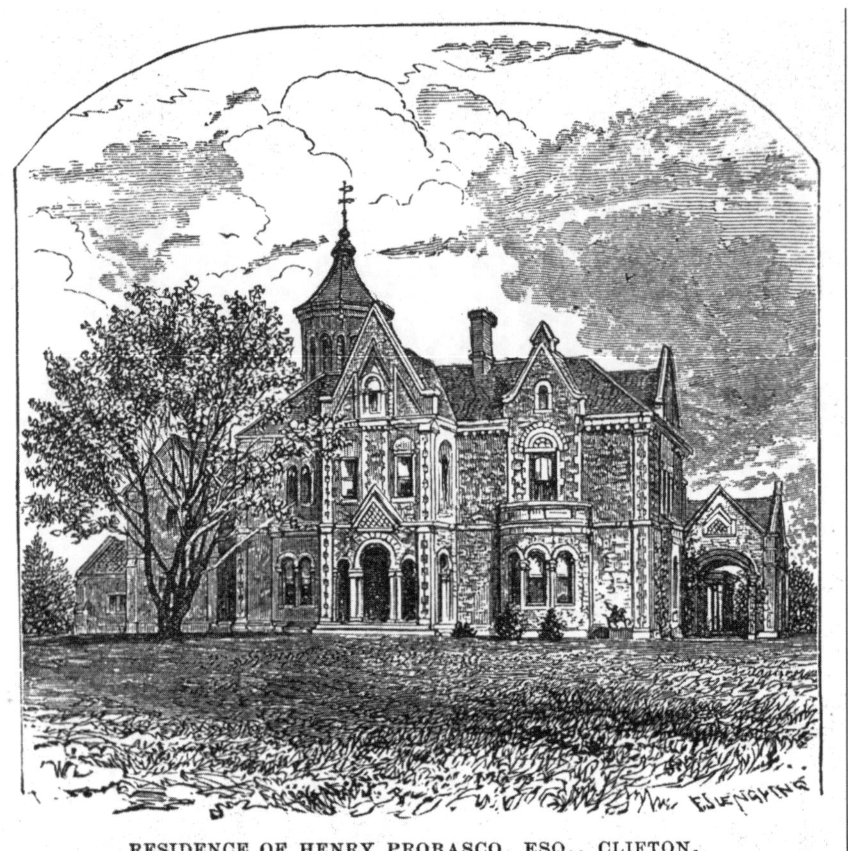

Fig. 7.3

Robert Clarke

Residence of Henry Probasco, Esq., Clifton. (fig. 7.3)

E. Juengling. Engraving. 1875. Image: 2.95 × 2.95 in (7.5 × 7.5 cm). Sheet: 11.1 × 7.72 in (28.2 × 19.6 cm). Daniel J. Kenny, *Cincinnati Illustrated: A Pictorial Guide to Cincinnati and the Suburbs . . .* (Cincinnati: Robert Clarke & Co., 1875), p. 34. Rare Books and Special Collections Department.

Donaldson

From Rags to Riches.

Lithograph. N.d. 30 × 20 in (76.2 × 50.8 cm). Newport, Ky.: The Donaldson Litho Co. Rare Books and Special Collections Department.

The Fast Mail (fig. 7.4)

Lithograph. N.d. 30 × 20 in (76.2 × 50.8 cm). Newport, Ky.: The Donaldson Litho Co. Rare Books and Special Collections Department.

[Race of the Natchez and the Rob't E. Lee]

Lithograph. N.d. 18 × 30 in (45.7 × 76.2 cm). Cincinnati: Donaldson Art Sign Co. Rare Books and Special Collections Department.

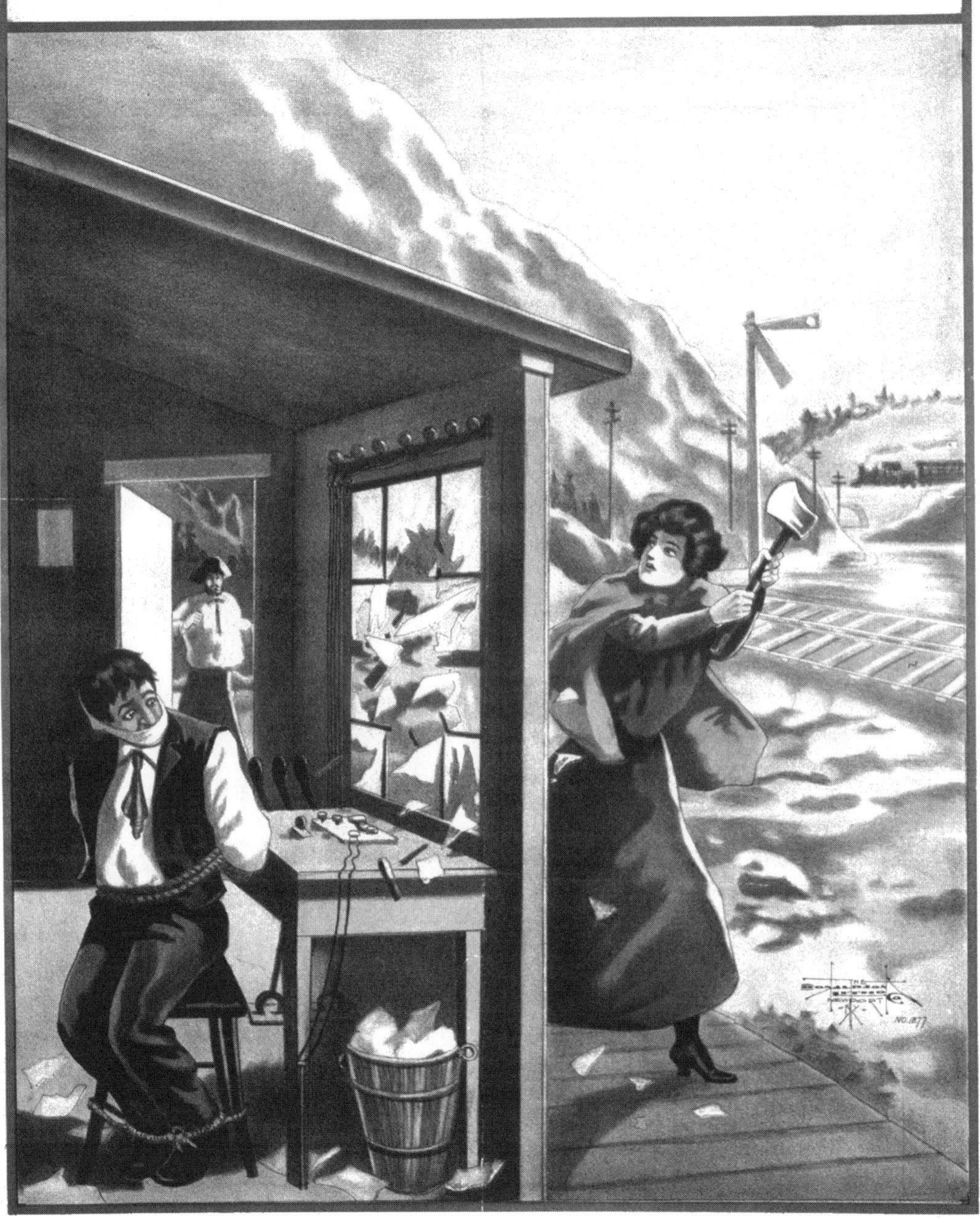

Fig. 7.4

Doolittle and Munson

Cincinnati Landing. (fig. 7.5)

Engraving. 1841. 3¼ × 6½ in (8.26 × 16.51 cm). Cincinnati: Doolittle & Munson. Charles Cist (1792–1868), *Cincinnati in 1841* (Cincinnati: Printed and published for the author, 1841), frontispiece. Rare Books and Special Collections Department.

Ehrgott & Forbriger

Bird's Eye View of Camp Chase Near Columbus, Ohio.

A. Ruger. Lithograph. [186–]. Image: 16½ × 24 in (41.9 × 61.0 cm). Sheet: 20 × 26⅞ in (50.8 × 68.3 cm). Cincinnati: Ehrgott, Forbriger & Co. Rare Books and Special Collections Department.

Edmund Dexter's Residence. / N.E. Corner of Fourth St. & Broadway, Cincinnati, O.

Lithograph. N.d. Image: 15¾ × 20¼ in (40.0 × 51.4 cm). Frame Opening: 21¾ × 25¾ in (55.2 × 65.4 cm). Cincinnati: Lith. & Print. in Colors by Ehrgott & Forbriger & Co. Rare Books and Special Collections Department.

Fort Washington / Erected 1790 in Cincinnati, / On the Ground Now Occupied As 3rd Street, East of Broadway.

H. W. Kemper, painter. Chromolithograph. At greatest extent: 8⅞ × 14⅜ in (22.5 × 36.5 cm). N.d. Cincinnati: Chromolithography of Ehrgott & Forbriger. Rare Books and Special Collections Department.

Hoffheimer Bro's. / Celebrated / Bavarian / Bitters / For Sale Here! (fig. 7.6)

Lithograph. Ca. 1862. Trimmed: 9¾ × $12\frac{15}{16}$ in (24.8 × 32.9 cm). Cincinnati: Ehrgott, Forbriger & Co. Lithogr. Langstroth Collection. Art and Music Department.

[Lady feeding animals]

Lithograph. N.d. $12\frac{11}{16}$ × 9⅝ in (32.2 × 24.4 cm). Cincinnati: Ehrgott, Forbriger & Co. Langstroth Collection. Art and Music Department.

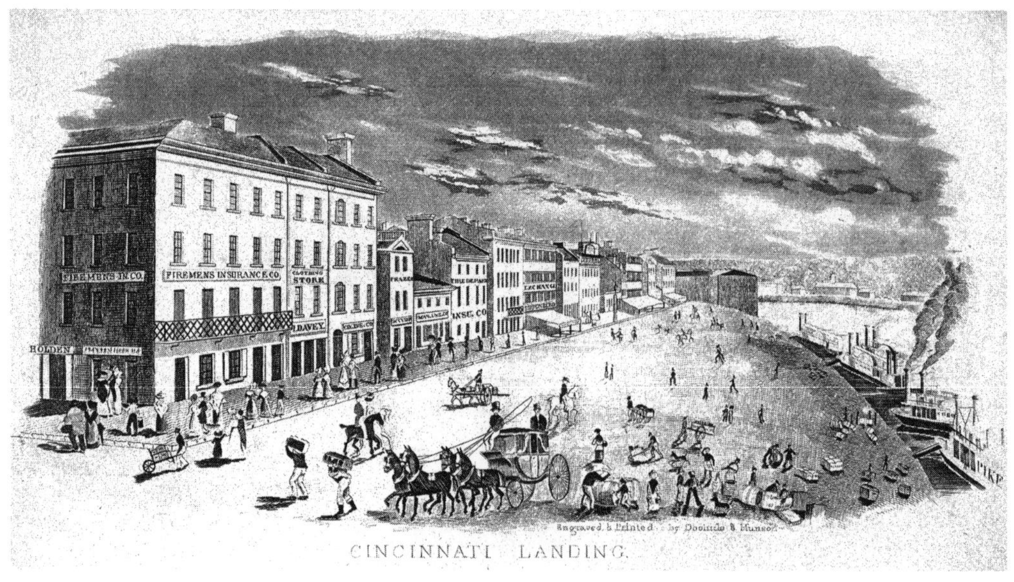

Fig. 7.5

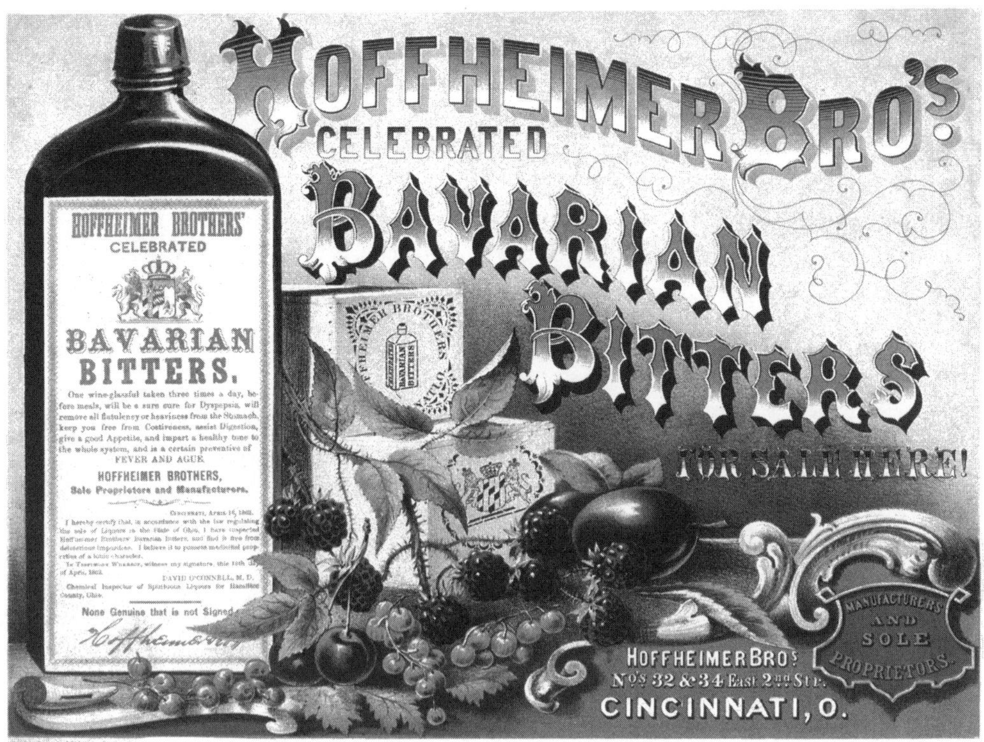

Fig. 7.6

M. Greiner & Son, / Manufacturers of the / Celebrated / Madison XX Ale. / Madison, Ind.
Lithograph. N.d. Trimmed: 17⅝ × 22 9/16 in (44.8 × 57.3 cm). Cincinnati: Ehrgott, Forbriger & Co. Lith. Langstroth Collection. Art and Music Department.

[Membership certificate] The / Cincinnati / Pioneer Association.
Henry Lovey, designer. W. Bucknell, delineator. Lithograph. Ca. 1858. 23¾ × 16½ in (60.3 × 41.9 cm). Cincinnati: Ehrgott & Forbriger Lith. Rare Books and Special Collections Department.

Norman House and Park.
Chromolithograph. 1857. 5½ × 8¾ in (14.0 × 22.2 cm). Cincinnati: Ehrgott & Forbriger. J. T. Crapsey, *Norman House and Park: Statement of the Plan and Prospects of the Norman Company* (Cincinnati: Wrightson & Co., Printers, 1857), frontispiece. Rare Books and Special Collections Department.

[Sheet music cover] To Mr. E. Cooley, / Jackson, Mich. / Sweet Bird of the South. / Sung with Great Applause by Miss Florence A. Rice / At the Brooklyn (N.Y.) Academy of Music, / By Frederic H. Peuse.
Lithograph. N.d. Trimmed: 13 5/16 × 10 5/16 in (33.8 × 26.2 cm). Cincinnati: Ehrgott, Forbriger & Co. Langstroth Collection. Art and Music Department.

[Sheet music cover] To My Friend / Alice Taylor / Boquet March. / By C. T. Lockwood.
Lithograph. N.d. Trimmed: 13⅜ × 10⅛ in (34 × 25.2 cm). Cincinnati: Ehrgott, Forbriger & Co. Lith. Langstroth Collection. Art and Music Department.

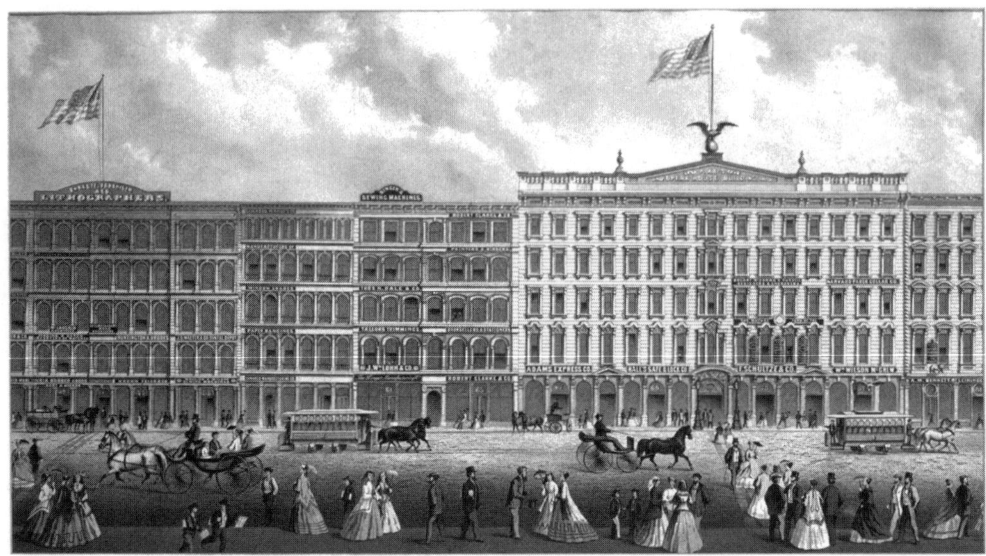

Fig. 7.7

South Side Fourth Street, between Walnut and Vine, Cincinnati, Ohio. (fig. 7.7)
Lithograph. N.d. Mat Opening: 11½ × 20½ in (29.2 × 52.1 cm). Cincinnati: Ehrgott, Forbriger & Co. Rare Books and Special Collections Department.

[Still life with fruit, wine, & fly]
Helen Searle, artist. Lithograph. 1869. Trimmed: 13½ × 11⅛ in (34.3 × 28.3 cm). Cincinnati: Ehrgott, Forbriger & Co. Langstroth Collection. Art and Music Department.

Ta Tsing Bitters / The Great Chinese Remedy. / For Sale Here.
Lithograph. Ca. 1862. Trimmed: 9 11/16 × 12 13/16 in (24.6 × 32.5 cm). Cincinnati: Ehrgott, Forbriger & Co. Lith. Langstroth Collection. Art and Music Department.

Tompkin's Farm. / (Camp Gauley Mount).
J. Nep. Roesler, artist. Lithograph. 1862. 12¾ × 16½ in (32.4 × 41.9 cm). Cincinnati: Ehrgott, Forbriger & Co. J. Nep. Roesler, *Camp Anderson, West Virginia: Lithographs of Civil War Scenes, Chiefly in West Virginia.* Binder's title: *Scenes of the Rebellion.* (Cincinnati: Ehrgott, Forbriger & Co., 1862). Unpaged. Rare Books and Special Collections Department.

[Two people at well]
Lithograph. N.d. 13⅜ × 10 1/16 in (34.0 × 25.6 cm). Cincinnati: Ehrgott, Forbriger & Co. Langstroth Collection. Art and Music Department.

Gest

[Evergreen]
Joseph Henry Gest, 1859–1935. 1901. Image: 4½ × 3¼ in (11.4 × 8.3 cm). Sheet: 7¼ × 6 in (18.4 × 15.2 cm). Joseph Henry Gest, *Typographical and Other Ornaments in Black and White* (Cincinnati: privately printed, 1902). Unpaged. Rare Books and Special Collections Department.

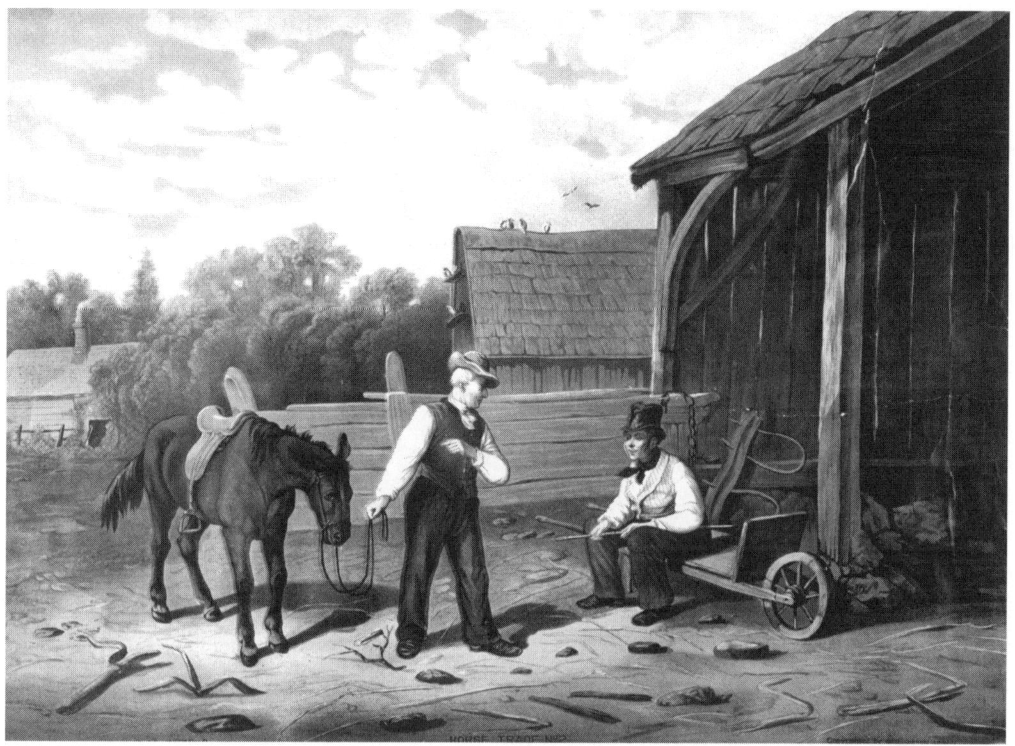

Fig. 7.8

Gibson

Cattle by the Stream.

William Eichner. Lithograph. N.d. Trimmed: 18$\frac{7}{8}$ × 24$\frac{7}{8}$ in (47.9 × 63.2 cm). Cincinnati: Gibson Litho. Langstroth Collection. Art and Music Department.

Horse Trade No. 2 (fig. 7.8)

Lithograph. 1881. 24 × 32$\frac{1}{4}$ in (61.0 × 81.9 cm). Cincinnati: Geo. Gibson. Langstroth Collection. Art and Music Department.

[Woman]

Lithograph. N.d. Trimmed: 16$\frac{5}{8}$ × 14 in (42.2 × 35.6 cm). Cincinnati: Gibson Litho. Langstroth Collection. Art and Music Department.

Henderson / Henderson-Achert

The Foss-Schneider / Brewing Co's / Bock / Cincinnati. (fig. 7.9)

Lithograph. N.d. Trimmed: 25$\frac{7}{8}$ × 20$\frac{1}{16}$ in (65.7 × 50.9 cm). Cincinnati: Henderson-Achert Co. Lith. Langstroth Collection. Art and Music Department.

[Still life with fruit]

R. LeRoy. Lithograph. 1896. 13$\frac{7}{16}$ × 17$\frac{11}{16}$ in (34.1 × 44.9 cm). Cincinnati: Henderson Lithography Co. Langstroth Collection. Art and Music Department.

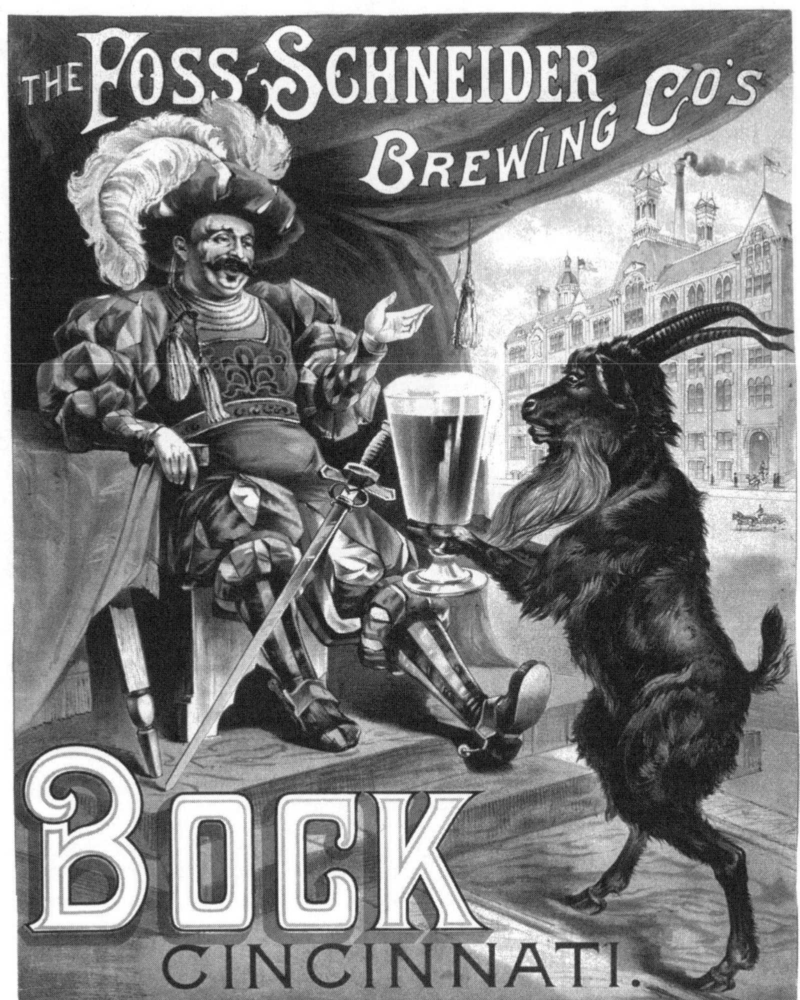

Fig. 7.9

Hennegan

Hennegan County / Fair / Cincinnati, Aug. 2, 3, 4 / Sample of Fence Streamer from Hennegan & Co., Cincinnati, Ohio.

N.d. Overall: 15¼ × 54 in (38.7 × 137.2 cm). Cincinnati: Hennegan & Co. Rare Books and Special Collections Department.

Kemper-Thomas

[Calendar 1906] Voss-Miller & Co. 819–821 Central Avenue, / Cincinnati, O. Opp. City Hall. / Furniture—Carpets—Stoves. / Phone Canal 2535.

Chromolithograph. [1905]. 15⅝ × 8⅝ in (39.7 × 21.9 cm). Cincinnati: Kemper-Thomas Co. Langstroth Collection. Art and Music Department.

Klauprecht & Menzel

Cincinnati in 1840 (fig. 7.10)

Lithograph. [1840]. 7⅝ × 15¼ in (19.4 × 38.7 cm). Cincinnati: Klauprecht & Menzel. David Henry Shaffer, *Shaffer's Cincinnati Directory for 1840* (Cincinnati: printed by J. B. & R. P. Donough, No. 106 Main Street, 1840), frontispiece. Rare Books and Special Collections Department.

Cincinnati. / Queen of the West.

J. Jelasso, delineator and lithographer. Lithograph. [Ca. 1841]. Image: 14⅝ × 10⅛ in (37.1 × 51.1 cm). Sheet: 17¼ × 22¾ in (43.8 × 57.8 cm). Cincinnati: Klauprecht & Menzel's Lith. Rare Books and Special Collections Department.

A. D. Kramer

Cincinnati U.S.A. [from Covington]

Charles F. Ulrich, engraver. Engraving. [1900]. Image: 7⅜ × 37½ in (18.7 × 95.3 cm). Sheet: 16⅜ × 44¾ in (41.6 × 113.7 cm). Cincinnati: A. D. Kramer. Rare Books and Special Collections Department.

Krebs

1888 / The / Centennial / Exposition / of the / Ohio Valley / and Central / States / at Cincinnati, U.S.A. / Opens July 4th / Closes Oct. 27th.

Lithograph. 1888. Frame Opening: 17¼ × 11¾ in (43.8 × 29.8 cm). Cincinnati: Krebs Lithographing Co. Rare Books and Special Collections Department.

[Calendar] Compliments of / The Geo. W. McAlpin Co. / Wholesale / Dry Goods and Notions.

Lithograph. N.d. 13⅜ × 9⅝ in (34.0 × 24.4 cm). Cincinnati: Krebs Lithographing Co. Langstroth Collection. Rare Books and Special Collections Department.

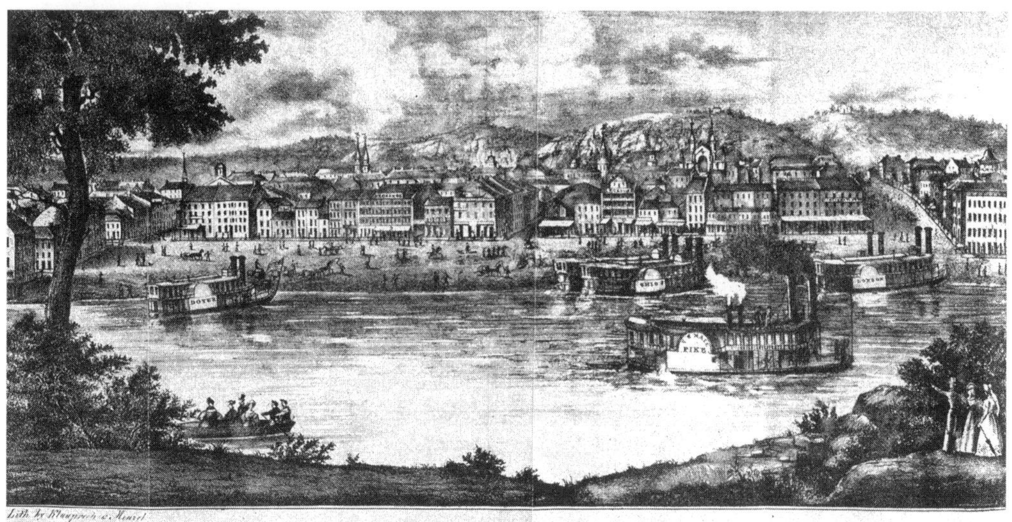

Fig. 7.10

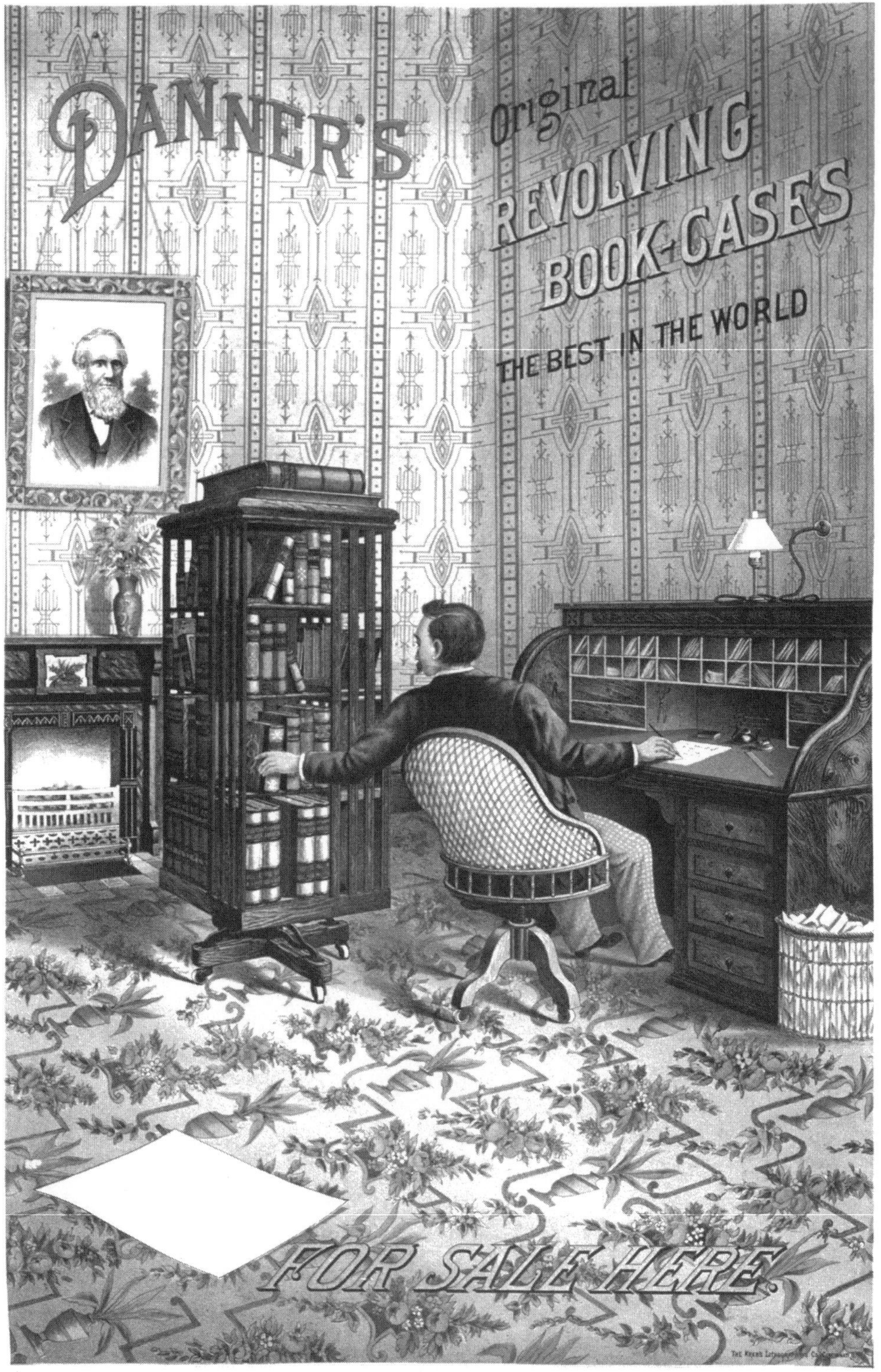
DANNER'S
Original
REVOLVING
BOOK-CASES
THE BEST IN THE WORLD
FOR SALE HERE

Fig. 7.11

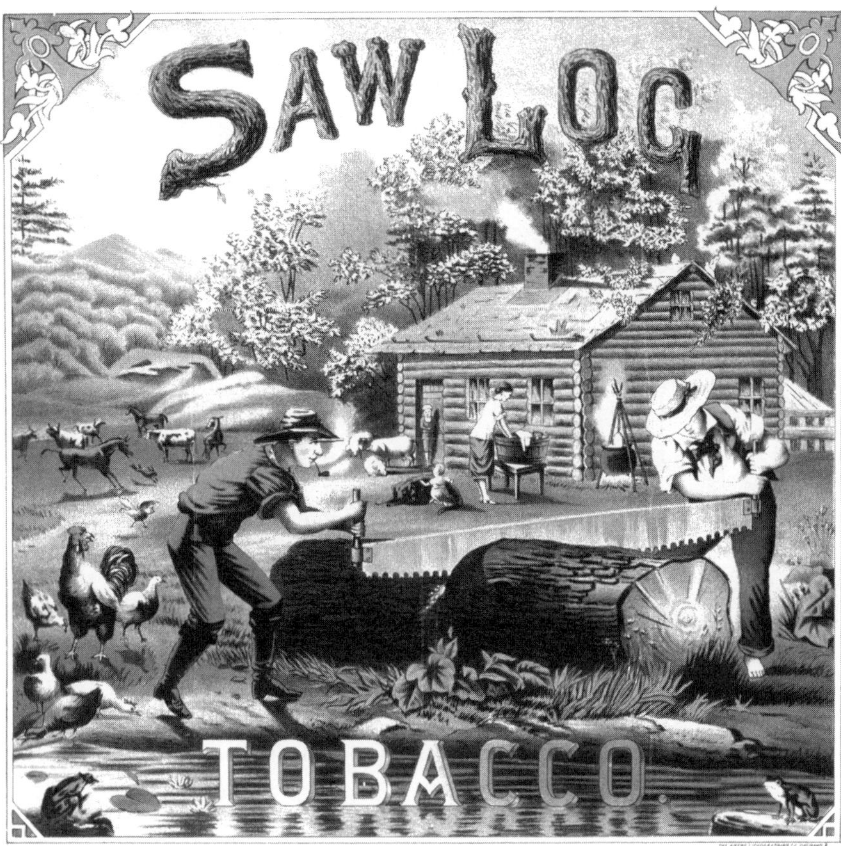

Fig. 7.12

[Calendar 1884] Swifts / Iron and Steel Works. / Incorporated 1866.

Lithographs—Black and white and colored. [1883]. Each 13$\frac{11}{16}$ × 10$\frac{9}{16}$ in (34.8 × 26.8 cm). Cincinnati: Krebs Lithographing Co. Langstroth Collection. Art and Music Department.

Danner's Original / Revolving / Book-Cases / The Best in the World / For Sale Here (fig. 7.11)

Lithograph. N.d. Trimmed: 19 × 12 in (48.3 × 30.5 cm). Cincinnati: Krebs Lithographing Co. Langstroth Collection. Art and Music Department.

[Falstaff]

Lithograph. N.d. 27$\frac{1}{16}$ × 11$\frac{15}{16}$ in (66.2 × 30.3 cm). Cincinnati: Krebs Lithographing Co. Langstroth Collection. Art and Music Department.

Ninth / Cincinnati / Industrial / Exposition / The National Exposition / of Art and Industry / Opens Sept. 7th / Closes Oct. 8th 1881.

Lithograph. 1881. Trimmed: 26$\frac{5}{8}$ × 20$\frac{7}{16}$ in (67.6 × 51.9 cm). Cincinnati: Krebs Lithographing Co. Langstroth Collection. Art and Music Department.

Saw Log / Tobacco. (fig. 7.12)

Lithograph. N.d. Trimmed: 10$\frac{7}{8}$ × 10$\frac{3}{4}$ in (27.6 × 27.3 cm). Cincinnati: Krebs Lithographing Co. Langstroth Collection. Art and Music Department.

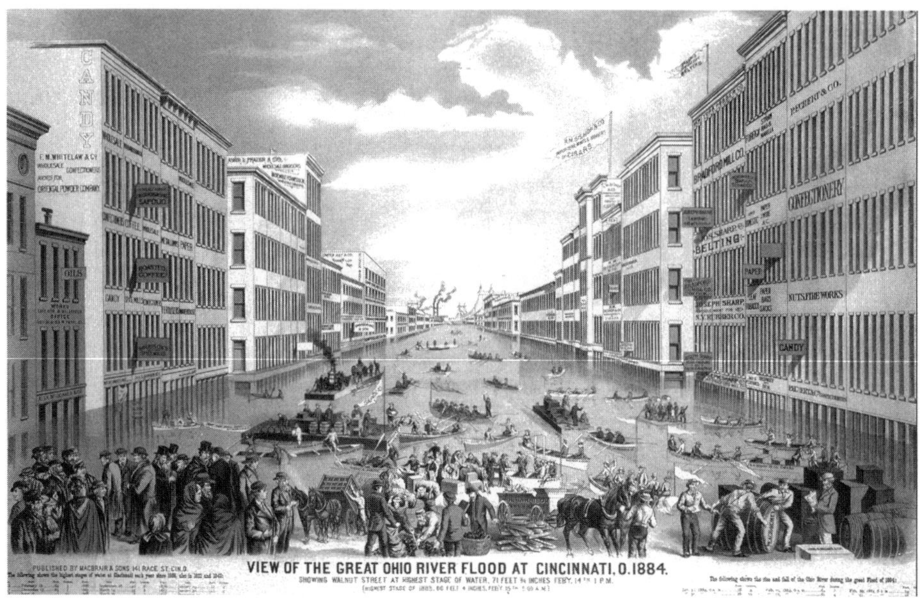

Fig. 7.13

Jeffras Seeley & Co. / 99 West Fourth St. / Cincinnati. / History of Ladies' Costumes from the Time of Eve.

F. Achert. Lithograph. 1876. 18¼ × 23¾ in (46.4 × 60.3 cm). Cincinnati: Krebs Lithographing Company. Rare Books and Special Collections Department.

Smoke El Burro / Manufactured by / The Wellman & Dwire / Tobacco Co. / Quincy, Ill.

Lithograph. Black and White and Colored. N.d. Each 13¾ × 10½ in (34.9 × 26.7 cm). Cincinnati: Krebs Lithographing Co. Langstroth Collection. Art and Music Department.

[Tobacco advertisement] Bright.

Lithograph. N.d. Trimmed: 10 × 11¾ in (25.4 × 29.8 cm). Cincinnati: Krebs Lithographing. Langstroth Collection. Art and Music Department.

[Trade card] Moerlein's / National Export.

Lithograph. N.d. 4½ × 3 in (11.4 × 7.6 cm). Cincinnati: Krebs Lithographing Co. Langstroth Collection. Rare Books and Special Collections Department.

Krehbiel

Ohio Valley Exposition.

Photolithograph. 1910. 8⅞ × 6 in (22.5 × 15.2 cm). *Prospectus. . .Exposition to be Held in the City of Cincinnati, August 29 to September 24, Inclusive, 1910* (Cincinnati: Krehbiel Press, 1910), title page. Rare Books and Special Collections Department.

MacBrair

View of the Great Ohio River Flood at Cincinnati, O. 1884. (fig. 7.13)

1884. Frame Opening: 24 × 34½ in (61.0 × 87.6 cm). Cincinnati: MacBrair & Sons. Rare Books and Special Collections Department.

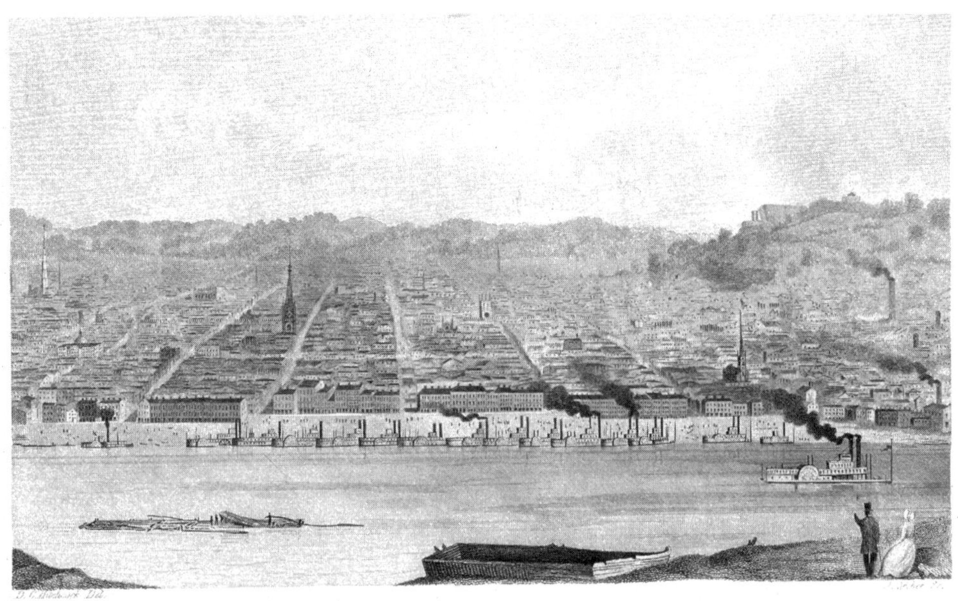

Fig. 7.14

McDonald

[Calendar 1907] An Example of Printing / Engraving / Advertising / As Produced by The / McDonald Press, / Cincinnati, U.S.A.

[1906]. 10 × 11¾ in (25.4 × 29.8 cm). Cincinnati: The McDonald Press. Langstroth Collection. Art and Music Department.

Mariemont Company

View of Mariemont, Ohio.

A. Aviroff, artist. Offset Lithograph. 1924. Image: 6.06 × 7.95 in (15.4 × 20.2 cm). Sheet: 8.07 × 11.06 in (20.5 × 28.1 cm). The Mariemont Co., *Mariemont, The New Town* (Cincinnati: The Mariemont Company, 1925), cover. Rare Books and Special Collections Department.

Middleton

[Book illustration] Infidelity.

Lithograph. N.d. Trimmed: 6¹¹⁄₁₆ × 4⅛ in (17.0 × 10.5 cm). Cincinnati: Middleton, Wallace & Co. Lith. Langstroth Collection. Art and Music Department.

[Book illustration] Intemperance. / The Road to Ruin.

Lithograph. N.d. Trimmed: 4¾ × 5⁹⁄₁₆ in (12.1 × 14.1 cm). Cincinnati: Middleton, Wallace & Co. Lith. Langstroth Collection. Art and Music Department.

Cincinnati. (fig. 7.14)

D. C. Hitchcock, delineator. J. Archer, sculptor. Engraving. N.d. 4⅝ × 7⁹⁄₁₆ in (11.7 × 10.2 cm). Cincinnati: Middleton Printer. Rare Books and Special Collections Department.

[Abraham Lincoln]

Lithograph. N.d. Oval Frame Opening: 16¼ × 13 in (41.3 × 33.0 cm). Cincinnati: Middleton, Strobridge & Co. Rare Books and Special Collections Department.

McAvoy's Superior. / Natural Size.

Lithograph. 1857. 7½ × 4⅞ in (19.1 × 12.4 cm). Cincinnati: Middleton, Wallace & Co. Edward James Hooper, *Hooper's Western Fruit Book* (Cincinnati: Moore, Wilstach, Keys & Co., 1857), facing page 292. Rare Books and Special Collections Department.

Map of Kansas / With Route from / Kansas City / To the / Gold Mines.

Lithograph. 1859. 10 × 24¾ in (25.4 × 62.9 cm). Cincinnati: Middleton, Strobridge and Co. *Guide to the Kansas Gold Mines at Pike's Peak, Describing the Routes, Camping Places, Tools, Outfits, &c., from Notes of Capt. J. W. Gunnison. . .* (Cincinnati: Mendenhall, 1859), frontispiece. Rare Books and Special Collections Department.

Mill Creek Valley at High Water, from Mt. Auburn Near Cincinnati.

Lovie, delineator. J. Archer, sculptor. Engraving. [1851]. 4¹¹⁄₁₆ × 7⅛ in (11.9 × 18.1 cm). Cincinnati: Middleton Printer. Rare Books and Special Collections Department.

Poesie.

M. Retzsch, artist. C. A. Jewett, W. Anderson, engravers. Engraving. [185–] 7¼ × 9⅛ in (18.4 × 23.2 cm). *Pictorial Album.* Cincinnati: E. C. Middleton, [185–]. Unpaged. Rare Books and Special Collections Department.

View on the Ohio, / (Below Cincinnati).

Nathl. Kinsey. Engraving. [1857]. 4¹³⁄₁₆ × 7⁹⁄₁₆ in (12.2 × 19.2 cm). Cincinnati: Middleton, Wallace & Co., Printers. Rare Books and Special Collections Department.

View on the Ohio [(Near Maysville, Kentucky)].

E. Bott, delineator. Nathl. Kinsey Jr., engraver. Engraving. [1856]. 4¾ × 7⁵⁄₁₆ in (12.1 × 18.6 cm). Cincinnati: [Middleton, Wallace & Co., Printers]. Rare Books and Special Collections Department.

[Woman—1]

Lithograph. 1849. 12⁷⁄₁₆ × 9 in (31.6 × 22.9 cm). Cincinnati: Middleton, Strobridge & Co. Langstroth Collection. Art and Music Department.

[Woman—2]

Lithograph. 1849. 12⁷⁄₁₆ × 9 in (31.6 × 22.9 cm). Cincinnati: Middleton, Strobridge & Co. Langstroth Collection. Art and Music Department.

Morgan, Lodge and Fisher

Medical College of Ohio Cincinnati.

William Woodruff. Engraving. 1827. 4½ × 7¼ in (11.4 × 18.4 cm). Benjamin Drake (1794–1841) and Edward D. Mansfield (1801–1880), *Cincinnati in 1826* (Cincinnati: Morgan, Lodge and Fisher, 1827), frontispiece. Rare Books and Special Collections Department.

[Map of Ohio River showing Cincinnati]

Engraving. 1825. 8¾ × 5½ in (22.2 × 14.0 cm). Samuel Cumings, *The Western Pilot* (Cincinnati: Morgan, Lodge & Fisher, Printers, 1825), facing page 16. Rare Books and Special Collections Department.

Nelson and Bolles

Landscape View of Madisonville.

W. R. McComas, delineator. Clegg, sculptor. Richard Nelson (1822–1900). 1874. Image: Oval: 5 × 7⅜ in (12.7 × 18.7 cm). Sheet: 5.87 × 8.98 in (14.9 × 22.8 cm). Cincinnati: Nelson & Bolles. *Suburban Homes for Business Men on the Line of the Marietta Railroad: A Description of the North-Eastern Suburbs* (Cincinnati: Nelson & Bolles, 1874), facing page 52. Rare Books and Special Collections Department.

Onken

Cincinnati, / Taken from Belle Vue on Sycamore Hill.

A. Forbriger, delineator. Lithograph. 1851. 8 × 10¹¹⁄₁₆ in (20.3 × 27.1 cm). William Franklin Wells, *Western Scenery, or Land and River, Hill and Dale, in the Mississippi Valley* (Cincinnati: published at the Lithographic Establishment of Otto Onken, 1851), frontispiece. Rare Books and Special Collections Department.

Flood of 1847. / A View of the City of Cincinnati and the Ohio River, Taken from / Mrs. W. W. Southgate's in Covington, Dec. 17 1847, At Which Time the Water Was about 61 Feet above Low Water Mark, and about 6 Inches Short of the Freshit [*Sic*] of 1832 (fig. 7.15)

J. B. Rowse, delineator. Lithograph. 1847. Image: 13⅞ × 24¼ in (35.2 × 61.6 cm). Sheet: 16¼ × 26⅛ in (41.3 × 66.4 cm). Cincinnati: Onken Print. Rare Books and Special Collections Department.

Milward & Oldershaw (fig. 7.16).

Lithograph. [1851]. 5 × 7⅞ in (12.7 x20.0 cm). Cincinnati: Onken's Lithography. Charles Cist, *Sketches and Statistics of Cincinnati in 1851* (Cincinnati: Wm. H. Moore & Co., Publishers, 1851), facing page 299. Rare Books and Special Collections Department.

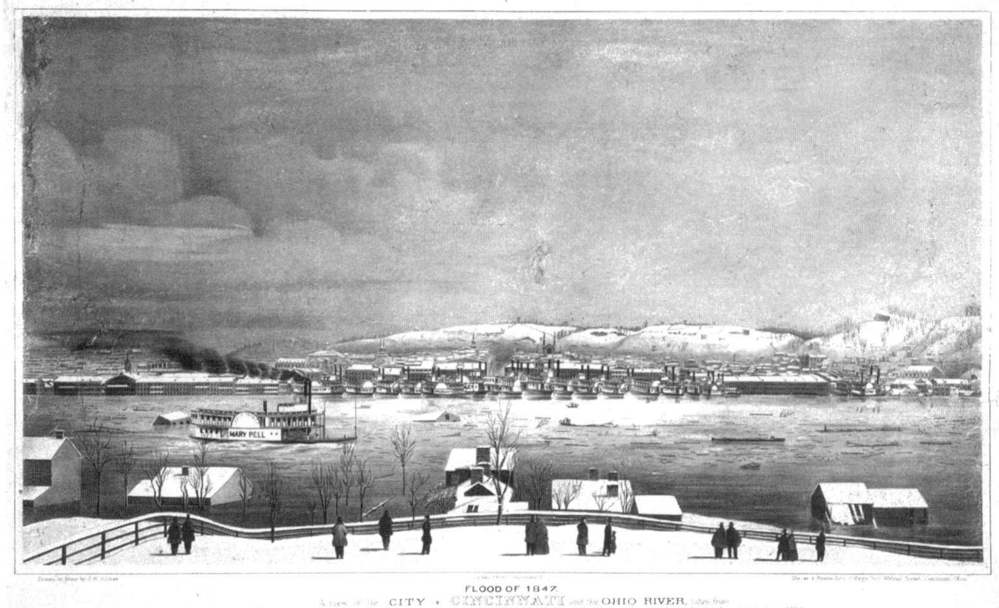

Fig. 7.15

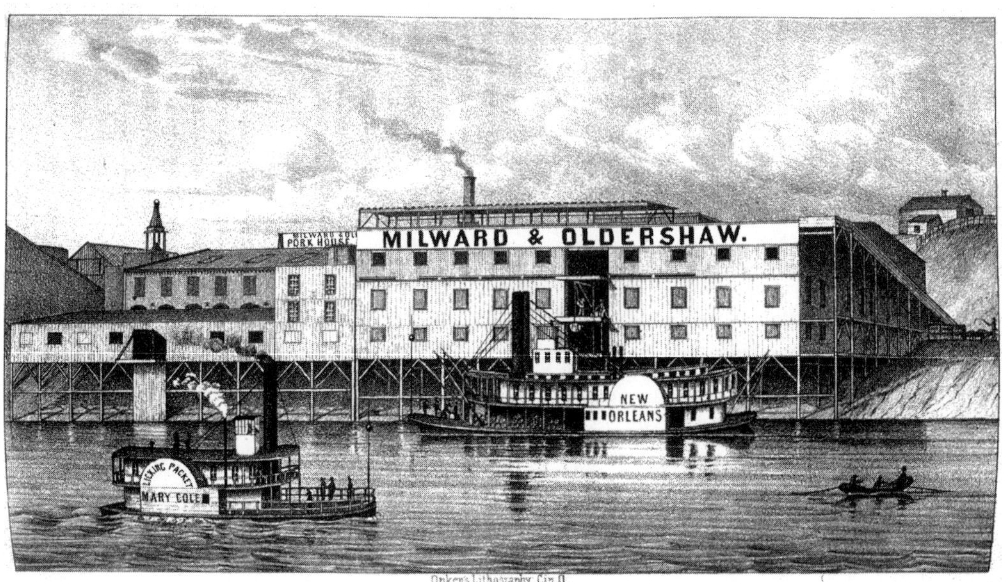

Fig. 7.16

St. Peter's Cathedral.

Lithograph. [1851]. 7⅞ × 5 in (20.0 × 12.7 cm). Cincinnati: Oncken's [*sic*] Lithography. Charles Cist, *Sketches and Statistics of Cincinnati in 1851* (Cincinnati: Wm. H. Moore & Co., Publishers, 1851), facing p. 29. Rare Books and Special Collections Department.

[Wells. Western scenery]

Lithograph. 1851. 10¹¹⁄₁₆ × 8 in (27.1 × 20.3 cm). William Franklin Wells, *Western Scenery, or Land and River, Hill and Dale, in the Mississippi Valley* (Cincinnati: published at the Lithographic Establishment of Otto Onken, 1851), title page. Rare Books and Special Collections Department.

Red Book Publishing

The Fosdick Building.

Shearer, delineator. Engraving. [1890]. 11½ × 6 in (29.2 × 15.2 cm). M. Retzsch, *The Illustrated Building, Business and Property Owners Directory of Cincinnati* . . . (Cincinnati: Red Book Publishing, [1890]), p. 293. Rare Books and Special Collections Department.

John Shillito Company

Interior of Public Library.

Plympton. Lithograph. 1883. 6¾ × 4½ in (17.1 × 11.4 cm). James W. Dawson, *Picturesque Cincinnati* (Cincinnati: The John Shillito Co., 1883), facing p. 170. Rare Books and Special Collections Department.

Rotunda / Of The / John Shillito Co.'s / Dry Goods Store.

Plympton. Lithograph. 1883. 5⅞ × 3⅝ in (14.9 × 9.2 cm). James W. Dawson, *Picturesque Cincinnati* (Cincinnati: The John Shillito Co., 1883), facing p. 188. Rare Books and Special Collections Department.

Strobridge (See also Middleton)

Adam Forepaugh & Sells Bros / The Ty-Bell Sisters / Beautiful Sensational Novelty / The Famous "Aerial Butterflies."

Lithograph. Ca. 1914. 40⅛ × 30 in (101.9 × 76.2 cm). Cincinnati: The Strobridge Lith. Co. Strobridge Poster Collection. Art and Music Department.

Barnum / and / Bailey / Greatest / Show on Earth (fig. 7.17)

Lithograph. Ca. 1917. 30 × 40⅛ in (76.2 × 101.9 cm). Cincinnati: The Strobridge Lith. Co. Strobridge Poster Collection. Art and Music Department. (Ringling Bros. and Barnum & Bailey Circus; Ringling Bros.; Barnum; Bailey; and, The Greatest Show on Earth are owned by and are trademarks and service marks of Ringling Bros.–Barnum & Bailey Combined Shows, Inc. All Rights Reserved.)

[Card calendars] The Strobridge Litho Co. (fig. 7.18)

Lithographs. 1906, 1907, 1910, 1911. Each 6⅛ × 3 7⁄16 in (15.6 × 8.7 cm). Cincinnati: The Strobridge Lithographing Co. Rare Books and Special Collections Department.

[Certificate of membership] Society of the / Army of the Tennessee.

Lithograph. [After 1864]. Image: 22¼ × 19 in (60.1 × 48.3 cm). Sheet: 24 × 19 in (60.1 × 48.3 cm). Cincinnati: Strobridge and Co. Lith. Rare Books and Special Collections Department.

Cincinnati—1800.

Lithograph. 1880. Frame Opening: 17⅝ × 28⅜ in (44.7 × 72.1 cm). Cincinnati: The Strobridge Lithographing Co. Rare Books and Special Collections Department.

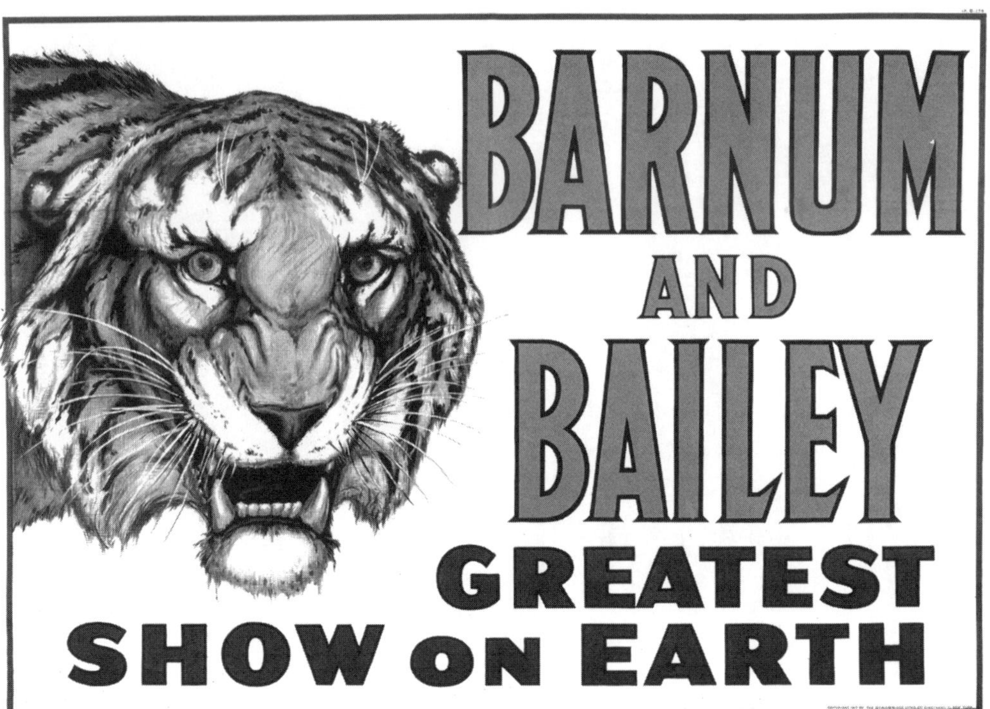

Fig. 7.17

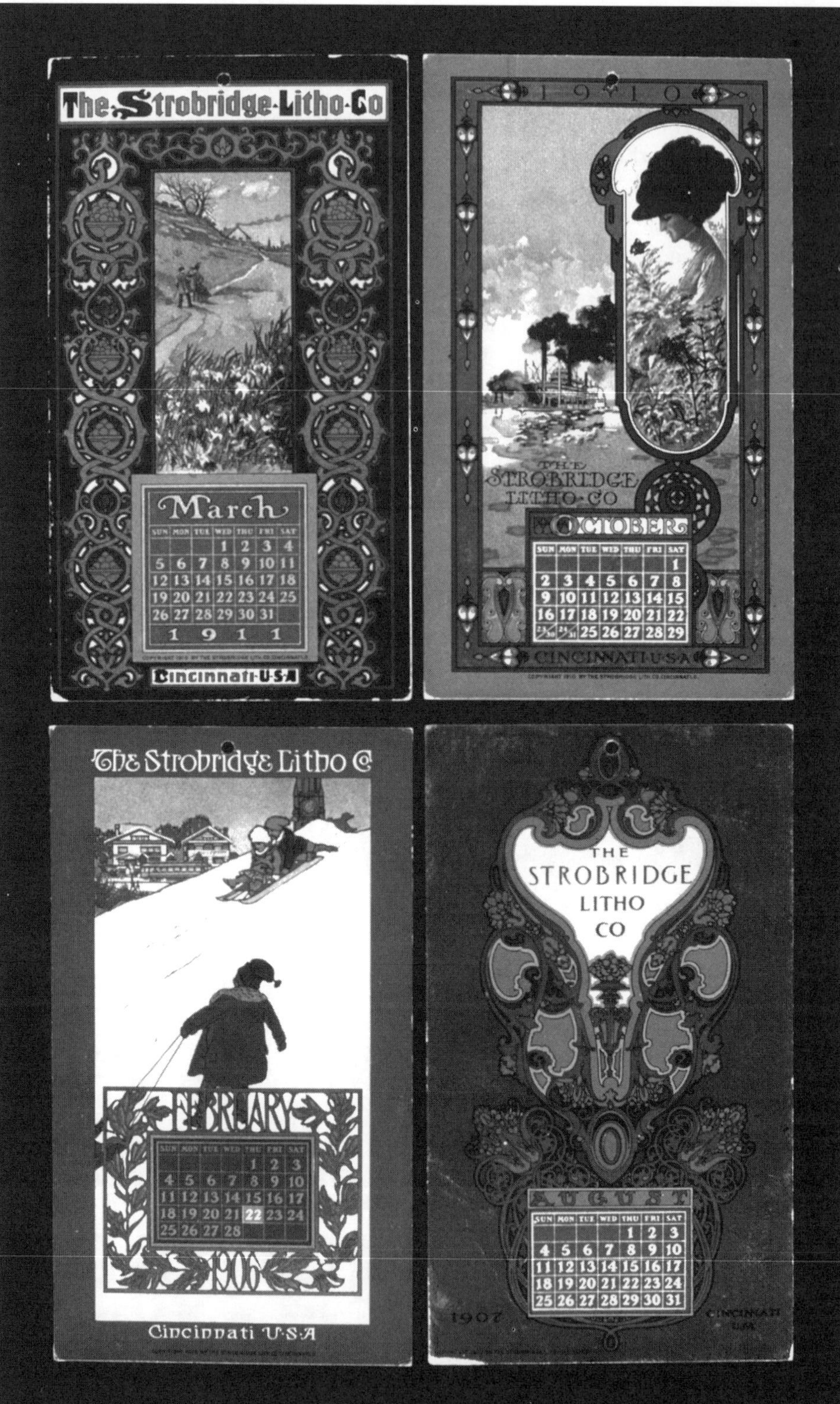
The Strobridge Litho Co
March
SUN MON TUE WED THU FRI SAT
1 2 3 4
5 6 7 8 9 10 11
12 13 14 15 16 17 18
19 20 21 22 23 24 25
26 27 28 29 30 31
1 9 1 1
Cincinnati U.S.A
1 9 1 0
THE STROBRIDGE LITHO CO
OCTOBER
SUN MON TUE WED THU FRI SAT
1
2 3 4 5 6 7 8
9 10 11 12 13 14 15
16 17 18 19 20 21 22
25 26 27 28 29
CINCINNATI U.S.A
The Strobridge Litho Co
FEBRUARY
SUN MON TUE WED THU FRI SAT
1 2 3
4 5 6 7 8 9 10
11 12 13 14 15 16 17
18 19 20 21 22 23 24
25 26 27 28
1906
Cincinnati U.S.A
THE STROBRIDGE LITHO CO
AUGUST
SUN MON TUE WED THU FRI SAT
1 2 3
4 5 6 7 8 9 10
11 12 13 14 15 16 17
18 19 20 21 22 23 24
25 26 27 28 29 30 31
1907

Fig. 7.18

New Map of / Cincinnati and Suburbs.

Engraving. 1875. 14⅛ × 17⅝ in (35.9 × 44.8 cm). Cincinnati: Strobridge & Co. Daniel J. Kenny, *Illustrated Cincinnati: A Pictorial Handbook of the Queen City* (Cincinnati: Geo. E. Stevens & Co., 1875), frontispiece. Rare Books and Special Collections Department.

[Ohio Valley Exposition]

Offset Lithograph. 1910. 9¼ × 6⅛ in (23.5 × 15.6 cm). *Official Catalogue and Guide: Ohio Valley Exposition, Cincinnati, 1910, Aug. 29–Sept. 24: Inclusive* (Cincinnati: The Strobridge Lithographing Co., 1910), cover. Rare Books and Special Collections Department.

Ringling / Bros and / Barnum / & Bailey / Combined Shows / Presenting / the Great / Arturo / in Hazardous High Jinks / Now Startling America.

Lithograph. N.d. 56 × 21 in (142.2 × 53.3 cm). Cincinnati: The Strobridge Litho. Co. Strobridge Poster Collection. Art and Music Department.

Ringling / Bros and / Barnum / & Bailey / Combined Shows / Presenting / Hubert / Castle / King of Tight Wire / in Comedy Tumbling, Somersaulting, / Acrobatic Achievements / without Parallel.

Lithograph. N.d. 42¼ × 14 in (107.3 × 35.6 cm). Cincinnati: The Strobridge Litho. Co. Strobridge Poster Collection. Art and Music Department.

Ringling Bros Shows / The Great Balkani Troupe / A Gorgeous Oriental Equestrian Sensation.

Lithograph. Ca. 1914. 40⅛ × 30 in (101.9 × 76.2 cm). Cincinnati: The Strobridge Lith. Co. Strobridge Poster Collection. Art and Music Department.

Ringling Bros / New / Gorgeous Spectacle / In Days of Old / A Colossal Production of Romance and Chivalry.

Lithograph. Ca. 1918. 42¼ × 30⅛ in (107.3 × 76.5 cm). Cincinnati: The Strobridge Lith. Co. Strobridge Poster Collection. Art and Music Department.

Victor / Allen & Ellis, Cincinnati, O.

Lithograph. 1872. Trimmed: 11¼ × 11¼ in (28.6 × 28.6 cm). Cincinnati: Strobridge & Co., Lith. Langstroth Collection. Art and Music Department.

View of Tell City, / Perry County, Indiana. / Praemie Zum Tell City Anzeiger.

Lithograph. N.d. Framed: 23½ × 29½ in (59.7 × 74.9 cm). Cincinnati: Strobridge & Co., Lith. Rare Books and Special Collections Department.

Peter G. Thomson

Annual Celebration of the / Order of Cincinnatus / At the Opening of the Eleventh Cincinnati Exposition September 1883.

Peter G. Thomson, designer and printer. Lithograph. 1883. Trimmed: 22½ × 33¼ in (52.7 × 84.5 cm). Cincinnati: Peter G. Thomson. Langstroth Collection. Art and Music Department.

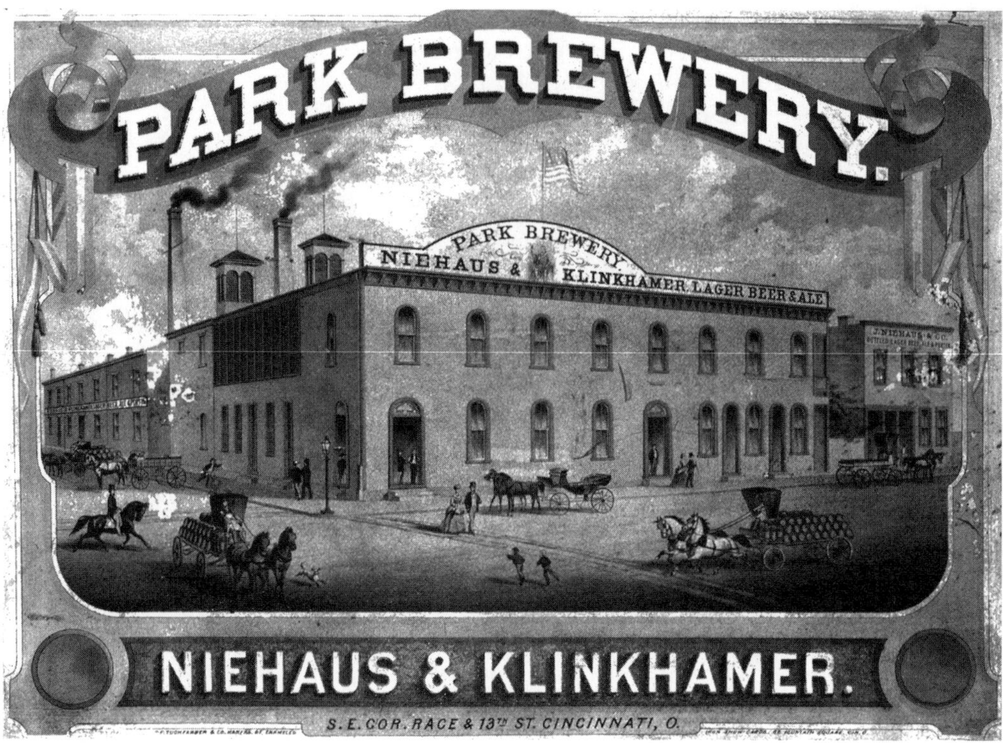

Fig. 7.19

A. E. Tripp

[Map of Cincinnati] Photo-Lithographed / from the Original / Platting Commission Map

Photolithograph. [187–]. 22⅜ × 54½ in (56.8 × 138.4 cm). Cincinnati: A. E. Tripp. Rare Books and Special Collections Department.

Tuchfarber

Hart & Gray / Unrivaled / Cherry Pounds / Cincinnati, Ohio.

Lithograph. Ca. 1870. 10 9/16 × 10⅝ in (26.8 × 27.0 cm). Cincinnati: Tuchfarber, Walkley & Moellmann Lith. Langstroth Collection. Art and Music Department.

Park Brewery. / Niehaus & Klinkhamer. / S.E. Cor. Race & 18th St. Cincinnati, O. (fig. 7.19)

Lithograph? on Metal. Frame Opening: 17¼ × 23¼ in (43.8 × 59.1 cm). Cincinnati: F. Tuchfarber & Co., Manfrs. of Enameled Iron Show Cards. Rare Books and Special Collections Department.

The United States Playing Card Company

[Monogramed deck of playing cards]

1905. Cincinnati: The United States Playing Card Company. Rare Books and Special Collections Department.

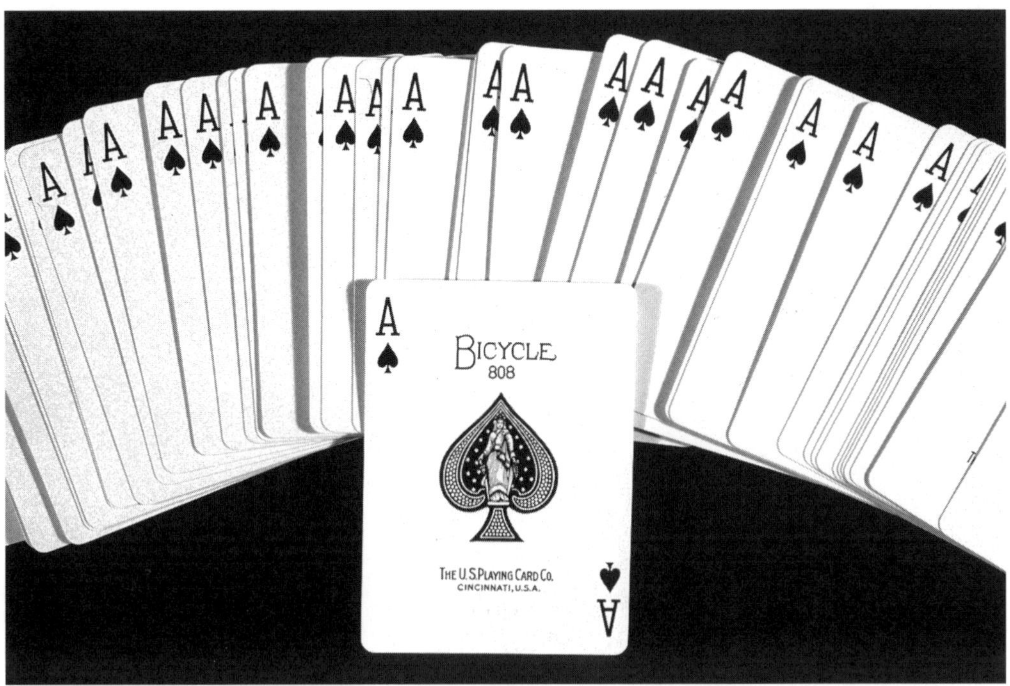

Fig. 7.20

[Pamphlets]

N.d., 1920, 1921. Cincinnati: The United States Playing Card Company. Rare Books and Special Collections Department.

Secret Weapon Bicycle aces of spades (Bicycle 808) (fig. 7.20)

[1966]. Cincinnati: The United States Playing Card Company. Rare Books and Special Collections Department. These cards were supplied to United States troops in Vietnam. To the Viet Cong, the ace of spades was a sign of death. As a female figure, the Goddess of Liberty appearing on the aces was another evil omen.

Steamboat playing cards, 999.

N.d. Cincinnati: The United States Playing Card Company. Rare Books and Special Collections Department.

Appendix A

Cincinnati Engravers, 1825–1860

Virginius C. Hall

Sources

CD	Cincinnati City Directory
GW	George C. Groce and David H. Wallace, *The New-York Historical Society's Dictionary of Artists in America, 1564–1860* (New Haven: Yale University Press, 1957).
Hamilton	Sinclair Hamilton, *Early American Book Illustrators and Wood Engravers, 1670–1870* (Princeton, N.J.: Princeton University Press, 1958).

Anderson, Walter W. Engraver, 1850–52. Neave's Building, northwest corner of Fourth and Race.

Archer, James. Engraver. Boston, 1835–49; Cincinnati, 1856–57.

Autenreith, Ludwig. Born ca. 1832 in Germany. Copperplate engraver in Cincinnati, 1853–60.

Balthis, J. Milton. Partner with George K. Stillman, 1851–52, in engraving firm Stillman and Balthis at 63 West Fourth Street, Cincinnati.

Barth, Frederick. Born ca.1804 in Germany. Engraver in 1851–52 with premises on east side of Vine between Twelfth and Thirteenth Streets.

Bauerle, Charles B. Wood engraver. Partner (1856) with Henri Lovie in firm Lovie and Bauerle; partner (1857) with Lovie and John C. Bruen in firm Lovie, Bauerle and Bruen.

Booth, T. Dwight. Apprenticed to an engraver in New York City in 1830. Copperplate engraver in Cincinnati, 1850–55, with residence in Newport, Kentucky. He worked in Chicago before returning to New York City in 1857.

Bowley, Charles. Born in England ca.1815. Lived in Alabama and New York City (1845–52) before coming to Cincinnati, where he was a copperplate engraver, 1855–56, with premises at 24 West Fourth Street.

BROWN, JOSEPH A. Copperplate printer, 1836–37, with a shop on Gano Street between Main and Walnut.

BRUEN, JOHN C. Partner, with Henri Lovie and Charles B. Bauerle, in engraving firm Lovie, Bauerle and Bruen (1857). Later moved to New York City.

BUTLER, CHARLES C. Partner, with Elisha C. Hussey, in an engraving firm Butler and Hussey, 44 West Fourth Street, which was advertised only in the 1853 CD.

CARLSON, EDWARD. Engraver, 1859–60+, at 27 East Fourth Street.

CLARKE, PETER. Born in Scotland ca. 1796; his only child was born in Ohio ca. 1841. Engraver in Cincinnati, 1858–60+, with premises at 28 1/2 West Third Street. He died March 14, 1864.

COCHEU, HENRY. Wood engraver. In New York City, 1851–54; in Cincinnati, 1856–60+. Formed, with Joseph W. Hart as partner, the firm Cocheu & Co., 1858–60+.

COLEMAN, JAMES B. Engraver listed in 1834 CD with premises on Front Street between Pike and Butler Streets.

CORDINGLY, JOHN L. Engraver, 1834, on Pike Street between Congress and Symmes.

CROOME, GEORGE L. Wood engraver at 114 Main Street in 1850–51; in Dayton in 1853.

DAVENPORT, JOHN D. Founder, with partner James P. Thomson, of wood engraving firm Davenport and Thomson, 1859–1860+, on the northeast corner of Fourth and Walnut Streets.

DENNIS, JULIAN. Partner, with Ephraim Frazer, in the wood engraving firm Frazer & Dennis, 1850–55.

DOOLITTLE, CURTIS M. Native of Connecticut. Formed, with Samuel B. Munson, also from Connecticut, engraving firm of Doolittle & Munson, 1831–46.

ERNST, THOMAS J. Born in Ohio ca. 1829 of German parents. Listed in 1850–51 CD as engraver at G. K. Stillman's, a manufacturer of window shades in 1855; a wood engraver at 63 West Fourth Street in 1856. Not in CD again until 1861, when he is listed as a general engraver.

EVENS, THEODORE. General engraver, 1858–60+ at 2 West Fourth Street.

FRAZER, EPHRAIM. Partner, with Julian N. Dennis, in wood engraving firm Frazer & Dennis, 1850–55, housed in the Gazette building. The partners advertised themselves, 1850–51 CD, as "successors to R. Vallentine." In 1856 William W. Waggoner advertised himself as the "successor to Frazer & Dennis." Frazer continued to be listed as wood engraver in CDs 1857–59.

GIBSON, GEORGE. Born in England ca. 1810, emigrated to America ca. 1848 with wife and five children. Established Gibson & Co., engravers and lithographers, about 1850. The firm, which came to include his sons, continued after 1860.

GREGSON, JAMES. Engraver, listed in 1859 CD. Gregson & Saver, engravers at the northwest corner of Court and Main, is in 1860 CD.

GRIDLEY, E. G. Engraver and copperplate printer in 1825, with premises on Sycamore, between Third and Fourth. He was born in Massachusetts. Possibly the same as Enoch G. Gridley listed by GW as a portrait and general engraver working in New York City, 1803–4, and thereafter in Philadelphia until 1818.

GROSVENOR, HORACE C. Employed, 1844–46, as engraver on wood at J. A. James's Type and Stereotype foundry. With Charles W. Thompson as partner, formed Grosvenor and Thompson, wood engravers, 1849–50. Subsequently, 1851–58, worked independently at the northeast corner of Fourth and Walnut.

HALL, C. F. Partner, with William and Henry H. Shipley, in engraving firm Shipley, Hall & Co., 1851–52. Premises at 22 West Fourth Street between Main and Walnut.

HART, JOSEPH W. Partner, with Henri Cocheu, in Cocheu & Co., 1858–60+.

HARTMANN, CONRAD FRIED. Copperplate engraver in Cincinnati, 1853–55; in New York City 1855–60.

HAVILAND, WILLIAM. Listed in 1834 CD (addendum, p. 267) as an engraver at Doolittle & Munson's.

HELM, AUGUSTUS L. Engraver, listed in CDs 1855–56, 1859–60, with first address at Fourth and Main, and later at 148 Main.

HITCHCOCK, DEWITT C. Illustrator and wood engraver. Worked in Boston, 1847–50; Cincinnati, 1850–51; Boston, 1852; and New York City in 1858 and after. He produced illustrations for *Harper's*, the *Illustrated-American News*, and numerous books (bibliography in Hamilton, pp. 148–49).

JEWETT, CHARLES A. Engraver, in Cincinnati 1845–56. Supervisor, 1845, at Toppan, Carpenter and Company, bank note engravers. Later he worked at premises on the northwest corner of Third and Walnut. Born in Lancaster, Massachusetts, began engraving ca. 1838 in New York City, and after his years in Cincinnati returned to New York City, where he died in 1878.

JONES, FITZ EDWIN. Started as a printer in Carlisle, Pennsylvania, then a copperplate printer in New York City in the 1840s. In Cincinnati, 1856–60, where he worked as an engraver and printer, some of the time at 148 Main Street.

JONES, GEORGE T. Engraver, 1850–57. His address, 148 Main Street, being the same as Fitz Edwin Jones (supra), suggests they were related. Born in Pennsylvania ca. 1818. He is listed in CDs with various middle initials.

JONES, THEODORE. Wood engraver, 1856–60+, with business address at the southeast corner of Fourth and Walnut.

KINSEY, NATHAN. Engraver, 1858–59. A Delaware native.

KINSEY, NATHANIEL. Born in Delaware ca. 1829. Engraver at Cincinnati bank note engravers Toppan, Carpenter & Co in 1850–51. Listed in CDs through 1859 (except 1855), sometimes as engraver and sometimes with no trade given.

KINSEY, NATHANIEL, JR. Engraver, listed, in addition to his father (?) and namesake, in the 1850–51 CD.

KNIGHT, EDWARD HENRY, 1824–. Born in England. In Cincinnati 1845–54, working as solicitor for patents and mechanical engineer. Later worked in D.C. for the Patent Office and was a commissioner to the Philadelphia Centennial Exhibition (1876) and to the International Exposition in Paris (1878). His papers are at the Cincinnati Historical Society.

LAYMAN, JAMES H. Wood engraver, 1855–59, with addresses given variously as 22, 24, and 25 West Fourth Street.

LENOBLE, AUGUSTE. Partner, with Henri Lovie, in designing and wood engraving firm Lovie and Lenoble, 180 Walnut Street, in 1853.

LEVI, ISAAC G. His entry in the 1836–37 CD is "engraver and circulating library," 107 Main Street. In New Orleans in 1852.

LINCOLN, HENRY P. Partner, with Phocion R. Way, in wood engraving firm Way & Lincoln, 24 West Fourth Street in 1855.

Lovejoy, John H. Wood engraver at Doolittle & Munson, 1835–37; proprietor of his own shop, 1840–44.

Lovie, Henri. Wood engraver and designer. Partner, with Auguste Lenoble, in firm Lovie and Lenoble (1853); partner, with Charles B. Bauerle, in firm Lovie & Bauerle (1856); partner, with Bauerle and John C. Bruen, in firm Lovie, Bauerle & Bruen (1857). Remained in Cincinnati until at least 1859. *Leslie's Magazine* employed him as a field artist during Civil War.

MacBrair, Archibald. Copperplate engraver and printer at 14 East Fourth Street. Listed in 1857, 1860, 1862, 1863 CDs.

Magnus, Leonard. Engraver, 1860, with premises at 51 West Fourth Street.

Martin, Ebenezer. Copperplate engraver and printer, 1825–31, with premises, 1825, on Sycamore between Third and Fourth; thereafter on Seventh between Plum and Western Row. A native of England.

Mason, Richard. Wood engraver, 1859–60+, with offices at 2 North Fourth Street.

Middleton, Elijah C. Listed as early as 1850 as engraver and bookseller, with premises in the Odd Fellows Building, 115 Walnut Street. Partner, with William R. Wallace and Hines Strobridge, in engraving and lithographing firm Middleton, Wallace & Co. (1855–58). Martin B. Ewing joined the company in 1857. In 1859 Wallace withdrew from the firm and the name was changed to Middleton, Strobridge and Company (1859–1864).

Mosler, Henry, Jr. Born and grew up in Richmond, Indiana; moved to Cincinnati ca. 1858. Listed in 1858 CD as wood engraver; in the early 1860s as portrait painter, engraver, and artist.

Munson, H. A. Wood engraver at Doolittle & Munson, 1831, possibly a son of Samuel B. Munson, a partner in the firm.

Munson, James A. Wood engraver at Doolittle & Munson, 1834 to 1836 or 1837, a native of Connecticut. Possibly a son of Samuel B. Munson, a partner in the firm.

Munson, Samuel B. Born, 1806, New Haven, Connecticut. Established in Cincinnati with partner Curtis M. Doolittle, engraving firm of Doolittle & Munson, 1831–46. In partnership with James E. Smith, 1851–52, with premises at 38 West Fourth Street. Thereafter, 1853–60+, he worked independently. He died April 6, 1880.

Nevers, Edward. Copperplate printer, 1840–46.

Norman, William T. Wood engraver. In New York City in 1850; in Cincinnati, 1857–60+.

Peck, W. H. Advertised in *Gray's Business Mirror*, 1851–52, as engraver on wood on Walnut Street opposite the Gibson House hotel.

Peticolas, Edward F. Wood engraver, 1857; engraver, 1860–61; assistant librarian at Young Men's Mercantile Library, 1863.

Reed, Edwin O. Born in Ohio ca. 1824. Engraver in Cincinnati, 1850–58.

Rhodes, George F. Engraver and die sinker, 1857–59, latterly with the Cincinnati Type Foundry.

Sanxay, T. Engraver on wood, 1834, at the bookstore of Morgan and Sanxay.

Seymour, John B. Wood engraver. In New York City 1852; in Cincinnati 1853–55 with premises in the Post Office Building.

Shipley, Henry H. Born in New York ca. 1830. Engraver in Cincinnati 1850–60+. In partnership with his brother William Shipley and C. F. Hall, 1851–52, under the name Shipley, Hall & Co. In partnership with his brother William Shipley and George K. Stillman under the name Shipley & Stillman, 1853. In partnership with his brother William Shipley under the name Henry H. Shipley & Bro. 1853–60+ with offices at 22 West Fourth Street.

Shipley, William. Partner, with his brother Henry H. Shipley, in the engraving firm Henry H. Shipley & Bro. (1853–1860+).

Smith, James E. Ohio native, son of Thomas Smith, in Cincinnati by 1850, aged twenty-two. Partner with Samuel B. Munson, 1850–51. Engraver, with premises at 38 West Fourth Street, 1851–53. The 1855 CD states that he "works for Shipley." In 1859 he was in Louisville, Kentucky.

Stillman, George K. Born in Massachusetts ca. 1821. Wood engraver. In Cincinnati by 1840 when he was working for Doolittle & Munson. In partnership with J. Milton Balthis, 1851–52 under name Stillman & Balthis; in partnership with Henry and William Shipley under the name Shipley & Stillman, 1853. Continued in business under his own name, 1855–60+.

Telfer, John R. Engraver at Grosvenor & Thompson's, 1850–51; wood engraver working under his own name, 1851–58. In 1855 "J. R. and J. Telfer" are listed as working together.

Thompson, Charles W. Partner, with Horace C. Grosvenor, in the wood engraving firm of Grosvenor & Thompson, 1850–51. A Charles W. Thompson is listed in New York City in 1840s and 1850s CDs as engraver, painter, etc.; possibly the same man.

Thomson, William S. Copperplate printer at C. W. James's, 1831.

Vallentine, R. Signed a woodcut in 1850–51 CD (p. 57). The same year Frazer & Dennis noted that they were "successors to R. Vallentine."

Waggoner, William W. Wood engraver in Cincinnati, 1853–56 and 1859.

Wagner, Andrew. Listed as wood engraver in 1860 CD. Before that time he worked, 1856–59, as a lithographer for Adolphus Menzel of Klauprecht & Menzel.

Walker, David S. Engraver, 1829.

Walker, David T. Engraver, 1829.

Way, Phocion R. Partner, with Henry P. Lincoln, in wood engraving firm Way & Lincoln, 1855. Listed, 1857–58, without partner as engraver with premises at the northeast corner Fourth and Walnut.

Wevill, George. Worked in Philadelphia 1850–57; in Cincinnati, 1858–60.

Whipple, George. Engraver, 1834–37, with premises, 1836–37, at the southwest corner of Eighth and Vine Streets.

Winans, William O. Born in New York ca. 1830; worked in Cincinnati as a wood engraver, 1853–55.

Woodruff, William. Engraver. Born in Pennsylvania; worked in Philadelphia, 1817–24; in Cincinnati, 1825–36.

Appendix B

Fliegende Blätter

A Checklist of Lithographs, 1846–1847

Alice M. Cornell

This checklist was compiled from the only known complete copy of the *Fliegende Blätter* in the Cincinnati Historical Society. Height and width dimensions for image sheets in this bound copy are given in that order. Beginning in January 1847, individual images or plates on a sheet were numbered. These numbers are indicated on the list. Four images do not include numbers. There is a break between issues 66 and 69. There are no images in the intervening issues in this copy.

Title Page: Fliegende Blätter 1ter Jahrgang.
10.4 × 7.9 in (26.5 × 20.0 cm). Vol. 1, no. 1 (August 17, 1846), p. 1.

Ibrahim Pascha bei der Revue in Hyde Park, London.
7.9 × 10.4 in (20 × 26.5 cm). Vol. 1, no. 1 (August 17, 1846), p. 4.

Mexicaner.
7.9 × 10.4 in (20 × 26.5 cm). Vol. 1, no. 1 (August 17, 1846), p. 5.

Drach's Belle Vue Bei Cincinnati.
7.9 × 10.4 in (20 × 26.5 cm). Vol. 1, no. 1 (August 17, 1846), p. 12.

Hermann zu Detmold.
10.4 × 7.9 in (26.5 × 20.0 cm). Vol. 1, no. 1 (August 17, 1846), p. 13.

Pious IX.
10.4 × 7.9 in (26.5 × 20.0 cm). Vol. 1, no. 2 (August 22, 1946), p. 20.

Kirmesstanz am Rhein.
7.9 × 10.4 in (20 × 26.5 cm). Vol. 1, no. 2 (August 22, 1846), p. 21.

Der Krieg im Kaffernlande.
7.9 × 10.4 in (20 × 26.5 cm). Vol. 1, no. 2 (August 22, 1846), p.28.

Musterung der Malayen in der Capstadt / 6th May 1846.
7.9 × 10.4 in (20 × 26.5 cm). Vol. 1, no. 2 (August 22, 1846), p. 29.

Abd-el Kader.
10.4 × 7.9 in (26.5 × 20.0 cm). Vol. 1, no. 3 (August 29, 1846), p. 36.

Hohenstauffen.
7.9 × 10.4 in (20 × 26.5 cm). Vol. 1, no. 3 (August 29, 1836), p. 37.

Flatboat Fahrt im Westen.
7.9 × 10.4 in (20 × 26.5 cm). Vol. 1, no. 3 (August 29, 1836), p. 44.

Der politisirende Alte.
10.4 × 7.9 in (26.5 × 20.0 cm). Vol. 1, no. 3 (August 29, 1846), p. 45.

Keokuk.
10.4 × 7.9 in (26.5 × 20.0 cm). Vol. 1, no. 4 (September 5, 1946), p. 52.

Meyerbeer.
10.4 × 7.9 in (26.5 × 20.0 cm). Vol. 1, no. 4 (September 5, 1846), p. 53.

Harem Scene.
10.4 × 7.9 in (26.5 × 20.0 cm). Vol. 1, no. 4 (September 5, 1846), p. 60.

Napoleon bei Lodi.
10.4 × 7.9 in (26.5 × 20.0 cm). Vol. 1, no. 4 (September 5, 1846), p. 61.

Lenore.
7.9 × 10.4 in (20 × 26.5 cm). Vol. 1, no. 5 (September 12, 1846), p. 68.

Der durstige Alte.
10.4 × 7.9 in (26.5 × 20.0 cm). Vol. 1, no. 5 (September 12, 1846), p. 69.

Wilde Fahrt im Westen.
7.9 × 10.4 in (20 × 26.5 cm). Vol. 1, no. 5 (September 12, 1846), p. 76.

Chamiso.
10.4 × 7.9 in (26.5 × 20.0 cm). Vol. 1, no. 5 (September 12, 1846), p. 77.

[Portraits] Halm—Ebert—Frankl—Grillparzer—Bauernfeld— A. Grün—Deinhardstein—Lenau.
10.4 × 7.9 in (26.5 × 20.0 cm). Vol. 1, no. 6 (September 19, 1846), p. 84.

[Portraits] Zedlitz—Feuchtersleber—Pyrker—Stelzhammer—Vogl— Castelli—Seidl.
10.4 × 7.9 in (26.5 × 20.0 cm). Vol. 1, no. 6 (September 19, 1846), p. 85.

Auto da Fe.
10.4 × 7.9 in (26.5 × 20.0 cm). Vol. 1, no. 6 (September 19, 1846), p. 92.

Marshall Bugeaud.
10.4 × 7.9 in (26.5 × 20.0 cm). Vol. 1, no. 6 (September 19, 1846), p. 93.

Kaffern Häuptlinge.
7.9 × 10.4 in (20 × 26.5 cm). Vol. 1, no. 7 (September 26, 1846), p. 100.

Grossfürstin Olga.
10.4 × 7.9 in (26.5 × 20.0 cm). Vol. 1, no. 7 (September 26, 1846), p. 101.

Ruinen von Ninive.
7.9 × 10.4 in (20 × 26.5 cm). Vol. 1, no. 7 (September 26, 1846), p. 108.

Arbeiter bei dem Ausgraben von Ninive.
7.9 × 10.4 in (20 × 26.5 cm). Vol. 1, no. 7 (September 26, 1846), p. 109.

Aufruhr in Coeln.
7.9 × 10.4 in (20 × 26.5 cm). Vol. 1, no. 8 (October 3, 1846), p. 116.

Lord Byron's Statue.
10.4 × 7.9 in (26.5 × 20.0 cm). Vol. 1, no. 8 (October 3, 1846), p. 117.

Der erste Kummer.
10.4 × 7.9 in (26.5 × 20.0 cm). Vol. 1, no. 8 (October 3, 1846), p. 124.

Walhalla bey Regensburg.
7.9 × 10.4 in (20 × 26.5 cm). Vol. 1, no. 8 (October 3, 1846), p. 125.

General Taylor.
7.9 × 10.4 in (20 × 26.5 cm). Vol. 1, no. 9 (October 10, 1846), p. 132.

Wettrennen von Sioux Indianern.
7.9 × 10.4 in (20 × 26.5 cm). Vol. 1, no. 9 (October 10, 1846), p. 133.

Festdesberliner Künstler Vereins.
7.9 × 10.4 in (20 × 26.5 cm). Vol. 1, no. 9 (October 10, 1846), p. 140.

Schiller's Denkmal zu Stuttgart.
10.4 × 7.9 in (26.5 × 20.0 cm). Vol. 1, no. 9 (October 10, 1846), p. 141.

Marmor Statue von Sir Walter Scott.
10.4 × 7.9 in (26.5 × 20.0 cm). Vol. 1, no. 10 (October 17, 1846), facing p. 156.

Enthüllung von Scott's Monument.
10.4 × 7.9 in (26.5 × 20.0 cm). Vol. 1, no. 10 (October 17, 1846), between pp. 156 and 157.

Schamyl der Tscherkessen Haeuptling.
7.9 × 10.4 in (20 × 26.5 cm). Vol. 1, no. 10 (October 17, 1846), facing p. 157.

Russische Truppen im Kaukasischen Feldzuge.
7.9 × 10.4 in (20 × 26.5 cm). Vol. 1, no. 10 (October 17, 1846), facing p. 158.

Hambacher Fest.
7.9 × 10.4 in (20 × 26.5 cm). Vol. 1, no. 11 (October 24, 1846), facing p. 165.

Aus dem Yankee Doodle.
10.4 × 7.9 in (26.5 × 20.0 cm). Vol. 1, no. 11 (October 24, 1846), facing p. 170.

1. Professor Schoenbein—2. Professor Grove—3. Sir F. W. Herschel—4. Dr. Daube—5. Professor Forbes—6. Prof. Heinrich Rose—7. Reverend Dr. Whewell—8. Professor Wheatstone—9. Obrist Sabine.
7.9 × 10.4 in (20 × 26.5 cm). Vol. 1, no. 11 (October 24, 1846), facing p. 175.

Deutsche Volksmänner. 1. P. J. Siebenpfeiffer—2. Dr. Wirth—3. J. L. Uhland—4. G. Fein—5. F. G. Welcker—6. D. V. Retteck.
10.4 × 7.9 in (26.5 × 20.0 cm). Vol. 1, no. 11 (October 24, 1846), facing p. 176.

Goethes Standbild zu Frankfurt A/M.
10.4 × 7.9 in (26.5 × 20.0 cm). Vol. 1, no. 12 (October 31, 1846), facing p. 186.

[Title in gutter—cartoon].
7.9 × 10.4 in (20 × 26.5 cm). Vol. 1, no. 12 (October 31, 1846), facing p. 188.

Fox Indianer.
10.4 × 7.9 in (26.5 × 20.0 cm). Vol. 1, no. 12 (October 31, 1846), facing p. 192.

Abdul Madian.
10.4 × 7.9 in (26.5 × 20.0 cm). Vol. 1, no. 12 (October 31, 1846), between pp. 192 and 193.

Wanderung einer Kalmuken Familie.
7.9 × 10.4 in (20 × 26.5 cm). Vol. 1, no. 13 (November 7, 1846), facing p. 204.

D'atteln-Verkäufer—Kammer-Jäger—Schuhflicker.
7.9 × 10.4 in (20 × 26.5 cm). Vol. 1, no. 13 (November 7, 1846), facing p. 205.

Aufzug des General Statthalters von Ostindien Zu Kurnaul.
7.9 × 10.4 in (20 × 26.5 cm). Vol. 1, no. 13 (November 7, 1846), facing p. 206.

Die Spanische Heiratsfrage.
7.9 × 10.4 in (20 × 26.5 cm). Vol. 1, no. 13 (November 7, 1846), between pp. 206 and 207.

Die Great Britain Gestrandet in der Dundrum Bay.
7.9 × 10.4 in (20 × 26.5 cm). Vol. 1, no. 13 (November 7, 1846), between pp. 206 and 207.

Die Französischerdeputirten Kammer.
7.9 × 10.4 in (20 × 26.5 cm). Vol. 1, no. 14 (November 14, 1846), facing p. 221.

Wasserscheu.
10.4 × 7.9 in (26.5 × 20.0 cm). Vol. 1, no. 14 (November 14, 1846), facing p. 222.

Wellington's Statue.
10.4 × 7.9 in (26.5 × 20.0 cm). Vol. 1, no. 14 (November 14, 1846), between pp. 222 and 223.

Dampfmaschine zum Auspumpen das Haarlemer Meeres.
10.4 × 7.9 in (26.5 × 20.0 cm). Vol. 1, no. 15 (November 21, 1846), facing p. 230.

General Taylor's Standpunkt zu Monterey.
7.9 × 10.4 in (20 × 26.5 cm). Vol. 1, no. 15 (November 21, 1846), between pp. 230 and 231.

Gutenberg's Standbild zu Mainz.
10.4 × 7.9 in (26.5 × 20.0 cm). Vol. 1, no. 15 (November 21, 1846), facing p. 232.

Die Spanishchen Heirathen. 1. Maria Isabella Louise Oder Isabella II, Königin Von Spanien—2. Maria Louise Ferdinanda, Infantin—3. Don Francois D'assis, Marie Ferdinand, Herzog V. Cadiz—4. Antoine-Marie Joseph Louis D'orleans, Herzog V. Montpensier.
10.4 × 7.9 in (26.5 × 20.0 cm). Vol. 1, no. 15 (November 21, 1846), facing p. 234.

Leipziger Messe. [Twelve vignettes].
10.4 × 7.9 in (26.5 × 20.0 cm). Vol. 1, no. 15 (November 21, 1846), p. 239.

Point Isabel.
7.9 × 10.4 in (20 × 26.5 cm). Vol. 1, no. 16 (December 5, 1846), facing p. 252.

Matamoras.
7.9 × 10.4 in (20 × 26.5 cm). Vol. 1, no. 17 (December 12, 1846), facing p. 267.

Künstlerfäsching in Munchen.
7.9 × 10.4 in (20 × 26.5 cm). Vol. 1, no. 17 (December 12, 1846): facing p. 268.

Jäger bei Thun.
7.9 × 10.4 in (20 × 26.5 cm). Vol. 1, no. 17 (December 12, 1846), facing p. 272.

Obrist Egloff / Commandeur der Zweiten Brigade—Schumacher Lagencomandant / Elgger Obristltnt—Obrist Gmür / Inspector.
7.9 × 10.4 in (20 × 26.5 cm). Vol. 1, no. 17 (December 12, 1846), after p. 272.

1. Mexicanische Reiterei—2. Das Kinderballet der Mad. Weis, Blumentanz—3. C. Spindler—4. F. Freiligrath—5. F. Mosen.
11.2 × 8.6 in (28.5 × 22 cm). Vol. 1, no. 18 (January 30, 1847), facing p. 8.

6. Wiener Shokoladmädchen.
11.2 × 8.6 in (28.5 × 22 cm). Vol. 1, no. 19 (February 6, 1847), facing p. 16.

7. Carneval zu Coeln—8. Don Montes.
11.2 × 8.6 in (28.5 × 22 cm). Vol. 1, no. 20 (February 13, 1847), facing p. 24.

Joh. Szerski—Joh. Ronge—A Theiner.
8.6 × 11.2 in (22 × 28.5 cm). Vol. 1, no. 21 (February 20, 1847), facing p. 32.

9. F. C. Dahlmann—10. G. Gervinius—11. L. Ranke—12. Wlhm. Grimm—13. Jakob Grimm.
11.2 × 8.6 in (28.5 × 22 cm). Vol. 1, no. 21 (February 20, 1847), after p. 32.

14. Der Abschied.
11.2 × 8.6 in (28.5 × 22 cm). Vol. 1, no. 22 (February 27, 1847), facing p. 40.

15. Baden Baden—16. Engländer—17. Russe—18. Franzose—19. Italiener.
11.2 × 8.6 in (28.5 × 22 cm). Vol. 1, no. 23 (March 6, 1847), facing p. 42.

20. Erwin's Denkmal—21. Strassburger Münster.
11.2 × 8.6 in (28.5 × 22 cm). Vol. 1, no. 24 (March 13, 1847), facing p. 50.

22. Fanny Gerito—Taglioni—Lucile Grahn—23. Thiers—24. Koletti.
11.2 × 8.6 in (28.5 × 22 cm). Vol. 1, no. 25 (March 20, 1847), facing p. 60.

25. Der Stamgast.
11.2 × 8.6 in (28.5 × 22 cm). Vol. 1, no. 26 (March 27, 1847), facing p. 72.

26. Schlacht bei Buena Vista.
8.6 × 11.2 in (22 × 28.5 cm). Vol. 1, no. 27 (April 3, 1847), facing p. 80.

27–42. Phrenologische Studien. [Sixteen cartoon vignettes].
11.2 × 8.6 in (28.5 × 22 cm). Vol. 1, no. 28 (April 10, 1847), facing p. 88.

43. Sängerfest am Rhein / R. Benedir.
11.2 × 8.6 in (28.5 × 22 cm). Vol. 1, no. 28 (April 10, 1847), after p. 88.

44. Auffahrt zur Ulm—45. Sennhütte.
11.2 × 8.6 in (28.5 × 22 cm). Vol. 1, no. 29 (April 17, 1847), facing p. 96.

46. Abfahrt von der Ulm.
11.2 × 8.6 in (28.5 × 22 cm). Vol. 1 , no. 30 (April 24, 1847), facing p. 104.

47–49. Des Herrn Barons Beisele und seines Hofmeisters Dr. Gisele / Krenz—un Onerzüge, / Havre. [Three cartoon vignettes].
11.2 × 8.6 in (28.5 × 22 cm). Vol. 1, no. 31 (May 1, 1847), facing p. 116.

50. Lola Montez.
11.2 × 8.6 in (28.5 × 22 cm). Vol. 1, no. 33 (May 13, 1847), facing p. 124.

51. General Scott.
11.2 × 8.6 in (28.5 × 22 cm). Vol. 1, no. 34 (May 22, 1947), facing p. 136.

52–54. New York. [Three cartoon vignettes].
11.2 × 8.6 in (28.5 × 22 cm). Vol. 1, no. 35 (May 29, 1847), facing p. 140.

55. Die blinde Mutter / Gretchen du spinnst ja nicht!
11.2 × 8.6 in (28.5 × 22 cm). Vol. 1, no. 36 (June 5, 1847), facing p. 152.

56. David Zeisberger, / 1er Ansiedler in Ohio.
11.2 × 8.6 in (28.5 × 22 cm). Vol. 1, no. 36 (June 5, 1847), after p. 152.

57. Das dritte Jahresfest der Liedertafel.
8.6 × 11.2 in (22 × 28.5 cm). Vol. 1, no. 37 (June 12, 1847), facing p. 160.

No Images. Vol. 1, no. 38 (June 19, 1847).

58. Sommer.
11.2 × 8.6 in (28.5 × 22 cm). Vol. 1, no. 39 (June 26, 1847), facing p. 174.

59–61. einem fashionable Neger Balle. [Three cartoon vignettes].
11.2 × 8.6 in (28.5 × 22 cm). Vol. 1, no. 40 (July 3, 1847), facing p. 180.

62. Der blinde Sieger.
11.2 × 16.9 in (28.5 × 43 cm). Vol. 1, no. 41 (July 10, 1847), facing p. 190.

63. Thal von Mexiko.
11.2 × 8.6 in (28.5 × 22 cm). Vol. 1, no. 41 (July 10, 1847), facing p. 192.

64–66. Tragische Geschichte (Chamisso). [Three vignettes].
11.2 × 8.6 in (28.5 × 22 cm). Vol. 1, no. 42 (July 17, 1847), facing p. 200.

No images. Vol. 1, no. 43 (July 24, 1847).

No images. Vol. 1, no. 44 (July 31, 1847).

No images. Vol. 1, no. 45 (August 7, 1847).

69. Nordamerikanisches Waldstück.
8.6 × 11.2 in (22 × 28.5 cm). Vol. 1, no. 46 (August 15, 1847), facing p. 230.

70–71. Schlacht bei Palo Alto, / 6 Mai 1846.
8.1 × 22.6 in (20.5 × 57.5 cm). Vol. 1, no. 47 (August 28, 1847), facing p. 234.

Schlacht bei Resaca de la Palma, / 9 Mai 1846.
10.0 × 21.1 in (25.5 × 53.5 cm). Vol. 1, no. 48 (September 4, 1847), facing p. 242.

No images. Vol. 1, no. 49 (September 11, 1847).

No images. Vol. 1, no. 50 (September 18, 1847).

No images. Vol. 1, no. 52 (October 2, 1847).

72. Cliff Mine / am See Superior.
8.6 × 11.2 in (22 × 28.5 cm). Vol. 1, no. 51 (September 25, 1847), facing p. 268.

Appendix C

Ehrgott, Forbriger & Co. Civil War Portraits

Christopher W. Lane

Key to locations:

CHS	Cincinnati Historical Society
CHS-	Listed in card catalog but missing
CHS+	In society collection but not from portfolio
CL	Cincinnati Library
CLM	Clements Library
LL	Lilly Library, Indiana University
LOC	Library of Congress
LOC-K	Listed in Milton Kaplan's article "Heads of State" in Library of Congress
NPG	National Portrait Gallery

Political Prints

Note: All the political prints have background P and no imprint, except as noted.

John Brough
"John Brough. / Governor Of Ohio."

Salmon P. Chase
"Salmon P. Chase. / Secretary Of The Treasury." [CHS-; CLM; LOC-K]

Andrew Johnson
"Andy Johnson. / Military Gov. Of Tenn." [CHS; CLM; LOC-K]

Abraham Lincoln
"A. Lincoln. / President Of The U.S." [LOC-K; NPG]

Oliver Perry Morton
"O. P. Morton. / Gov. Of Indiana." [CHS; LOC-K]

Two variants exist of this print, one with the head redrawn on the same body. In the later variant the head is set a bit higher in the print and shifted slightly to the left, so that it covers the "s" at the end of "United States" in the map title; this "s" is not covered on the earlier variant of this print. The title of the later variant is also redrawn, for it is set slightly lower to the image and at something of an angle. Perhaps the head was redrawn when Morton was reelected in 1864.

William Henry Seward
"Hon. William H. Seward. / Secretary Of State."

Edwin McMasters Stanton
"E. M. Stanton / Sec. War." [CHS; CLM; NPG]

One example of this print has the imprint "Lith. v. Ehrgott, Forbriger & Co. Cincinnati." This example also has a sepia tint stone.

David Tod
"David Tod. / Gov. Of Ohio." [CHS; CLM; LOC-K]

Gideon Welles
"Hon. Gideon Welles. / Secretary of the U.S. Navy."

Military Officers

Note: At least one example of all the military prints has an imprint for Ehrgott & Forbriger & Co., except as noted.

Nathaniel Prentiss Banks
"Nathl. P. Banks. / Maj. Genl. U.S.A." Background S1. With sepia tint stone. [LL]
"Nathl. P. Banks. / Maj. Genl. U.S.A." Background S6b. [CHS; LOC]

Louis Blenker
"Louis Blenker. / Brig. Genl. U.S.A." Background S6a. With sepia tint stone. [LL; NPG]

Ambrose Everett Burnside
"A. E. Burnside, / Maj. Genl. U.S.A." No imprint. Background S10. [NPG]
"A. E. Burnside / Maj. Genl. U.S.A." Background S14a. [LOC-K]

Burnside is listed in the card catalog as being part of the CHS portfolio, but this print is missing, so it is not certain which of these images it was.

Benjamin Franklin Butler
"B. F. Butler. / Maj. Genl. U.S.A." Background S2. [CHS; LL; NPG]
"B F Butler / Maj. Genl. U.S.A." No imprint. Background S3c. [LOC-K]

The example in the Lilly Library has a sepia tint stone.

Michael Corcoran
"Corcoran, Col. 69th. Reg^{t}. N.Y.S.M." Background S1. [CHS; NPG]

The blanket has two stars despite Corcoran being a colonel, probably because it was taken from the Banks impression and never changed.

Samuel Ryan Curtis
"S. R. Curtis / Major General U.S.A." Background S3a. [CHS; LL; LOC-K; NPG]

Jefferson C. Davis
"Jefferson C. Davis. / Brig. Genl. U.S.A." No imprint. Background S10. [CHS; LOC-K; NPG]

John Adams Dix
"John. A. Dix. / Maj. Genl. U.S.A." No imprint. Background S2. [CHS+; LOC-K]

Ebenezer Dumont
"E. Dumont. / Brig. Genl. U.S.A." Background S13b. [LL; NPG]

Ephraim Elmer Ellsworth
"E. E. Ellsworth. / Col. Ellsworth's N.Y. Zouaves." No imprint. Background S3b. [CHS; LOC-K]
"E. Elsworth.[*sic*] / Col. N.Y.Z." No imprint. Background S6b.

William Buel Franklin
"W^m. B. Franklin. / Maj. Genl. U.S.A." Background S3a. [CHS; LL; LOC-K; NPG]
The example in the Lilly Library has a sepia tint stone.

John Charles Frémont
"John C. Fremont. / Maj. Genl. U.S.A." Background S3a. [CHS; CLM; LL; LOC-K; NPG]
The example in the Lilly Library has a sepia tint stone and an accented "é."

Quincy Adams Gillmore
"Q. A. Gilmore [*sic*] / Maj. Genl. U.S.A." No imprint. Background S15. [LOC-K]

Ulysses S. Grant
"Ulysses S. Grant / Maj. Genl. U.S.A." Background S11. [CHS; NPG]
"U.S. Grant / Maj. Genl. U.S.A." Background S14a. [LOC-K; NPG]

Henry Wagner Halleck
"Henry W. Halleck / Maj. Genl. U.S.A." Background S3e. [CHS; CLM; LOC-K]

Samuel Peter Heintzelman
"S. P. Heintzelman / Maj. Genl. U.S.A." Background S4c. [LL]
"S. P. Heintzelman / Maj. Genl. U.S.A." Background S5b. [CHS; NPG]
"S. P. Heintzelman. / Maj. Genl. U.S.A." No imprint. Background S6b.

Joseph Hooker
"Joe. Hooker. / Maj. Genl. U.S.A." No imprint. Background S10. [CHS; LOC-K; NPG]
"Joe. Hooker. / Maj. Genl. U.S.A." Background S15.

David Hunter
"D. Hunter. / Maj. Genl. U.S.A." Background S2. [CHS; CLM; NPG]

Frederick West Lander
"Fred. W. Lander, / Brig. Genl. U.S.A." Background S6a. With sepia tint stone. [LL]

John Quincy Lane or James Henry Lane (?)
"Jim. Lane / Brig. Genl. U.S.A." Background S6a. With sepia tint stone. [LL]
James H. Lane, leader of the Free State movement in Kansas, was ranked only as high as major general and during the war was a senator, not an officer. There was also a James H.

Lane, who was a Confederate brigadier general. However, this image might be John Q. Lane, who was from Ohio and who was breveted as a brigadier general; the first name on the print may be a mistake.

John Alexander Logan (?)

"Joseph A. Logan. / Maj. Genl. U.S.A." No imprint. Background S4b. [CHS+; CLM]

No Joseph A. Logan has been found, so this is probably John A. Logan, who was appointed as a major general on November 29, 1862, and who commanded the Army of Tennessee.

Nathaniel Lyon

"Nathl. Lyon. / Brig. Genl. U.S.A. / Killed at the Battle of Springfield Mo Aug 10 1861 / After life's fitful fever, he sleeps well, / Treason has done his worst." Background S7. [CHS; CL; CLM; LOC-K; NPG]

William Haines Lytle

"W. H. Lytle / Colonel. Tenth Ohio." Background S13b. [CHS-; NPG]

George Brinton McClellan

"Geo. B. M^{c}.Clellan. / Maj. Genl. U.S.A." Background S8. Chromolithograph.

"Geo. B. M^{c}.Clellan. / Maj. Genl. U.S.A. / And Staff." Background S14a. [NPG]

"En Avant!" A music sheet with unattributed image of McClellan by Ehrgott & Forbriger. Cincinnati: A. C. Peters & Bro., 1862. Same face as other McClellans, with horse and body from background S10, but figure is about two-thirds the size of the regular portraits.

McClellan is listed in the card catalog as being part of the CHS portfolio, but this print is missing, so it is not certain which of these images it was.

John Alexander McClernand

"Jno. A. M^{c}.Clernand, / Brig. Genl. U.S.A." Background S7. [CHS; LOC-K; NPG]

Alexander McDowell McCook

"A. M^{c}. D. M^{c}.Cook. / Brig. Genl. U.S.A." Background S13a. [CHS; CLM; NPG]

Robert Latimer McCook

"Robt. L. M^{c}.Cook / Co^{l}. 9th. (First German) Reg^{t}. / O.V.U.S.A." Background S13b. [CHS-; CLM; LOC; NPG]

Irwin McDowell

"Irwin M^{c}.Dowell, / Maj. Genl.. U.S.A." No imprint. Background S12. [NPG]

George Gordon Meade

"Geo. G. Meade. / Maj. Genl. U.S.A. / Commander Of The Potomac Army." Background S14a. [CHS+; CLM; LOC-K; NPG]

Thomas Francis Meagher

"Thos. Fr. Meagher / Brig. Genl. U.S.A." Background S7. With sepia tint stone. [LL; NPG]

Minor Millikin

"Minor Millikin. / Co. First Ohio Cavalry." No imprint. Background S13c. [CHS]

Ormsby McKnight Mitchel

"O. M. Mitchell [*sic*] / Brig. Genl. U.S.A." Background S4b. [CHS-; LL; LOC]

William Nelson

"William Nelson / Brig. Genl. U.S.A." Background S6b. With sepia tint stone. [LL]

Peter Joseph Osterhaus
"P. J. Osterhaus / Brig.Genl.U.S.A." Background S15. [CLM]

William Starke Rosecrans
"W. S. Rosecrans. / Maj. Genl. U.S.A." No imprint. Background S10. [CHS; CLM; LOC-K; NPG]
"W. S. Rosecrans. / Maj. Genl. U.S.A." Background S15.

L. S. Rosseau (?)
"L. S. Rosseau / Maj. Genl. U.S.A." Background S5a. [CHS; LL; NPG]
This may be a mistake for L. H. Rousseau.

Lovell Harrison Rousseau
"Lovell H. Rousseau, / Maj. Genl. U.S.A." Background S14c. [CLM]

Robert Cumming Schenk
"Robert C. Schenk. / Maj. Genl. U.S.A." Background S14b. [LOC-K]

Carl Schurz
"Carl Schurz. / Maj. Gen. U.S.A." No imprint. Background S5b. [CHS]

Thomas West Sherman
"T. W. Sherman. / Brig. Genl. U.S.A." Background N4. With sepia tint stone. [LL]
Though in the army, T. W. Sherman is shown on a ship.

William Tecumseh Sherman
"W. T. Sherman. / Maj. Genl. U.S.A." No imprint. Background S2. [CHS+; LOC-K]

James Shields
"James Shields / Brig. Genl. U.S.A." Background S6a. With sepia tint stone. [NPG]

Daniel Edgar Sickles
"Dan. E. Sickles / Maj. Genl. U.S.A." Background S15. [CHS; CLM; LOC-K]

Franz Sigel
"Franz Sigel. / Brig. Genl. U.S.A." Background S9. A chromolithograph. [CL; LL]
"Franz Sigel. / Maj. Genl. U.S.A." Background S9. [CHS; LL; LOC; NPG]
This is from the same stone as above, but with the change of rank, more stars on the saddle blanket, and it is not a chromolithograph.

George Stoneman
"Geo. Stoneman. / Maj. Genl. U.S.A." Background S15. [CHS; CLM; LOC-K]

Jeremiah Cutler Sullivan
"J. C. Sullivan. / Brig. Gen'l U.S.A." Background S3a. [CHS]

Edwin Vose Sumner
"E. V. Sumner / Maj. Genl. U.S.A." Background S12. [CHS; NPG]

George Henry Thomas
"George H. Thomas. / Maj. Genl. U.S.A." Background S15. [CHS+; CLM; LOC-K]

Lewis Wallace
"Lewis Wallace / Maj. Genl. U.S.A." Background S3d. [CHS-; NPG]

William Harvey Lamme Wallace
"W. Y. L. Wallace / Brig. Gen[l]. U.S.A." Background S4c. With sepia tint stone. [NPG]
"W. H. L. Wallace / Brig. Gen[l]. U.S.A." Background S4c. With sepia tint stone. [LL]
These prints differ only in the middle initial.

August Willich
"August Willich / Brig. Gen[l]. U.S.A." Background S5b. [CHS-; LL; LOC; NPG]

John Ellis Wool
"John E. Wool. / Maj. Gen[l]. U.S.A." Background S4a A chromolithograph. [CHS; LL; NPG]

Naval Officers

Note: At least one example of all the naval prints have an imprint for Ehrgott, Forbriger & Co., except as noted.

John Adolph Dahlgren
"Com. Dahlgreen. / U.S.N." No imprint. Background N1. [LOC-K; NPG]

Samuel Francis Du Pont
"S. F. Dupont, / Adm. U.S.N." No imprint. Background N4. [CHS; LOC]

David Glasgow Farragut
"Commodore Farragut / U.S. Navy." Background N5.

Andrew Hull Foote
"Commodore Foote, / U.S.N." Background N1. [CHS; LOC-K; NPG]

Louis Malesherbes Goldsborough
"Louis M. Goldsborough / Flag Officer U.S. Navy." Background N2. [CHS; LOC; NPG]

David Dixon Porter
"Admiral D. D. Porter / U.S. Navy." Background N1.

William David Porter
"Commodore W. D. Porter / U.S. Navy." Background N1. [CHS; CLM; NPG]

John Lorimer Worden
"John L. Worden. / Commanding the Monitor." No imprint. Background N3. [CLM]
"John L. Worden. / Commanding the Montauk / Capt. U.S. Navy." No imprint. Background N3. [CHS; LOC; NPG]

Appendix D

Ehrgott, Forbriger & Co. Backgrounds

Christopher W. Lane

Background P
A political figure is seated in a carved chair, facing to the left. His right hand holds a pen to a document which rests on a cloth-covered table, upon which sits an Indian-figure inkstand. From left to right behind the subject are a curved arch through which can be seen a field filled with troops in a battle; a bust of Washington mounted high in a corner; a wall map on rollers—"Map of the United States"—drapery, and a floor-standing globe. The only differences in the divers prints are the heads, collars, and ties (if any), with the coat and vest remaining the same. The stone is signed with initials, possibly "JS," but these are not visible in every impression. This background corresponds to Kaplan's group A.

Background S1
A figure is shown riding to the left on a horse which has two hooves off the ground. The foreground is flat, with woods behind, a fort just visible in the brush at the left, and a flag flying above.

Background S2
The main figure stands next to and holds the reins of a horse which faces to the left. Behind on the left is a formation of soldiers with their flag flying; behind on the right are three ships just off a coastline. This corresponds to Kaplan's group G.

Background S3a
A figure is shown sitting on a horse trotting to the right along a hilly path in the foreground. A rocky ledge is shown to the left and a small hill to the right. In the distance vague shading might indicate hills. A small white dot—a blemish in the lithographic stone—appears below the back left hoof. This corresponds to Kaplan's group E, which also includes a print of Ellsworth that actually has background S3b.

Background S3b
This background is a transfer from S3a, with the addition of Zouave troops marching from left to right. One can see a small bit of the old background shading at the right of the image and also some blemishes in the stone that first appear in S3a.

Background S3c
This background is also a transfer from S3a, with the rocky ledge on the left cut off halfway down and augmented by two bushes. Most of the background behind the main figure was removed and a river scene added, showing a double-stacked steamship on the river, with houses and steeples on the far bank. This corresponds to Kaplan's group I, which also includes a print of Halleck that actually has background S3e.

Background S3d
This is another transfer from S3a, with the same horse and body of the main figure but with the foreground modified. The rocky ledge at the left has been redrawn as a flat path, and the hill at the right has its top wiped out. The horse's back left hoof, not shown in S3a, is drawn in. The background has the same shading as S3a, except at the far right, where the shading in the sky is gone.

Background S3e
This background is a transfer either from S3a or S3d. Other than the main figure and his horse, at least from the top of its legs up, the background has been completely redrawn. The new foreground is fairly bare and level, with a tall bush shown at the left and a stump or basket at the right. In the distance is an army encampment, with wagons, tents, a flagpole, and troops in formation.

Background S4a
This is a chromolithographic background of a mounted figure on a standing horse facing to the left. The ground is a flat coastline leading up to the sea. A fort and lighthouse are shown on the right, a paddlewheel steamship is depicted at left, and a fleet of sailing ships and steamships is drawn in the distance.

Background S4b
This background is a transfer of the black image only from S4a. The same mounted figure on his horse is shown, and the flat foreground is the same, but this now leads down to a river rather than to a seaside as in S4a. On the right, the form of the fort from S4a is turned into a hill, with the tip of the lighthouse from S4a now shown as a vague building on top of the hill. At the left a row of tents and trees replaces the paddlewheeler, and in the middle a river scene is drawn with an ironclad sailing along. Masts of the ships from S4a can be seen faintly, looking somewhat like the ships might be docked at the town in the distance.

Background S4c
This is a transfer of the horse and rider from either S4a or S4b but with all else completely redrawn. The foreground is a slightly raised flat area with grass, stones, a few plants, and a tree stump. In the distance a formation of troops, led by two mounted figures, marches in rank in front of a rail fence. In some of the prints with this background a sepia tint stone has clouds in the sky and hills on the left.

Background S5a
A mounted figure sits facing to the right on a dark horse with two hooves off the ground. The figure holds the reins in his left hand, and his right arm is extended back to the left, with a cap held in that hand. The foreground is flat, with some woods shown in the middle distance and a hill in the back on the left. Troops are shown marching from left to right in front of the woods.

Background S5b
This image is a transfer from S5a, with the horse shown as dappled white rather than dark. The only other difference is that on S5b there are two light lines, clearly unintended blemishes, which run between the front two hooves of the horse.

Background S6a
In this two-tone background, a figure sits on a horse charging to the right, all four hooves in the air, holding a tasseled sword or hat aloft in his right hand. Behind to the left is a bugler and at the right is a marching rank of troops, one of whom turns around to cheer the general. The cheering soldier holds his cap in his hand just under the horse's nose. A script "A" is signed in the stone at the lower left. All these images have a sepia-tinted sky with clouds.

Background S6b
This is a transfer from S6a. The bugler is gone, though the faint outline of his horse's head and a disembodied leg can still be seen. The troops on the right have been completely redrawn, with the cheering soldier eliminated, though the faint outline of his cap can still be seen just under the horse's nose. The sword in the main figure's hand now has no tassel. This image appears both with and without a tint stone. The script "A" still appears. Blemish marks, shaped like facing "L"s, appear at the bottom center of the image.

Background S7
A figure, facing right, sits on a horse with its front right and back left hooves off the ground. The figure is turned slightly to his right, his right hand raised and holding a hat, straight sword, or curved sword. The ground is grassy and there is no other detail besides shading. One print with this background includes a sepia-tint stone, which adds clouds and a faint figure behind the tail of the main horse. This corresponds to Kaplan's group H.

Background S8
This is a chromolithographic background showing a figure, his right hand on his hip and his left holding the reins, mounted on a white horse facing left. In the distance is an encampment with many tents.

Background S9
A figure sits on a standing horse facing to the left. Hills are shown in the mid-distance, while the foreground is barren with some rocks. The horse has its front right hoof lifted high and its back left hoof just touching the ground.

Background S10
A general, his cape flying off his shoulders, sits on a horse charging to the left with all four hooves off the ground. The figure's left hand holds the reins and his right hand points forward.

In the left foreground is a cannonball and just behind it some bramble. Smoke fills the background. This corresponds to Kaplan's group F.

Background S11

This is a winter scene with a figure standing on a rise in the foreground, holding in his right hand a sword pointing down, his left hand pointing to the right. A sword, basket, cannonball, and cannon lie discarded in the foreground. Behind the main figure some troops are shown attacking to the right. At the left a soldier holds a flag, and at the right another tries to support a companion who has just been shot.

Background S12

A mounted figure, looking to the right, rides a white horse facing to the left. The horse has its front left and back right hooves lifted off the ground and it stands in a flat area with hills and a gully behind. To the left, at the foot of a hill, is some small brush, and to the right, in the distance, is a stand of trees.

Background S13a

A figure sits on a horse charging to the left with all of its hooves off the ground. The figure holds the reins in his left hand and his right hand extends straight out, holding a hat. Troops are drawn behind the figure on the left, and on the right are some more troops shown charging with a flag flying above the horse's tail. Signed "JS" in the stone.

Background S13b

This is a transfer from S13a, with a bugler replacing the flag on the right. The charging troops on the right are faintly visible, though it looks as if they are not supposed to be there. The main figure holds either a hat or a sword. Signed "JS" in stone.

Background S13c

This background was modified from S13b. The charging troops on the left are replaced by charging cavalry. However, still visible just below the charging horses is a faint image of the legs of the troops which were removed. The bugler is still shown on the right, but he is very worn. Signed with "JS" in the stone.

Background S14a

A figure, looking over his left shoulder and pointing with his right arm, sits on a horse facing to the left. Different figures hold different objects in the pointing hand. Behind the main figure, to the right, are four mounted soldiers, though the back figure is never strongly depicted and fades in later strikes. The horse of the front figure in this foursome is drawn with its two front legs showing between the back two legs of the main figure's horse. Behind and to the left are the butt end of a cannon, two horses, and a mounted figure. This corresponds to Kaplan's group B, which also includes Schenk, who actually has background S14b.

Background S14b

Transferred from S14a, this is a slightly more worn image. The two most distant figures of the group on the right are eliminated and the other two figures have redrawn heads, the officer on the far right now having a brimmed hat rather than a cap.

Background S14c
This is a transfer from S14b, even more worn. Added to the foreground are a cannonball and some scruffy grass. To the left is the butt end of a cannon and two horses with mounted figures. The figures on the right, shown on previous versions, are completely gone, but the two front legs of one of these figures' horse are still there, making it look like the central figure's horse has six legs.

Background S15
A mounted figure sits on a horse rearing on its two hind legs and facing to the left. The figure looks toward the viewer, his left hand holding the reins while his right hand is outstretched and pointed ahead. In the foreground, at the bottom left, is a prone body with a knapsack on its back and a hat lying behind its head; a cannonball is to the right. In the distance at the left are several marching figures with knapsacks and bayoneted rifles, and at the right are two mounted figures. This print includes square framed shading around the print, with clouds in the sky. This corresponds to Kaplan's group C.

Background N1
A figure stands on the cabin of an ironclad, holding a sword in the crook of his left arm. Behind him are three other ironclads steaming along the river, and a fort is shown on the shore in the distance on the left. The stone is signed with a script "JS." This corresponds to Kaplan's group D.

Background N2
A figure stands on the deck of a ship, holding a sword hilt in his left hand while his right arm is extended off to the left, holding a cap. Behind the main figure is a mast at left, a capstan behind, a flag in lower left corner, and two soldiers by the mast.

Background N3
A figure stands on the deck of an ironclad ship with shell fragments at his feet. He looks straight out, his left hand pointing across his body and his right hand holding a telescope. Behind him a rowboat passes a floating log, and on the farther shore is a fort on the right and an encampment on the left, with an ironclad ship just off the shore near the encampment.

Background N4
A figure stands on the deck of a ship, holding a sword hilt in his left hand, with his right hand behind his back. A sailor, shown slightly behind on the left, raises a flag on a pole, and a cannon covered by a coat is depicted slightly behind on the right. In the distance, across the water, is a shoreline with a ship, a fort, and tents at the right. The stone is signed with a script "JS." One of the prints has a sepia-tint stone, which adds a sail extending from the main figure's left shoulder to the upper right corner.

Background N5
A figure stands on a ship deck, before a mast, with his left arm hanging by his side and his right hand holding a telescope. The ship deck has a cannon at the left, a stool with a map of the Mississippi River on it at the right, and a sailor talking to two soldiers behind. In the distance at the left are a number of ships with their sails furled.

Appendix E

Artists and Publishers Represented in the Smithsonian's Graphic Arts Exhibit at the Ohio Valley Centennial Exposition, Cincinnati, 1888

Helena E. Wright

Note: This listing has been compiled from Koehler's 1888 catalog of the exhibition, plus catalog and accession files. Titles are supplied when they can be determined from these sources.

Actinic Engraving Co., photomechanical relief
Adams, J. A., wood engraving for *Harper's Illuminated Bible*, 1843
Albert, Dr. E., photogravure
Alt, Rudolf, etching
Amand-Durand, photogravure
American Photolithographic Co., photolithography
Amman, Jost, etching
Anderson, Dr. Alexander, eleven wood engravings, including *Waterfowl*, after Teniers (see fig. 6.25)
Andrew, George T., wood engravings
Andrew, John, wood engravings, including *Bull's Head* (see fig. 6.12)
Angerer, V., photogravure
Annan, T. & R., photogravure
Annan & Swan, photogravure
Annin, G., wood engraving after Landseer, 1852
Anthony, A. V. S., wood engravings
Asser, photolithography
Auer, machine engraving and galvanography

AUTOTYPE CO., photogravure

BACHER, OTTO, etchings
BALDUNG, HANS. *See* Grien, Hans Baldung
BARON, HENRI, lithograph
BARTOLOZZI, F., stipple engraving after A. Kauffman, purchased from Wunderlich, $10
BAUDE, CHAS., wood engraving
BAYER, T., lithograph
BEHAIM, HANS SEBALD, two engravings purchased from Wunderlich: *Mascaron*, $6; and *Hercules killing Caius*, $4
BELLOWS, A. F., etchings
BERGHEM, NICOLAS, etching, *Flute Player,* purchased from Wunderlich, $6
BERNSTROM, VICTOR, wood engravings
BEWICK, THOS., wood engraving
BLUM, ROBERT, etching
BOGART, J. A., wood engravings for *The Aldine*, 1872, and others
BOLSWERT, SCHELTE A., engraving, *Christ Crowned with Thorns*, purchased from Wunderlich, $67.50
BOOKHOUT, E., wood engraving for *Women of the Bible*, 1868
BOSTON PHOTOGRAVURE CO., collotype
BOULLONGNE, L. DE, etching
BOURDON, SEBASTIEN, etching
BOURGEOIS, C., lithograph
BOUSSOD, VALADON & CO., photomechanical relief and photogravure
BRACQUEMOND, F., etching
BRADFORD, L. H., photolithography
BRENNAN, ALFRED, etching
BROWN, GEORGE L., etchings
BROWN, J. G., etching

CALLOT, JACQUES, etchings, *Les Petites Miseres*, purchased from Wunderlich, $12
CANALE, ANTONIO [Canaletto], etching
CANTARINI, SIMONE, etching
CASSATT, MARY, eight etchings and drypoints, lent by S. P. Avery
CHAPMAN, J. G., etchings
CHARLET, N. T., lithograph
CHASE, WILLIAM MERRITT, etching
CHAUVEL, THEODORE, etching
CHIFFLART, F., etching
CHILDS, B. F., wood engraving, *Two Watchers*
CHURCH, F. S., etchings
CLAUDIUS, wood engraving
CLEMENTS, GABRIELLE, four etchings
CLOSS, A., wood engraving

Closson, William B., wood engravings
Cole, Timothy, wood engravings
Collas, A., machine engraving
Colman, Samuel, etchings
Corot, J. B. C., *cliché-verre*
Corwin, Chas., etchings
Crosscup & West, photomechanical relief, Ives process

D'Orschwillers, lithograph
Dallas, photogravure
Dana, William J., wood engravings
Danhauser, Jos., lithograph
Davis, J. P., wood engravings
Delacroix, Eugene, etching
Demarteau, Gille, crayon manner
Dielman, F., etching
Dietterlin, Wendel, etching
Dillaye, Blanche, four etchings
Dochy, wood engraving
Doms, A., wood engraving
Drevet, Pierre Imbert, engraving, *Cardinal Dubois*, purchased from Wunderlich, $16
Dujardin Heliogravure, photogravure
Dujardin, Karel, etching, *Donkey between Two Sheep*, purchased from Wunderlich, $9
Duperac, Etienne, etching
Dupont, H., aquatint and proof, *Cromwell at coffin of Chas I*, purchased from Wunderlich, $38
Durand, Asher B., engraving, *Ariadne*, 1835, after Vanderlyn (see fig. 6.14)
Durer, Albrecht, four woodcuts purchased from Keppel: *Death of the Virgin*, $12; *Virgin Crowned*, $4; *Coat of Arms of Nuremberg*, $6; *Supper at Emmaus*, $5. Two engravings, purchased from Wunderlich: *The Great Horse*, $16; *St Jerome*, $170. One etching, purchased from Wunderlich, *The Cannon*, $10 (see fig. 6.16)
Duveneck, Frank, etchings
Dyck, Anthony van, etching, *Justus Suttermans*, purchased from Wunderlich, $40

Earlom, Richard, three mezzotints
Egloffstein, von, photogravure
Elten, Kruseman van, etchings

Falconer, J. M., etchings
Farinati, Paolo, etching
Farrer, Henry, etchings
Feckert, G. H. G., lithograph after Knaus
Felter, J. D., wood engraving, for *Women of the Bible*, 1868
Ferris, S. J., etchings

FILLEBROWN, F. E., wood engravings
FILMER, JOHN, wood engravings for *The Aldine*, 1872
FLAMENG, LEOPOLD, etching
FORBES LITHOGRAPHIC CO., collotype (see fig. 6.21)
FOSTER, J., wood engraving for *Women of the Bible*, 1868
FOURNIER, U., wood engraving
FRENCH, FRANK, wood engravings
FRISCH, ALBERT, collotype
FROMENT, wood engraving

GAUGENGIGL, I., etchings and collotype after his painting (see fig. 6.21)
GAVARNI, lithograph
GEBBIE & HUSSON, photogravure (see fig. 6.23)
GEIGER, P. J. N., lithograph
GENDALL, lithograph
GETCHELL, EDITH L., six etchings
GIBBONS, P., photolithography
GIFFORD, R. SWAIN, etchings
GOLTZIUS, HENDRIK, engraving, *Son of Frisius*, purchased from Wunderlich, $75
GORDON, J. G., wood engraving for *Women of the Bible*, 1868
GOUPIL & CO., photogravure
GRAPHOTYPE COMPANY, graphotype
GREATOREX, ELIZA, five etchings
GREEN, VALENTINE, mezzotint
GRIEN, HANS BALDUNG, woodcut, *Horses Fighting*, purchased from Wunderlich, $9
GUTEKUNST, F., collotype
GUY, S. J., etching

HADEN, SEYMOUR, three etchings, purchased from Keppel: *Sunset on the Thames*, $13; *Scotch Firs, Inveroran*, $13; *Kilgaren Castle*, $8 (see fig. 6.8)
HALE, ELLEN DAY, two etchings
HAMILTON, HAMILTON, etching
HAMILTON, JAMES, *cliché-verre*
HANFSTAENGL, photogravure
HARLEY, wood engraving
HARROUN & BIERSTADT, collotype
HAYES, E. D., wood engravings for *Women of the Bible*, 1868, and others
HECHT, WILLIAM, etching and wood engraving
HEINEMANN, E., wood engravings
HELIOGRAPHIC ENGRAVING COMPANY, photogravure
HELIOTYPE PRINTING COMPANY, photolithography and collotype (see fig. 6.22)
HERKOMER, HUBERT, etching
HERRICK, H. W., wood engravings
HEYWOOD, TOM, lithograph

Hill, John Henry, etchings
Hinshelwood, Josiah, engraving
Hopfer, Daniel, etching, *Ornament*
Hopkins, G. E., etchings
Hoskin, Robert, wood engravings
Hovenden, Thos., etching
Howland, William, wood engraving

Illman & Pillbrow, engraving, *Jane's Cottage*
Ives & Barrett, photomechanical relief

Jacque, Chas., two etchings, purchased from Wunderlich: *Feeding Pigs*, $2.50; *La Rentrée*, $2.50
Jacquemart, Jules, etching
James, Col. Henry, photolithography
Jewett & Chandler, wax engraving
Johnson, G. E., wood engraving
Johnson, T., wood engravings
Josey, Richard, mezzotint
Juengling, Frederic, wood engravings

K. K. Militar-Geog. Inst., photogravure
Karst, F., wood engravings
Kiessling, lithograph
Kilburn, S. S., wood engravings
King, F. S., wood engravings
King, Jas. S., etching
Kingdon, wood engraving for *Women of the Bible*, 1868
Kingsley, Elbridge, wood engravings
Kinnersley, A. F., wood engraving for *Women of the Bible*, 1868
Klic, lithograph
Klinkicht, M., wood engraving
Kobell, F. von, galvanography
Kretzschmar, Edward, wood engraving
Kriehuber, Jos., lithograph
Kruell, G., wood engravings, including *Phorcydes*, after Vedder
Kurtz, William, photomechanical relief

Lalanne, Maxime, etching
Langridge, J. L., wood engraving for *Women of the Bible*, 1868
Lasalle, Emile, lithograph, *Faust and Mephistopheles*, after Scheffer
Leggo Bros., photomechanical relief
Leibl, William, etching
Lemercier, Lerebour and Barreswill, photolithography

Le Mousseu, photogravure

Le Prince, J. B., aquatint

Leyden, Lucas van, engraving, *David before Saul*, purchased from Wunderlich, $43; etching, *Self-Portrait*, purchased from Keppel, $11.40 (now recognized as after a drawing by Dürer, not Lucas)

Linton, Henry, wood engraving for *Illustrated London News*

Linton, W. J., nine wood engravings for *Appleton's Art Journal*, *American Art Review*, and *Bacchus in America*, after Hennessey, 1869; wax engravings (see fig. 6.26)

Lippincott, Wm H., drypoint

London Stereoscopic & Photographic Co., Woodburytype

Lorraine, Claude le, etching, *Apollo and Muses*, purchased from Wunderlich, $20

Mansion, L., lithograph

Mante, photogravure

Mantegna, A. engraving, *Christ Descending into Limbo*, purchased from Keppel, $39.90

Maratti, Carlo, etching

Marsh, Henry Harris, wood engraving from *Insects Injurious to Vegetation*, 1862

Marvy, Louis, two soft-ground landscape etchings, purchased from Keppel, $1.75

Mason, wood engraving for American Tract Society

Masson, Antoine, engraving, *Comte d'Harcourt*, purchased from Wunderlich, $14

McLaughlin, M. Louise, etching and two drypoints

Meisenbach Co., photomechanical relief

Menzel, Adolf, two lithographs

Merritt, Anna Lea, five etchings, including *Ophelia* (see fig. 6.10)

Miller, Chas. H., etchings

Miller, Willy, wood engravings

Millet, F., etching

Minor, Robert C., etching

Mitchell, J. A., etchings

Monks, J. A., etching

Moore, Charles H., mezzotint

Moran, Leon, etching

Moran, Emily, four etchings (probably including *Long Beach, York Harbor, Maine*) (see fig. 6.28)

Moran, Mary Nimmo, seven etchings, including *Old Oaks*

Moran, Percy, etching

Moran, Peter, etchings (probably including *The Pool*) (see fig. 6.13)

Moran, Thomas, etchings

Morin, Jean, etching

Moss Engraving Co., photomechanical relief

Mouilleron, A., lithograph after Delacroix

Muller, Friedrich, engraving, *Sistine Madonna*, after Raphael, purchased from Wunderlich, $200 (see fig. 6.18)

Muller, R. A., wood engravings

Nanteuil, R., engraving, *Pompone de Bellievre*, purchased from Wunderlich, $47
Nesbit, Charlton, wood engraving
Nicoll, J. C., etchings
Niepce de St Victor, photogravure

Oakford, Ellen, seven etchings
Oertel, K., wood engraving
Orr, J. W., wood engraving
Orr, N., wood engravings
Osborne, H. Frances, five etchings
Osborne, J. W., photolithography
Ostade, Adriaan van, etching, *The Family*, purchased from Wunderlich, $8

P. [Parmegiano?], F., etching
Pannemaker, wood engraving
Parrish, Stephen, etchings
Patin, P., Woodburytype (photoglyptique)
Pennell, Joseph, etchings
Photo-Engraving Co., photomechanical relief (see fig. 6.24)
Photo-Galvanograph Co., photogravure
Photographische Gesellschaft, photogravure
Photogravure Co., photogravure and collotype
Piloty, Carl, etching
Pisan, H., wood engraving after Doré
Pitteri, G. M., engraving, *Self-Portrait*, after Piazetta, purchased from Wunderlich, $4
Platt, C. A., etchings and drypoint
Ploos van Amstel, *Cornelis*, crayon manner
Poitevin, Alphonse, photolithography
Pontius, Paul, engraving, *Thomiris*, after Rubens, purchased from Wunderlich, $32
Potter, Paul, etching, *Cow Resting by a Fence*, purchased from Wunderlich, $4.50
Powell, Caroline A., two wood engravings for *Harper's Magazine* (see fig. 6.27)
Prestel, Maria Catharina, aquatint
Pretsch, Paul, photomechanical relief and photogravure
Prout, Samuel, lithographs
Putnam, S. G., wood engravings

Quartley, F. W., wood engravings for *The Aldine*, 1871–72

Raimundi, Marcantonio, engraving, *Madonna on Clouds*, purchased from Keppel, $68.40
Rajon, Paul, etching, *Cardinal Newman*, purchased from Wunderlich, $9
Ramage, Jas., photolithography
Reichsdruckerei, photogravure
Rembrandt, etching, *Christ Preaching*, purchased from Wunderlich, $350 (see fig. 6.17)
Reni, Guido, etching

Ribera, Giuseppe, etching
Roberts, C., wood engraving for *London Graphic*
Rosa, Salvatore, etchings, *Oedipus*, plus another
Rosenberg, H., etching
Russell & Richardson, wood engravings
Ruysdael, Jacob van, etching, *Two Peasants*, purchased from Wunderlich, $6
Ryland, Wynne, stipple engraving, *Achilles Mourning Death of Patrocolus*, purchased from Wunderlich, $9

Santo Bartoli, Pietro, etching
Sartain, John, mezzotints, *Robert Gilmor Jr.* and others (see fig. 6.19)
Saxton, Joseph, machine engraving
Schmidt, G. F. etching, *Self-Portrait*, purchased from Meder, $10; engraving, *Pierre Mignard*, after Rigaud, $40
Schoff, Stephen A., etchings
Schongauer, Martin, engraving, *Christ before Pilate*, purchased from Wunderlich, $93
Schoninger, galvanography
Schwarzburger, C., wood engraving
Sharp, William, engraving, *Dr. John Hunter*, after Reynolds, purchased from Wunderlich, $105
Shirlaw, Walter, etching, *The Reprimand*, after Eastman Johnson (see fig. 6.29)
Silvestre, Israel, etching
Simoneau & Toovey, photolithography
Sirani, Elisabetta, etching
Smillie, Jas D., etchings
Smithwick & French, wood engravings
Smithwick, J. G., wood engraving
Speer, wood engravings for *The Aldine*, 1873, and others
Spiegle, C., wood engraving for *The Aldine*, 1872
Sprague & Co., photolithography
Staudenbaur, Robert, wood engravings
Storm van's Gravesande, Chas., drypoint
Strange, Robert, engraving, *Charles I*, after Van Dyck, purchased from Meder, $20
Strixner, N., lithograph
Struthers (Jos.) & Co., wax engraving
Strutt, J. G., etching
Sylvester, H. E., wood engravings

Taber (Chas.) & Co., collotype
Talbot, Henry Fox, photogravure
Teel, George A., wood engravings
Thiriat, H., wood engraving
Thomas, George, vignettes for wood engravings
Thomas, W. L., wood engraving

THOMPSON, JOHN, wood engraving
THURWANGER, PETER, lithograph
TIETZE, R., wood engravings
TINKEY, JOHN, wood engravings
TISCHBEIN, J. H., JR., etching (sand manner)
TOOVEY, W., photolithography
TURNER, J. M. W., etching, *Woman and Tambourine*, purchased from Wunderlich, $20 (see fig. 6.15)
TWACHTMAN, MARTHA SCUDDER, four etchings
TYPOGRAPHIC ETCHING CO., photomechanical relief

UNGER, WILLIAM, etching (possibly *The Wallachian Team* after Schreyer) (see fig. 6.7)

VAILLANT, WALLERANT, engraving, *Boy Carrying Game*, purchased from Wunderlich, $8.50
VANDERHOOF, C. A., etching
VISSCHER, CORNELIS DE, engraving, *Gellius de Bouma*, purchased from Wunderlich, $20
VOGEL, A., wood engraving

WALDHEIM, wood engraving
WALKER, CHAS A., etchings and monotype
WALTNER, C. A., etching
WARD, GEO M., wood engraving for *Women of the Bible*, 1868
WELCKE, ROBERT, photolithography
WELLINGTON, FRANK H., wood engravings
WENDEL, T. M., etching
WHISTLER, J. A. M., three etchings purchased from Wunderlich: *Eagle Wharf*, $9; *Big Mast*, $25; and *Kitchen*, $24; and two others (see fig. 6.5)
WHITNEY, E. J., drawing for photomechanical relief work and wood engravings
WHITNEY, J. H., wood engraving for *Women of the Bible*, 1868, and others
WILLE, J. G., engraving, *Satin Gown* or *Parental Advice*, purchased from Wunderlich, $245
WINHAM, E., wood engraving, *Niagara, the Rapids*
WOLF, HENRY, wood engravings
WOOD, T. W., etching
WOODBURY PERMANENT PHOTOGRAPHIC PRINTING CO., Woodburytype
WOOLLETT, WM. ET AL., engraving, *Dido & Aeneas*, purchased from Keppel

Index

Page references in **boldface** type denote illustrations.

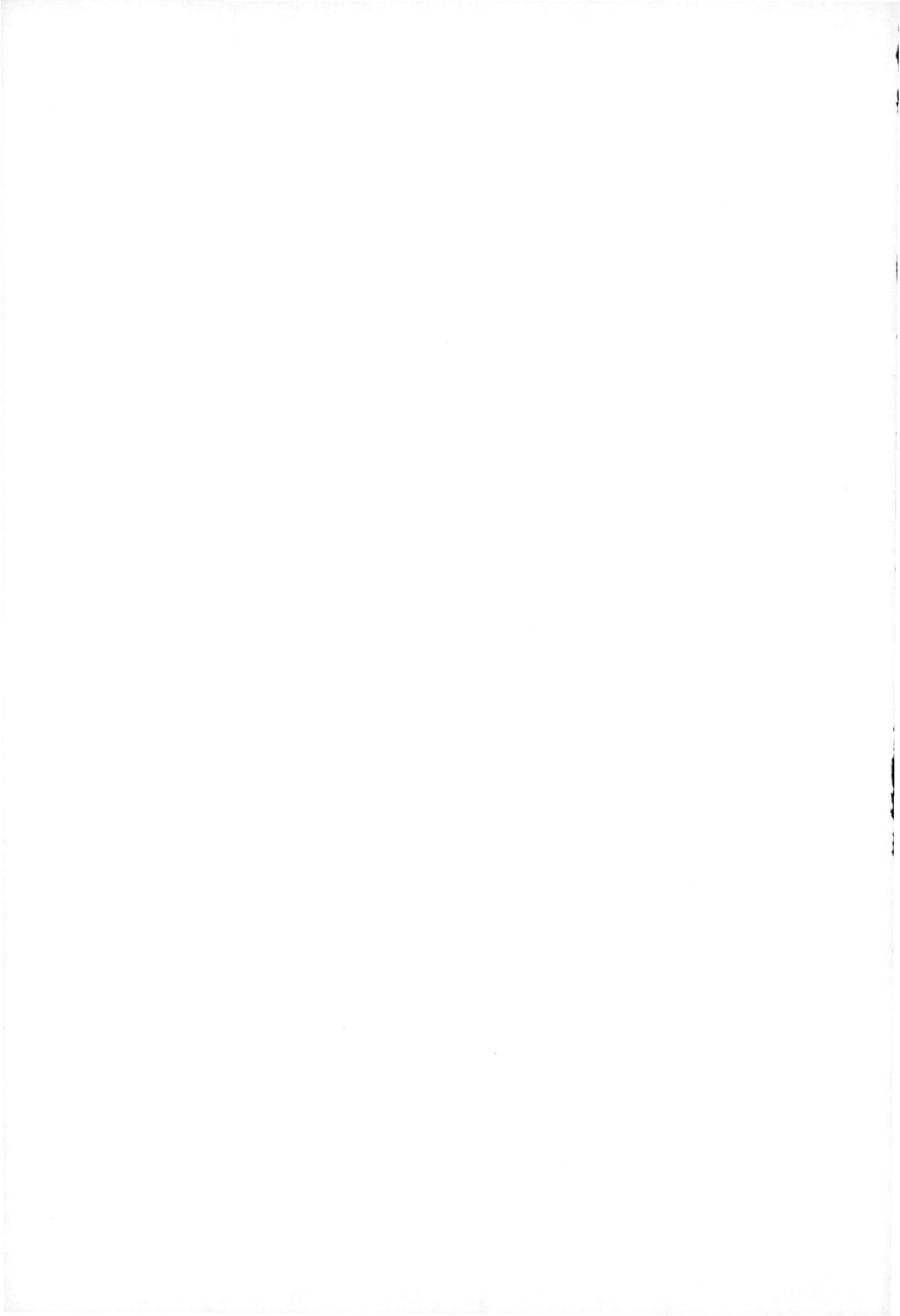